VENGEANCE
OF THE
VICTIM

D1520621

Minnesota Publications in the Humanities, Volume 5

A series of books published with
the financial assistance of the Graduate School
and the College of Liberal Arts of
the University of Minnesota

VENGEANCE
OF THE
VICTIM

History and Symbol in Giorgio Bassani's Fiction

Marilyn Schneider

University of Minnesota Press, Minneapolis

Published by the University of Minnesota Press
2037 University Avenue Southeast, Minneapolis MN 55414.
Published simultaneously in Canada
by Fitzhenry & Whiteside Limited, Markham.
Printed in the United States of America.

Library of Congress Cataloging-in-Publication Data

Schneider, Marilyn.
    Vengeance of the victim.

    (Minnesota publications in the humanities ; v. 5)
    Bibliography: p.
    Includes index.
    1. Bassani, Giorgio. Romanzo di Ferrara.
2. Bassani, Giorgio—Symbolism. 3. Jews in literature.
I. Title. II. Series.
PQ4807.A79R637 1986   853'.914   85-28866
ISBN 0-8166-1512-8
ISBN 0-8166-1513-6 (pbk.)

Illustrations and photographs by Herb Schneider.

The University of Minnesota
is an equal-opportunity
educator and employer.

Ogni parete, ogni angolo, ogni più piccola cosa portavano la traccia del dolore. La verità è che i luoghi dove si ha pianto, dove si ha sofferto, e dove si trovarono molte risorse interne per sperare e resistere, sono proprio quelli a cui ci si affeziona di più. . . . E adesso questa terra, questa vecchia città dove [Lei] è nato, dove è cresciuto e si é fatto un uomo, sono diventate doppiamente sue. Lei non le abbandonerà mai più.

"Gli ultimi anni di Clelia Trotti"

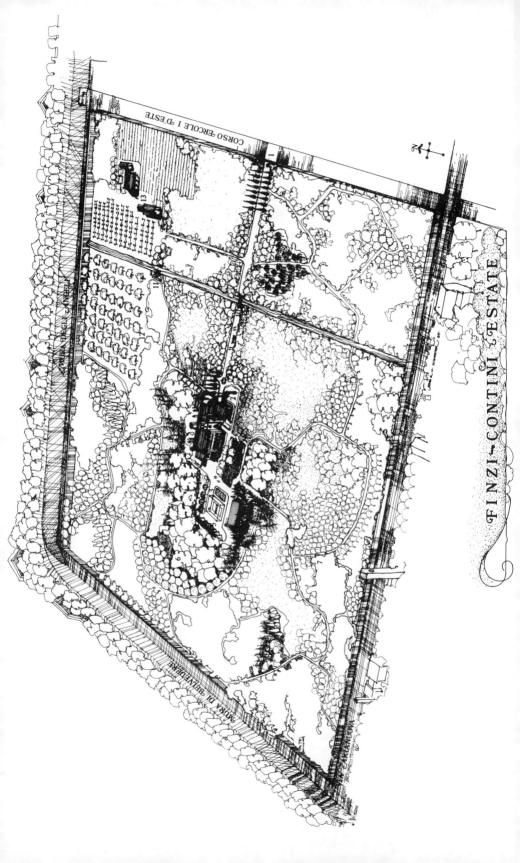

CORSO ERCOLE I D'ESTE

MURA DI BELVEDERE

FINZI-CONTINI ESTATE

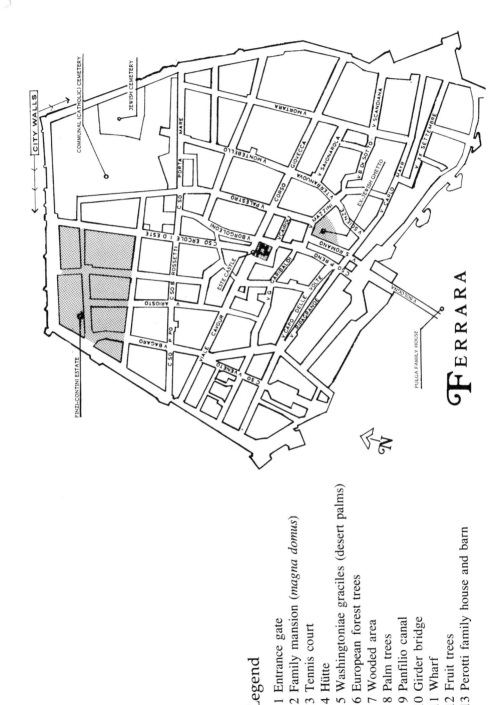

Legend

1 Entrance gate
2 Family mansion (*magna domus*)
3 Tennis court
4 Hütte
5 Washingtoniae graciles (desert palms)
6 European forest trees
7 Wooded area
8 Palm trees
9 Panfilio canal
10 Girder bridge
11 Wharf
12 Fruit trees
13 Perotti family house and barn

CITY WALLS

COMMUNAL (CATHOLIC) CEMETERY

JEWISH CEMETERY

FINZI-CONTINI ESTATE

V. MORTARA

V. MONTEBELLO

GIOVECCA

CORSO

V. TERRANUOVA

V. SAVONAROLA

V. SCANDIANA

V. B. DI SOTTO

EX-JEWISH GHETTO

V. XI SETTEMBRE

PORTA MARE

V. PALESTRO

C.SO ERCOLE I D'ESTE

V. BORGOLEONI

V. MAZZINI

C.SO ROMANO

V. SCIENZE

V. CARLO MAYR

C.SO B. ROSSETTI

ESTE CASTLE

V. G. GARIBALDI

V. SARACENO

V. RIPAGRANDE

V. CARLO DELLE VOLTE

C.SO P. RENO

V. ARIOSTO

VIALE CAVOUR

C.SO V. VENETO

C.SO P. PO

V. BAGARO

V. PO BOLOGNA

PULGA FAMILY HOUSE

N

ℱERRARA

Contents

Acknowledgments

I wrote an essay on the *Giardino dei Finzi-Contini* during a research leave in the 1970s. Later grants enabled me to develop that initial effort into a book. During a month's leave in Ferrara (1980), I acquired invaluable knowledge of places and people related to the *Romanzo di Ferrara*. Giorgio Bassani gave generously of his time, talking about and guiding me through Ferrara, Codigoro, Cerveteri, and other places germane to his fiction. The *ferraresi* friends I made on that trip have enriched my life forever. I am grateful to them and to the University of Minnesota for its crucial contribution of the paid research leaves that led me to an unusually enriching intellectual and social experience.

Finally, my thanks go to my daughter, Karen, who read an early version of the manuscript with a critical eye and helped me improve some rough edges, and to the whole family for their support and interest in the project. Herb's help was indispensable.

Biographical and Historical Chronology

1916   Giorgio Bassani is born on March 4 in Bologna, Italy, of upper middle-class Jewish Ferrarese parents and is raised and schooled in Ferrara. His grandmother is Catholic; his grandfather, of Jewish origin, is a prominent surgeon in Ferrara.

1922   Mussolini becomes prime minister after the march on Rome.

1925   The Italian government becomes a one-party, dictatorial Fascist state.

1933   The Fascist party initiates an intense and successful membership campaign.

1935–36 Mussolini wages a successful war on Ethiopia, gaining popular support. The Italian king is declared emperor.

1935–39 Bassani attends the University of Bologna, commuting by train from Ferrara. Although he is a student of literature, he is most influenced by his art history professor, the eminent Roberto Longhi; also important is his contact with the painter Giorgio Morandi. But it is the philosophy and outspoken anti-Fascism of Benedetto Croce that most broadly affect Bassani's intellectual and artistic formation. His first poems and short stories are written during this period. He graduates with a thesis on the nineteenth-century writer and patriot Niccolò Tommaseo. By the late thirties, he is a committed anti-Fascist involved in clandestine political activity.

1936   Mussolini and Hitler aid Franco in the Spanish civil war. The Rome-Berlin Axis is declared, establishing a military pact between Italy and Germany.

1937   Mussolini visits Germany.

1938   Hitler visits Rome in May. In September anti-Jewish laws are decreed in Italy, imposing severe restrictions on Jewish civil rights.

1939   Bassani teaches school in the Jewish community of Ferrara because Jewish children are no longer admitted to public schools. The Pact of Steel formalizes the Axis agreements of 1936. A few months later, Germany attacks Poland. Two days later, Great Britain and France declare war on Germany.

1940   *Una città di pianura* appears under the pseudonym Giacomo Marchi (the surname is his grandmother's) because Jews can no longer publish. On June 10 Mussolini joins the war on the side of Germany. Bassani's brother, Paolo, is expelled from the University of Grenoble when Italy declares war on France.

1942   Bassani is among the founders of the *Partito d'Azione*, one of the most effective political parties in the Resistance.

1943   On July 25, days after the Allied invasion of Sicily, the Fascist Grand Council votes Mussolini out of office; King Vittorio Emanuele III arrests Mussolini; the new prime minister, Pietro Badoglio, outlaws the Fascist party. In prison since May for anti-Fascist acts, Bassani is now liberated. He marries Valeria Sinigallia in August and moves to Florence and then to Rome (where he still lives) with his wife and parents. On September 8 Badoglio announces an armistice; German troops immediately occupy northern and central Italy; Bassani goes into hiding under a false name; partisan warfare commences. On October 13 Italy declares war on Germany. On November 14 Fascists in Ferrara slaughter innocent compatriots in an act of vengeance.

1945   On April 25 northern Italy is liberated, bringing the war in Italy to an end. *Storie dei poveri amanti*.

1946   Elections are held to form a Constituent Assembly. A national referendum ends the Italian monarchy and institutes a republican government.

1948   Bassani becomes editor of *Botteghe Oscure*, an international literary journal that publishes work by unestablished young writers, such as Italo Calvino and Pier Paolo Pasolini, until it closes in 1960. In these same years, he contributes articles to many important periodicals and newspapers and also writes filmscripts. Postwar elections are held for the first time.

1949   Bassani spends three years in Naples, teaching at the Nautical Institute, then returns to Rome.

1953   *La passeggiata prima di cena*. Bassani invites Pasolini to collaborate with him on filmscripts. They work together for several years and become good friends as well as firm admirers of each other's fiction and poetry. Bassani teaches theater history at the National Academy of Art in Rome; he becomes a director and vice-president of Italian public radio and television.

1955   Bassani is a founder and animator of *Italia Nostra*, an association dedicated to the protection of Italy's natural and cultural monuments.

1956   *Cinque storie ferraresi.*

1958   *Gli occhiali d'oro.* As director of the Library of Literature series for the publisher Feltrinelli (a post he keeps until 1963), Bassani advises publication of Tomasi di Lampedusa's *Il Gattopardo* (The Leopard), a novel turned down by other publishing houses but destined for literary and international fame.

1960   *Le storie ferraresi.* Bassani joins the editorial staff of *Paragone*, the art and literature journal directed by Roberto Longhi and Anna Banti.

1962   *Il giardino dei Finzi-Contini.*

1963   *L'alba ai vetri.*

1964   *Dietro la porta.*

1965   Bassani serves as president of *Italia Nostra* until he resigns in 1980; he then becomes president emeritus.

1966   *Le parole preparate.*

1968   *L'airone.*

1970   Vittorio De Sica produces a film based on *Il giardino dei Finzi-Contini*, which displeases Bassani despite its box office success.

1974   *Il romanzo di Ferrara; Epitaffio.*

1975   Bassani is a visiting professor at Indiana University. Three years later he teaches at the University of California in Berkeley and at McMaster University in Canada. Some of the poems of *In gran segreto* are inspired by his experiences in the United States.

1978   *In gran segreto.*

1980   Revised edition of *Il romanzo di Ferrara.*

1982   *In rima e senza.*

1984   *Di là dal cuore.*

Note on Citations of Bassani's Work

The edition of Giorgio Bassani's fiction used in the text is *Il romanzo di Ferrara* (Milan: Mondadori, 1980). Parenthetical references to the *Romanzo* give page numbers only. Page references to the earlier edition (1974) and to other books of Bassani's prose, poetry, and essays are preceded by an abbreviated title and the year of publication or, where warranted, by the title or year alone. Close ellipses in citations are always the author's.

A list of works by Bassani cited in this study follows. It gives titles, abbreviated titles (used frequently in textual references), and translations of full titles. The order of the texts given below matches the table of contents in the 1974 edition of the *Romanzo*. Bassani trimmed the table of contents in the 1980 edition to include only the titles of the six books that make up the collected volume, preceded by "Libro primo" (First Book), etc. He also replaced the short-story titles of *L'odore del fieno* (1974) and the roman numerals preceding them with arabic numerals in the later edition. These appear internally to the text. The streamlining emphasizes the author's conception of the *Romanzo* as a single, unified text.

Each principal entry below corresponds to a title of a book published earlier that is now part of the *Romanzo* — except for *Dentro le mura*, a title Bassani substituted for the original *Cinque storie ferraresi*. I use the latter, original title in references (both titles appear below). Book titles (*L'airone*, for example) correspond to chapter titles in the *Romanzo* and are italicized; section titles placed beneath chapter titles are italicized and indented (*Due fiabe*, for example); individual short-story titles, including the essay that closes the text, are in quotation marks ("Lida Mantovani," for example).

Il romanzo di Ferrara (Romanzo) (The Novel of Ferrara), contains the following texts:

   Dentro le mura (Within the City Walls); orig. title, *Cinque storie ferraresi: Cinque storie* (Five Ferrarese Stories)
   "Lida Mantovani": "Lida" (Lida Mantovani)
   "La passeggiata prima di cena": "Passeggiata" (The Walk before Dinner)
   "Una lapide in via Mazzini": "Lapide" (A Plaque on Mazzini Street)
   "Gli ultimi anni di Clelia Trotti": "Anni" (The Last Years of Clelia Trotti)
   "Una notte del '43": "Notte" (A Night in 1943)
Gli occhiali d'oro: Occhiali (The Gold-rimmed Eyeglasses)
Il giardino dei Finzi-Contini: Giardino (The Garden of the Finzi-Continis)
Dietro la porta: Porta (Behind the Door)
L'airone: Airone (The Heron)
L'odore del fieno: Odore (The Smell of Hay)
   Due fiabe: "Fiabe" (Two Fables)
      1. "La necessità è il velo di Dio": "Necessità" (Necessity is God's Veil)
      2. "Ai tempi della Resistenza": "Resistenza" (During the Resistance)
   Altre notizie su Bruno Lattes: "Notizie" (More News about Bruno Lattes)
      1. "L'odore del fieno": "Odore" (The Smell of Hay)
      2. "La ragazza dei fucili": "Ragazza" (The Rifle Girl)
      3. "Una corsa ad Abbazia": "Abbazia" (A Dash to Abbazia)
   Ravenna (Ravenna)
   Les neiges d'antan: "Neiges" (The Snows of Yesteryear)
      1. "Cuoio grasso": "Cuoio" (Fatty Hide)
      2. "Pelandra" (Pelandra)
   Tre apologhi (Three Apologues)
      1. "Apologo" (Apologue)
      2. "Un topo nel formaggio": "Topo" (A Mouse in the Cheese)
      3. "Le scarpe da tennis": "Scarpe" (The Tennis Shoes)
"Laggiù, in fondo al corridoio": "Laggiù" (Way Down, at the End of the Corridor)

Other works by Bassani cited in this study

Fiction

Le storie ferraresi: Storie (The Ferrarese Stories)
   "Il muro di cinta": "Muro" (The Enclosing Wall)
   "In esilio": "Esilio" (In Exile)

Essays

> *Le parole preparate: Parole* (Prepared Words)
> *Di là dal cuore: Di là* (Beyond the Heart)

Poetry

> *L'alba ai vetri: Alba* (Dawn in the Windowpanes)
> "Te lucis ante": "Lucis" (Before the Dawn)
> *Epitaffio* (Epitaph)
> *In gran segreto: Segreto* (In Utmost Secrecy)
> *In rima e senza: Rima* (In Rhyme and Not)

Translations

For English translations other than my own, an abbreviated title and page reference follow each translation. Sometimes, because translators worked from earlier editions of texts than the 1980 text I quote from, I insert a word or phrase in brackets or else insert ellipses to keep the translation consistent with the language of the Italian quotation. Listed below, with the names of the translators and the books they translated, are the full and abbreviated titles of the works cited.

Isabel Quigly: *The Garden of the Finzi-Continis* (Q:*G*)
                  A Prospect of Ferrara (Q:*P*)
William Weaver: *Behind the Door* (W:*D*)
                  The Heron (W:*H*)
                  The Smell of Hay (W:*S*)

VENGEANCE
OF THE
VICTIM

Introduction

"Only the dead are well off." During the course of his uncle's funeral, Bruno Lattes recalls the time when, as a little boy, he repeated this family proverb while attending his grandfather's funeral. The episode, from one of Bassani's short stories, exemplifies not only a dominant thematic mode of memory, but also a narrative architecture of concentric circles expanding outward to the enclosing city walls of a Ferrara-"tomb" (Bassani's metaphor) and outward further to the book that encompasses the author's extended narration of death, *Il romanzo di Ferrara*, which is the specific subject of my study. Death—or, better, the burial of the dead—preserves the memory of life. Bassani enmeshes the limit case of death and, with it, the urgency of funerary ritual, in the hundreds of pages of his global "novel." He has stated the case explicitly in interviews; one word suffices: Buchenwald.

The *Romanzo* contains images and signs, sometimes veiled, of the wartime situation of the Jews: ostracism, persecution, death in concentration camps. One of my aims is to draw out from hidden linguistic signs the author's imprint—scattered and surreptitious—of death camp configurations. The presence of this subliminal imagery is not only startling but the more commanding in its rhetorical indistinctness, a sign itself of unutterability. Bassani's themes, grounded in death and memory, encompass humiliation, estrangement, victimage, and betrayal. Not infrequently, victimizers and victims exchange roles. A countertheme, more dynamic than the themes of death, is grounded in life and the narrative present. It patterns a paradigmatic journey of life, from pubescence to maturity, from spiritual and artistic death to rebirth. The achievement of this journey is the vengeance of the victim.

> Non è possibile immaginare la vita senza la morte, e non è possibile immaginare l'arte, che è il contrario della verità, senza la verità.
>
> Giorgio Bassani
>
> (It is impossible to imagine life without death, and it is impossible to imagine art, which is the opposite of truth, without truth.)

The major purpose of this study is to analyze the layers of text that interfold in the *Romanzo*: historical, spatial, autobiographical, temporal, mythical, linguistic, sexual, symbolic, metatextual. I shall be exploring how the text works and how it signifies, hoping to communicate as well the "poetry" of this richly inventive and meticulously organized work of fiction. More profoundly than any documentary record, the *Romanzo* captures a very particular and powerful historical reality: Jewish life under Fascism and Nazism, especially between the years of the Italian "racial" laws[1] and the end of World War II; that is, from 1938 to 1945. A sketch of each chapter in my study will indicate my approach to the text.

Chapter 1 examines several aspects of the thematic of death: social ostracism, the significance of tombstones, the author's experience of persecution, the postmortem structure of the authorial persona, the dialectic of death and survival. This chapter underpins and anticipates the subject matter of the remaining chapters.

Chapter 2 provides the historical background implicit but not usually elaborated in the fiction. Although the main historico-narrative fulcrum is on the Fascist era, two other periods are textualized and, if scarcely recognized in the critical literature, significant: the Renaissance in Ferrara, dominated by the Este court, and the Risorgimento. Into this context I introduce fictional events and characters of the *Romanzo* that illustrate the considerable depth added to the narrative field by certain patriarchal and matriarchal figures. A filament of Jewish history woven through the chapter further deepens narrative meaning. All the historical strands serve a social history embedded in the fabric of the text. Throughout the *Romanzo*, historical facts are cut up into textual swatches and processed for the pivotal drama of the narrating subject confronting both himself and the chaotic world of late Fascism in which he lives.

Chapter 3, the central chapter, explores the spaces of Ferrara (the author's home for the first twenty-seven years of his life), from street names, houses of prostitution, the former Jewish ghetto, and the Este Castle to sacralizing, sacrificial, and transformative spaces and symbolic spaces that separate "outsiders" from "insiders." This chapter, a mapping of both the mythopoeic center and the conjuncture of the real and the invented city, repeats itself to some extent in a different discourse in the following chapter, which considers sexual symbolism.

In chapter 4 my thesis is that sexual relations are metaphors of personal and social identity, indicators of health and sickness. Implicated in erotic desire are, for example, "Aryan"-Jewish political relations, Jewish self-humiliation, artistic creativity. The erotic in Bassani's fiction is essential; a generally neglected element in commentaries on the *Romanzo*, it here receives careful attention.

Chapter 5 is dominated by the figure of the authorial persona. Several third- and first-person male subjects interfuse across the texts in a gradual narrative construction of a persona on a sinuous existential, moral, and artistic journey from symbolic death to rebirth. In a parallel movement, the narratives themselves are viewed in their progress toward self-reflexivity and metanarrative. The achieved prominence of the writer and his writing climaxes this chapter (and the entire *Romanzo*) and focuses attention on the creation of the text in the first place. The pattern of circularity prevails through an echoing of the first text of the *Romanzo* in the final one.

A consummate work of fiction that calls out to be read as historical memory, the *Romanzo* is also a symbolic autobiography: a closed world of entwining historical and personal crises, reflecting and emblematizing one another. Bassani's literary transformation of exceptional history and simple city streets into myth and symbol—not diminished but enriched by the realist strength of his writing style—is a process that hinges on the textualized persona: a Jew, a writer, and an autobiographical narrative subject.

All writers occupy marginal positions in society as commentators on a world they both experience and observe. But Bassani is more marginal than most. As a Jew in a Catholic country, an elitist among iconoclastic intellectuals, a renowned writer whose style and conception of narrative fit neither the postwar mold of neorealism nor the post-postwar mold of neoexperimentalism, a "provincial" more attuned to Rome than to his native Ferrara, and a member of the Jewish community who keeps his distance from it, Bassani stands apart, an eternally displaced person. Yet, as a founder and longtime president of *Italia Nostra*, the cultural organization dedicated to the protection of Italian historic buildings and landscapes, as a political candidate for national office, as a publisher's consultant who "discovered" Lampedusa's *The Leopard*, and, most of all, as a superb epic novelist of modern Italy and a critically acclaimed poet, Bassani obviously enjoys a privileged and central status in his native country. The comprehensive editions of his fiction, *Il romanzo di Ferrara*, his poetry, *In rima e senza*, and his essays, *Di là dal cuore*, which crown his career, reaffirm his eminence as a writer and his centrality in Italian culture. Thus his privileged status is as precarious as it is secure. At no time was his separation from the mainstream more intensely lived than during the late thirties and the decade that followed: the years that inspired his best work.

Nella musica straordinariamente sapiente che è *Il romanzo di Ferrara*, l'orchestrazione della frase principale procede per accenni, per suggerimenti, per infinite presenze misteriose di una intensità che ha pochi riscontri nella letteratura contemporanea.

Luigi Bàccolo

(In the extraordinarily profound music that is the *Romanzo di Ferrara*, the orchestration of the principal line proceeds by allusion, by suggestion, by infinite and mysterious displays of an intensity rarely encountered in contemporary literature.)

Two conflictive personae speak simultaneously in the fiction: the one, an authoritative spectator-witness censuring his community like an Old Testament prophet; the other, an outcast censured and victimized by a calamitous social order. In mythopoeic terminology, Bassani's invented Ferrara is a polluted community. Only a single, exceptional, inevitably female personage is untainted: the young Micòl Finzi-Contini, who is enclosed almost always in the Edenic space of the garden-estate that is her home, and who is destined to die a sacrificial victim without a home. The concept of pollution predicates a moral vision, to which Bassani gives narrative voice in varying modalities—of victim and judge, witness, survivor, bard—but always in a penal language of admonition and revenge: the insistent dialogue between the persona of conscience and the community in crisis hones the text into a moral weapon, one that wounds but also cleanses. In the long and violent shadow cast over his writing by personal experience and recent Jewish history, the author clears an uncontaminated space of love and creativity, inhabited by Micòl and eventually earned by the authorial "I."

The texts that constitute the *Romanzo* originated shortly after World War II, in a moment when new as well as established writers felt a vital need to communicate their war experiences as anti-Fascists and Resistance fighters. In the late forties and the fifties, the mode of communication—that is, the nature of narrative—assumed the characteristic of historical chronicle, often imbued with confessional ardor and moral certitude. Optimism and pride ruled during Italy's return to a democratized government; among intellectuals a Marxist fervor of renewal cast the future as bright and fruitful. But Bassani's vision was out of that focus. Scarred by his persecution as a Jew and by the larger persecution in extermination camps, his sense of the future was pessimistic; his passion, to memorialize; his place, apart; his obsession, of death and truth; his literature, symbolic and sacramental. Fully assimilated all his life into the upper middle class—which included Jewish writers such as Natalia Ginzburg, Carlo Levi, Alberto Moravia, and Primo Levi—Bassani alone (with the clear exception of Primo Levi, whose books include narratives that reflect his life in Auschwitz) makes the Jewish condition the very ground of his fiction.

In 1955 a moribund neorealist literature reached a bitter ideological crisis that focused on Vasco Pratolini's novel *Metello*, which recounts the birth of Socialism and unionism in Italy. Marxist critics entered into internecine battle, with the offensive faction criticizing *Metello* as "idyllic" and "counterrealistic," its hero as antiheroic. Bassani, at this time, was about to publish his first collection of short stories. Two years later he would recommend publication of a first novel by an unknown writer, a work which had much in common with his own lyrical-realistic, "late nineteenth-century" style of narration. The novel was *Il gattopardo* (The Leopard) by Giuseppe Tomasi di Lampedusa. With its "retrogressive" nature and immense appeal, it joined *Metello* in sounding the death knell for neorealism.

Interlacing historical, political, and concentrationary victimage and violence, Bassani's early tales had an uncommon vision of ambiguity that would remain constant in his work. Most clearly emblematic of this vision is a later story, "Ai tempi della Resistenza," the single fiction that Bassani dedicates to the Resistance movement. Constructed on the baroque topos of life as a dream, "Resistenza" undercuts any heroic or public action expected in its partisan contents; instead, it is a tale infused with the mystery of fable. Although the very title and the naming of places in Ferrara (where the story is set) convey precise images of historical and factual reality, a contrary ambiguity pervades the action, giving to reality a quality of unreality, or metaphor. Pier Paolo Pasolini, in an essay of the late fifties, pointed to a "contradiction" between Bassani's writing style—which he characterized as a "linguistically noble mannerism"—and his mimetic representation of a "passionately political" world of persecution and antagonisms in provincial Ferrara under Fascism.[2] Bassani's mannerist—or, better, baroque—approach to signification is not to explain, but to problematize, to leave his reader with important moral, existential, and linguistic questions begging for resolution. The characteristic ambiguity of his narrative endings alerts the reader to metaphysical and metastorical problems and not to fluctuating political and social issues. In Pasolini's words, Bassani's fictive world is "always seen under the aspect of eternity, and [is] therefore lyrical."[3] The baroque lyricism of long, hypotactic sentences that characterizes Bassani's style deftly executes willful contradictions, shifts in perspectives, disorderings, and a heightened recognition of narrative subjectivity. These stylistic choices bothered Marxist critics in Italy, such as Gian Carlo Ferretti and Giuliano Manacorda, who condemned Bassani for his "idyllic" and "elegaic" prose (as others had shortly before condemned Pratolini) and for his lack of historical "maturity." Not open to a literature that fused history and myth, that formed new metaphors and symbolic systems expressive of allegorical as well as historical truths, that sought the "aspect of eternity," these critics disparaged Bassani's narratives as literature of consolation.[4]

In the sixties another breed of writers and critics, avant-garde neoexperimentalists called the *Gruppo 63*, waged an ostentatious, if legitimately self-invigorating, campaign against Bassani and one or two other prominent fiction writers they considered old-fashioned. Experimentalist writers such as Edoardo

Sanguineti, Luigi Malerba, and Giorgio Manganelli, who formed the vanguard of Italian postmodernist fiction, strove to enlarge our way of reading; their method was aggressive—and comic. They shattered conventional rules of narrative with bold new formulas of linguistic play and narrative decomposition, poking fun at physical laws, objectivity, and logic. But Bassani regarded such writers as ivory-tower theoreticians, found their combative spirit banal, and refused unflinchingly even to recognize their existence.[5] One of the original enthusiasts of the *Gruppo 63* was a young Umberto Eco. Eco today sees the old polemics as a meaningful exercise past its usefulness. Those polemics defined a successful book (such as Bassani's *Giardino* or Lampedusa's *Gattopardo*) as a book lacking quality, or, in the then-favored Marxist term of disapproval, as a "consolatory" book. Eco summarizes: "One can say that the equation 'popularity = lack of value' was encouraged by certain polemical positions that we, of the *Gruppo 63*, took even before 1963, when we identified a successful book with a consolatory book, and a consolatory novel with a novel with a good plot, while we celebrated the experimental work, that scandalizes and is rejected by the vast public." Of the writers scorned in the sixties, Eco singles out Bassani for special reevaluation: "Regarding Bassani . . . I would act very much more cautiously today, and if I were back in 1963 I would accept him as a fellow traveler (*compagno di strada*)."[6]

Perhaps Bassani's greatest objection to the *Gruppo 63* was their rejection of history. For history, according to Bassani, is the means by which we come to understand the world. On a linguistic level, however, Bassani's writing is not totally out of step with the neoexperimentalists. If the latter's aims were to explode and ironize such realist conceptions and fluent stylistic devices, Bassani's increasing use of transgressive language and situations in the *Romanzo* and the self-reflexivity of his later metanarratives, especially of *L'odore del fieno*, reveal untraditional stylistic tendencies. While his complex sentences "of Proustian expanse, but Manzonian cadence"[7] weave a sometimes-elegaic prose (that a few critics find objectionable), they also employ the homely syntax and lexicon of bureaucracy and banality. The final effect of the prose is a finely balanced, ironic tension: on the one hand, a spectacular sweep of a narration that encompasses the ways of human destiny; on the other, a crowded, crisply detailed little picture of small-minded troubles and fears. Unmoved by neoexperimentalist oddities and attacks, Bassani kept the faith of his originary, Olympian view of literature as a moral as well as artistic calling, a view shaped not only by traumatic times, but also by Crocian idealist principles of historicism and truth.

For the whole of Italy in the early twentieth century, Benedetto Croce was an exemplum of moral and intellectual stature absolutely without equal—the lay pontiff (in Antonio Gramsci's words) of national culture. By the time of the philosopher's death in 1952, Bassani had published four volumes of poetry and was just beginning to turn decisively to prose. Already influenced by the hermetic poets of the previous generation, most notably by Eugenio Montale, Bassani found a still more compelling teacher in the rationalist, secular, iconoclastic, and antimetaphysical sage of philosophical idealism. Bassani has spoken frequently of the centrality of Croce's influence on his artistic and ideological development and even on his techniques of narrative and poetic construction. His antipathy to turn-of-the-century psychological analysis and his aspiration to objectivity are clearly in keeping with Crocian principles. Bassani ranks modern European writers like Proust, James, the early Joyce, Mann, Musil, and Svevo — all of whom he has read and with whom he is frequently and reasonably compared — of considerably less importance to his writing than Croce. And next in importance, he claims, is the renowned art historian Robert Longhi, with whom he studied while a student at the University of Bologna. Without doubt, Bassani translated the lessons of Longhi — as well as the austere, subtle metaphysical paintings of both Giorgio De Chirico (who lived a while in Ferrara) and the Bolognese Giorgio Morandi — into poetic and novelistic verbal paintings that add an introspective element to the clarity, precision, and realism the author holds as his poetic goals. Alessandro Manzoni, too, the source of profound, perhaps the greatest, literary influence on Bassani, has been repeatedly invoked to suggest Bassani's grand vision and writing style. For in Bassani's work, "objective," "knowable," historical truth has an obverse side, the subjective, incomprehensible, "metaphysical" truth that only the "heart" can know (see the Manzonian epigraph to the *Giardino*, 1974 ed. and the Chekovian epigraph to "Notte," 1974 ed.). The influence of Manzoni, the patriarchal master of modern Italian literature, infiltrates Bassani's texts not only through epigraphic and unmarked textual quotations, but also through stylistic techniques, irony, history's imprint on ordinary individuals, and the force of moral and social problems.

The subjective world of ineffable human desire and fear is a fundamental element of the *Romanzo*; it is implied in the enigmatic endings of several narratives, as if interrogating text and reader alike and admitting indirectly the impossibility of conclusion. A paradoxical hallmark of the *Romanzo*, such signs of interpretive struggle surface in the fiction as occasional cracks in the normally realistic narration, intimating moral imperatives or mythic moments that stop the flux of narrative time.

Like other paradoxical elements in the *Romanzo*, a breached moral order represents both punishment and liberation: Micòl's defiance of family codes of behavior and her refusal to marry are signs of her individualistic freedom; Edgardo Limentani's biological disorder and lack of appetite are signs of his loss of moral will and his estrangement from the social order, for social eating represents a moral bond. By the sleight of hand at which a writer excels, the sterile Edgardo becomes the instrument of his creator's artistic vitalization: *L'airone*, Edgardo's novel and the final novel of the *Romanzo*, is both a narrative of deadening self-alienation and, from another angle of vision, a metanarrative transcription of authorial rebirth. The project of the entire *Romanzo*, in the process of breathing life into a universe of individuals and communities afflicted by historic upheaval, is to record the birth of its poet. *Epitaffio* and *In gran segreto*, the two volumes of poetry published after the *Romanzo*, voice a lyrical postnarrative epitaph and a secret spoken aloud to the world. Together they reaffirm narrative completion and engrave a poetic tombstone that keeps alive the memory of the poet's beginning.

Chapter 1
Death and Survival

Subito dopo aver chiuso gli occhi per sempre / eccomi ancora una volta
chissà come a riattraversare Ferrara . . .

Epitaffio

After publishing short stories, novels, and poems for some forty years, Giorgio
Bassani collected his major works of fiction, somewhat revised, under the title
Il romanzo di Ferrara (1974). In 1980 the volume appeared again, newly and
notably retouched and surely the last redaction. Following publication of this
second edition, the author affirmed in an interview what his writing practice had
already affirmed: that he had rewritten his book from "the first line to the last,
because I am at the end of my work." The same assertion of completion characterizes a discerning comment he made a year later:

> Altre cose ambientate a Ferrara potrò scriverne: ma non apparterranno più
> al *Romanzo di Ferrara*, che è compiuto; né saranno più opera di quell'Io
> scrivente che è sempre diverso dopo le poesie di argomento ferrarese di
> *Epitaffio* e *In gran segreto*.[1]

> (I may write about other things set in Ferrara, but they will not belong to
> the *Romanzo di Ferrara*, which is done; nor will they any longer be the
> work of that writing "I" that is always different after the poetry dealing
> with Ferrara in *Epitaffio* and *In gran segreto*.)

Articulated in this statement is a rupture between an "old" and a "new" person,
"quell'Io scrivente" of the past and the writer now. To claim hyperbolically a to-

tal rewriting of the *Romanzo* is to emphasize the end of writing, to proffer a rhetorical assertion of authorial death, an image of a spectral writer confronting his already completed work. Logically enough, the book of poems following the *Romanzo* the same year is called *Epitaffio*. In notable contrast to the earlier collected fiction, *Cinque storie ferraresi* and its expansion into *Le storie ferraresi* — whose titles are plural and partial, announcing incompletion — a title in the singular for the *Romanzo* (and for *Epitaffio*) declares itself a recognition of completion, that is, "epitaphic" closure. The visual appearance of the poems of *Epitaffio* and *In gran segreto* imitates the design of funerary epitaphs, and a postmortem voice dominates their contents.[2]

Images of Disfranchisement and Death

If a postmortem image of the author surfaces in some terse published remarks, it saturates the narrative fabric of the *Romanzo*. Two terrible moments of Bassani's memory — one personal, the other historical — inform a dialectic of death and survival that generates a literary tension greater still than the archetypal dyad of life and death his texts also celebrate. The first of the two moments is traceable to the spring of 1943, when the twenty-seven-year-old author, captured and imprisoned in Ferrara for anti-Fascist deeds, faced for three months the daily prospect of death. The second and public event is the Nazi near-annihilation of European Jewry. This is the supreme historical event generating Bassani's fiction, and although it establishes the limit condition of his central thematics of (Jewish) estrangement and betrayal, its textual voice is hushed almost to silence. One task of the chapters that follow is to isolate and contextualize the subnarrative presence of death camp images in the *Romanzo*.

In a limpid essay written twelve years after World War II, Bassani insisted that the writer's "destiny of intimate solitude" has to reckon with the force of history:

> Lo so bene: *bisogna* servire. Abbiamo alle spalle quello che abbiamo: il fascismo, il nazismo, immani sterminii. Nelle carceri, ai confini di polizia, sui patiboli, nei Lager, milioni di uomini, e insieme con essi alcuni dei migliori fra noi, hanno lasciato miseramente la vita. Un tale passato, noi non possiamo obliterarlo. Esso è l'amara traccia, l'orma sanguinosa che segna per sempre il nostro cammino.[3]

> (I well know: one *must* serve. We have behind our backs what we have: Fascism, Nazism, monstrous slaughter [lit., exterminations]. In the prisons, in political exile, on the gallows, in the concentration camps, millions of individuals, and along with them some of our best, have wretchedly left their lives. We cannot obliterate such a past. It is the bitter trace, the bloody track that marks our way forever.)

This violently incised text is a gem of poetic expression: a bare list of the human suffering caused by Nazism and Fascism explodes eloquently through figure and alliteration into a moral burden. Three duplicative words—"trace," "track," "marks"—press into a scarred authorial consciousness an indelible Holocaustic stain that permanently changes ("che segna per sempre") the writer's—and "our"—postwar course. Just a delicate yet essential tracing in the lines cited above, the memory of the blood-stained concentration camp victim is one that Bassani superimposes throughout his texts. The dark image of historical victimization—which also reflects one face of the author's own outcast and "slaughtered" self-image—has another side and character in the *Romanzo*: the strongly voiced capacity to survive.

Over and over, Bassani marks his fiction with two historical signifiers in the form of dates: the years 1938 and 1943. All the narrative events produce signification in some manner related to these dates. The earlier year is when Fascist Italy instituted the so-called racial laws (following the German example of 1935, with its division of Europeans principally into two races, "Aryan" and "Jewish"); the later year dates the beginning of the German occupation of northern and central Italy and the subsequent roundup and deportation of Italian Jews to concentration camps. Not surprisingly, Bassani's characters—"per me . . . persone vere, che abitano una certa strada, che appartengono ad una sfera sociale determinata" (for me . . . real people, who live on a certain street, who belong to a particular social sphere)—are destined to die, as he told an interviewer, "in Buchenwald."[4] In a later interview, while on the subject of his concern with narrative "objectivity," he related, almost parenthetically, his subjective need to tell certain stories right after the war:

> La mia massima aspirazione è al tempo oggettivo, al tempo cartesiano della conoscenza, ma come Proust e come Joyce io so di non avere il diritto di raccontare delle storie. A chi potrei raccontarle? L'ho fatto subito dopo la guerra, in un momento eccezionale, dopo che eravamo tutti, *non solo io*, usciti da Buchenwald. Tutti venivamo di là, in qualche modo.[5] [emphasis added]

> (My greatest aspiration is to objective time, the Cartesian time of cognition, but like Proust and Joyce, I know I don't have the right to tell stories. To whom could I tell them? I did tell them right after the war, in an exceptional moment, when all of us, and *not only I*, had come out of Buchenwald. All of us came from there, one way or another.)

Extraordinary words are these, weighted by the immeasurable tragedy that the name "Buchenwald" revives and by the writer's ethnic identification with the persecution of his people; nor do they exclude the personal injuries he suffered for political and religious reasons. All this provides a ready apparatus for a literary posture of survivorship. The textualized survivor—always a male, always self-reflexive—is not explicitly a victim, however, but rather a resuscitated former (younger) self visited by the present one: an "io sdoppiato, vivo/morto"[6] (split "I," alive/dead) who nonetheless cannot be detached from the persona who returns from Buchenwald. The clearest embodiment in Bassani's texts of a survivor burdened by surviving the death camps comes not from the later books of poems, which are filled with ghostly doubles, but from his last major piece of fiction, *L'airone*, whose protagonist, Edgardo Limentani, fled safely to Switzerland after the Nazis invaded his homeland. Totally out of joint upon return to Italian postwar life, Edgardo commits suicide. Reserving the relation of Edgardo and the Holocaust for later chapters, I here comment briefly on the immplications of the novel's third-person narration in the context of survivorship. Since it is obviously impossible (at least in realist literature) for a narrator to relate his own death, the narrative locates its speaker entirely inside Edgardo's mind, *as though* the narrator were Edgardo. Thus there is no separation of the suicide and his storyteller, or in other words, of the suicide and his surviving self: the narrator is the posthumous voice of Edgardo, facing himself as an Other from beyond the grave. All the more interesting in this context is a remark Bassani makes in the preface to his book of essays, *Le parole preparate*: "Riguardo alla disposizione della materia, confesso di essere stato a lungo incerto. Alla fine, scartata l'idea, abbastanza lugubre, di atteggiarmi a postero di me stesso, ho preferito tenermi a un ordine non cronologico" [*Parole*, p. 9] (Regarding the arrangement of the material, I confess that I was in doubt for a long time. In the end, rejecting the rather gloomy idea of assuming a stance posterior to myself, I have preferred to follow an order that was not chronological). The non-fiction of *Parole* is not to nurture fictionalized and especially epitaphic self-portraiture: let the real man and his persona, Bassani suggests implicitly, double each other where they more comfortably and productively belong: in the world of literature and poetry.

As a foundational signifier of a new era of social wrong—of "anticommunity"—the anti-Jewish laws play a principal part in Bassani's narratives. But the fiction does not ignore the deportations and exterminations. The story of Geo Josz, for example, originates in the character's unexpected return home from Buchenwald after the war; its concern is with the effects of the survivor's experience on himself and the effects of his "intrusion" upon the citizens of Ferrara. Nowhere in the *Romanzo* does any episode occur inside a *Lager* (as the Italians called the camps, using the German word). The reason cannot be simply that Bassani was not himself a captive of the camps. At the time of the massacre in Ferrara (an event described at length in "Una notte del '43"), Bassani was in Bologna learning about it second-hand, the same way he learned about the concentration camps. He chooses deliberately to leave the experience of the *Konzentrationslager* at the level of textual subterfuge—an unuttered truth expressed through indirection and subliminal signs, a rhetorical structure dramatized "silently."

The anti-Jewish laws of the late 1930s made Jews into dispossessed foreigners in their own land. Disfranchisement ranged from the removal of Jewish names in telephone directories to the expulsion of Jewish students and teachers from public schools and universities. It meant restrictions on professional and business rights, as well as prohibitions against marrying "Aryans," working as public officials, publishing. Following Mussolini's declaration of war in June of 1940, internment camps were created for Jews and anti-Fascists; a couple of years later, Jewish men were conscripted into slave labor.

In his book on Italian Jews under Fascism, the renowned historian Renzo De Felice discusses Italy's exceptional integration of its Jewish citizens, a rare European phenomenon that Fascism's pro-Nazi accommodations aimed to destroy:

The great majority of Italian Jews were taken completely by surprise by the adoption of the early "racial" measures. If you leave out the few Jewish anti-Fascists who clearly understood where the road that Fascism had taken might lead, with its steady movement toward Germany, not even the rekindling in the beginning of 1938 of the anti-Jewish press campaign and the publication of the virulent Diplomatic News Report #14 sufficed as "factual data" to convince the majority of Jews as much as most Italians, moreover, that Fascism had decided to follow the German example even in the matter of anti-Semitism. (p. 319)

Persecution was so far from the mentality, history and tradition of Italians, so unjustified from every point of view, that the majority of Italian Jews could not even conceive of the idea. . . . For a very great many Italians the anti-Jewish campaign unleased in 1938 was the first true political shock following the assassination of Matteotti, the first event that really opened their eyes to Fascism and marked the beginning of their divorce from it. . . . Hadn't Mussolini in fact helped the refugees from Germany, treated the Jews as few other European governments treated theirs and, at least officially, always denied the existence in Italy of a "Jewish question"? . . . Italians through and through, by birth, by culture, by education, and in a certain sense doubly Italian because Italy for [the Jews], beyond being what it was for the rest of the Italians, was also emancipation and civic equality granted just a few decades earlier. (p. 321)[7]

The Fascist policy of anti-Semitism was for the Italian Jews, including Giorgio Bassani, an act of unbelievable emargination, humiliation, and betrayal. In a sense, all Bassani's fiction is a response to this radical social displacement. Wrenching the then-twenty-two-year-old, assimilated, unreligious Jew from the heart of bourgeois, provincial Ferrara, the oppressive laws showed Bassani "what, until that moment, his society had been, [unjust, cruel, vulgar]" and what he himself had been: egotistical, indifferent, cynical.[8] Also emblematic of the author's "destiny of intimate solitude," the revelational moment of alienation is, among other things, his textualized moment of despair, a precondition of his pursuit of writing.

It is not surprising to find that the composition of the *Romanzo* – the author's spiritual as well as artistic autobiography – follows a confessional schema. One of the particularly important instances of the pattern may be discerned in the juxtaposition of the opening and closing moments of the volume, the first of which adumbrates a literal and arduous labor of birth-giving ("Lida") fulfilled in the second, metaphoric and artistic birth ("Laggiù"). By conflating the opening sentences of the first and last texts, Bassani effects a convergence/conversion of the third-person, experiencing persona *inside* the narrative (the aimless character David) and the first-person, writing persona *outside* the text (the purposeful author Giorgio Bassani). The structure is familiar in confessional literature, from Augustine on. In a Bassanian frame of reference, a death of the self leaves a ghostly residue of death in the reborn – or, better, surviving – spirit. In the *Romanzo* a telling marker of postmortem presence is Emily Dickinson's poetry, to which I shall shortly return. If Bassani's writing is a valiant exploration of the humiliated self rising to a glorious (re)birth, it also nowhere proposes that life or moral certitude squarely triumphs over death or spiritual vacuity in the manner of christological conversion. In the forms of a corrupted yet kindred community and a self-lacerating yet robust communal victim, the shadow of death spreads steadily across the pages of our text.

Death and survival assume various, even conflicting, narrative forms. Death, for example, may be healthy, unhealthy, artistic, sacrificial, real, symbolic. Similarly, survival – real or symbolic – may be individual, communal, a sign of decay or rebirth, a testimony to moral certitude or political oppression, or Jewish history. Death and survival always occupy a liminal space; the foremost textual occupant of that space is the narrating subject. The conflict *between* death and survival and *within* each of these states parallels the conflict between and within the (composite) authorial persona and the turbulent social universe that Bassani calls "Ferrara" and describes as the "piccolo, segregato universo da me inventato" [p. 734] (small, segregated universe that I invented). While this spare, self-confident authorial affirmation bodies forth a living universe, a contrary moment of restive self-interrogation, like a drifting echo of Henry James, summons forth a deathly silence that convulses Bassani's sentient universe. In the American writer's words: "Why does my pen not drop from my hand on approaching the infinite pity and tragedy of all the past? It does, poor helpless pen, with what it meets of the ineffable, what it meets of the cold Medusa-face of life, of all the life *lived*, on every side. *Basta, basta!*"[9]

James's "cold Medusa-face of life" is an apposite paradoxical metaphor of the agonistic relationship between death and life, but it is also a sexual metaphor in which the Medusa kills the men she "seduces."[10] Precisely in accord with a concept of sexual relations does Bassani organize his own narratives of death and survival. Like the Medusa-face, erotic discourse in the *Romanzo* points to male psychic affliction. Male impotence and female lust constitute the coordinates on Bassani's axes of male humiliation and despair. Sexual discourse also functions to gauge social disintegration. But in privileged relational and sexual narrative events, erotic discourse mediates the textual recuperation of a "sacred" past and the attainment of artistic creation.

The *Romanzo* plays out a variation on the themes of solitude and exclusion in terms of homelessness. Rooted in the raw material of social history and especially in the effect of society on events and individuals, the theme of homelessness often translates into confrontational tropes of insider and outsider. A conversation in the short novel *Dietro la porta* may serve to exemplify how sharply in Bassani's Ferrara the sides are drawn between the entrenched "ruling" class and its impotent and vilified "inferiors." This particular play of power unfolds in the small social universe of school children:

> Sta' sicuro. Pur di intrufolarsi nelle case degli altri, chissà quanti chilometri sarebbe disposto a macinare in un giorno, quello lì, con quei suoi due stecchi di gambine. Sai certi cani bastardi che basta fargli un fischio e subito accorrono, trottando e scodinzolando? *Da autentico meteco*, Pulga è proprio così. Smania d'intrufolarsi, capisci?, e mica tanto perché abbia bisogno di qualcosa. È soltanto questione di carattere. Io, vedi, sarà perché non sono un bastardo e nemmeno un meteco, e le mescolanze non posso soffrirle, mi fanno venire una specie di pelle d'oca, *io non sto bene che a casa mia*, mentre al contrario c'è al mondo gente che a casa propria non ci si può vedere. [p. 514; emphasis added]

> (Don't worry. To pry his way into other people's houses, he would walk for miles, that one, with those toothpick legs of his. You know how certain mongrels are? You just have to whistle and they come trotting up, wagging their tail. That's Pulga. *A real mongrel*. [The italian term, *meteco*, means "vile foreigner."] Dying to force his way inside, you understand? And not because he really needs something. It's simply a question of character. . . . Look, maybe it's because I'm not a bastard and not a mongrel, either, and to tell you the truth, I can't stand them, they give me goose flesh, *I'm only happy in my own house*, whereas, on the contrary, there are people in this world who can't stand their own homes.) [W:*D*, p. 98; emphasis added]

Speaking the above is Carlo Cattolica, star student in the *liceo* class that includes the story's first-person protagonist. It is the latter whom the esteemed Carlo addresses. Although the object of his scorn is a Bolognese newcomer to class named Luciano Pulga, Carlo's truer target is the narrator himself. The Jewish protagonist—*second*-best in class—and the obsequious Luciano are identical in the eyes of the (before the fact) "Aryan" Carlo. Both are illegitimate (*bastardi*) and foreign (*meteci*).[11] Though for Carlo they are equally deplorable, the central character suffers the singular weakness of being Jewish. Elsewhere the text is clear that the latter's religion constitutes otherness; this, too, explains the narrator's desire to slip into (*intrufolarsi*) "legitimate" (Catholic middle-class) society. But slipping in is not unaffected inclusion; it is, rather, intrusion (another meaning of *intrufolarsi*). Only a "Cattolica" can be perfectly "at home" at home. The tension of place—second place, which is equivalent to the exclusion of place—preoccupies the narrating "I" of all Bassani's fiction.[12] The fate of second place in the schoolboy's universe of *Dietro la porta* is no less than a harsh and humiliating case of social and moral failure. Indeed, the main action of the short novel is the narrator's tortuous and unredeeming death of the self. Only metatextually does this moment of death become a moment of value; that is, when it becomes the precondition of rebirth.

The postscript to *L'alba ai vetri*, the volume containing his poetry of the years 1942–50, evokes a fugitive, endangered, anonymous Bassani in occupied Florence, seeking solace in the memory of his native Ferrara. One of the poems he wrote in that "atrocious" time recorded the calm engendered by his recollection:

> Il sonetto . . . lo scrissi nell'autunno del '43, a Firenze, con facilità estrema: caso raro, per me. Ma ormai lontano—e per sempre—dai luoghi dov'ero nato e cresciuto, nascosto com'ero, in quel tempo atroce dopo l'8 settembre [when the Nazis seized most of Italy], sotto falso nome, il paesaggio della mia pianura tornava a me con la stessa calma che le immagini dei morti famigliari talvolta sanno infonderci.[13]

> (I wrote the sonnet in the autumn of 1943, in Florence, with extreme ease: a rare case for me. But far away now—and forever—from the places where I was born and grew up, in hiding and under a false name in that atrocious time following September 8, the flat land of my countryside came back to me with the same calm that the images of dead relatives can inspire.)

There is a strange sense of self-abandonment in this discursive fragment that blends loss of identity and infused calm, as if the persona has assumed a ghostly form and is suspended in a temporal and spatial moment of transmutation.[14] As time passed and the war ended, Bassani felt an overpowering need to embrace a "new reality," to break away from the "ritagliato paradiso del gusto e della cultura" (cut-out paradise of good taste and culture) and the "facile paradiso degli affetti primordiali" (ready paradise of earliest affections): "Soltanto se avvertivo la vita abbandonarmi, soltanto in questo caso potevo consentire a me stesso di volgere attorno, sulla scena del mondo, lo sguardo sereno, 'da artista,' d'una volta" [*Alba*, p. 88] (Only if I felt life abandoning me, only that way could I allow myself to cast a serene glance again, "like an artist's," on the stage of the world). The image of "morti famigliari" returns ten years later, in the *Giardino*. Here it assumes universal significance and receives an eternal space, "protected, sheltered, privileged." To reach this sacred ground, one must cross over from one world to another—from present-day Rome to ancient Etruria (in the action of the novel) and from life to art (in the discourse of writing):

Varcata la soglia del cimitero dove ciascuno di loro possedeva una seconda casa . . . l'eternità non doveva più sembrare un'illusione, una favola, una promessa da sacerdoti. Il futuro avrebbe stravolto il mondo a suo piacere. Lì, tuttavia, nel breve recinto sacro ai morti famigliari; nel cuore di quelle tombe dove, insieme coi morti, ci si era presi cura di far scendere molte delle cose che rendevano bella e desiderabile la vita; in quell'angolo di mondo difeso, riparato, privilegiato: almeno lì (e il loro pensiero, la loro pazzia, aleggiavano ancora, dopo venticinque secoli, attorno ai tumuli conici, ricoperti d'erbe selvagge), almeno lì nulla sarebbe mai potuto cambiare. [p. 252]

(Once inside the cemetery where each of them owned a second home . . . eternity must no longer have seemed an illusion, a fairy-tale, a priests' promise. Let the future overturn the world, if it care to; but there, whatever happened, in that small space sacred to the family dead; in the heart of those tombs where they had the foresight to take, not only their dead, but everything that made life beautiful and desirable; in that sheltered, well defended corner of the earth, there at least nothing would change, and their thoughts, their madness, still hovered round the conical mounds covered in coarse grass after twenty-five centuries.) [Q: *G*, pp. 11–12]

This eulogy to the Etruscan necropolis at Cerveteri, near Rome, predicates death as the preserver of life. Similarly, the poet himself needed to "die" in order to preserve the vitality of his art. And now, through the medium of fiction he freely returns, reborn "da artista," to recreate and thus to preserve in absolute and purified form the "facile paradiso degli affetti primordiali" (ready paradise of earliest affections). Needless to say, the Edenic return in this case is specifically the return to Micòl, the "sacred" occupant of the paradisiacal Finzi-Continian garden. Again the author's own testimony is trenchant. Speaking to an interviewer about the *Giardino* as the story of a voyage, Bassani points out that the novel

inizia ai margini, inizia a Cerveteri, ma inizia ai margini anche della città di Ferrara. . . . il romanzo non è altro che la storia di quest'andata fino ai margini [d'un certo giardino], e poi dell'essere entrati oltre le mura di quel giardino . . . essere finalmente arrivati alla cameretta di Micòl. Ed entrare nella cameretta di Micòl non ha voluto dire possedere tutta la verità, tutta la realtà: *ché se l'autore avesse posseduta tutta la realtà, ciò che sta oltre, dentro il corpo stesso di Micòl, non sarebbe stato qui a raccontare questa vicenda.*

Lei mi chiede se in Micòl si sarebbero annullati il tempo e lo spazio, se in Micòl il protagonista avrebbe potuto raggiungere la vita; ebbene, esattamente, avrebbe raggiunto sicuramente la vita, ma avrebbe però rinunciato ad essere un artista. È questo il punto, non avrebbe più scritto il *Giardino dei Finzi-Contini.*[15] [emphasis added]

(begins on the margins, begins in Cerveteri, but it also begins on the margins of the city of Ferrara. . . . the novel is nothing else but the story of this going to the margins [of a certain garden], and then of going beyond the walls of that garden . . . to arrive finally in Micòl's bedroom. And arriving in Micòl's bedroom did not mean possessing the whole truth, the whole reality: *for if the author had possessed the whole reality, everything that is beyond and inside the very body of Micòl, he would not be here to tell the story.*

You ask me if through Micòl time and space would disappear, if through Micòl the protagonist could have reached life; well, exactly, he would have surely reached life, but he would, however, have renounced being an artist. That is the point, he would not have written *The Garden of the Finzi-Continis*.)

Commemorations of Life

The literal preservation of life in Bassani's texts has its best symbol in the figure of a dead creature "returned" to life by taxidermic art; the stuffed heron, in the novel named for the creature, is the *image* of life. Death always begins the process of life in Bassani's art:

I romanzi generalmente finiscono con la morte. Tutte le storie di Bassani con la morte cominciano, anzi solo a questa condizione Bassani può cominciarle, trovando la sua ispirazione, se il richiamo non è troppo letterario e scolastico, nel rito del vate che abbraccia le urne e le interroga.[16]

(Novels generally end with death. All Bassani's stories begin with death. Indeed, Bassani can begin them only on this condition, since he finds his inspiration [if the reference isn't too literary and bookish] in the bard's ritual of grasping cinerary urns and questioning them.)

In the *Giardino*, the competing and interfused claims of death and life are spelled out, in large yet finely traced letters, in the (female) voice of Micòl. With Emily Dickinson, the subject of her *laurea* thesis, Micòl shares both a joy in living and a sense of pervasive death. "Anche le cose muoiono, caro mio," she calmly notes. "E dunque, se anche loro devono morire, tant'è, meglio lasciarle andare" [p. 327] (Things die, too, you know. And so, if they too have to die, well there it is, it's so much better to let them go [Q:G, p. 119]). Micòl's quiescent acceptance of death is the obverse of her zeal for life and present time. Dickinson's verses focalize the fictional heroine's boundless love of life: "I find ecstacy in living—the mere sense of living is joy enough." Like Dickinson in postmortem ecstacy, Micòl prefers arrested (recurrent and ever-the-same) time, without future but subsuming an always already sanctified ("holy," that is, allegorized) past. Like Bassani in the act of inventing history, the realm of the past demarcates the only temporal arena in which unstructured, purely objective, and therefore aimless reality becomes history/story—becomes, that is, a *meaningful* temporality; in other words, a significant and allegorical discourse.

Micòl translates and sends to her aspiring lover, the novel's narrator, one of the American poet's lyrics on death, "I Died for Beauty."[17] From the vantage point of eternity, Dickinson describes a "marriage" between Beauty and Truth, which Micòl playfully claims is the only kind of compensation "su cui è costretto a puntare l'abbietto zitellaggio!" [p. 353] (poor wretched spinsterhood is forced to! [Q:G, p. 156]. Virginal and Jewish, Micòl already reads her destiny of unwedded (unerotic) life and premature, sacrificial death. Deported with her family to a Nazi concentration camp, she is invested by her author's discourse with purifying symbolic meaning. The narrator's failed erotic union with her, however—that is, his arrested state of ontological completion—represents a death of the self.

The Etruscan necropolis at Cerveteri, situated in the novel's prologue, quickens the narrator's will to write down Micòl's story; and the image of a tomb, the Finzi-Continis' multicolored marble mausoleum, opens the novel's first chapter. With the Nazi extinction of Finzi-Contini posterity, the ancestral tomb outlasts its purpose of burial and is supplanted by the family mansion, the *magna domus*, the true tomb, an Etruscan-style, "living" necropolis that survives its narrative demolition by virtue of its privileged literary inscription. The intended monument to memory (the theatrical "husk" of a tomb carved of indestructible rock) is an empty signifier while the materially emptied space (the demolished mansion) is reoccupied, that is, recuperated as memorial inscription.[18]

Diseased Alberto Finzi-Contini, the sole discredited member of the family, is interred young in the garish sepulcher that, until now, has known decades of disuse. He is its final occupant and, along with the decayed and neglected monument itself, stands for useless survival. More important than the emblematic thorns, weeds, and wild flowers grown high around its sides is the fact that the author's detailed visual description of the monument excludes any mention of an epitaph. This is an eloquent lack, especially since the two pages dedicated to the tomb (the opening pages of the novel) do take note of a commemorative plaque (*lapide*, which also signifies an inscribed tombstone) that the Jewish community has placed on a wall of the Jewish temple in honor of the tomb's respected founder, Moisè Finzi-Contini. Further, the text juxtaposes the *Tempio* of Via Mazzini (the synagogue) with the pretentious pastiche of "una *specie* di tempio" (a *kind* of temple): the tomb (emphasis added). The latter betrays its inauthenticity as a shrine and burial place by its lack of graphic inscription. Paradoxically, only an inscription signifies absence. Thus Micòl's death, marked neither by stone nor by words, and hardly retrievable by the theaterpiece her great-grandfather erected, is sacralized in the *magna domus*, whose funerary inscription is the entire text of the novel. Only this enormous body of words suffices to mark the memory and measure the irrevocable loss of the textually revered, indomitable, and Jewish Micòl.

Sepulchral imagery reappears in various guises in the *Romanzo*. One pattern, dominant in *L'airone*, constellates a series of images of wells into which the spiritually dead protagonist sinks metaphorically on almost every page of the novel. Another is the underground passage (*cunicolo*) of the *Giardino*, in which the school-aged protagonist, having "buried" his depression over a poor grade, fantasizes a new, erotic life with Micòl. Also in the *Giardino*, the real Jewish cemetery of Venice collapses into an image of decadent aestheticism, the locus of betrothment and theater — "il Prati fa cominciare la sua *Edmenegarda* proprio lì" [p. 314] (Prati starts his *Edmenegarda* right there [Q:*G*, p. 100]) — and thus ironizes the literary and pseudohistorical archival pretensions of old Professor Ermanno, himself an image of a dead culture.[19] In the terminating essay of the *Romanzo*, "Laggiu, in fondo al corridorio," Bassani describes Pino Barilari's small bedroom (see "Notte") successively as a "cameretta-prigione," "cameretta-cella," and "cameretta-tomba" [p. 733] (bedroom-prison, bedroom-cell, and bedroom-tomb). The same essay recounts the author's satisfaction in creating a narrative structure for the "Passeggiata" that makes one think "proprio attraverso la forma della sua struttura, per mezzo di essa, a una lunga, lunghissima carrellata cinematografica" [p. 732] (precisely through the form of its structure, and by means of it, of a long, really long cinematic tracking shot). The very long tracking shot tropes the essay's title-image, already metaphoric, putting into focus this idea:

> Il passato non è morto . . . non muore mai. Si allontana, bensì: ad ogni istante. Recuperare il passato dunque è possibile. Bisogna, tuttavia, se proprio si ha voglia di recuperarlo, percorrere una specie di corridoio ad ogni istante più lungo. Laggiù, in fondo al remoto, soleggiato punto di convergenze delle nere pareti del corridoio, sta la vita, vivida e palpitante come una volta, quando primamente si produsse. [ibid.]

(The past is not dead . . . it never dies. It moves away, to be sure: every moment. To recover the past is therefore possible. You must, nonetheless, if you truly desire to recover it, go down a kind of corridor that gets longer every minute. Down there, at the end of the distant, sunny point of convergence of the corridor's black walls, is life, as vivid and as palpitating as it once was, when it was produced in the first place.)

"Lighted" by the memory of "throbbing" life, the black-walled, sepulchral corridor projects a dynamic figuration of death *as* life. The moving dolly-shot gives luminous temporality to the dark corridor, the temporality required, precisely, for the reading—and writing—of a work of literature. Ordinary tombs only bear epitaphs. For those like Micòl Finzi-Contini, slaughtered in a "concentrationary universe" in which not even an ordinary tombstone is available, death becomes "anonymous, ubiquitous and unceremonialized."[20]

Two other characters belong to that universe. Each of them, according to the same essay, is a "protagonista assoluta" and "*monstre sacré*" (ibid.). One, Elia Corcos, modeled on Bassani's grandfather, dies anonymously, as Micòl does, in an extermination camp; the other, Geo Josz, "dies" a survivor of the camps, too polluted for his neighbors to countenance. Bassani writes the epitaphs for the two victims on the funerary monument he fashions of the "long corridor" populated by the inhabitants of the entire book: "Elia Corcos, il medico curante ferrarese ed ebreo venerato per decenni all'intera cittadinanza [e] Geo Josz, il ragazzo ferrarese ed ebreo reduce lui solo dall'inferno dei campi di sterminio nazisti" [ibid.][21] (Elia Corcos, the Jewish family doctor of Ferrara, venerated for decades by the entire citizenry [and] Geo Josz, the Jewish boy from Ferrara who was the only one to return from the hell of the Nazi extermination camps.)

What tombs most immediately signify is a form of radical absence which is not simply immediately or directly represented. If a tomb represents, first, the empty, hollow void which lies at its center, it then becomes a pretext for a second representation, which through graphic inscriptions upon tombs transforms the latter into funerary monuments. Through graphic inscriptions, that is to say, that which is most inimical to presence, funerary monuments are the twice-removed representation of an empty center. Inscriptions on funerary monuments refer to the absence of absence in the present. Funerary monuments do not, simply, indicate absence; what they signify is that the irrevocable nature of absence is repeated by the inevitable mediation of graphic representations.[22]

Micòl's deprivation of a tomb is an ideological violation of her person. Nazi politics aimed to obliterate the memory, as well as the existence, of Jews through the instrument of silent and undifferentiated mass interments and incinerations.[23]

Bassani's narrator understandably wonders about Micòl and her family: "Chissà se hanno trovato una sepoltura qualsiasi?" [p. 253] (Who knows if they found any burial place?). After posing it in the novel's prologue, the narrator answers his own question affirmatively with the entire text that follows. Nor does Bassani's "tomb" for Micòl not vividly recall the act of Nazi profanation. Time and a "città lasciva" (wanton city), like Foscolo's conceptual innovation in *Dei sepolcri*, serve Bassani, too, as demystifying replacements for the conventional locus of burial: pastoral and transcendent Nature, given form in the country churchyard.[24] The transformation of the Finzi-Contini home into a memorial tomb takes place after the family's deportation in 1943 and after the postwar appropriation of their untended, isolated house by mythicized "subproletarian" refugees, "gente inasprita, selvaggia, insofferente" (embittered, primitive, and intolerant people), who settle in permanently ("ancora adesso") [p. 258]. These violent usurpers ravage the home and pollute the city by their effective obliteration of the *magna domus* from public memory (ibid.). The destroyed trees and house historicize but also allegorize the Jewish experience during the Nazi-Fascist era. The mythopoeic garden of the novel's title points to a mystified narrative center inhabited by Micòl. A mystified Micòl is the author's portrayal of inextinguishable vitality, in the mode of female ideality. But when the paradisiacal garden is destroyed, its mythopoeic cycle completed, history takes over to vest the garden's ashes and to claim Micòl as its victim: a sacrificial figure bloodied for a twentieth-century "racial" ideology.

Running along Corso Ercole I is the eastern perimeter of the extensive Finzi-Contini property. The far side of the avenue faces the city cemetery, behind which is the small Jewish cemetery. The combined land of these three properties fills the northern limits of Ferrara. With the Corso splitting the area equally in two, the cemeteries project a mirror image of the Finzi-Contini property, like an oracular premonition of the great home's destiny. The boundary space far from the city's center that is shared by the three "necropoli" is a sacred space — for ancient, communal reasons on one hand and by dint of literary valorization on the other.

Right before the conclusion of the *Giardino*, the narrator recalls Micòl's attitude toward time — her loathing of the future, her delight in the "virgin," "vivacious" present, her greatest preference for the "sweet" and "holy" past (p. 450). Like Bassani's, Micòl's stance privileges the past, though she moves spiritedly within the present, for her an uncharted ("virgin") and fertile ("vivacious") time. For Bassani that time is also uncharted and fertile, a marginal space of writing in which to record the "bloody track" of recent Jewish history. Micòl's abhorrence of the future — a direct response to the Communist Giampiero Malnate's naive faith in it but more fundamentally an aesthetic disposition against the void of future time — echoes her creator's persuasion: "La mia poesia poi, così come la narrativa, parla del passato, del presente, e non del futuro, perché il futuro non c'è"[25] (So my poetry, like the narratives, speaks of the past, the present, and not the future, because there is no future). Present and past time arrest time, causing the future to cease existing. From another angle, taken by the narrator-husband of "Ravenna" (in *Odore*)—as will be seen in chapter 5—the future, for one who senses everywhere the presence of death, is a time of exclusion; thus it is a meaningless time.

Love, Art, and Survival

Micòl's "sweet" past makes the presence and knowledge of death a daily and natural experience. She is Bassani's untarnished emblem of an uncorrupted "vierge . . . vivace, et . . . bel aujourd'hui."[26] Her tenderness for the persons and objects of her early years can find no correspondence in the author's post-Holocaustic memory—except in Micòl herself, who becomes a sweet and pious past that inspires the author, paradoxically, to record a bitter and impious time and so terminate his own amorous and artistic despair. On the level of plot, Micòl participates in a warm and vaguely romantic friendship with the first-person narrator, and then peremptorily refuses the erotic relation he ardently desires. Her nonconsent, however, ultimately leads to his liberation ("reanimation") and the writing of the novel. The novel's last sentence, an enigmatic gloss of its broad significance, images a union of erotic love and the act of writing that retrospectively allegorizes the narrator's fitful erotic attachment as the necessary and reinforcing struggle of the writer with his craft. This allegorical struggle subsumes, as well, the author's fitful attachment to the Jewish community and his survival of persecution. At the end of the novel, the narrator, as lifeless as *acqua morta*—"still (dead) water"—imagines Micòl making love "every night" with the Milanese engineer Giampiero Malnate, whom they have both befriended. Suddenly he overcomes his passion: " 'Che bel romanzo,' sogghignai, crollando il capo come davanti a un bambino incorreggibile" [p. 448] ("A fine novel," I grinned, shaking my head as if before an incorrigible child [Q:*G*, p. 290]). The presumed romance between Micòl and Giampiero, ironized as a piece of fiction, is a child's foolish fantasy, to be displaced by an adult's work of art, the "true" fiction of Micòl. Following a concluding opinion of hers on the merits of present, past, and future time, the narrator ends his story: "E siccome queste, lo so, non erano che parole, le solite parole ingannevoli e disperate che soltanto un vero bacio avrebbe potuto impedirle di proferire, di esse, appunto, e non di altre, sia suggellato qui quel poco che il cuore ha saputo ricordare" [p. 450] (And as these, I know, were only words, the usual desperate, deceptive words that only a real kiss would have stopped her uttering: let them, just these and no others, seal the small amount the heart has managed to remember [The Italian term, *ricordare*, means both "remember" and "record"] [Q:*G*, p. 293]). The narrator's inability to stop Micòl's "deceptive" and "desperate" words enables *him* to appropriate them as a sign of his inadequate ("that little bit") yet artistically skilled ("that my heart has learned to remember") representation of her.

An autobiographical pattern concealing itself in the unlikely hideaway of Bassani's book of essays *Le parole preparate* compels the deliberate nonchronological ordering of the book into a linear, poetic autobiography that, repeating the pattern of the *Giardino*, culminates in artistic success. Since the author rejected the "rather gloomy" idea of assuming a "posterior" temporal attitude toward himself (*Parole*, p. 9), the essays stop the artistic journey at its height and thus avoid the undesirable prospect of the writer's postmortem self-visitation. As we have seen, the final prose of the *Romanzo*, too, which is in essay form, uses a veiled discourse to etch the figure of a newborn but fully mature writer. The nonfictional essays of *Parole* adumbrate an authorial persona between the lines. But the design of the essays, as the title indicates, is knowingly prepared, and the sense of artistic dominion that climaxes the text must surely be experienced by every reader. Published in 1966 and composed of essays that date from the dark years of war (1942) to the glittering years of authorial fame (1964), *Parole* seems an appendix to the *Giardino*, published only four years earlier.[27]

On the other side of the persona medallion drawn briefly in the preceding paragraph is a female form of desire, embodied in Micòl and symbolizing artistic life. As already suggested, Micòl occupies a sacred space in Bassani's fictive universe, a space of ennobling love and creative inspiration. This love, however, also contains a disquieting counterforce of artistic anguish and alienation. In an intertextual episode linking the *Giardino* to *Occhiali*, Micòl's narrator-lover is moved to defend the middle-aged Doctor Fadigati, who fell in love with a young and handsome male scoundrel and eventually committed suicide (this is the climaxing event of *Occhiali*). The narrator of Micòl's story maintained that

> l'amore giustifica e santifica tutto, perfino la pederastia; di più: che l'amore, quando è puro, cioè totalmente disinteressato, è sempre anormale, asociale, eccetera: proprio come l'arte . . . che quando è pura, dunque inutile, dispiace a tutti i preti di tutte le religioni. [p. 431]

> (love justified and sanctified everything, even pederasty; indeed that love, when it is pure, that is totally disinterested, is always abnormal, asocial, etc.: just like art . . . which, when it is pure and therefore useless, no priest of any religion . . . ever approves of.) [Q:*G*, p. 265]

This little credo is double-edged. On the one hand, it elevates the work of art to a form of "pure" love that is generally misunderstood and undervalued; on the other hand, it is a parable of the outcast, for abnormality and asociality outline the contours of the Jew in Fascist Italy. Jewishness and art constitute the two sides of the Bassanian coin, the currency of which the dominant social body rejected ("no priest of any religion . . . approves") during the young artist's slow-moving years of struggle and pain toward artistic maturity and social reintegration. Paradoxically, the enactment of anti-Jewish legislation helped lay the ground of a literary formation that radically altered Bassani's vision of literature. To conclude this chapter I shall retrace some of that early history and its translation into literary matter.

In 1935, aged nineteen and a freshman at the University of Bologna, Bassani was already a fledgling writer publishing short literary pieces in the local press and simultaneously being initiated into politics. A group of young anti-Fascist Sardinian schoolteachers newly arrived in Ferrara, just a few years older than he, and writers as well, became instrumental in nurturing the college student's literary-political development. These new friends included the now-esteemed novelist Giuseppe Dessì and the literary critic Claudio Varese. By 1937 Bassani was participating in clandestine political acts, which continued until his arrest in 1943. Those six years, dedicated

> quasi del tutto all'attività antifascista clandestina . . . furono tra i più belli e più intensi dell'intera mia esistenza. Mi salvarono dalla disperazione a cui andarono incontro tanti ebrei italiani, mio padre compreso, col conforto che mi dettero d'essere totalmente dalla parte della giustizia e della verità, e persuadendomi soprattutto a non emigrare.[28]

> (almost totally to clandestine anti-Fascist activity . . . were among the most beautiful and intense of my entire existence. They saved me from the desperation that so many Italian Jews, including my father, were facing, through the comfort they gave me of being completely on the side of justice and truth, and especially of persuading me not to emigrate.)

Bassani's moral decision not to emigrate resonates in several of his fictional characters who, through inaction, fail to emigrate and are swept into concentration camps. In sharpest contrast to Bassani's position of public resistance is the personal and amoral decision of his autobiographical character Bruno Lattes, who choses emigration—in other words, flight from political danger (see "Anni"). The torment of imprisonment for Bassani was undoubtedly mitigated by his conviction that he was serving justice and truth. For Bruno the same difficult years resulted in a loss of faith in political ideals. "Tutto quello che è accaduto a Bruno Lattes, sono io . . . soltanto che mentre Bruno Lattes era uno che era un niente, io invece . . . m'interessavo seriamente alla politica prima e anche dopo le leggi razziali"[29] (Everything that happened to Bruno Lattes happened to me . . . only that while Bruno Lattes was someone who was nothing, I instead . . . took a serious interest in politics before and also after the anti-Jewish laws). Thus Bruno's creator condemns his character.

Bassani's toughened mind and elated sense of cause are manifest in his fiction. So, too, however, is the anguish—political and personal—that informs much of it. The anti-Jewish legislation cut two ways: it nurtured not only a feeling of hu-

Figure 1. Jewish school building on Vignatagliata Street. Giorgio Bassani taught Jewish children here in 1939, following anti-Jewish legislation. The situation inspires a scene in "Gli ultimi anni di Clelia Trotti."

miliating (self-)isolation, but also a sense of increased moral strength—at least in some of its victims. Bassani's literary creativity, somewhat paradoxically, burgeons in response to the lethal decrees, whose sheer facticity motivates both the structure of an entire novel (*Giardino*) and a whispered distillation inside another narrative event ("Lida"). While numerous self-reflexive characters stun the reader with their self-mortifications (which are tied to religious identification), out of their depths a countervoice or presence, eventually an autobiographical "character," takes narrative shape and overpowers (survives) the weaker selves. The metamorphic interchange of victim and victimizer is effected not only within the fiction, but also implicitly in the comparison of autobiographical data and textualized models. Consider, for example, a particular episode of "Anni" that focuses on Bruno Lattes some years before his unheroic emigration. Bruno, like Bassani in 1939, began teaching in the school on Via Vignatagliata in the old ghetto (p. 123), opened for Jewish pupils suddenly barred from the public schools by Fascist legislation. The school building—which in real life was a spiritual shrine for Bassani—in the short story is reduced to a situational prop for Bruno Lattes. For Clelia Trotti, who is subjected to police surveillance, the building has the quality of a sanctuary; on its walls she sees plaques commemorating her own glorious socialist history. Although at this stage of her advanced life Clelia is but a pathetic relic of idealistic militancy, Bruno has no history whatsoever. He is an empty shadow of a person in this period, a wasted shell of political and erotic anguish. The author, a known anti-Fascist activist and already experiencing some literary success by the time of "Anni's" publication in 1955, constructs Bruno as a fictive double representing his own moral opposite. The negative specular persona seems to embody a moment of weakness overcome or exorcised by his creation of the character. Perhaps beneath the fictive Bruno's existential crisis of the years 1939–43 lurks the historical period of Bassani's withdrawal from active political resistance during the time he lived pseudonymously—and fearfully—in Rome, during the German occupation. By contrast, the Bassani of the Bruno years was a forceful "anti-Bruno."

Paolo Ravenna, one of Bassani's adolescent pupils in the makeshift Jewish school from 1939 to 1943, has attested to his former teacher's invigorating strength of mind and to the sudden stress that befell Jewish life at that time. Recalling the inside reaction of the student "group of the excluded" (in which he was numbered), Ravenna maintains that the new anti-Jewish mood of the time, "destined to humiliate and estrange [the schoolchildren] from civic life," did not succeed. And thanks go to Bassani for having played an instrumental part in strengthening their young minds and spirits:

> Bassani fu tra coloro che nel modo più efficace contribuì ad evitare che noi giovani potessimo cadere in un, del resto comprensibile, complesso di persecuzione. . . .
>
> Intendiamoci, Bassani poco parlava con noi di politica e Dio sa quanto in noi urgeva l'avvenimento quotidiano. Eravamo in guerra, i tedeschi sembravano invincibili, le conseguenze per il nostro futuro erano abbastanza buie. Ma di ciò forse Bassani non parlava perché la politica, quella vera, la cospirazione, la faceva altrove. . . .
>
> Ma un'altra politica Bassani faceva, e molto vivamente. Nella nostra scuola ormai sempre più ridotta nel numero degli allievi e dei docenti, entrava la voce di una cultura italiana e straniera ignorata nei testi ufficiali. Sentivamo parlare di sfuggita . . . dei fratelli Rosselli, di Giustizia e

Libertà, mentre faceva una rapida apparizione un giornale clan-
destino . . . .

E quando, ormai rimasti in due soli allievi, ci spostavamo per le lezioni
nel silenzioso studio di Bassani, già eravamo in grado di apprezzare ed
amare l'opera degli autori allora esclusi dall'arte ufficiale [per esempio
Montale, Vittorini, Chekhov, Croce]. . . .

Questo suo lucido atteggiamento, che poi esprimeva i contenuti della
resistenza, rispondeva anche . . . ad una esigenza di allenare noi ragazzi
ad una sorta di "autodifesa psicologica" dal pericolo del vittimismo, dalla
paura dell'ignoto domani; stato d'animo ben comprensibili in tempi di persecuzione quali erano i nostri.[30]

Bassani was among those who in the most effective way helped us
young people from falling into what was in any case an understandable
persecution complex. . . .

Let us be clear, Bassani hardly spoke about politics to us and God
knows how much daily events pressed on us. We were at war, the Germans seemed invincible, the consequences for our future were rather dark.
But perhaps Bassani didn't talk about that because he was involved elsewhere in politics, the real politics of conspiracy. . . .

But Bassani practiced a different kind of politics, and in a very lively
way. Into our school, now with fewer and fewer pupils and teachers, came
the voice of an Italian and foreign culture ignored in official texts. We
heard hurriedly . . . about the Rosselli brothers, about Justice and Liberty, while a clandestine newspaper made a hasty appearance . . . .

And when, with only two pupils left, we moved our class to Bassani's
quiet study, we were already able to appreciate and love the works of
authors who were then excluded from official art [for example, Montale,
Vittorini, Chekhov, Croce]. . . .

His lucid manner, which voiced resistance subject matter, responded
also . . . to a need to prepare us children for a sort of "psychological
self-defense" against the danger of scapegoatism, against the fear of the
unknown tomorrow—a state of mind very comprehensible in such times
of persecution as ours were.

With the arrest of Bassani and other teachers in the spring of 1943, the school
on Via Vignatagliata "ceases to exist" (ibid.). Although just twenty-two when he
began teaching as an outcast citizen, Bassani had a vision of civilized humanity
that not only strengthened his pupils but also forged his own spiritual armor. In
Ferrara between 1938 and 1943, he was like a prophet crying in the wilderness.
Fear silenced most of his compatriots, and apocalypse seemed on the edge of
explosion. Not surprisingly, the voice that narrates the "novel" of Ferrara carries
overtones of prophetic castigation and self-righteousness. Embodied in diverse

characters internal to the narratives, it arches over the entire fiction, casting an image of despair and spiritual death that slowly metamorphoses—unambivalently, in the end—into a self-constructed, self-possessed, invulnerable authorial figuration.

This fractionated yet epic narrative voice becomes a powerfully lean and lyric one in the poetry.[31] A proper analysis of Bassani's poems needs a separate space; now collected in *In rima e senza*, the poems from 1939 to 1981 constitute a major poetic statement.[32] Analogous in both voice and composition to the *Romanzo*, the title of the poetry volume also inscribes completion: *rima* and *senza* demarcate bipolar coordinates of the poetic axes. Included in this publication (and others) is a very early poem, "Te lucis ante," closely connected with the drama of death and survival the poet experienced as a prisoner of the Fascist regime, an experience that shaped his maturing years. Devoid of the exhilarating spirit of combat that made the years between the anti-Jewish laws and imprisonment "the most beautiful and intense" of his whole life, "Lucis" records the anguish of a young man daily fearing execution. In fact a series of poems, it is organized into two sections: the opening one contains two relatively long poems that frame the historical and locational circumstances of Bassani's incarceration; the second one consists of sixteen short, poetic units. "Lucis" marks a watershed in Bassani's poetic vocation; it can be read not only as an intimate cry of despair, but also as a record of the poet's literary and ideological conversion from subjective, impressionistic writing to a poetical rendering of historical truths.[33] Bassani had some striking words to say about his prison poem many years ago, in the aftermath of the critically acclaimed *Giardino* and the earlier *Cinque storie*: "Non avrei mai potuto scrivere niente se non avessi, prima, scritto *Te lucis ante*. In un certo senso, è dunque questo il mio libro più importante"[34] (I would never have been able to write anything if I hadn't, beforehand, written "Te lucis ante." In a certain sense, then, this is my most important book).

The placement of this citation in Bassani's own book of essays is significant: it forms part of the closing (and only) section of the volume addressed entirely to himself and his own work, and it appears in the dramatic form of a dialogue—a dialogue, furthermore, in which the secondary interlocutor (the interviewer) has been erased, transformed into a depersonalized "D" (*Domanda*). Bassani as "R" (*Risposta*) clearly remains himself, by the nature of the interview as well as the nature of the book. Paradoxically, by diminishing himself relative to his writing, he asserts his artistic maturity and the primacy of the text. At the bottom of the page that includes the "Lucis" citation, Bassani responds to a question about the *Giardino* by agreeing that the success of the latter novel most certainly includes reasons "that go beyond my 'personal merit'. I'm worth much less than *The Garden of the Finzi-Continis*" [*Parole*, p. 247; *Di Là*, p. 268]. The self-diminishing sign of achievement parallels *in nuce* the large structure of the *Romanzo*, still to be discussed.

"Te lucis ante" is a purgatorial cry that rises from a "profondo carcere" (deep prison) located in an estranged, terrestrial valley (the Aniene Valley around Rome). It reiterates the thematics of its Dantean model (Purgatorio VIII): the exiled soul's longing for home; the presence of a potent serpent-adversary; holy and redeeming prayer. The great political leaders of the purgatorial valley (Dante's "essercito gentile") invest Bassani's narrating persona analogically with political nobility.[35] But notwithstanding its sacred poetic referent (Ambrose's original hymn and Dante's citation of it) and its address to the Hebraic God, Bassani's poem is secular, his speaker burdened with earthbound self-doubt and, in fact and figure, totally alone in his purgatory. If Dante's *terza rima* reflects the Trinity, Bassani's *quarta rima* "answers" with a trope that traces Earth's four corners. The modern poet's verses, predominantly septenarii, with harsh, imperfect rhymes, are a dark interrogation (framing no fewer than seventeen questions in its brief structure) of a "tu" that seems a despairing *alter ego* and another one (originally capitalized) forged as the great and wrathful God of Israel:

> Dormo: o sei tu che pungi
> il mio sonno quieto?
> Tuo il grido che di lungi
> cerca me, il mio segreto?
>
> Se fosse questa veglia
> perché tu sia! L'aceto,
> tutto il fiele che al vino,
> al forte vino tuo aggiungi,
>
> chi non berrebbe, e lieto? [*Rima*, p. 70]

> I sleep: oh is it you who pierce
> my quiet sleep?
> Yours the cry that from afar
> seeks me, my secret?
>
> If only this watch were
> for you to be! The vinegar,
> all the bile that to the wine,
> to your strong wine you add,
>
> who would not drink it, and happily?

These stanzas portray deep anguish desiring contentment—a thematic conflation of the Dantean pilgrim's infernal journey leading to purgatorial hope. The speaker's conflictive cries, like the medieval poet's, are aroused by political and religious questions that spark the potential of self-renewal. Like the Finzi-Continis' *magna domus* and the communal and Jewish cemeteries of Ferrara, the poem of confinement represents a sacred space. Picturing a windswept valley and two dark towers, the prologue poems define a space of dislocation and fear, an abyssal edge where weeping never rests and prayer receives no response. Here is the prisoner-persona's greatest locus of emargination, and the fall over the edge seemingly imminent. In the subsequent short poems, the "io" becomes humbled, confessional; the lyrical discourse, religious – imaging forth demons and angels, light and shadow, vengeance and the Kingdom of God, Moses, a cross in a field "awakened" by a loving sun/voice, a shadow seeking a loving, final dawn. As the lyric narrative reaches silence, the sacred space is transformed, the original purgatorial plain and prayer recuperated; the space becomes, in short, "Te lucis ante," the poet's own answer to his brush with death. The figure emerging from the purgatorial/poetic plain speaks a new language.

Curiously, the difficulty of prison life, affirmed in essays and interviews and transcribed into poetry and fiction, seems discredited by fourteen letters Bassani wrote at the time to his family. (The letters – discovered recently, it seems – appear in the opening section of *Di là.*) There is little sense of hardship and none of fear in these homely, affectionate notes that give advice to his young sister on her painting, appreciation to the family cook for hot meals sent to him, and news of how well and how long he sleeps at night. "Sto bene, sono calmo e tranquillo" [p. 9] (I am well, calm, and peaceful) is his message home. Where, then, is the truth of his prison experience: in his retrospective writing, or in his contemporary letters? Was the young prisoner hiding his fears from his family, or was he, simply, not so uncomfortable under Fascist confinement? The only clue to an answer might be contained in Bassani's well-known statement just quoted in the context of "Lucis": "I am worth much less than *The Garden of the Finzi-Continis.*"

Chapter 2
Ferrara, Real and Invented

Ferrara, il piccolo, segregato universo da me inventato.

L'odore del fieno

Ferrara Revisited

The city of Ferrara received its definitive and characteristic form in the Renaissance, when its medieval contours were expanded northward by an urban development larger than the whole of the earlier city. At the new center, Duke Ercole I governed and resided in the sumptuous castle his ancestors had built a century earlier to be an inviolable fortress. At the periphery, imposing brick walls thickened by bastions gradually rose before and after Ercole's life to encircle the city limits. For Giorgio Bassani, growing up in Ferrara four centuries later, the city plan afforded a natural and felicitous setting for the stories he was to write of the daily life, history, and social and civic politics of its modern citizenry.

The ancient streets and walls of Ferrara still circumscribe well-defined neighborhoods and historical memories and inscribe intrinsic symbolic vectors among its social spaces. Bassani uses and reinvents city life to heighten the relation of history and symbolic representation, conjoining the two perspectives so well that non-Ferrarese readers are seduced by the fiction's illusory historicity and the *ferraresi* are duped by its illusory credibility.[1] In both cases the author's underlying patterns of rhetorical structure may go unheeded, though not unfelt. Ferrara's topography, in Bassani's hands, is a map of sacred spaces that plots the author's idea of history's meaning. And history is of the essence. The attention Bassani gives to other cities in literature, in several essays of his *Parole preparate*, may be read as his poetics of literary urbanization. Paying homage to Croce, to whom the book is dedicated, Bassani in fact describes *Parole* as "anche, e forse soprattutto . . . una continua, indiretta dichiarazione di poetica" [*Parole*, pp. 9–10] (also, and perhaps above all . . . a continuous and indirect declaration of poetics).

An example to be avoided, according to the author in his lengthy essay on Venice, is Ben Jonson's recreation of Piazza San Marco, "uno spazio convenzionale, astratto: un palcoscenico, e basta, disposta com'è, oramai, a essere saccheggiata dalle più private e assurde immaginazioni" [p. 25] (a conventional, abstract space – a mere stage that's set up now to be plundered by very private and absurd fantasies). To be avoided as well is the nineteenth-century Venice of two other famous writers, both foreign novelists:

Che cosa ha a che fare la Venezia storica, reale, *italiana*, della fine dell' Ottocento, con quella, squisitamente putrida, che affascina gli eroi di James e di Mann? . . . La Venezia di James resta "l'antro" niente affatto metaforico da cui guata . . . la mitica signorina Bordereau, decrepita ex amante del non meno mitico Jeffrey Aspern: il cupo, insondabile, immemoriale antro veneziano di sempre. [p. 30]

What does the historical, real, *Italian* Venice of the end of the nineteenth century have to do with the other, exquisitely putrid one that fascinates the heroes of James and Mann? . . . The Venice of James remains the not at all metaphoric "cavern" from which . . . the mythical Miss Bordereau, decrepit ex-lover of the no less mythical Jeffrey Aspern, watches suspiciously: the same old dark, unfathomable, immemorial Venetian cavern.)

Similarly, Mann's Venice is "una specie di *suk* medio-orientale, di viscido bordello, o addirittura di impietrata cifra del sesso" (a kind of Middle-Eastern *suk*, or slimy bordello, or even petrified cipher of sex); and its cholera, "non si sa poi se reale o ipotetico, a quale altra malattia alluda, della psiche e dell'anima. Sta di fatto, ad ogni modo, che la città che lo cova, in segreto, dentro il suo seno guasto, non è e non può essere di questo mondo" [p. 30] (you don't know if it's real or hypothetical, nor to what other illness of the psyche or soul it may allude. Anyway, the fact remains that the city that nurtures it secretly within its wasted breast is not and cannot be of this world). To be attained, on the other hand, with poetic power is "truth" and "concreteness" (p. 24), by which Bassani means a rigorously historical imagination. Disparaged in the cited passages, mythic and spatial structures then are able to have a crucial literary function – as my reading of Bassani's narratives attempts to verify, though I am unaware of statements by the author on this question. In this light, the reader might wish to consider Bassani's depiction of the Venetian Doctor Fadigati of *Occhiali* (a character who has been compared to Mann's Aschenbach) and the rank streets of Ferrara where Fadigati wanders, looking for homosexual companions.

Bassani constructs a Ferrara – that is, a society – that is tested to its limit by the Fascist regime. Diseased beyond recuperation, the city discloses its contaminated condition. The author's voice, ironic and moralizing, tunes its rhetoric to the sounds of a chastising Old Testament prophet. The sometimes submerged parameters of community life – moral feebleness, guilt and shame, sacrificial slaughter and redemption, erotic love and literary redemption – catalyze the broad range of narrative action across the total corpus.

Although modern Ferrara – the Ferrara defined by Fascism – is at the heart of Bassani's fiction, Ferrara as text extends its embrace to a substructure of historical and geographical preconditions that predate even the founding of the city in 1208. Renaissance Ferrara, one of the capital cities of Europe, like its mighty neighbors Milan, Venice, and Florence, determines the modern city's physical character and embeds its legacy of politics and social structure in the city's streets and buildings. The aristocratic Este dynasty, though only lightly remarked in the fiction, claims important textual status as the privileged and violated origin of the modern city. The small Jewish community of Ferrara, whose first settlers date back to Roman times,[2] is part of, yet distinct from, the Ferrarese populace. The streets that once delimited the tiny ghetto reify the religious and social ostracism never entirely absent from pre-1870 Italy and reinstituted under Fascist rule. The streets also mark the loss of Risorgimental assimilation and recall, farther back, the unique toleration and defense of the Jews by the Este rulers. Fascism, taking possession of the city, forges it into a topsy-turvy world, sacrificed, impotent, and shamed – harshly unredeemed because of its fruitless sacrifice. The public voice, once gossipy, merely provincial, is now silenced by its fear of Fascist violence, and that silence bespeaks an "infernal" communal descent. Only the voice of the "prophetic" persona-narrator intrudes unrelentingly on the silence, proclaiming the community's shame.

Bassani's modern Ferrara is a twilighted city, qualified by its recent past and by "intrusive" neighbors – Bologna, Venice, and Milan – that represent, as cities and through particular fictive inhabitants, outsiders who disrupt Ferrara's social equilibrium. Finally, there is a transcendent Ferrara, beyond the narrative "now" of fictive experience, beyond the reflective time of remembering and writing, a Ferrara that encloses the historical and imaginary constituents of Bassani's narrative, and by which the invented city attains meaning and totalization: the Ferrara-mosaic formed of the discrete, enchained, cumulative, completed texts bounded by their nontextualized referent.

All these Ferraras participate in forming an organic literary body. Like Dickens's London or Proust's Paris, this imaginative reconstruction threatens or nurtures in insuppressible ways. The name of the universe, *Il romanzo di Ferrara*, signals its preeminently social nature; of the inexhaustible parts acted out in this social biography, the most prominent and polymorphous is reserved for the narrating subject.

The city of Ferrara is also a semiotic labyrinth, summoning the reader to traverse the spaces, histories, and myths that fabricate the text's thickly interwoven layers of meaning. The authorial persona, in diverse embodiments, traverses the city/novel from within: on foot, by bicycle, by train, by car, on a tortuous journey of self-knowledge. A naive reader who responds to the call of the text may move (read) through it unaware, like a tourist in town. As the narrator of "Una notte del '43" observes, casual strangers, in contrast to the uneasy, alert inhabitants, arrive in the city with no recollection of the wartime massacre at the castle wall they pass by. The alert reader, of course, does not assume the tourist's posture, but instead studies the facade of the castle wall as if it were a textual wall and comprehends (reads), for example, certain holes in it as a sign not of time but of gunfire. So ordinary, otherwise, can the moment seem that "alla persona di fuori . . . sarà consentito di passare dinanzi alle piccole targhe marmoree che portano incisi i nomi dei fucilati *senza che il corso dei suoi pensieri abbia a soffrire del minimo turbamento*" [p. 136; emphasis added] (some stranger . . . could walk in front of the small marble plaques engraved with the names of the men gunned down, *without his train of thought having to suffer the slightest disturbance*). The tourist/reader must scrutinize/suffer the city's monuments/signposts to detect their engraved and not touristic sense – to respond affirmatively to the unuttered question of the watchful townspeople (the author traceable beside them): "Alzerà o non alzerà finalmente la testa, colui, dalla Guida del Touring?" [ibid.] (Will he or will he not finally lift his head from the Touring Guidebook?).

The relations of modern Ferrara to its properous neighbors, of Bassani to his city, and of the author to his text are all of marginality. The spatial metaphor, with its implication of "inside" and "outside," orients the structure and symbolism of the whole of the *Romanzo*; history and topography – referential and textual – orient the narrative action. Not only in its topography, but also in its landscape, Ferrara lends itself to a symbolism of spiritual or moral testing. The "landscape" is largely brick buildings set close to the street, their rooms and courtyards concealed from public view by facades and high walls. The impression is a lack of human activity and natural vegetation. The fog of the Po River valley beyond its borders envelops the city much of the year. Federico Fellini, traveling in this area after the war with Rossellini to film *Paisà*, likened the land to "that wretched Holland." "In the Po Delta," Fellini recalled, "misery had a wild and silent quality."[3] D'Annunzio lyricized the city's "melanconia divina" in a poem beginning "O deserta bellezza di Ferrara" (Oh barren beauty of Ferrara) and ending in praise of its "vie piane, grandi come fiumane" (streets as straight and grand as broad streams) and its "silenzio."[4] Goethe, more desolate, confessed, "Per la prima volta mi sento sorpreso da non so che uggia, in questa [Ferrara] che è pur una grande città, ma tutta in piano e spopolata"[5] (For the first time I am surprised to feel a certain gloom in [Ferrara], which is still a great city, but completely flat and unpopulated). Giorgio De Chirico painted his disquieting "metaphysical" canvases in Ferrara.

The silence and emptiness of the city, felt by these and other poets and artists, lends itself to metaphor, mystery, and, most important, the materialization of creative potentialities.[6] The symbolization of the urban spaces — from the thick outer walls to the narrow inner streets — is a fundamental literary operation by which the author exploits Ferrara's fecund silence to structure his tales and to conjure mythopoeic figures of suffering and death. The autobiographically privileged fictional character, who frequently traverses Ferrara and "tests" his life in its outlands, recharts the ancient topos of a heroic journey in a modern, deheroicized modality. Topographical spaces are transcribed into literary topoi in a process that entails historical metamorphosis along with the invention of characters; artifice such as this supports an edifice of "truth."

Let us now look more closely at the historical material that spans the author's novelistic universe — Renaissance, Risorgimento, Fascism, post-Fascism — and note in each the crucial Jewish history, especially as interpreted by key characters, that subtends these periods.

Renaissance Ferrara

From the illustrious Este dynasty that ruled Ferrara for three centuries derive the three most important Renaissance imprints on Bassani's textual Ferrara: the Este castle at the center of the city, the swampy wilderness called "Il Barco del Duca" (The Duke's Park) at the city's northern extremity, and the ruling family itself. As an embodiment of the *polis*, the Este castle symbolizes good (if somewhat mystified) government, which is, however, defiled by a chilling political crime that takes place in 1943 at the castle wall. The historical drama is reconstructed in the short story "Una notte del '43." In the *Giardino*, the Estes and some of the property they owned are linked to the Finzi-Contini home and family.

The land that was to become Finzi-Contini property was purchased by Micòl's great-grandfather Moisè in 1850. It contained an orchard and ruins that "inalberavano *ab antiquo* il molto decorativo nome di Barchetto del Duca" [p.259] (brandished *ab antiquo* the highly decorative name of The Duke's Little Park). The "diminutive" Barchetto, consuming almost a quarter of the entire Herculean addition to Ferrara, brandishes, in essence, its identity with the Estense Barco del Duca,[7] a large stretch of uninhabited wilderness (including the later Finzi-Contini estate) contiguous with the northern border of medieval and, later, Renaissance Ferrara, where the Este dukes and their company would ride

Figure 2. Ariosto's house in Ferrara. His inscription on the facade begins "Small but suited to me" (Parva sed apta mihi).

and hunt for amusement. Bassani's "first family" thus become heirs to the ducal rulers. In addition to the aristocracy they assume by association, they inherit the material isolation and dank air of the heavily wooded wilderness. Their house, "isolata laggiù fra le zanzare e le rane del canale Panfilio e dei fossi di scarico, e soprannominata invidiosamente la '*magna domus*' " [p. 259] (isolated over there among the mosquitoes and frogs of the Panfilio canal and the drains, and enviously nicknamed the *magna domus* [Q:*G*, p. 22]), was built in a part of the city "fuori mano, insalubre . . . deserta, malinconica, e soprattutto inadeguata" [p. 260] (so much out of the way, so unhealthful . . . so deserted besides, so melancholy, and above all, so very unsuitable [Q:*G*, p. 23]). Yet, enclosed on two of its vast sides by the city walls and on a third by a high garden wall abutting Corso Ercole I,[8] the estate seems to the Ferrarese to confirm the Finzi-Continis' haughty and excessively private ways: what one might expect from royalty. But this perception, as the reader comes to know, is inadequate; the wealthy and cultured Finzi-Continis prove to possess strong moral qualities of fearlessness and loyalty to their religious group.

   Bassani's identification of the Finzi-Continis with the Estes enhances the qualities of the former less by facile glamorization than by hard historical accounts of the latter. The ubiquitous Este shadow aggrandizes the personal and civic qualities of the Finzi-Continis.

The Este dynasty, while hardly guiltless of violence and exploitation, enjoyed a reputation as honorable and benevolent rulers very popular with their subjects. Celebrated patrons of the arts and urban development, they also demanded respect for the people from their soldiers and welcomed fugitives from other Italian cities as well as from foreign countries. A good number of those fugitives were Jews fleeing intolerable conditions. By the mid-fifteenth century, the Jewish residents of Ferrara, with the Estes' promise to accept their services and skills rather than ostracize them, were able to establish a proper community. In 1448 Lionello d'Este succeeded in persuading the pope to halt anti-Jewish slander in church sermons, and three years later his successor, Borso, made it known that he would act as the protector of all Jews seeking refuge in his lands. Ercole I, in 1473, not only resisted suggestions by papal delegates to expel the Jews, but also defended their rights as his subjects. He further authorized for his Jewish subjects the purchase and conversion of a Ferrarese *palazzo* into the synagogue that still stands on Via Mazzini. When the Sephardic Jews were expelled from inquisitional Spain in 1492, Ercole admitted some of them to his city, where they, too, soon set up their own synagogue. And following nightmarish oppression of Jews in central Europe, his successor, Ercole II, in 1532 announced his guarantee of safe passage westward for the refugees, some of whom settled in Ferrara and established a German-language synagogue. In the next few years, exposed *marrani* (Jews practicing Catholicism) from Portugal and elsewhere found shelter and protection in Ferrara. By the mid-sixteenth century, the city boasted ten synagogues for some 2,000 Jews (in a population of approximately 50,000). This was a time when Estense Ferrara was a center of both Christian and Jewish culture; the latter, for example, produced a still-prized Spanish translation of the Bible. But the light of civilized society soon dimmed. In 1598 Este rule passed to the Church, and the 1,500 Jews who chose not to follow their rulers out of Ferrara lost most of their civil rights; they were also forced to wear a yellow identifying badge and, some twenty-five years later, were locked every night into the ghetto.[9]

Risorgimento Ferrara

The Ferrarese mock the Finzi-Continis by calling their home the *magna domus*, in ironic contrast to Ariosto's famous *parva domus*, but the very choice of their model unwittingly forges another link in the Renaissance myth of nobility that encircles the privileged Jewish family. Micòl's paternal grandmother, Josette Artom, reaffirms in the late nineteenth century the family's affiliative touch of royal lineage. A supercilious woman of titled ancestry (barons of the Treviso line), Josette was a "donna magnifica, ai suoi dì: bionda, gran petto, occhi celesti" [p. 260] (magnificent woman in her time: blond, buxom, blue-eyed). Bassani models her on her contemporary, Margherita di Savoia, queen of Italy, whose grace and blond beauty were legendary. Those attributes were celebrated by the great poet and patriot of Risorgimental Italy, Giosue Carducci, who appears as a character in the *Giardino*. In 1875 he spends ten days as the houseguest of Josette and her husband, Menotti. According to Micòl's father, Carducci's inspiration for the famous verses of the "Canzone di Legnano" was not after all Queen Margherita, but Josette. Evidence of the poet's devotion to Josette is the pack of letters the family preserves that Carducci wrote to her, using terms such as "charming baroness" and "most gracious hostess." But, like the queen, Josette was also "notoriously a bigoted conservative" (a modern historian's assessment of Margherita): Josette adored the House of Savoy, hated the fomenting Socialists and Anarchists, loved Bismarckian Germany, and could not conceal her distaste for the tight little (*ristretto*) Ferrarese Jewish milieu to which her husband had brought her.[10] Moreover, she could not conceal "*il proprio fondamentale antisemitismo*" [p. 260; Bassani's emphasis] (*her own fundamental anti-Semitism*). The half-German Josette looked upon her new home, the Barchetto del Duca, as her Valhalla (ibid.). There is textual irony in her bleak assessment of the Barchetto, for in the narrator-author's view, too, the estate is a hall of death, but a humanizing one that preserves the daily life of its inhabitants, in the manner of Etruscan necropoli.[11] Josette's Berliner mother infuses the Finzi-Contini lineage with German (Ashkenazic) blood; the next generation, in the person of Olga Herrara, Micòl's mother, infuses it with Hispanic (Sephardic) blood. Like a microcosm of the Jewish fugitives from Western and Eastern Europe who found a home in Estense Ferrara centuries earlier, Western and Eastern Jewish in-laws intermix with Italian stock in the Finzi-Contini family: a maternal "foreign" side splices into the paternal "native" side. The females contribute to the real and metaphoric family attribute of nobility. Olga, of Venetian origin, is born of a "famiglia sefardita ponentina *molto buona . . . però* piuttosto dissestata, e d'altronde osservantissima" [p. 260] (*very* good Sephardic family . . . but one that was financially not too sound, although fearfully orthodox [Q:*G*, p. 24]). There is a strange tension between the figures of the anti-Semitic Josette and her daughter-in-law, the orthodox Olga. Bassani wishes, it seems, to internalize in his privileged fictive family not only the principal sects of European Judaism but even the Hebraic anti-Christ: the Jewish anti-Semite. The Finzi-Continis synecdochize the ethnic case *par excellence*.

The founder of the "dynasty," Moisè Finzi-Contini, precedes Micòl by just three generations. The "ancient" roots of this family go back only to the time of the founding of the Italian nation. This draws a sharp line of origin from which not only the history of the nation, but also the history of a people (the Jews), flows in rapid retrogradation. Moisè is a magnificently conceived patriarch. He is called "il rigido patriarca" (p. 255) in the positive sense of being resistant to external pressures and asserting his right of self-determination, even if to excess. Thus he spares no expense to build (in bad taste) the first Finzi-Contini "house," the massive, multicolored marble tomb resembling "una specie di tempio tra l'antico e l'orientale, come se ne vedeva nelle scenografie dell'*Aida* e del *Nabucco*" [ibid] (a kind of vaguely ancient and vaguely oriental temple, the kind you saw in the productions of *Aida* and *Nabucco* [Q:*G*, p. 17]) in the Jewish cemetery. Like his biblical namesake, Moisè is a figure of deliverance denied domicile in the land promised to his people. He dies in 1863, shortly after the annexation of the Papal States to the Kingdom of Italy, "e la conseguente, definita abolizione anche a Ferrara del ghetto per gli ebrei" [ibid.] (as a result of which the Jewish ghetto in Ferrara was abolished, once and for all [Q.*G*, p. 17]). When, in 1850, while still an inhabitant of the ghetto, Moisè buys from the Marquis Avogli the "historic ruins" of a sixteenth-century Estense residence set on nearly twenty-five acres of unhealthful, marshy land, he not only makes a good monetary deal, but he also invests his family with a mythic as well as aristocratic space. The thickly wooded land cut by canals represents a border state between wet and dry, an arduous and sacred space associated with both fertility and decay. During the Middle Ages, Ferrara entrusted its northern defense principally to this land, "to natural hostilities, the impassability of the terrain and the absence of practicable crossings."[12] The estate spatializes both a timeless (universal) condition and a historical, optimistic epoch of national transition in which Moisè participates. A plaque on the synagogue of Via Mazzini, praising him for his "meriti di 'italiano e di ebreo' " [p. 255] (virtues "as an Italian and a Jew" [Q:*G*, p. 18]), attests to the pride among Jews of Moisè's time in gaining full acceptance into Italian life and being able, from a humble origin, to rise to a position of wealth and esteem.

> Gli anni parevano belli, floridi: tutto invitava a sperare, a osare liberamente. Travolto dall'euforia per la raggiunta eguaglianza civile, quella stessa che da giovane, all'epoca della Repubblica Cisalpina, gli aveva consentito di far suoi i primi mille ettari di terreno di bonifica . . . [ibid.]

> (Things seemed fine and flourishing in those days: everything about the times encouraged hope and daring. Swept up into a mood of euphoria by his newly acquired civil equality, the same that as a young man, at the time of the Cisalpine Republic, had allowed him to reclaim his first substantial piece of land . . .) [Q:*G*, p. 18]

Moisè is as much a patriot of Italian liberation as a "prophet" of Jewish liberation.

Jewish social progress in the late nineteenth century was a tremendous victory over the days of papal rule in northern and central Italy, when Jews were prohibited from acquiring or continuing to own land, not to mention their forced domicile within the ghetto. This state of affairs had endured in Ferrara (and in other cities such as Rome, Bologna, and Venice) throughout the seventeenth and eighteenth centuries, securing for most of the Jews (2,000 of whom were Ferrarese) extreme economic hardship. Another century and the Napoleonic occupation of Ferrara (1796) needed to pass before the ghetto gates were to be demolished, the yellow cloth insignias discarded, and equal rights again decreed. By 1815, however, papal rule along with ghetto life and the old interdictions returned. Only in the wave of the revolutionary spasms of the thirties and forties were Jewish rights gradually restored. With the admission of Ferrara into the Kingdom of Italy (1859–60), the good times under the Estensi seemed reborn. Jewish citizens like Moisè Finzi-Contini (and the fathers of Edgardo Limentani [*Airone*] and Giorgio Bassani) eagerly claimed their right to proprietorship of land, farms, and other real estate, while others took their places in industry, especially in textile production.[13] Still others, like Dr. Elia Corcos ("Passeggiata"), were now free to practice their professions for the community at large, no longer restricted to employment by Jews.

The figure of Moses is deeply etched in Bassani's imagination: as a child, an antique engraving of "law-giving Moses" hung over his bed. While he was imprisoned during the war, the print came back to his mind as a sign of divine judgment. To the child, the face of Moses had been the very face of God.[14] No wonder that the adult Bassani made "Moses" the fountainhead of his fiction's most prized family, the Finzi-Continis. But whereas the Biblical Moses led his people truly to the promised land, the Ferrarese Moisè leads his descendants to a "garden of Eden" (the Barchetto del Duca) destined in two generations to burn as firewood, its inhabitants dispossessed and destroyed. In this way, Bassani articulates the failure of a historical, utopian vision of national unification and Jewish assimilation.

The author borrows another great Biblical figure, the prophet and king Solomon, to father the second most important family of the *Romanzo*. This family, centered in Elia Corcos, dominates "Passeggiata," which is the second of the two foundational texts of Bassani's collected work. Extratextual, autobiographical information enriches the reader's understanding of the Corcos family, headed by Salomone, as the generic founding family of the narrating subject. Bassani's maternal grandfather, who became a prominent doctor in Ferrara and lived almost a hundred years, provided the model for Doctor Elia Corcos, Salomone's youngest son and Ferrara's most prominent (fictive) surgeon. Owing to the esteem of the real doctor, Bassani's parents were spared many abuses suffered by other Jews during the last years of Fascism. After the German occupation of Ferrara, the doctor's influence and the brave assistance of non-Jewish neighbors enabled them to escape capture and rejoin their son Giorgio in Florence. All of them, including the old doctor (unlike the old Elia), suffered but survived the war.[15] A portrait of this ancestor hangs on the living-room wall of Bassani's childhood home.

Elia's father, Salomone, was an old grain merchant who lived "nel cuore di quello che fino a non molto avanti era il ghetto" [p. 57] (in the heart of what until recently had been the ghetto). The narrative time is about 1888, only two-and-a-half decades after the restrictive ghetto rules were abolished, and the year in which Elia becomes engaged. He is the youngest of Salomone's twelve children (eleven sons and one daughter). A "half-dozen" years (p. 57)–originally a full dozen (1974, p. 62)–go by before the young doctor can afford to purchase his own home. His sons, Jacopo and Ruben, are born in their grandfather's rented apartment on former ghetto ground where the old man has lived since the early 1840s (p. 62). The Biblical names and numbers, along with the ghetto-space of origin, are markers of a "sanctified" Jewish origin. Only the Finzi-Continis share the Corcos family's aura of Jewish authenticity, that is, its inherent and constant religious faith. Rooted in the oppressive and humiliating ghetto that persists into the years of national unification, the purest embodiments of historical Jewish character are Bassani's two fictional patriarchs: Moisè Finzi-Contini and Salomone Corcos. Their patriarchal grandeur passes pristinely through a clamorously unorthodox filter to their descendants Micòl and Elia. Individuals such as these form the touchstone that releases Bassani's rage against inauthentic–that is, "metastorical"–Jews: those who lack a historical understanding and therefore (presumably) a genuine religious soul.[16]

    The fruitful Salomone, a *grain* merchant, resembles in more than name ancient Israel's first dynastic king, who ruled over twelve tribes, had many wives (Salomone had three), was blessed with a God-given understanding heart, and wrote impassioned love poetry (1 Kings 3, 9). Elia, in an early version of the text, ironically speaks some lines from *Aida* to his unloved wife–"vieni, diletta, appressati / schiava non sei, né ancella" [1953, p. 118] (come, my beloved, draw close / you are neither slave nor maid-servant)–that seem to mock the holy Salomonic love song. Even more, Elia's words mock himself, for he feels shackled by his choice of spouse and lacks the kindhearted simplicity of his father. Another ironic allusion to *Aida* occurs in the opening chapter of the *Giardino*, where Moisè Finzi-Contini's new family tomb is compared to *Aida's* stage sets. The intertextual decision not only pairs the two principal family lines of the *Romanzo* but also elicits political issues. Men like Moisè and Salomone, liberated ghetto Jews of the Risorgimento and Italian patriots–indeed, founding fathers of a new Jewish social order–revered Verdi's operas, including *Aida*, for the political message in them obvious to all Italian patriots of that time. *Aida* premiered in 1871, in the very dawn of Italian nationhood; its creator is as much the greatest embodiment of Risorgimental pride as he is Italy's most beloved composer. Salomone is another Mosaic figure. The engraving of Moses that fascinated the very young Bassani (and became the subject of a poem) reappears in the first version of Elia's story: "lassù, in cima in cima alle scale, sopra la porta del granaio, una solenne immagine di Mosè legiferante" [1953, p. 117] ('way up at the top of the stairs, over the granary door, a solemn picture of law-giving Moses). Although the author expunges the direct reference to Moses subsequently, the image juxtaposed with the granary leaves its mark in Salomone's work with grain. The merchant's very clothes give off the smell of grain, and his sole being, without need of words, bespeaks piety, sanctity, and simplicity:

> Quantunque religiosissimo e praticante . . . pure, in casa, non parlava mai di religione. . . . Si limitava a esprimersi nel particolare dialetto, simile a quello ferrarese ma pieno di parole ebraiche, d'uso normale dalle parti di via Mazzini. . . . Fatto si è che in bocca sua nemmeno le parole ebraiche avevano niente di misterioso, di strano. Chissà come, acquistavano anche quelle il colore del suo perpetuo ottimismo, della sua bontà. [p. 62]

> (Even though he was religious and observant . . . he never spoke of religion at home. . . . He limited himself to speaking in the special dialect—similar to *ferrarese* but full of Hebrew words—that was normally used in the neighborhood of Via Mazzini. . . . The fact is that in his mouth even Hebrew words didn't sound mysterious or strange. However it happened, they too took on the coloring of his perpetual optimism and goodness.)

Salomone, his head encircled by white curls as shiny as silk, his age nearly a hundred, affirms his great mythical-religious stature through the life-sustaining "manna" (Mosaic grain) whose aroma he exudes:

> Misto di vaghi effluvi di agrumi, di fieno appassito e di grano, era il medesimo odore che sfogliando certi libretti di devozione ebraica, da lui portati con sé nella casa di via della Ghiara [la casa di Elia] in vista di una loro "eventuale" distribuzione fra i convitati delle due successive cene di Pasqua, lei [Ausilia, sorella della moglie di Elia] aveva sempre sentito sprigionarsi da quelle vecchie pagine indecifrabili . . . le dieci piaghe d'Egitto, Mosè dinanzi a Faraone, il passaggio del Mar Rosso, la caduta della manna . . . e così, di seguito, fino allo svelarsi a Giosuè della Terra Promessa. . . . Dai panni e dall'intera persona di Salomone Corcos spirava . . . un profumo che . . . faceva subito pensare a quello dell'incenso. [p. 64]

> (A mixture of vague emanations of citrus, dry hay and grain, it was the same smell that, while leafing through certain little Hebrew devotional books he had brought along to the house on Via della Ghiara [Elia's home] in expectation of their "eventual" distribution among the guests of the two Pasqual suppers, [Ausilia, Elia's wife's sister] always felt radiating from those old, undecipherable pages . . . the ten plagues of Egypt, Moses before Pharoah, the passage through the Red Sea, the rain of manna . . . and so on, to the revelation of the Promised Land to

Joshua. . . . From his clothes and the entire being of Salomone Corcos emanated . . . a perfume that . . . made one think immediately of incense.)

The smell of grain that anoints Salomone as a sacred forefather returns in a much later text as a smell of hay that pacifies mourners attending the funeral of Bruno Lattes's uncle; the olfactory leitmotiv in turn diagrams the funeral scene allegorically as artistic, creative power. The Bassanian smell of hay is as material as the grain Salomone handles and as ethereal as the breath of inspiration that the author tries to subdue (see "Odore" in the book homonymously titled, and my discussion in chapter 5).

Salomone is also a political patriot. Although he was "certainly the mildest man in the world," he often recounted his memories of Ferrara under Austrian domination, its streets full of mounted soldiers brandishing bayonets: "La gente questi soldati li guardava con disprezzo, con odio. E anche lui—ammetteva—, che a quell'epoca, cioè prima del '60, era ancora abbastanza giovane, aveva talvolta fatto altrettanto" [p. 63] ("the people looked at these soldiers with scorn and hatred. And Salomone admitted that he too—who in that period, that is to say, before 1860, was still quite young—had sometimes behaved the same way"). More often Salomone would talk about Giuseppe Garibaldi, "the sun, the idol of his youth," who spent a week in Ferrara and "on a starry night of June 1863" addressed an enthusiastic crowd that included Salomone (ibid.). The patriot talked to his child Elia about "another marvelous night" a few years later, when the ghetto gates were pulled down by a violently aroused public ("a furor di popolo"), so that the little boy would always retain the image of the fair-haired Man ("Uomo biondo") in the red shirt who had created Italy: "Garibaldi!" (ibid.). Salomone embodies the inflamed spirit of the Italian Risorgimento, soaring to its highest reach by dint of his brand-new and joyous liberation as a Jew.

In the original version of the narrative, the location of Salomone's home is "in the narrow and unhealthful heart of the ghetto." (1953, p. 103). The squalid ghetto environment shares with the resplendent Finzi-Contini estate an original condition of unhealthfulness, whose surpassing is all the more remarkable for the original debilitation. In both cases the eventual homes—the one inherited by Micòl's father and the one purchased by Elia outside the ghetto—are airily rustic: "wholesome," though tinged with sadness. The definitive fate of the privileged inhabitants is, the reader knows, to be chased from their homes, to die in concentration camps. During the days of prosperity, both homes are tagged with the Ariostean epithet of *magna domus*. In the case of the Finzi-Continis, the epithet voices the resentment of gossipers; in the case of Elia Corcos, it is self-created and gently self-mocking, uttered "fra il serio e il faceto" [p. 57] (half-seriously and half-facetiously). Previous writings of the text curiously had Elia reciting the exact (*un*ironized) Ariostean inscription "*parva* sed apta mihi" (1974, p. 62; 1953, p. 104; emphasis added). The later alteration suggests a strong identity between the two families, but at the same time the difference in their social status is heightened: the half-joking tone of Elia asserts a personal self-awareness that humanizes him, whereas the public belief in Finzi-Continian self-containment transforms the family into super-human victims of (sacral) ostracism.

As Elia ages, he comes to resemble his father physically, but the generation that separates them casts them into different worlds. Salomone's old-fashioned ways are epitomized in his religious devotion and in his earthen aroma. The modern Elia, on the other hand, is a creature of science who smells of mercuric chloride and phenic acid (p. 64)—a Positivist (1953, p. 112), of course. He refuses to contribute his monetary obligation to religious education in the Jewish community because his conscience does not permit him to pretend a faith he does not have (p. 59); and yet, in the final analysis ("venendo al dunque"), he conforms in the main to Jewish customs (p. 60). In time of crisis, such as the funeral of his eight-year-old son, Ruben, Elia adheres to "the most orthodox rites" (ibid.). This unconventional man rises socially and professionally from the humblest of origins to great distinction, thanks in large part to the accident of his birth during the birth of the Liberal Italian state. His hard-earned bourgeois home "so out-of-the-way" (p. 58)—most of all, out of the ghetto neighbor-hood—and his marriage to a Gentile (as his disapproving relatives remark) acclaim his uprootedness and his modern views. At the same time, facing rustic fields on one side and urban traffic on the other, the house concretizes a histori-cal moment of enormous political change. The promise of a new political dawn reaches the meridian neither for Elia nor for Ferrara. With regretful memories of the eclipsed Estense Renaissance, the contemporaries of the elderly Elia look upon the glittering career of their homegrown "genius" as "inadequate, only pro-vincial" (p. 54), like Ferrara itself. The destiny of Elia to "soar" is borne in his Hebrew name: the prophet Elijah, perhaps best known for his fiery translation to heaven but also for his similarity to Moses (at whose side he appears on the mount of transfiguration), bears a name that in its Greek transcription spells "sun." The imagery that Bassani employs to narrate Elia's (and Ferrara's) less-than-splendid achievement fuses the Hebraic narrative with the Greek myth of Icarus, channeling a reader-response of ironic pathos. "Around 1880" (the vague date signals the storyteller's fabulation of past time), when both the physician and the city are ripe for momentous, lifetime eminence, an "obscure" Bolognese deputy manages to gain governmental approval for "the most important railway junction of northern Italy," to be constructed in Bologna rather than in Ferrara. As a result of "that fatal resolution" (according to Bassani's historical invention), Bologna becomes, "in the twinkling of an eye," the greatest city of Emilia (ibid.):

Che cosa era stato infine anche Elia Corcos, come tanti altri suoi concit-
tadini, come tanti altri galantuomini suoi pari, di niente altro colpevoli che
d'essere nati e cresciuti a Ferrara, se non una vittima innocente degli in-
trighi della politica? Anche lui, non diversamente da innumerevoli altri
suoi compatrioti degni di miglior sorte, proprio quando già stava per spiccare il volo (Potere, Gloria, Felicità, eccetera: oh le grandi, eterne parole . . .), anche lui sul più bello aveva dovuto rinunciare, ritirarsi, ar-
rendersi. [pp. 54–55]

(What after all had even Elia Corcos been—like so many of his compatriots, like so many other honorable men of his kind, guilty only of having being born and grown up in Ferrara—if not an innocent victim of political intrigues? He too, no differently from any number of other
compatriots worthy of a better fate, just when he was about to take flight
[Power, Glory, Happiness, and so forth: oh, those grand and eternal
words . . .], he too, just at the right moment, was obliged to renounce,
withdraw, and surrender.)

This little account of second-class municipal and occupational status is an
ironic, pseudohistorical parable of the inner contradictions of an individual and
a social history. Nonetheless, it attests also to the ineradicability of vigorous free
thought and fantasy: Icarus downed but not drowned. The author's earlier writing of this narrative guides the reader explicitly to the delicate patterns of contradictory meaning in Ferrara's late nineteenth-century historical rise that falls;
to Elia Corcos's professional brilliance that illuminates a miniscule sphere; and,
perhaps most of all, to his robust imagination, which preserves a glow in his
otherwise dimmed spirit (this latter attributed to his unfortunate marriage to an
unlearned and Catholic peasant girl):

[I ferraresi], Corcos in prima fila, avevano avuto le ali mozzate! Ciò che
spettava loro di diritto . . . altri, ormai, se l'era appropriato! Senonché,
allo stesso modo che il canto consola e ripaga la cecità del poeta, ecco che
negli offesi, nei derelitti, quasi a compenso dell'enorme sopruso, sorgeva
potente la consapevolezza d'un tesoro che mai nesssun furto avrebbe
potuto alienare. Tutto, essi avevan perduto; ma non già, grazie a Dio, il
vigore della fantasia, la forza indagatrice e chiarificatrice del libero pensiero. [1953, p. 97]

([The Ferrarese], Corcos in the front row, had had their wings clipped!
What was theirs by right . . . others had now appropriated! Except that
in the same way a song consoles and repays the poet's blindness, in the
offended and the forlorn—as if to compensate for the enormous political
abuse—arose the powerful awareness of a treasure that no theft could ever

remove. They had lost everything; but not yet, thank God, the vigor of imagination, the probing and clarifying force of free thought.)

With a leap of imagination, it is also possible for the reader to "spremere una lacrima generosa sul contemporaneo e interdipendente attentato che avevan subito le carriere parallele del dottor Corcos e della città [antica e nobile] che gli aveva dato i natali" [p. 98] (squeeze out a generous tear for the contemporaneous and interdependent outrage suffered by the parallel careers of Doctor Corcos and the [ancient and noble] city that had given him his birthplace).

Elia straddles the old and the new, the fragile and the strong, the scientific and the imaginative. A kind of Janus figure (like his house), he looks backward to his father, Salomone, and the founding of a "tribal" family and ahead to the textual fulfillment of the family in the persona of the author, an inferred descendant who recounts their stories and his own. The Biblical names of Elia's children, Ruben and Jacob, his own Hebraic prophet's name, his place as the twelfth-born child, and his father's name delineate a sacralizing family foundation. However, the blatancy and slight imprecision of the allusions, that is, the presence of one female among the twelve siblings, also gently ironizes the parallels. The echo of the Biblical story of Joseph and his brothers is nonetheless essentially mystifying and endows the death-burdened Corcos family with mysterious vitality. The death of his child Ruben verifies the atheist Elia's strong sense of Jewish identity (p. 60). His own octogenarian death in a concentration camp is a "kingly" sacrificial slaughter that in this collected fiction compares only to the similar fate of Micòl Finzi-Contini. Both are children of Italian patriots impoverished by repressive ghetto life; both lavishly evidence the economic and social success of Jewish assimilation following national unification and liberation. The three-generational, unnatural extinction of these families (Salomone's only son dies with him) forms the ancestral and artistic bedrock of the regenerative journey of the self that threads together the project of the *Romanzo*. Whereas Micòl is the artistic inspiration for the narrator, Elia bequeaths to the latter, his symbolic "son," an artistic disposition. The image of the young doctor sitting at a kitchen table among incredulous strangers, isolated under a bright electric light and irrationally asking for Gemma Brondi's hand in marriage, deepens in time to image the mature doctor sitting alone at his desk in a corner of his own kitchen, concentrated on inner visions: both etch the lonely and troubled (and illuminated/illuminating) figure of the writer at work. Symbolizing the writing persona in any of his guises, Elia Corcos, with his face "più fragile e delicata di quella normale" (more fragile and delicate than was normal), is (in the eyes of the Brondi family) "diverso, fondamentalmente estraneo" [p. 53] (different, fundamentally alien). Elia's "difference" bears first of all on his social status, but also on his religion (ibid.). The particular author, of course, to whom Elia's posture leads us is also bourgeois and Jewish. Estrangement is the historical Jewish burden; neither Estense aristocratic nor Risorgimento liberal ideology was capable of eradicating it. The narrative of Elia's social rise in Italy's modern Golden Age attains its full meaning only retrospectively; that is, in the "epilogue" of his success story, his senseless death in Auschwitz.

Fascist Ferrara

The demolition of the ghetto gates inaugurated an era of social, economic, and political opportunity that instilled nationalistic pride in Jews as different from each other as the financially wise Moisè Finzi-Contini and the politically zealous Salomone Corcos. Their identification of themselves as Italians was a joyous act of self-esteem and social contract. A euphoric pride in country led some of these Jews, and even more non-Jews, in the first decade of the new century to form a political party; the members of this Nationalist party, founded in Florence in 1910, were "not without a certain admirable idealism," but they were also "inebriated with the vulgar imperialism of violence and conquest."[17] They preferred discipline and obedience to liberty and equality, aggression to moderation. Many of their numbers, including Jews, moved eagerly into the ranks of the budding Fascist bands of 1919. World War I, as the fictive Clelia Trotti knew, was a tremendous catalyst of right-wing politics ("Anni"): "Come avevamo ragione, noialtri socialisti . . . di sentire nelle campane che salutavano la vittoria italiana del '18 le nostre campane a morto!" [p. 125] (How right we were, we Socialists . . . to hear in the bells that were saluting the Italian victory of 1918 our own death-tolls!). The "arrogant rhetoric" (ibid.) of that time, she goes on to say, was already Fascism's claim, and the ruinous war thrust Socialists, too, into many errors (p. 126). Modeled on Ferrara's famed revolutionary Alda Costa, Clelia embodies the idealism, courage, and persecution endured by the Socialists during their more than half-century of militant action, originally against economic injustice and later against Fascist tyranny. The narrative's mere notation that Clelia "had discussed socialism" with no less than the party's revered historical leader, Filippo Turati (p. 117), is ample intimation of her place of political honor.

The Jewish Moisè and Salomone and the Catholic Clelia are figures of ancestral authority and reverence, without peers in the *Romanzo*. They form a "sacralized" archetype of moral as well as familial origins. Curiously, the pairing of a Jewish husband and a Catholic wife, a Bassanian leitmotiv, functions textually both *in bono* (regarding parental figures) and *in malo* (regarding spouses). Some instances of the latter marital configuration will be examined in later chapters.

Beyond their function as founding figures relative to the fiction's "universal" narrator, the three characters mentioned embody great historical moments in twentieth-century Italy. History, in fact, is the cement that holds together Bassani's narrative building blocks. Historical facts permeate the fiction in many forms, from news reportage (invented conversations on the likelihood of war, for example) and fictionalized real events (the 1943 massacre at the Este Castle in "Notte") to, finally, semiotic clues or symbols (Edgardo Limentani's passing mention of his three years in Switzerland—an "unspeakable" semiotic allusion to his frantic flight from Nazi deportation [*Airone*]). Bassani's narratives, even ones like "Lida" and "Passeggiata," produce their meanings in reference to their characters' experience of Italian Fascism and World War II. Lida's marriage in 1929 is related symbolically to the concordat ("marriage contract") signed in the same year by Mussolini and Pius IX. Dr. Corcos's story, though set primarily around the turn of the century, leaps suddenly ahead to his death in Auschwitz. Although Bassani's textualization of Fascism provides the reader with a good history lesson, the author deliberately falsifies some facts, such as the date of the 1943 slaughter, and contrives others, such as the postwar governance of Ferrara by former Resistance leaders. Still others are left out or are pure invention. Historical and fictional discourse interpenetrate, each sharpening the significance of the other. Later chapters will examine crucial instances of this interaction in various narratives. What is in order now is a brief chronological overview of the particular historical happenings that helped determine and shape the texts.

Invented and led by Mussolini, the Fascist movement came into being on March 23, 1919, in Milan's San Sepolcro Square. In the turbulent years following World War I, Fascist combat teams strove to eliminate the Socialist threat by intimidation, bludgeoning, and murder. Political agitation and violence provide the backdrop for the arrival in Ferrara of an exceedingly bourgeois and peace-seeking doctor, Athos Fadigati (*Occhiali*). On October 28, 1922, the march on Rome persuades Italy's King Vittorio Emanuele III to appoint Benito Mussolini as prime minister. Bassani depicts the disorderly and sadistic side of the momentous march in "Notte." The train ride of Ferrarese Fascists to Rome is both the factual basis and the calculated origin of his fictionalized drama of a massacre; the drunken rioting of the marchers gathered in Rome from numerous cities is a matter of history. The principal object of amusement in Bassani's account is Pino Barilari, whose father was a Freemason. Italian patriotism and Freemasonry once were synonymous: from Mazzini to Garibaldi, men who sought to liberate their nation from foreign or oppressive rule joined the society. Mussolini outlawed this liberal and anticlerical organization in 1925, in good part to assuage the pope, whose political support he keenly desired. The politics paid off in 1929, with the pact that conciliated Church and State and greatly satisfied the Catholic populace. The promise of "new life" fires the very Catholic imagination of the seminary-schooled Oreste Benetti, who in the year of the concordat marries the much younger and "fallen" protagonist of "Lida." This tale of broken promises is a bitterly ironic political allegory. In the same year of Fas-

cist triumph, Dr. Fadigati is disgraced: he is identified as a homosexual (a criminal offense during the regime). For six so-called years of consensus following
the Lateran Pacts, the Italian nation hails Mussolini for bringing it first stability,
then the Church, and finally the Empire. The Ethiopian War of 1935–36, the
last imperialist campaign of modern times, was enormously cheered by the
Italians and instrumental in moving Mussolini aggressively into Franco's war
and Hitler's lap; it plays no role in Bassani's fiction. On that historical horizon,
however, rises the storm of Italian-legislated anti-Semitism—the most noxious
of the Duce's accommodations to Hitler. This legislation, to which most Italians
reacted with disbelief and repulsion, is the archhistorical event of the *Romanzo*:
it constitutes the humiliating and treacherous plunge into nonbeing into which
the Ferrarese (and all other Italian) Jews were incredulously compelled. Numerous characters embody aspects of a conglomerate authorial persona whose
reconstructed experience of institutionalized anti-Semitism is the organizing
principle of the confessional *Romanzo*. Catastrophe moved at a swift pace in
these years, from the 1936 war in Spain, the 1938 anti-Jewish laws, and the 1939
Pact of Steel (which obliged Italy to fight with Germany if war broke out) to
the declaration of war on May 10, 1940, the disaffection of his ministers that
brought Mussolini down in July of 1943, the Duce's partial resurrection by the
Germans a month and a half later (along with the latter's occupation of northern
Italy), and the start of Italian Jewish deportation in September of 1943, marking
the "fulfillment" of the nefarious anti-Jewish laws. The two acts of religious oppression shape the fiction both as major elements of plot (*Giardino*) and as underlying metaphors of extreme victimization. Inversely, some of the narratives
trace classical *topoi* of death and unspeakability (*Porta*).

The early Fascists, from the *sansepolcristi* who founded the *Fasci italiani di
combattimento* at their first meeting in 1919, to those who signed up during the
early years of the regime, were later to be honored and decorated (with special
red fringes on their uniforms) as "first-hour" Fascists. The Jews among the early
believers (and there were many) enjoyed certain rights that would be denied to
their coreligionists by the anti-Jewish laws. Along with Jewish soldiers who
fought in the Italian wars of the century,[18] these Jews were granted
discriminazioni—a distinction that began to dissipate as Berlin's pressure on
Rome increased; it assumed its entirely negative meaning once the Nazis took
control in late 1943. Bruno Lattes's father typifies this group: a volunteer soldier
in 1915 and a combatant on the Carso, he acquires his Fascist *tessera* soon after
the war, expecting (wrongly) that his special status will facilitate his son's
emigration to Palestine (see "Anni," pp. 122, 125 and *Giardino*, p. 440). His
enthusiasm, like that of many Italians, wanes as the Duce's alliance with Hitler
grows. The father of *Occhiali*'s schoolboy protagonist embodies this later disil-
lusionment:

Romantico, patriota, politicamente ingenuo e inesperto come tanti altri ebrei italiani della sua generazione, anche mio padre, tornando dal fronte nel '19, aveva preso la tessera del Fascio. Era stato dunque fascista fin dalla "prima ora," e tale in fondo era rimasto nonostante la sua mitezza e onestà. Ma da quando Mussolini, dopo le baruffe dei primi tempi, aveva cominciato a intendersela con Hitler, era diventato inquieto. Non faceva che pensare a un possibile scoppio di antisemitismo anche in Italia; e ogni tanto, pur soffrendone, si lasciava sfuggire qualche amara parola contro il Regime. [p. 204]

(Romantic, patriotic, ingenuous, and politically inexperienced like so many Jews of his generation, my father, too, on his return from the front in 1919, had taken out a Fascist card. He was, therefore, a Fascist "of the first hour," and so he remained, basically, in spite of his gentleness and honesty. But ever since Mussolini, after the quarrels of the early days, had begun to agree with Hitler, my father had grown uneasy. He thought only of an outbreak of anti-Semitism in Italy, too; and every now and then, though it upset him, he came out with some bitter remark against the regime.) [(W:S, p. 136)]

The narrative ends in 1937. One rendering of a generic fictional father, the same character a couple of years later (in "Anni") is a changed man, physically as well as spiritually. The anti-Jewish laws have become history, and his emaciated "tempia fragile fragile, più cartilinagine che osso" (extremely fragile temple, more cartilage than bone) and "capelli bianchi e leggeri come piume" (white hair, as light as feathers) [p. 121] signal his state of ostracism and mortification; more, they image annihilation: a (death-camp) skeletal specter is being blown away like a feather. The place of the Jew in the Fascist regime has radically shifted from a centrality grounded in nationalistic pride, prestige, and participation to the shameful marginality of the dispossessed.

The first-hour Fascist Geremia Tabet, one of the numerous characters appearing in various narratives, exemplifies the extreme case of Jewish belief in Fascism. His intimacy with Fascist high officials ("era sempre stato 'dentro alle segrete cose' " [Occhiali, p. 243] (he had always been "in on the secrets") convinces him as late as November of 1937, owing to the "guarantee" of his friend, the federal chief of police, that an anti-Jewish law will never be passed (ibid.). Geremia seems to project Bassani's most profound contempt of Jewish political assimilation. Another text, "Lapide," casts Geremia—named cynically for the Old Testament prophet of uncompromising enmity toward false prophets and idolators—as the uncle of Geo Josz, survivor of Buchenwald. Such a relation, balancing the extremity of Nazi-Fascist victimization against the extremity of Nazi-Fascist collaboration, symbolizes the European community's failure to be the keeper of its Jewish brothers and sisters. Within the bounds of the Jewish community, the innocent, slaughtered Geo becomes a symbol of Abel; his uncle, who betrays the justice his name stands for, symbolizes fratricidal Cain. The Biblical tale, in which a brother's murderer founds a prosperous city, has an ironic, despairing counterpart in the rubble of unredeemed Ferrara.

To the townspeople's perplexed and self-insulating questions about Geo back in Ferrara, the answer might have come (the text conjectures) in the form of "un urlo furibondo, disumano" (an inhuman form of rage [Q:*P*, p. 123]) that they would have heard "con orrore" [p. 96]. This scream, a hypothetical one, ends the text. Geo's actual scream responds to the first sight of his uncle, upon Geo's return home from the concentration camp: "Ebbene, non era stato enorme che Geo, quando lo zio fascista aveva messo il naso fuori da una finestra del primo piano, fosse uscito in un grido acutissimo, ridicolmente, istericamente appassionato, quasi selvaggio?" [p. 81] (Well, wasn't it inconceivable . . . that Geo, the minute his Fascist uncle appeared at a window on the first floor, came out with a piercing shriek, ridiculously, hysterically passionate, almost savage? [Q:*P*, p. 104]). If the communal voice ignores the obvious motives of Geo's "inhuman" screams, for Geo the mere sight of Geremia and the Fascist-style beard he still flaunts[19] evokes the specter of death camps. Bassani ironizes Geremia's Fascist patriotism and assigns him behavior that reveals his moral indifference to the rest of Ferrarese Jewry: "talmente benemerito del Regime, quello là, da riuscire per almeno due anni, dopo il '38, a continuare a frequentare di tanto in tanto addirittura il Circolo dei Negozianti" [p. 81] (he was so esteemed by the regime, such a Fascist hero, that even after 1938, he was able for at least two years to continue patronizing the Merchants Club every now and then). This is the very club from which Bruno Lattes's father is expelled for being Jewish (p. 121).

Countervailing the ex-Fascist and maternal uncle, Geremia, is the nephew's ex-partisan and paternal uncle, Daniele Josz. The latter is linked onomastically to the royal Israelite prophet who, mortally endangered by conspirators, miraculously returned safely to his land from exile: the exalted outline of Daniele's safe return home despite the Nazi-Fascist plan to slaughter Jews and partisans. The only partisan whom the author depicts with no touch whatsoever of blemish, Daniele seems to represent a warning, by noble example, against the moral weakness that Bassani detects in his Jewish neighbors (and in himself?). Daniele's righteousness, confirmed by his continuing "indignation" and "polemical inclination" toward the most notable exponents of the "primissimo squadrismo ferrarese" [p. 90] (earliest and best known of the local Fascists [Q:*P*, p. 116], is confirmed more deeply and symbolically by his singular role in Geo's only (albeit temporary) reintegration into a family unit. The two relatives, but not Geremia, also bear the same surname. Geo's mother, father, and younger brother are all killed in Buchenwald, and the Ferrarese community shuns the returned survivor. Geo refuses his ex-Fascist uncle's invitation to live with him, sharing instead with his equally family-denuded Uncle Daniele a single, tiny room of his large house that has been expropriated by the governing Communists.

For Bassani, the rise of Fascism in Ferrara is an exacting measure of the Jews' communal standing and imperative moral choices. Jewish pride in assimilation and achievement and despair in persecution and death are the parameters within which the "prophetic" author's didactic voice grows sympathetic (for Bruno's father), scornful (for Geremia Tabet), and outraged (for Geo's persecution and forced homelessness, first in Buchenwald and then in Ferrara). Geo's sudden and definitive departure from his native city reiterates the forcible deracination of the proverbial wandering Jew. Later chapters of this book will examine Bassani's judgmental literary inscription of the intense moral responsibility that historical circumstances forced on Italians—and Italian Jewry—during this century's reign of Nazi-Fascist tyranny. Under Fascist rule prior to World War II, only two government acts truly stunned the nation: the 1924 assassination of the Socialist deputy, Giacomo Matteotti, and the 1938 anti-Jewish legislation.[20]

By the first half of 1938, the newspapers were vilifying the Jews. Month after month, newspaper and government announcements addressed "the Jewish question." In the middle of the year, a diplomatic fact sheet (*Informazione diplomatica, n. 18*) reaffirmed the government's concern with "the health of the [Italian] race" while insisting: "Discriminare, non significa perseguitare. . . . Come fu detto chiaramente nella nota n. 14 dell'*Informazione diplomatica* e come si ripete oggi, il Governo Fascista non ha alcun speciale piano persecutorio contro gli ebrei in quanto tali" (Discrimination does not mean persecution. . . . As was clearly stated in note 14 of the *Diplomatic News* and as repeated today, the Fascist government has no special plan to persecute Jews as such). Yet it reminded its readers of the "equazione storicamente accertata, in questi ultimi venti anni di vita europea, fra ebraismo, bolscevismo e massoneria"[21] (equation, historically proven in these last twenty years of European life, among Judaism, Bolshevism, and Masonry). Notwithstanding the unusually antagonistic tone of this document, Italian Jews still reined in their apprehension. Mussolini had repeatedly maintained that in Italy there never was a "Jewish question," but he began in 1938 to contemplate the merits of an isolated Jewish colony or even nation. One in already-colonized Ethiopia (with a native Jewish population of ancient origin) seemed particularly suitable. The duke of Aosta, his viceroy there, encouraged the idea, especially for foreign Jews residing in Italy and the more recent refugees (since 1933) from Germany, Austria, and Czechoslovakia. The duke left instructions, in the latter part of 1938, for the "discovery of a true little 'terrestrial Paradise' ":

La zona doveva essere ottima dal punto di vista sanitario . . . avere un clima moderato, risorse idriche abbondanti, terreno suscettibile di un ot timo sfruttamento agricolo-industriale, non essere sulle direttrici di traffico principali ed abitata da popolazioni pacifiche, prevalentemente pagane, dove esistessero il minor numero di chiese Copte e di Moschee, onde evitare dissidi di carattere religioso.[22]

(The area had to be of the highest quality regarding sanitation . . . and should have a moderate climate, an abundant water supply, and land suitable for high-quality agricultural-industrial development; it should not be on main traffic roads and should be inhabited by peaceful natives, predominantly pagan, so that there would be very few Coptic churches and mosques around, in order to avoid religious friction.)

This "humanitarian" impulse to empty Europe of the Jews soon gave way to a harder line. A manifesto written by "racial scientists" and approved by the Fascist party in July of 1939 stated in part that the concept of race was purely biological, that Italy's population and civilization were of Aryan origin, that the Jews did not belong to the Italian race, and that the physical and psychological European characteristics of Italians must not be altered in any way. Anti-Semitic statements from diverse sources kept appearing in print, and finally, during the night of October 6–7, Mussolini's Grand Council approved an anti-Jewish document. Its first sentence read: "Il Gran Consiglio del Fascismo, in seguito alla conquista dell'Impero, dichiara l'attualità urgente dei problemi razziali e la necessità di una coscienza razziale"[23] (The Fascist Grand Council, in consequence of imperial conquest, proclaims that racial problems and the need for racial awareness are of pressing moment). Among its numerous provisions, it prohibited marriages of Italians to "non-Aryans"; expelled foreign Jews (many of whom just five years earlier had found refuge in Italy from Nazism); granted "discriminations" to Jewish citizens whose families included distinguished or mortally wounded soldiers or Fascist party members enrolled in the years 1919–22 (a provision which, though it applies, is never awarded in the fiction to the ex-combat officer, Lattes père, and his son Bruno); prohibited military service and membership in the Fascist party; prohibited landholders from owning more than a certain number of acres of land (wherefore Edgardo Limentani signs his property over to his Catholic wife); denied Jews the right to attend any schools other than those set up by the Jewish community (Clelia Trotti goes to Ferrara's Jewish school to see Bruno, who teaches there). Although the great majority of Italians, including the arch-Fascist Filippo Tommaso Marinetti, strongly opposed the views of the council, its anti-Jewish measures—with some addenda that, inter alia, closed off many professions to Jews—became law on November 17, 1938, under the name "Measures for the Defense of the Italian Race."[24] Refined and more restrictive decrees followed one after another until the war was almost over, except for the brief hiatus of Mussolini's loss of power and the outlawing of the Fascist party in the summer of 1943. The first months of the legislation – fall and winter of 1938-39 – were especially traumatic for the Jews and for the direction of Bassani's fiction. The Fascist alliance with Nazism delayed the "final solution" for Italian Jews until September of 1943, when the Germans took total command of northern Italy. Exceptional efforts of other Italians to protect their Jewish compatriots in occupied zones allowed many of the latter to stay alive. Of the entire population of Italian Jews at the start of the war – about 40,000 – relatively few – some 7,500 – were deported; of them, however, only 610 returned home. In Eastern Europe, of course, the situation was much worse. From Kiev alone, in late 1941, almost 34,000 Russian Jews were murdered by special Nazi squads at Babi Yar. Ninety percent of the Polish and German Jews (totaling more than 3,500,000 people) were annihilated.[25] Bassani's narratives, by fabricating lives of a very small number of Italian victims and by almost suppressed yet dramatic instances of the "final solution," uniquely delineate an inexpressible reality.

In the city of Ferrara, the Jewish population at the end of 1938 numbered between 700 and 900. With the Nazi occupation of the city, some eighty-seven of them were deported, only five of whom returned.[26] The Fascist concentration camp at nearby Fossoli, which had interned anti-Fascists (with relative humanity) since the early years of the regime, became a clearinghouse not only for political prisoners but also for Jews rounded up from the cities and mountains within the puppet Republic of Salò by Mussolini's *repubblichini* and their German comrades. Each prisoner was identified by a number and a small emblem: a yellow rectangle for Jews, a blue rectangle for foreigners, a red triangle for politicals. Fossoli rapidly became a horrifying *Durchgangslager* (assemblage and sorting camp), a "waiting room of death" before the last stop at Auschwitz, Mauthausen, Buchenwald, and so on. With the front line advancing northward beyond Florence, all the remaining internees had been deported by August 1, 1944, and the camp closed.[27] All told, 10,000 people passed through Fossoli, about a third of them Jews. Among these Jews was the distinguished writer Primo Levi. Others, in fiction, were Micòl Finzi-Contini, her mother, father, and grandmother, who, "nel settembre del '43, furono presi dai repubblichini. Dopo una breve permanenza nelle carceri di via Piangipane [in Ferrara], nel novembre successivo furono avviati al campo di concentramento di Fossoli, presso Carpi, e di qui, in seguito, in Germania" [p. 449] (in September '43, were taken by the *repubblichini*. After a short stay in the prison at via Piangipane [in Ferrara], they were sent to the concentration camp at Fossoli, near Carpi, the following November, and thence to Germany [Q:*G*, p. 291]).

Bassani's microcosmic Ferrara magnifies the tragedy of the exterminated lives through the figure of one who survives: Geo Josz. Through the unrivaled and youthful dynamism of the ineffable Micòl, who does not return, Bassani leaves a delicate yet profound textual imprint of Holocaustic loss and sacrifice. Through the almost subliminal history of Edgardo Limentani, the author adumbrates the survivor spared by timely flight (to Switzerland). Thus the concentration-camp image diffuses the *Romanzo* interstitially, as it were. By Bassani's nonfactual literary calculation, almost half of Ferrara's Jewish population— 183 of 400—are deported, and only Geo returns (p. 73). Through numerical power, the author underscores the effectiveness of the massive annihilation process. But he reserves the greater instrument of narrativization for Italy's unique drama of the anti-Semitic decrees: the omen of the death camps. As much as the German model synthesized that country's long and sad history of anti-Semitism, the Italian copy stunned and saddened the vast and unbigoted majority of its citizens.

After the War

The postwar era of the fifties opens an authorial space of memory, self-reflexivity, and writing: an epilogic space. The *Giardino* duplicates this structure, for its first and last sections explicitly frame the narrative action within a postnarrative time. Its very first paragraph sets the "old" story against a much later writing time: "Da molti anni desideravo scrivere dei Finzi-Contini. . . . Ma l'impulso, la spinta a farlo veramente, li ebbi soltanto un anno fa, una domenica d'aprile del 1957" [p. 249] (For years I have wanted to write about the Finzi-Continis. . . . But the urge, the impulse to get down to doing so, I had only a year ago, one April Sunday in 1957 [Q:*G*, p. 7]).

The writing time—resurrection time ("an April Sunday")—is further distanced by the narrator's location in Rome; the story he writes takes place in Ferrara. The first of the *Romanzo* stories ("Lida") also ends with an epilogic reflection (Lida's self-disarming recognition of her husband's long and unconfessed unhappiness) that distances itself from the story's final narrative action, Oreste's death in the spring of 1938. "Lida" underwent five redactions between 1937 and 1955. The last one implicitly mirrors the retrospective period of authorial writing in the narrative time of Lida's final rumination. Similarly, the last chapter of "Passeggiata" recollects a much earlier time, the primary narrative time of Elia Corcos's engagement and marriage. These early stories, both narrated in the third person, adopt a technique of temporal distancing that will become the hallmark of Bassani's major narratives, all in the first person, and all the critical core of the *Romanzo*. Focusing on the decades before and after the dawn of the new century and thus having a unique background function relative to the others, the first two short stories are conspicuously intruded, even "scorched," by the crucial temporality of the anti-Jewish legislation and the concentration camps. With the lightest of touches, Elia's narrative foretells his extermination in Germany, and with an indirect but clear sign, Lida's narrative locates Oreste's death at a time—spring of 1938—that no reader of the *Romanzo* can fail to associate with the imminent anti-Jewish legislation. The fourth of the grouped Ferrarese stories opens with an epilogue: the main narrative matter, Clelia Trotti's last years, follows retrospectively. This structure resembles that of the *Giardino*, and the texts also share the depiction of the (archetypal) narrator's fundamental attributes: his self-liberation from erotico-political bondage and, by "disappearing" from the narrative stage of Nazi-Fascist persecution, his survival. The survivor-narrator is a category of authorial representation that subsumes every other depiction of authorial figures in the *Romanzo*. It is a figure of absolute centrality, provided with inextinguishable strength (unlike the survivor of Buchenwald, Geo Josz) that enables—even requires—him to remember (write). The survivor in Bassani's representation is a metaphor of the writer.

Unlike the thematically central period of persecution under Fascism, the postwar, it must be stressed, is less important for its events than for its status as a creative space. The later Ferrara of remembering and writing frames the earlier, foregrounded Ferrara of the narrative "now" of experiencing. The concentric contours of the spatial construct called Ferrara begin to touch tiny Codigoro and distant Rome and Naples. These latter, destabilizing *dramatis urbes* cast an anamorphic shadow across Ferrara, calling the city newly into question. Also from outside the city, the narrating "I," with an ever more stabilized angle of vision, rearticulates the question.

The years of the *dopoguerra*, with its backward-gazing need to remedy war wounds, both material and social, and its ceremonious close, finally, with the national elections of April 18, 1948,[28] play a part in the plotted sorrow of the *Romanzo*, but one that paves a path of retrospection and continuity with the past. Like the reflective years of the fifties and sixties, the late forties constitute a postnarrative time. But while the texts that encompass the postwar decades are discontinuous with the events that occur earlier, in the strained quadrennium of the war's postlude, survivors play out lives shaped by the violence of events: Geo Josz (who returns to Ferrara in 1945 only to depart in rage in or shortly after 1948), Pino Barilari (who after the 1948 trial of war criminals becomes obsessed with the time of the 1943 massacre), and Edgardo Limentani (the most self-conscious survivor of them all, whose narrative of self-disintegration takes place in 1947) are both victims and survivors. Edgardo's and Geo's social alienation is the product of an energized political climate intent on exoricism of the past and purification by communal renewal. The presence of these men, as well as of Pino and his crazed descent into himself, stains their compatriots' effort of renewal.

The "second" Risorgimento began with the Resistance and was to be fulfilled in a new order of social justice, under the leadership of the political Left. Resistance leaders commanded perhaps as many as 200,000 clandestine fighters in northern Italy, most of whom were "well to the Left."[29] Their ruling body was called the Committee of National Liberation (CLN); after the war its members became the authorized civil government, with headquarters in Milan. These men represented six political parties: Socialist, Communist, Christian Democrat, Actionist, Republican, and Liberal (Bassani was a founding member of the much-respected though short-lived *Partito d'Azione*). Leftists became the influential local administrators of many northern cities, such as Ferrara (they carry out their work, for example, in "Lapide" and "Anni"). The central command of the Resistance forces, led by the Communist Luigi Longo, the Actionist Ferruccio Parri, and the army general Raffaele Cadorna, was a paradigm of heterogeneous political unity. Parri served a brief term as prime minister; the Christian Democrat who succeeded him in December of 1945, Alcide de Gasperi, became firmly entrenched in that post. De Gasperi's coalition cabinet of Christian Democrats, Communists, Socialists, and Republicans collapsed in January of 1947 but was immediately resuscitated as a three-party system (without the Republicans), still under his aegis. Another government crisis, which erupted on May 31, 1947, led to another cabinet formation and another prime ministership for De Gasperi, who this time formed a one-party council of Christian Democrats and "technical" personnel. This move, which came soon after De Gasperi's visit to the United States, inaugurated the Catholic-dominated Christian Democratic party's hegemony in Italy.[30] A shred of newspaper that Edgardo Limentani picks up while seated on a toilet in a hotel announces De Gasperi's trip abroad: "   SPERI A NEW YORK, diceva un titolo a grossi caratteri" [p. 573] (SPERI IN NEW YORK, a large-type headline declared). Another fragmented headline alludes to the anger of the excluded leftists: "   ENNI E TOGLIATTI - ATTACCANO IL GOVER   " [ibid.] (ENNI AND TOGLIATTI - ATTACK THE GOVERNM   ). These disjointed scraps recalling critical national events are also temporally disjointed over some months of 1947: " 'Doveva essere appartenuto a un giornale di qualche mese avanti,' " rifletté [Edgardo], considerando il colore giallino della carta" [ibid.] (It must have been part of a newspaper of some months ago, he reflected, considering the yellowish color of the paper [W:*H*, pp. 38–39]). De Gasperi's triumph and the reduction of Nenni's Socialist party and Togliatti's Communist party to voices of opposition crystallize the social pressures bearing down on Edgardo, who reads the old news on the December day of his suicide. The last headline to catch his eye refers to the continued flowing of Jewish blood: "   RRE SANGUE EBRAICO - A POLONIA D'OGGI" [ibid.] (TH JEWISH BLOOD - IN TODAY'S POLAND). This montage of oppressive (particularly to him) political ideologies and persistent anti-Semitism flashes itself upon his own shredded self-image as he sits in an environment aptly dedicated to waste matter.

A month before De Gasperi's American trip, the Constituent Assembly, headed by the Christian Democrat and indispensably aided by the Communist party, incorporated Mussolini's papal concordat into the new republic's constitution. Thus the nation vigorously restored political power to the Catholic church, disfavored for decades by the pre-Fascist Liberal governments. In the June 1946 elections that created the Constituent Assembly (and the republic), Communists and Socialists outnumbered the Christian Democrats. The greatest leftist vote in the nation came from the four so-called red regions of Tuscany, Umbria, the Marches, and Emilia-Romagna. Emilia, where Ferrara is located, cast the strongest of these votes, electing 5,356 left-wingers, primarily Communists, to the Constituent Assembly but only 1,595 Christian Democrats. While nationally more votes went to Socialists than to Communists, Emilia elected more Communists.[31] Edgardo's lost sense of power is, of course, due in good part to this massive Communist presence surrounding him.

One privilege of the old regime that the new one wished to eliminate was the *latifondi*, the enormous estates that men like Moisè Finzi-Contini acquired in the late 1800s and that men like Edgardo Limentani inherited in the following century. The Assembly Left succeeded in "irrevocably" abolishing the *latifondi* and in guaranteeing the right of workers to share in profits and management of the smaller lots into which the estates would be divided.[32] The constitution became effective in January of 1948, one month after Edgardo's suicide. During the many months of Assembly debate leading to legislation, this affluent landowner, in confrontation with the inflamed Emilian workers on his land and with Communist party youths such as his duck-shooting guide Gavino, witnesses the uprooting of "his" world in the national tensions of the swiftly altering Italian society of the late 1940s. Edgardo's world of power and hierarchy collapses first under Fascism, when he is cast out as a Jew, and again after Fascism, when he is cast out as a landlord: the ideologies of both Right and Left leave no room in between for him. Nor can the national domination by the Christian Democrats (with the Church on their heels) ameliorate his feeling of hollow survivorship. And although he tries to minimize it, Poland's ancient history of anti-Semitism, practiced bloodily now under Communism like a diabolical resurrection of Nazism, is a further sign of his vulnerability, his utter homelessness. Edgardo's day-long constipation, which sets the scene of the torn newspapers, is a metonym of his ontological burden of stultifying immobility. Still seated, he looks out from the top-floor bathroom window and sees all of Codigoro before him. Image by image, another montage of history coalesces, evoking memories of his own recent life: the anti-Jewish laws that annihilated his once-uncontested authority and power; his expedient marriage; his refuge in Switzerland; his separation from his close friend and cousin, Ulderico. Like a "surveyor without instruments," Edgardo attempts to measure distances and proportions (p. 574). This ill-equipped (now ontologically unfit) Edgardo contrasts with Bassani, who measures the distances and proportions of his texts with the accurate instrument of his creative imagination. In this perspective, Edgardo, seated in a private space and surveying an infinite one, is a parodic anti-image of the writer at work. Edgardo's backward glance reaches from the 1940s to the 1930s. Bassani "retrieves" this narrative material with a 1960s retrospection. Through the precision instrument of his book, the author quickens his own, present-time artistic inertia.[33] The retrospective measure characterizes all Bassani's writings; like the "geometer" Edgardo, but even more like the metaphoric geometer who tries to square the circle in the last lines of the last canto of the *Divine Comedy*, Bassani has a geometrical imagination:

> A ciascun racconto la sua struttura, in ogni caso. Quella degli "Ultimi anni" non presentava nulla che avesse a che fare con le linee convergenti in prospettiva della "Passeggiata," o con le sfere ruotanti della "Lapide." Si trattava di quattro rigidi elementi verticali di una materia opaca e translucida, più vicina alla carta o alla stoffa che non alla pietra o al metallo: larghi e piatti, tutti e quattro questi elementi, divisi ma paralleli. Se non proprio alla sfera, però, la struttura della "Notte" si ispirava di nuovo al cerchio. Avevo immaginato dei cerchi, tanti: uno dentro l'altro. [p. 733]

> (In any case, for each story its own structure. "Ultimi anni" had no connection with the converging perspective lines of "Passeggiata," nor with the rotating spheres of "Lapide." It was characterized by four rigid vertical elements of an opaque and translucent material, closer to paper or cloth than to stone or metal: wide and flat, all four of these elements, and separate but parallel. Though not exactly spherical, the structure of "Notte," too, was inspired by the circle. I had invisaged many circles, one inside the other.)

Like Edgardo and even like Dante's pilgrim in Paradise, Bassani takes the measure of a certain city. For Edgardo it is Codigoro. Words of distance encompass his observations: *oltre, là, da un lato, dall'altro lato, in mezzo, quasi su una stessa linea, ben più alte, più in là, fra le due rive, più in là ancora, molto più in là, il confine nord, ai margini meridionali del paese* [p. 574] (beyond, there, on one side, on the other side, in the middle, almost on the same line, much higher, farther away, between two banks, still farther away, much farther away, the northern boundary, at the southern edges of the town). Edgardo wonders how far an edge of the city is from the central square and whether the statue of an unknown soldier in the square is larger or smaller than life-size. His seemingly supererogatory reflections on the city's measurements retrace, in fact, his history and its meaning in the mute geometric forms of a social space. Spiritually inert, Edgardo makes a Christmastime "pilgrimage" to Codigoro/Dis on a gloomy day that will offer him a luminous and suicidal vision of a taxidermic Heavenly City. The irony of Edgardo's conversion to death dissipates in the narration's completion, itself a sign of authorial reanimation or conversion to life.

Around *Cinque storie ferraresi*, published in 1956, and *L'airone*, published in 1968, are circumscribed the principal years of Bassani's narrative writing.

The creativity of these two decades contrasts with his literary inscriptions of moral malignancy, both psychic and political. With interludes of two and four years, he composed the books that now appear as "chapters" of the Romanzo. The last book ("chapter") incorporated into the Romanzo, *L'odore del fieno* (1972), heralds in its title a definitive, that is, victorious, creative afflatus. The motive force of this liberating vitality, as already argued, derives from artistic acts structured as moral explorations. Bassani's geometric conception of his five Ferrarese stories is a prelude to his grand construct of encircled Ferrara, a geometrical center and circumference no less symbolic, moral, and whole than Dante's sacralized spheres.

Utopian Ferrara

Having recalled some of the historical circumstances that became grist for Bassani's narrative mill, I shall conclude this discussion of the invention of "Ferrara" with some observations on its utopian and allegorical parameters.

Ferrara is both a utopia and a dystopia. The characteristics of a utopia are a love of nature and natural scenes, self-sufficiency, a rural agricultural life, stability, cyclical temporality, an absence of history, a mental state at or beyond the frontiers of human knowledge and desire, and a physical location in a remote, inaccessible place.[34] The *Giardino* represents a utopian mental state as well as a utopian state of nature. The prominence of "garden" in the title immediately clues the reader to an Edenic textual environment. From the location of the walled and verdant estate at the northwest limit of the city walls ("remote" from the city proper, at the time the family dwelled there) to Micòl's passionate love of the "pious" (eternalized) past and abhorrence of the future (linear, unpredictable temporality), the Finzi-Continis and their property meet the conditions of a utopian community. Micòl's love of the past is an expression of her attachment to memory, the very marrow of artistic creation. Thus the novel is also a testament to the author's labor of art. The dialectical relation between the author/narrator of the novel and the completed book/Micòl is intrinsic to any discussion of the book's meaning. At the present juncture, let us limit our focus to the significance of the Finzi-Contini family, especially Micòl, within the context of Fascist Ferrara.

Beyond the structural requirements of utopia, the Finzi-Continis represent moral, scapegoated leadership, to the same extent that the ancient Este family, whose castle-home still stands at Ferrara's historical center, represents the public good. A number of fictional characters in the *Romanzo* manifest aspects of utopian behavior. One is Bruno Lattes, who flees the Nazis across the Atlantic Ocean on a life-regenerating journey of purification ("Anni"). Another is Salomone Corcos, the grain merchant ennobled textually by his natural simplicity and affection, his farinaceous body smells, and his mane of snowy hair ("Passeggiata"). Micòl, who wears earthen colors and animal skins, whose special places exude fruity and vinegary fragrances, and who might herself be described as "pungent" or "bittersweet," is Bassani's poetic ideal, the exemplar not only of health and natural beauty, but also of the civilized virtues of intellect and charm. For as long as they can, Micòl and her family cultivate an aristocratic isolation in their autarchic home. Isolation is a requirement of utopia, for it cannot survive in propinquity with an alternative way of life.[35] The imposed way of life that destroys the Finzi-Continian world is Nazi-Fascism — the collaboration of the Fascist (puppet) government with Nazi brutality, in the regions of Northern Italy — which deports and slays the family. Italian Fascism, with its anti-Jewish decrees, creates the breach in the family's walled security. Total destruction is achieved by the Nazis who exterminate them, and by the large number of impoverished refugees who demolish their home. Fascism and Nazism build dystopia, the violent urban world that is a Finzi-Continian antiplace and that successfuly dis-places utopia. The Finzi-Continian society is both bourgeois and Jewish. Its extinction signifies Italian Jewry's loss of the Eden that modern, pre-Fascist Ferrara was quite capable of representing. When the 1938 anti-Jewish laws become effective, the degeneration of the city into a dystopia affects Ferrara's entire citizenry. The would-be Fascist autarchy[36] reaches its topsy-turvy peak as a nation of vacuous servants and fearful subjects mortally threatened by hunger and bombings. But out of the ashes of a terrible war, utopia can rise again.[37] In Bassani's scheme, the purification and rebirth of the Fascist-polluted city is essentially the task of the writer. The narrator of the *Giardino* enacts this project by "resurrecting" Micòl and her family through his written memory of them. The extinction of the family, particularly Micòl, triggers its rebirth in language: the narrator/writer's book is the mythical phoenix. Extended to the *Romanzo*, the writer's inscription of dystopic Ferrara — the "ashes" of a city — is an instrument of self-reflection and moral growth. Bassani uses the medium of his book to help reconstruct, in an unending past that is present, a utopic Ferrara. The author's role is thus to be a "visionary leader — messiah or prophet — who evokes the 'sense of time' required for a difficult journey to moral worth."[38] Ultimately, the "perfect place" to which the "worthy" reader-pilgrim must travel is a state of mind. But the spatialized "perfect place" ("perfectly" exemplary) Bassani offers his reader is his invented Ferrara. The spatial symbolization of invented Ferrara maps out a moral landscape. Its polysemous features are the subject of the next chapter.

Chapter 3
Center, Periphery, Boundary, Outside

For without a cement of blood (it must be human, it must be innocent) no
secular wall will safely stand.

W. H. Auden

Four areas of Ferrara mark off city spaces saturated by Bassani with mythic
meaning. No less than in a primitive culture, the center and circumference of
Bassani's Ferrara function as sacred spaces. The Este castle at the center of the
city and the Renaissance wall which still surrounds the city are potent indicators
of social conditions. Between the center and the periphery are two more spaces
that have mythopoeic value: the boundary (by which I mean an interior space,
as opposed to the periphery, at the edge of the city) and the outside (any part
of Ferrara built up beyond the walls). Four different narratives of the *Romanzo*
use these spaces to enhance the meaning of social and historical events. "Una
notte del '43" describes a wartime Fascist massacre at the Este castle wall
(sacrificial ritual to restore the public order); *Il giardino dei Finzi-Contini*
describes a family's splendid home located at the very edge of the city wall, far
from its central neighborhoods (isolation and separation of divinities from mor-
tals); "Una lapide in via Mazzini" names the street that bounds the main section
of the historical Jewish ghetto and on which the Jewish synagogue still stands
(exclusion of community outcasts); and *Dietro la porta* describes a shabby
neighborhood outside the city wall, where the novella's principal antagonist lives
(a profane wilderness).

The first city space I examine corresponds to a historical one. It is the site of the Renaissance Este castle: the geographical center of the city and the historical center of local government, past and present. In 1943 Italian Fascists executed eleven Ferrarese men, four of them Jews, at the castle wall. Via Mazzini, the second and also historical space, is the "Main Street" of the old Jewish ghetto. It intermediates materially and figuratively between "il nucleo più antico e la parte rinascimentale e moderna della città" [p. 68] (the ancient center and the Renaissance and modern part of the city); more significantly, if nowadays only symbolically, Via Mazzini intermediates between Jewish and non-Jewish Ferrara. In 1945, shortly after the end of the war, Geo Josz returns home from Buchenwald to find his name among those of the 183 exterminated Ferrarese Jews memorialized by the plaque on the synagogue of Via Mazzini. The principal fictive element in the scene is Geo. The third space, contiguous with a segment of the Renaissance wall that bounds the city, locates the Finzi-Contini estate. Entirely invented, the house and garden of the fictive Finzi-Contini family can nonetheless be pinponted on the city map by topographical markers in the fiction. The fourth space, invented and only approximately placeable on Via Bologna but definitely located beyond the city walls, is the rented apartment of the crude Pulga family, non-Jews who live for a while in Ferrara before returning to their native Bologna. The young son, Luciano Pulga, is Bassani's most unlikable (profane) character.

Bassani's mythologizing conflates reality and fiction with the result that reality itself seems the author of myth, and street locations become an animating source of narrative energy.

"Una notte del '43"

The narrative chronology of the short story "Una notte del '43" wrenches backward and forward, as if straining in many directions to make sense of its central event, the massacre of innocent Ferrarese citizens in December of 1943. Uninvolved yet bound to the crime is Pino Barilari, a paralyzed pharmacist whose disease seems but one symptom of a greater communal sickness that begins to spread (*serpeggiare*), especially in Ferrara, in the summer of 1939. Narrative composition juxtaposes Pino's bodily condition and Ferrara, which as a locus of Fascist brutality suddenly becomes "a kind of inferno" (p. 139). The Fascist massacre scorches the minds of the Ferrarese, causing them to behave,

> per mesi e mesi, per tutto il tempo che occorse alla guerra per risalire adagio la penisola italiana: come se l'immaginazione collettiva avesse bisogno di ritornare sempre là, a quella notte tremenda, e di riavere uno per uno davanti agli occhi i volti degli undici fucilati quali nel punto supremo il solo Pino Barilari li aveva avuti. [p. 154]

(for months and months, for all the time it took for the war to rise slowly up the Italian peninsula: as if the collective imagination needed to keep returning to that horrible night, to see again – one by one – the faces of the eleven men gunned down at the supreme moment as only Pino Barilari had seen them.)

Pino eventually becomes the one most obsessed with the slaughter. After the war, having become a totally isolated, harping, "polluted" outcast, he calls to strangers from his apartment window with ear-piercing verbal allusions to the terrible event. This story, which depends more fully than any other in the *Romanzo* on a historical event, exposes with singular distinctness the author's reworking of historical material and offers an excellent example of his rhetorical practice.

First the historical situation needs to be recalled. The newly resurrected Fascist government, the so-called Italian Social Republic, held its constitutive assembly in Verona on November 14, 1943, about two months after the Germans occupied northern and central Italy, which followed immediately upon the Grand Council's constitutionally legal ouster of Mussolini and the subsequent armistice between the Badoglio government and the Allied Forces. Fascist emotion was high and of a vindictive bent.

During the Verona meeting, two *repubblichini* rushed in announcing the assassination the night before of Igino Ghisellini, the national secretary of Ferrara's Fascist party. A group of Venetian and Paduan *squadristi* (blackshirted Fascist terrorists organized after World War I to silence political foes) set out in trucks for Ferrara, arriving there at night, barely visible under the cover of the city's fog and drizzle. From a list of eighty-four "suspected" anti-Fascists supplied to them by local party officials, the *squadristi* gathered a large group in the military barracks, a disproportionate number of them Jews. Because the local Fascists refused to select specific victims for the *squadristi*, the outsiders (Venetians and Paduans) acted: four men were seized from the barracks before dawn on November 15, and four others, imprisoned a month earlier for anti-Fascist activities, were pulled from jail. The eight were led to the Este castle and shot in front of its wall. The executioners then seized a young railroad worker from the train station and shot him near the castle. Two final victims were taken from their homes and shot some distance from the castle, at the city walls. Later in the day, the police commissioner telegraphed the judiciary: "This morning eleven unidentified corpses were found. The motives and the authors of these deaths are unknown." From that moment on, "the night of Ferrara" became infamous; the Fascist press coined the word "ferrarrizzare" to describe it, and "ferrarrizzare l'Italia" became the Fascist battlecry for a reign of terror.[1]

For a long time there were two views on the killing of Secretary Ghisellini.

One placed the blame on the Ferrarese Fascists themselves, one faction of whom was antagonistic to the somewhat conciliatory Ghisellini. The other view pointed to partisan warfare. A Communist leaflet circulated right after the murders claimed responsibility for Ghisellini's death and reaffirmed the partisans' pledge to kill all "Fascist traitors."[2] More than twenty years later—and more than a decade after the writing of "Notte"—two other Communist publications refuted the theory of Fascist internecine fighting by supplying the details of the partisan assassination plan; they identified its moment of origin (November 13, in Bologna) and the assassin (a Bolognese Communist, then also a soldier in the Italian Air Force, who operated in collaboration with a comrade from Ferrara).[3] Bassani's dramatization in "Notte" incorporates the first, more shocking and ironic version: that Fascists executed one of their own. The sacrifice of the victims, in Bassani's account, thus serves both to deepen the sense of Fascist treachery and to arouse a collective cry for vengeance and justice after the war. The cry for vengeance becomes a critical narrative element and an intrinsic part of the ritualistic plotting.

Disregard for historical accuracy in Bassani's version of the massacre begins with the event's date. Instead of November 14–15, the author chooses December 14–15. This allows him first of all to set the scene against a very cold, snow-covered city. He takes the further liberty of substituting a crystal-clear night for the actual foggy one. Returning home in the early hours of the morning, one of the characters notices that Corso Roma, the street that runs in front of the castle, is "tutto vuoto sotto la luna piena, la neve, indurita dal gelo, sparsa come una specie di polvere brillante su ogni cosa, talmente limpida e chiara l'atmosfera da poter leggere le ore all'orologio del Castello (le quattro e ventuno, esatte)" [p. 162] (empty under the full moon; the snow, hardened in the cold night, scattered like a kind of shining powder over everything, the atmosphere so clear and so transparent that you could read the time on the Castle clock above—4:20 exactly [Q:P, p. 218]).

The character returning home is Anna Repetto, the young wife of the paralyzed and ridiculed pharmacist, Pino Barilari. She is returning from an illicit night visit. Her accidental crossing of Corso Roma immediately after the executions imposes major roles upon her and her husband within the historical event. Indeed, Bassani's narrative explores the meaning of the massacre through an elaboration of the personal lives of the fictitious couple. In order to understand the full history of "December 14, 1943," the author is telling us, we must examine the Ferrarese community in relation to it. In this way others (readers) may see the event with the same clarity that the townspeople could have seen the bodies of the men under the full moon and did see them the following morning and afternoon, outlined dramatically against the newly fallen snow. Bassani's invented weather casts a metaphoric chilling light on the scene. The intense clarity of the moonlight invokes the mythopoeic status of the noonday sun, offering its

Figure 3. Corso Roma, now Corso Martiri della Libertà. On the left is the Este castle wall, site of the infamous massacre of 1943 restaged in "Una notte del '43." After the war the character Pino Barilari, "as if from a box seat," looks down from his corner window across the street on the "animated theater" of Corso Roma.

"chilling" insight in lieu of the energizing, even erotic impulse that the sun's blaze traditionally generates.

The mythologizing technique Bassani employs for revealing the "truth" and outlining the principal protagonist of "Notte"—the Ferrarese community—led him to the invention of another character, the local Fascist leader and central villain of the narrative, Carlo Aretusa, better known as "Sciagura" (Calamity). The lives of Sciagura and Pino intertwine from their early youth, the Fascist as political and sexual master of the pharmacist. Their relation of victimizer to victim is inseparable from the story's central drama of community guilt.

The place of the massacre as a sacred space is established in the opening lines of the story, which also establish Pino's function as "guardian" of the space. Only twelve years after the executions (that is, at the narrative present), the event already belongs to a "distant," in other words mythicized, past.[4] The place of the executions has become a tabooed space, sacred and dangerous, not to be trespassed. Tourists and other outsiders may walk there with impunity, but the Ferrarese must scrupulously avoid it: a person seen on the sidewalk in question could be "chiunque, insomma, ma non un ferrarese" [p. 135] (anyone, in short, but not a *ferrarese*).

Figure 4. The Este castle, facing Corso Roma. In "Una notte del '43" "a rapid burst of a Fascist machine gun . . . cuts down eleven citizens" on the sidewalk by the castle wall. In view of "the high clock tower and, a bit to the right, the crenellated terrace of the orangery" postwar customers across the street at the Caffè della Borsa (under the arcade where Pino Barilari's pharmacy is located) thus face the scene of the massacre.

Figure 5. the plaque in the photograph names four men actually shot at the castle wall as well as three others killed in nearby streets; a second plaque (outside the frame) shows where the remaining four actually fell.

QUI CADUTI PER LA LIBERTA
ARLOTTI sen. EMILIO - HANAU VITTORE
ZANATTA avv. MARIO - HANAU MARIO
SUGLI SPALTI DELLE MURA DI SAN TOMASO
SAVONUZZI ing. GIROLAMO
TORBOLI rag. ARTURO
IN VIA BOLDINI
BELLETTI CINZIO

On certain occasions during the day, "Gli occhi si fissano, i respiri si moz-zano" [p. 136] (eyes narrow, as people watch breathlessly [Q:*P*, p. 18]). The regular customers in the cafe hear the cracking voice of an "invisible" Pino Barilari, who watches over the sacred stretch of pavement through large binocu-lars from a window of his apartment above the pharmacy: "La voce dice: 'Badi a lei, giovanotto!'; oppure: 'Attenzione!; oppure: 'Ehi!' " [ibid.] (The voice says: "Look out, young man!"; or: "Watch out!"; or "Hey!"). Despite his high-pitched, ineffectual voice, the frail Pino assures *local* adherence to the mysterious taboo. As we later realize, his power derives from his double function as a voice of public conscience and the embodiment of collective guilt.

The postwar attempt to reconstruct Ferrarese life rouses the desire to avenge the Fascist crimes; in particular, the desire to convict Sciagura for his manifest participation in the massacres. A trial takes place in 1946 (in Bassani's story, not in fact) and occasions the final, definitive conjoining of Sciagura and Pino. Now, however, their roles invert, for Sciagura is the victim (the accused) and Pino the potential victimizer – the putative single living witness to the Fascist's participation in the crime. Sciagura stands accused of collaborating with the Ve-netian and Paduan Fascists to the extent of identifying and selecting the victims (his own neighbors), some of whom could not have been found without local as-sistance.

Bassani's insertion of the trial completes the ritualized structure of the mas-sacres that began with the sacrifice of innocent victims to protect the power of the ruling body. The message of scapegoatism is delivered by life as well as by Bassani's fiction in this case, even to the inclusion of an arbitrary victim, the rail-road worker who seems to have been an unpolitical person who just happened by at the wrong time. Bassani accentuates the role of the worker as *random* vic-tim in his text, that is, as the only kind of victim who could cause terror in the whole populace, the nonpoliticals as well as the anti-Fascists. History, in staging the sequence of the event, was less careful than Bassani. The actual Fascists shot their victims in three different places, thereby losing some of the mythic power of the space of the castle. But they soon grouped the eleven bodies at the castle wall; Bassani's victims are shot as well as displayed there. The Este castle represents, historically, the good government of the renowned Renaissance dy-nasty; it rises at the spatial center of the city and symbolizes the collective unity. The bloodying of this monument – by the real executioners as by Bassani's in-vented ones – is an act of violence that implicitly mocks the traditional founda-tion rite of the *polis*.[5] For the Fascists, the massacre explicitly expresses their contempt for the old order and their imposition of a new, tyrannical one.

A customary part of sacrificial ritual, the random victim functions as a sur-rogate for the whole community. Because of its arbitrariness, the ritual serves a public and not a private interest. Through sacrifice, archaic communities aimed to ensure divine assistance in restoring disrupted prosperity and peace.

Fascist rule in Ferrara inverts the normal order that seeks the public good. In a despotic society the random victim exemplifies the breakdown of communal unity – the impotence of the collectivity – and thus embodies the impossibility of communal escape from violence. Bassani, in posing the question of moral responsibility within a society denied sacrificial cleansing, phrases the question to consolidate the historical (unique) with the mythic (archetypal) dimension. On "the night of 1943," in addition to the random victim – by definition an outcast without history – are "persone a Ferrara *troppo* note . . . persone delle quali, oltre ai nomi, si conoscevano *troppo* bene infinite particolarità del fisico e del morale, perché la loro fine non apparisse di primo acchito un evento spaventoso, di una efferatezza *quasi incredibile*" [p. 148; emphasis added] (people *too* well known in Ferrara . . . people whose detailed physical and moral characteristics, not to mention their names, were *too* well known for their fates not to seem terrifying right away, and of an *almost unbelievable* savagery [emphasis added]). These deaths alarm the populace with a sense of personal danger, for the victims are people whose lives intermeshed with their own. A line that appears in an earlier version of this passage is very explicit on the similarity between the victims and the survivors: "troppo *intrecciate*, le loro esistenze modeste, alle modeste esistenze di ognuno" [1974, p. 170; emphasis added] (their modest lives too closely interwoven with the modest lives of everyone else [Q:*P*, p. 197]). Paradoxically, the actual deaths seem unreal (an event "quasi irreale" [ibid.]), whereas their symbolic (arbitrary) value affirms the reality of a hovering human hecatomb: the slaughter at the castle threatens to extinguish the whole city.

The long, silent lines of townspeople in front of the Fascist headquarters the next day, waiting to register for party memberships, constitute an expression of communal shame that will remain beyond the hope of cure until a proper sacrificial slaughter can atone for it. The end of societal contamination must await the end of the war and of Fascism, and the establishment of guilt upon a surrogate victim.

The postwar trial is the hoped-for vehicle of public purification and restoration to health. Its potential as theater – ritualistic celebration – is not overlooked by its organizers. The Committee for National Liberation of the now-governing Communist party extends the courtroom, located conspicuously in the ex-Fascist headquarters, directly to the center of town, that is, back to the scene of the crime, by means of a string of loudspeakers (p. 154). First some twenty accused ex-Fascists rounded up from assorted hiding places in Italy are quickly released for lack of evidence. On Sciagura alone depends the assumption of guilt that can paradoxically transform him into a savior and release the Ferrarese from their burden of shame. But "Calamity" is not easily subdued. Sciagura's ability to domineer is no less as a defendant on trial than it was when, as a rising Fascist, he forced the teenaged virgin Pino at gunpoint to copulate with a prostitute while he, Sciagura, stood by as a spectator. In the courtroom teeming with spectators "thirsty for vengeance" (p. 155), Sciagura insists upon his innocence. Worse, his words and gestures condemn the others:

Ma ogni volta era come se insinuasse che no, non si illudessero i suoi persecutori odierni di far dimenticare, condannando lui, quello che ieri erano stati. Tutti al pari di lui erano stati più o meno fascisti: e nessun verdetto di tribunale sarebbe mai riuscito a cancellare una verità come questa. [pp. 155-56]

(But every time he seemed to insinuate that no, his present persecutors needn't think that, because they condemned him, what they'd been themselves only yesterday would be forgotten. All of them, like himself, had been Fascists more or less: and nobody's verdict was ever going to wipe out a truth like that.) [Q:P, pp. 208-9]

Sciagura refuses to play the role of scapegoat. His self-confident performance dominates the spectacular trial, and only when Pino Barilari makes his way through the crowded chamber is Sciagura shaken for a brief moment. Pino, summoned to testify, is the image of physical infirmity and clownishness: victimage incarnate. The condemnatory eyewitness testimony his compatriots yearn to hear is instead a self-obliterating "dormivo": "I was sleeping" (p. 158).

Sciagura averts sacrificial victimage and thereby maintains his status as personified communal disaster and ill fate, a status borne proudly in his nickname. Pino, socially earmarked for humiliation, is forced into the uncomfortable role of potential savior. Both Sciagura and Pino refuse the ultimate roles that society requires of them for its own well-being. Ferrara remains wounded and bound to the past, its longing for rebirth, restored innocence, and receptivity to the future thwarted. The spirit of vengeance sides with the appointed victims. The sole suggestion of propitiation arising from the trial conjoins Sciagura and Pino through the former's "almost imperceptible wink of understanding" (p. 158) that responds to Pino's exonerating "dormivo."

Thus concludes the courtroom drama and narrative chapter, arrested at a point of enigma and inconclusion. Pino, Sciagura's longtime victim, once again chooses victimage but this time, in so doing, becomes the victimizer's savior. The motive for Pino's refusal to bear witness is not articulated, but at stake in testifying is a virtual admission of still another, perhaps more terrible, witness: to his wife's infidelity. For Pino to have seen Sciagura among the executioners during the infamous night would imply also having seen his wife returning home in the darkness of predawn.

From the perspective of his marriage, Pino's "dormivo" is self-defensive, one more closing of his eyes to an ugly reality. Pino's lack of witness absolves Sciagura and thereby confers authentic power upon Pino, converting his outcast position of ridicule to one of dread—the *threshold* position of guardian of the sacred space that memorializes the loss of the social good. Pino, in this light, is a figure of the author, who, concealed behind his text like Pino behind his window, preserves—the one through the text produced, the other through the shame proclaimed—the memory and moral taint of collective criminality.

Il giardino dei Finzi-Contini

Pino's window, elevated above the castle wall across the street, in more traditional lore might have been a tower window. In his "watchtower" Pino fittingly rises above the level of ordinary (in this case, immoral) life to become its sentinel of conscience. In some fanciful tales the tower is inhabited by a virgin, often a princess. She and the tower symbolic of ascent signify metamorphosis or transformation. Pino as embodied social conscience suggests a way to communal release from shame and guilt through unrelenting self-knowledge. In the *Giardino*, Bassani endows the novel's heroine, Micòl, with a real tower. Her tower-bedroom, at the top of a spiral staircase of 123 steps, is part of the neogothic family "manor house" situated within a vast and verdant estate—the garden of the book's title. Micòl functions as the principal transformative agent in the narrator's growth to manhood.[6] She represents more than a mythic power, however. The entire Finzi-Contini family—wealthy, well-bred, aloof, Jewish—represents marginality on a social, political, religious, and moral plane in relation to the community of Ferrara. Their marginality is a positive force; Micòl is Bassani's most energized character. The valorization of the family includes one negative component, Micòl's brother, Alberto, who dies of disease before his kin are deported to Germany. Alberto may be viewed as a negative image of his sister, a diseased young shoot that withers and dies without contaminating the others. Indeed, of the many characters created by Bassani, the Finzi-Continis are almost unique in avoiding communal contamination. (The only other case is that of the protean authorial persona, about whom more will be said later.) The superiority of the Finzi-Continis is indicated even by the author's location of their home at the edge of the city, a place of limit and separation, an "empty" space such as one finds surrounding holy objects. During the Renaissance, the outlying section of Ferrara was swampland the Estes used for pleasure. We have already seen that elliptically, as well as directly, Bassani informs his reader of the copresence of the two noble families across time.

Although the Finzi-Continis are a fictitious family, they, like almost all of Bassani's other characters, bear traces of actual people. A newspaper article entitled "The Finzis Do Not Forgive Bassani for His 'Betrayal' of Micòl as a Character" opens with these words: "The real garden of the Finzi-Continis—or, better, Finzi-Margrinis—rises not at the city wall, but in the very heart of Ferrara, on Via Borgoleoni."[7] The article goes on to report the family's displeasure over Bassani's disregard of their daughter Giuliana's real history, that is, her marriage and early death, which had nothing to do with Nazism. "I hate your son," Giuliana's father is quoted as saying to Bassani's mother in the same article. Of primary interest here is the displacement of the "real" home, for it signals Bassani's mythologizing technique. Micòl, inspired least of all by Giuliana Finzi, is a vibrant blond "princess" who as both child and young woman tantalizes, tests, soothes, and snubs into maturity the novel's unnamed narrator. With her mother, father, and grandmother, the ebullient Micòl disappears from Ferrara and the fiction following news of their deportation during the war. The house, too, "disappears" but survives in memory/writing, not only as an object of personal sentiment, but also as a complex symbol of the social good—specifically, political and moral. Located at the end of Corso Ercole I d'Este, the house sits

> proprio nel cuore di quella parte nord della città che fu aggiunta durante il Rinascimento all'angusto borgo medioevale, e che appunto per ciò si chiama Addizione Erculea. Ampio; diritto come una spada dal Castello alla Mura degli Angeli; fiancheggiato per quanto è lungo da brune moli di dimore gentilizie; *con quel suo lontano, sublime sfondo* di rosso mattone, verde vegetale, e cielo, *che sembra condurti davvero all'infinito*. [pp. 256–57; emphasis added]

> (in the heart of the northern part of the city that was added to the small medieval town during the Renaissance by duke Ercole, and named after him. Wide and straight as a [sword] from the Castle to the Wall of the Angels, with dark, imposing dwelling-houses on either side of its entire length, and, high in the distance, a [sublime] backdrop of brick red, leafy green, and sky that seems to lead you into infinity.) [Q:*G*, pp. 19–20]

The Finzi-Contini house,

> sebbene vi si acceda anche oggi da corso Ercole I—salvo però, per raggiungerla, *dover poi percorrere più di mezzo chilometro supplementare attraverso un immenso spiazzo poco o nulla coltivato*—; sebbene essa incorpori tuttora quelle storiche rovine di un edificio cinquecentesco, *un tempo residenza o "delizia" estense* . . . ad onta di tanti superstiti motivi d'interesse, chi ne sa niente, mi domando, *chi se ne ricorda più*? [p. 257; emphasis added]

> (must be approached [even today] from Corso Ercole I—except that today, to reach it, you must cross more than half an extra kilometre across a huge stretch of mostly untilled ground; although it still includes the historic ruins of a sixteenth-century building, at one time a residence or "pleasure ground" of the Este family . . . in spite of so much that is of interest in it still, who now knows anything about it, I wonder, and who still remembers it?) [Q:*G*, p. 20]

The mythicizing factors of house and setting are manifold: remoteness, sublimity, isolation, suggestions of infinity, vagueness of communal memory. The implied family succession to the Este dynasty is clear, and especially prized by Micòl, who proudly states that one of her favorite trees in the garden is an enormous and ancient plane tree, planted not by "grandmother Josette" but rather by "Ercole I d'Este himself, perhaps, or Lucrezia Borgia" (p. 320).

Although the Touring Club guidebook of the early 1900s "never failed" to mention the home and gardens, the latter were laid waste by the war, and the home, badly damaged by bombs in 1944, is "still" (in the narrative present of 1957) occupied and *being ravaged* by hundreds of "beggarly sub-proletariat" refugees. By the time the reader reads about the house, it is already destroyed; "history" provides the confirmation: nowhere along the famous Corso or along the decaying Renaissance city walls can any sign of it be found. The "mythic" home functions as a transformative, higher-than-ordinary (human) power. Although as distant as possible from the city's center, the house is nonetheless joined to the center; that is, to the Este castle, literally by the Corso. By legacy, that is, by the ruins and ancient trees still standing on the property, the Finzi-Continis join the Este family. Topographically, onomastically, and historically, through the urban expansion initiated by the Este rulers and named for them in the sixteenth century, the contemporary Finzi-Continis are assimilated into Renaissance aristocratic leadership, courtly life, and good government: they are at once center and periphery, "rejected" good government, in contradistinction to the Fascist regime and communal collaboration and cowardice that have usurped the center. The Finzi-Continis "see" accurately and courageously: they scorn membership in the Fascist party when, during the membership campaign of 1933, ninety percent of their coreligionists rush to join (p. 261); they respond to the repressive anti-Jewish laws of 1938 by ending their sectarian (Sephardic) religious worship and rejoining the main (Italian) synagogue; they relax in general their preferred private ways and invite other Jews (and non-Jews) into their home. They continue to manifest a joy toward life while keenly aware of its pain, whereas their compatriots show signs of inner despair and judge the perplexing family with resentment and misunderstanding. In a manner that endows the family with the special grace and saving power customarily reserved for mythic heroes and regal victims, the Finzi-Continis accept the ultimate scapegoatism of the concentration camps forced upon the Jews. They, too, become noble outcasts scorned and sacrificed symbolically—and in fact—like Christ, outside the city limits; outside, ironically, the arena of contagion.

The peripheral Finzi-Contini home is the locus of grace, the alternative to the "center"—the locus of unredemptive slaughter—and the alternative to the "boundary"—the marker of Jewish exclusion. The periphery is a transformative point of potentiality, the sacred space of the "divinities" inhabiting Bassani's fictive universe, and of ennobling, unselfish love and creative inspiration. Marginal, dynamic, regally "abnormal," Micòl is the sovereign icon of Bassani's novel of Ferrara, a figure of love and the spirit of creativity and life.

The lowly outcasts, Sciagura and Pino Barilari, also serve the good of the populace by reflecting, like a Luna Park mirror, a deformed, exaggerated self-image that stands for the community. One a pompous Fascist, the other a would-be Fascist, they form a composite image of the threat to the social order that Fascism was and could again become, perhaps under a different name. Victimizer and victim form an infertile, "homosexual" partnership that could accommodate as well the diseased and cryptohomosexual Alberto Finzi-Contini.[8] The sacrificial offerings that the other, lifeloving Finzi-Continis become constitute the opposite coordinate of scapegoatism, the erotic, fertile pole symbolized primarily by Micòl but also by the happy marriage of her parents and the generational continuity that includes her aged grandmother. Their shared victimage, though it brings to an end the Finzi-Contini lineage, offers potential rebirth to a disarrayed society, and psychic and literary birth to the writer who resuscitates the family through his art.

The Este castle and the Finzi-Contini home delineate the radical symbolic urban spaces of Bassani's fiction and represent the extreme violation of social order, as well as the limit of societal salvation in Bassani's Ferrara. The symbolic value of the Jewish Finzi-Contini family transcends their religious affiliation and marks them quintessentially as archetypal "despised and rejected" social leaders. The community's disdain is clearly expressed in its adoption of the term *magna domus* to describe the house Finzi-Contini ancestors had constructed upon the ruins of an original Estense residence. Contemptuously "offended" by the family's *nouveau riche* status and "rude" disregard of all others, the local populace "enviously" gives the house its sardonic nickname in extravagant contrast with Ariosto's celebrated *parva domus* in Ferrara (p. 259).

"Una lapide in via Mazzini"

The ill fortune of the Jewish community as such—its persecution by Nazis and Fascists and the discomfort it provokes in its non-Jewish neighbors during and after the war—is starkly embodied in the character Geo Josz, who is mistakenly listed with the Ferrarese Jews exterminated in the death camps. The commemorative plaque on the synagogue epitomizes the fate of the Jews as outcasts; Via Mazzini literally draws the line of their exclusion, whereas the synagogue and Geo's return symbolically affirm their almost miraculous survival.

Like the narrative of a night in 1943, "Lapide" bespeaks Ferrara's act of "infernal" descent. The principal character in each story is a figure of ridicule—an outsider—and an uncomfortable reminder of the city's past cowardice and want of the spirit of Christian *caritas*. In "Notte," the absolute turning point in Pino Barilari's life—his testimony in court—is foreboded by his physical appearance. Comical, even grotesque, Pino has the look of a medieval court fool: "aggrappato con una mano al braccio della giovane moglie, con l'altra a un grosso ba-

Figure 6. Mazzini Street, the main street of the former Jewish ghetto.

Figure 7. The synagogue on Mazzini Street. The plaque on the right lists the names of Ferrarese Jews who died in German concentration camps. In "Una lapide in via Mazzini" the deportee Geo Josz returns home to find his name among those memorialized.

stone nocchieruto dal puntale di gomma (magre come stecchi dentro le brache alla zuava, le gambe gli uscivano nello sforzo del passo in una specie di curiose falciate laterali) [p. 157] (one hand clutching his wife's arm, the other a thick rubber-tipped walnut walking-stick [with the effort of walking his legs, matchstick thin in zouave trousers, made an odd sort of sidelong kicking or scything movement] [Q:*P*, p. 211]). Similarly, Geo Josz enters Ferrara enormously fat and of an "indefinable" age (p. 67), his head covered "fin sotto gli orecchi da uno strano berretto di pelliccia" [p. 69] (down to his ears with an odd-looking fleecy cap). In an earlier version, he looks like a harlequin clown: "rivestito di una sorta di campionario di tutte le divise militari del momento, cognite e incognite" [1974, p. 76] (dressed in an outfit that seemed pieced together from sample swatches of military uniforms of every known and unknown stripe). His body strangely bloated, Geo looks like a fattened lamb. In spite of the intense August heat, he keeps a large lambskin cap on his head, pulled down over his ears, concretizing, as it were, his status of sacrificial victim. Everything about him is abnormal and suspect. His appearance, just four months after the war's end, signals entrapment for his compatriots—condemnation to their recent history—though he himself, clownlike, laughs to find his name listed among those of the slaughtered Jews. Too much the Fool, too sober his jokes, he represents to the community a threatening inversion of its values. As does the author.[9]

Geo is a dark counterimage of Micòl Finzi-Contini. The latter's story ends with her deportation to a concentration camp; Geo's begins with his return from one. Micòl's death, which occurs in the margin of her narrative, is dignified, sanctified by its silence and sacrificial impact on the survivors, especially the readers. In contrast, Geo's presence, close up on narrative center-stage in the first pages of "Lapide," is grossly material—repugnant and enigmatic, a still-bleeding wound in the reconstructive tissue of Ferrarese postwar society. Like Micòl, Geo is young, the child of a prosperous Jewish family whose home was purchased from nobility during the post-Risorgimental, anticlerical time of largesse toward the long isolated and oppressed Jews. And like the Finzi-Continis' *magna domus*, the Joszes' "palazzo gentilizio" [p. 74] (noble mansion) includes "un vasto, traboccante giardino" [ibid.] (a great and superabundant garden) and a tower rising some hundred steps above ground level. The displaced refugee—homeless in his own home—is obliged to inhabit this "remote" and tiny space of confinement to satisfy the needs of the "liberating" Communist government now holding office in the house. But Geo's high room, like Micòl's, is a (literal) indicator of proper perspective, in contrast with the moral nearsightedness of the collectivity at street level.

Geo's youth, like Micòl's, is nipped in the bud—his despite (in fact, because of) his survival. Returning to Ferrara on the verge of chronological maturity, he is frozen into that fruitless moment by the memory of his holocaustic experience and even more so by his own compatriots' refusal to allow him to survive (be) among them. His presence is an effective slap in the face to them; his grotesque bloatedness and ragbag dress are vulgar signs of his insistence on being alive. His actual slap to the face of the ex-Fascist Count Scocca—the narrative's climaxing episode—is the logical consequence of Geo's tattered and deformed return, which the townspeople refuse to understand. Their incomprehension, beyond simple puzzlement, constitutes a symbolic slaughter of their compatriot. What the Nazis did not carry to completion the Ferrarese, in spirit, do. The public act of rejection, which is equivalent to betrayal, assumes official validity through the governing body's appropriation of Geo's home. The youth is a painful goad, insisting on keeping the past still present. One method he employs is to show the residents "chilling" photographs of his deported parents and ten-year-old brother, whose very names (see below) signify God's affection. But his former neighbors remain unmoved. They wonder why Geo has returned and whether, fat as he is, he has actually suffered:

> Possibile che dopo essere sceso all'inferno e per miracolo esserne risalito, in lui non ci fosse altro impulso all'infuori di quello di rievocare immobilmente il passato, secondo ciò che testimoniava l'agghiacciante serie di fotografie di tutti i suoi morti—Angelo e Luce, i genitori, e Pietruccio, il fratellino appena decenne—delle quali un giorno che di soppiatto era salito su, nel suo stanzone, [zio Daniele] aveva trovato tappezzate le quattro pareti del medesimo? [p. 81]

> (Could he possibly, after going down to hell and by a miracle coming up again, want nothing but to conjure a frozen past again, as the chilling collection of photographs of his dead family proved (poor Angelo, poor Luce, and little Pietruccio, born ten years after Geo . . .); photographs which, one day he crept secretly upstairs to his nephew's bedroom, Uncle Daniele found covering the four walls?) [Q:P, p. 104]

Geo seeks to recover his lost adolescence in the city he calls home, just as the Italian Jews nostalgically sought to recover their seventy-year-long "homecoming" between national unification and the anti-Jewish legislation. Geo finds, instead, only estrangement and change. His family home has been converted into headquarters for the post-Fascist partisan government. Allowed to occupy only the "narrow, Ghibelline tower" (p. 74) more than a hundred steps above the rest of the house, Geo spends three years there as a government "guest," whose presence, however, immediately bothers the occupants below. The light in Geo's tower disturbs the people outside. As if reflecting words expressed in a similar context by Pino Barilari, the illuminated window seems a veritable heavenly body, a light that manifests a watchful conscience: " 'Badate a voi!' " ammoniva il lume del reduce sospeso a mezz'aria nel cielo stellato" [p. 78] ("Watch out, there!" the survivor's lamp warned everyone, as it hung mid-air in the starry sky). For three years Geo walks the streets, wanting to belong.

Everyone else is concentrating on rebuilding and forgetting. The townspeople's unyielding attention to the future isolates and suffocates the returned displaced person. The scarred city streets constitute a parable of Geo's social estrangement and the unity of the others. So disfigured by bombardments as to be almost unrecognizable to Geo (1974, p. 83), the streets spur the residents to social and political development. The detritus that is *Geo*, however, appears to them as a face of evil omen ("faccia di malaugurio" [p. 72]): between the community and Geo is a perception of reciprocal disfigurement, each a stranger to the other. The community reacts with irritation and puzzlement; Geo, with irony, even amusement. The story's narrator, revealing his fraternity with his rejected character, singles out (in the 1974 edition) Via Mazzini among the many streets of Ferrara for its immunity to the bombs: "Nemmeno la guerra, l'ha toccata: come a significare che nulla, mai, potrà accadervi!" [p. 76; note the *un*conditional, *future* tense] (Not even the war touched it. As if to signify that nothing, ever, will happen to it!). The beloved temple ("nostro caro, vecchio Tempio") on the street also stands as "una delle rare cose rimaste *grazie a Dio* identiche a 'prima' su cui a Ferrara uno potesse ancora contare" [p. 70; emphasis added] (one of the rare things left, thank God, the same as "before" in Ferrara, and which someone could still count on). The polar views of the community and narrator toward Geo and the urban wreckage form a pattern of fugue-like inversion that elevates Geo above the scarred debris of Ferrara's streets and citizens, valorizing his survival, together with Via Mazzini's and the synagogue's, as impermeable, virtually sacred. In actual fact, though not recorded in Bassani's story, the temple's interior was severely damaged several times during the Fascist years by bludgeon-swinging Fascist gangs. Yet the temple itself did and does survive, like Geo, despite considerable internal damage. Among the "countless warehouses, stores and shops" of Via Mazzini, Bassani places a warehouse owned by Geo's father. At the time of the son's return it is used to store whatever the Jews were able to recover of their Fascist-confiscated property. In this detail, too, is imaged the remnant of survival.

Dietro la porta

Of the three symbolic spaces just reviewed, the first—the space of the Este castle—is the most hallowed, the center of the center that the entire city represents in traditional literature and societies. Itself the symbol of the whole city, the castle embodies the city's origin and its foundation in good government. Beyond the city is a "heathen" wilderness, a profane world from which the "sacred and ordered" urban space is walled off.[10] Bassani's Ferrara belongs to this historical tradition, and clearly its walls rise to shut out the Pulga family: non-Jews, non-Ferrarese, unrefined bourgeois. Luciano Pulga, who spends part of a school year as a first-year *liceo* classmate of the story's narrator, even enters the narrative late (in the fourth chapter), after school has been in session for the three months that occupy the first three chapters. The absolute degree of Luciano's negative otherness is implied in the opening paragraph of the short novel, in terms of the narrator's own remembered state of extreme dejection:

> Sono stato molte volte infelice, nella mia vita, da bambino, da ragazzo, da giovane, da uomo fatto; molte volte, se ci ripenso, ho toccato quello che si dice il fondo della disperazione. Ricordo tuttavia pochi periodi più neri, per me, dei mesi di scuola fra l'ottobre del 1929 and il giugno del '30, quando facevo la prima liceo. Gli anni trascorsi da allora non sono in fondo serviti a niente: non sono riusciti a medicare un dolore che è rimasto là come una ferita segreta, sanguinante in segreto. Guarirne? Liberarmene? Non so se sarà mai possibile. [p. 453]

> (I have been unhappy many times in my life, as a child, as a youth, as a grown man; many times, when I think about it again, I have touched what is called the depth of despair. Yet I remember few periods bleaker for me than the school months between October of 1929 and June of 1930, when I began high school. The years that have passed since then have, after all, done no good: they have not been able to heal a sorrow that has remained in me like a secret wound, secretly bleeding. Be cured of it? Freed of it? I don't know if it will ever be possible.)

The intertwining of the lives and characters of the narrator and Luciano Pulga is central not only to *Porta*, but equally so to the total fiction, signaling in this context the self-contradictory and dialectical features of the authorial persona that is assuming greater textual delineation. From one viewpoint, Luciano represents a psychological projection of the narrator's worst self. From another, more important, perspective, he progressively signifies ugliness, defilement, deception, betrayal, unsociability, a rupture in the continuity of life and society. In symbolic opposition to Luciano is Carlo Cattolica, the indisputable whiz of the *liceo* class. Bassani's penchant for spatial symbolism informs not only the urban location of Luciano's home, but also the schoolroom spaces. Tall, thin, handsome, quickminded, graceful Carlo Cattolica sits in class in the second of three rows, as close as possible to the row's midpoint, in direct line with the teacher's desk — thus claiming the privileged center: a location analogous to that which the castle occupies in the city. The narrator chooses to sit in the third and last row — the "girls' " row — in the end seat, which is farthest from the door and at the greatest possible distance from the teacher's desk. The same seat will be selected by the entering Luciano three months later. A small, skinny boy with pale blond hair and cold, blue eyes, Luciano always perspires. His strongly accented *bolognese* speech provokes giggles from the class: he is relentlessly an outsider.

The Pulga family's first stop in Ferrara, following the father's sudden transfer there, is the Hotel Tripoli, a cheap place behind the castle whose main service is hourly rental for sexual dalliances. The family's more permanent move takes them from the center of town to outside Porta Reno, that is, beyond the city walls, to the lower-class *sub*-urb near the Foro Boario. Just as Luciano is a negative *alter ego* of the narrator as a young boy, so too is his father, Osvaldo, a negative image of the narrator's father. A civil service doctor (*medico condotto*) who barely earns enough to support his family, Luciano's father (according to the narrator's) is a boor, a hypocrite, a name-dropper, and a zealous Fascist. A doctor by training but long not in practice, the narrator's father, by contrast, lives on private income. The differences in the status and comportment of the two families place them at extremities from each other, both social and spatial. The regard of the one begins in condescension; of the other, in subservience. Luciano's flattery of his chosen friend (the narrator) inflates the latter's sense of self-importance, leading him to believe that he has achieved an authority to rival Carlo Cattolica's. This self-elevation ineluctably leads to a self-lacerating fall, of which the boy's uneasy fascination with Luciano's "otherness" is the instrument. Spatial separation is a distinctive metaphor of alterity in the novella and is also the voyeuristic means of recognizing it. Whereas the narrator's mother eavesdrops "behind the door" in approval of her son's studying with his new friend, the narrator eventually eavesdrops behind a door in Carlo Cattolica's house, to hear Luciano betray him.

In addition to flattery, Luciano employs comedy to ingratiate himself. He has an endless repertory of jokes and amusing anecdotes about the mountain towns outside Bologna. What he reserves for his own part in the jokes is always the same, the role "del furbo, del sagace, dell'abile; dello svelto, oltre che di cervello, di mano e di piede" [p. 486] (of the sly one, the wise, the clever one, quick not only with his wits but also with his hands and feet [W:*D*, p. 53]). In brief, Luciano assumes the role of court jester to his young "prince." In this role Luciano affirms his status as the outsider in relation to the narrator (the insider). Soon the jester adds to his tricks the dangerous fascination of transgression. First, social intimacy: "Sentii a un tratto [richiama il narratore] che stavamo scivolando verso una intimità dalla quale fino allora ci eravamo tenuti lontani, una intimità che *dovevo* ad ogni costo rifiutare" [p. 487] (All at once [recalls the narrator] I felt we were sliding toward an intimacy that, until then, we had kept at a sufficient distance: an intimacy I *had* to refuse at all costs [W:*D*, p. 55]). Next, familial disrespect: Luciano, unruffled, calls his father "an obstinate idiot" ("testardo di un cretino" [ibid.]) and coolly claims that his mother enjoys being beaten by his father (p. 488). The boy further claims that the "high-society" women who frequent the Hotel Tripoli are mothers, perhaps grandmothers, who may be seen in a box at the Teatro Comunale immediately after their sexual frivolities. With the same dispassion, Luciano relates his voyeuristic delight in peeking at copulating couples in the hotel room next to his. The boy's detailed accounts of what he has seen and heard captivate the narrator, as do the accounts of his pornographic readings accompanied by masturbation. The totally ignorant and inexperienced narrator absorbs Luciano's "instruction" with absolute faith, even consenting, though embarrassed, to a mutual exhibition of their sexual parts. His initiation into sexual knowledge is attended by the sensation of being "sospinto a grado a grado verso qualcosa di ignoto e di minaccioso" [p. 492] (thrust gradually toward something unknown and threatening [W:*D*, p. 62]). Luciano assumes a serpentlike quality: "La sua voce mi teneva fermo, mi chiudeva dentro le sue spire basse e ronzanti. . . . Vivevo come dentro una galleria sotterranea" [ibid.] (His voice held me fast, it gripped me in its low buzzing coils. . . . I lived as if in a tunnel [ibid.]). The narration contrasts a "day" world of soccer games under a bright, gladdening sun with the "night" world of Luciano's seductive, sexual storytelling. A serious case of tonsillitis soon allows the narrator time to reflect on the "dark tunnel" (p. 495) of the last months; the disease itself is a sign of the acute assault of incipient self-awareness, and thus also already a sign of the potential for moral recuperation:

> Io, per me, mi ero sentito afferrare allo stomaco da un senso irrefrenabile di disgusto. D'allora in poi non avevo pensato che a quel sesso oscenamente, paurosamente enorme, e al mio disgusto. Disgusto, schifo. Se avessi ricominciato con Luciano era allo schifo di ogni minuto trascorso con lui che sarei andato incontro. [p. 495]

> I, for my part, had felt my stomach seized by an irresistible disgust. After that, I had done nothing but think of it, really: of that sex, obscenely, frighteningly enormous, and of my disgust. Disgust, revulsion. If I were to begin again with Luciano, I would have to face the disgust of every minute spent with him.) [W.*D*, p. 68]

The narrator's private pain is intensified by the public situation, that is, by his schoolmates' (particularly Carlo Cattolica's) knowledge of his friendship with (in their words) "quel leccaculo del Pulga" [p. 496] (that ass-licker, Pulga). The series of broken taboos leads to a final one that marks a profound turning point for the suffering narrator. As a result of the tonsillitis, he must refrain from gymnastics in order to avoid perspiring:

> La proibizione assoluta di sudare . . . tornava a riempirmi di un'invidia struggente, dolorosa. . . . continuavo a guardarli correre, gli altri, saltare, gridare, sudare, e mi sentivo più che mai un reietto, un debole, un meschino: degno in tutto e per tutto di fare il paio con un Luciano Pulga. [p. 497]

> (The firm order that I was not to become overheated . . . now filled me again with painful, searing envy. . . . I went on watching the others run, jumping, shouting, sweating, and more than ever I felt an outcast, a weak-

ling, a wretch. Completely worthy of making a pair with somebody like Luciano Pulga.) [W:*D*, p. 70]

The prohibition against perspiring consciously stimulates desire for and envy of his classmates' beaded brows and no doubt recalls Luciano's constant and repulsive sweated face. Athletic or healthy opposes uncontrollable or unhealthy exudation, as well as the narrator's own exclusion from the healthy: he is now a repugnant outcast.

The timorously but deeply admired Carlo Cattolica turns up at this moment, not unlike a fairytale prince, to assist the diseased protagonist's physical and moral recovery. Assistance takes the form of an invitation to Carlo's home, for the purpose of studying together; it is an invitation, in the eyes of the invited, tantamount to a supreme privilege. But with the guest's suggestion that his regular studymate, Luciano, join them (a request Carlo scornfully rejects), the narrator's physical disease again declares itself as a sign of his willful moral disease: "La peste Luciano ce l'aveva davvero, e ormai, a forza di stargli vicino, me l'ero presa anch'io" [p. 500] (Luciano really did have the plague, and I, too, from being with him, had caught it [W:*D*, p. 75]. Disease and contagion are privileged metaphors of social and political disorder in these texts. The exclusion in *Porta* of direct attention to the presence of Fascist life in Ferrara—the political lodestone of Bassani's work—operates to allegorize the factor of failure in the authorial construct that, distinct from elsewhere in the fiction, is here modeled to fill the entire narrative stage. The youthful persona is at once an allegorical representation of social corruptibility by Fascist flattery and intimidation and an enlarged close-up of mature self-reflexivity: Bassani's boldest and bravest public confessional.

Luciano Pulga and his unappealing family intrude on Ferrara and a young boy's inexperience for the duration of a school year (1929–30), a year that coincides with the bloom of the Fascist regime about to enjoy the years of so-called consensus—that is, about to seduce and betray a society beyond healing: "Gli anni trascorsi da allora non sono in fondo serviti a niente: non sono riusciti a medicare un dolore che è rimasto là come una ferita segreta, sanguinante in segreto. Guarirne? Liberarmene? Non so se sarà mai possibile" [p. 453] (The years that have passed since then have, after all, done no good: they have not been able to heal a sorrow that has remained in me like a secret wound, secretly bleeding. Be cured of it? Freed of it? I don't know if it will ever be possible). The narrator's self-evaluation speaks as well for a social one. The well-educated, respectful, and responsible young boy mirrors the Ferrarese bourgeoisie of the Fascist years; his acceptance of Luciano signifies his transformation *into* Luciano. The classroom seat the young protagonist first occupies—the corner seat at the farthest end of the room—is soon exchanged for a center seat next to Carlo Cattolica, the class hero, statuesque idol, and vain and contemptuous rival. The exchange allows Luciano, on his first day in school, to choose the vacated seat as his own. Following Carlo's climactic "behind-the-door" exposure of Luciano as disloyal to the narrator and denigrating to his mother, the narrator decides to change his seat again, even though school is about to end; he requests to return to his former seat, still occupied by Luciano. Bassani stages this little scene deftly, accentuating the "metamorphosis" of the narrator into Luciano and the transgression that the request signifies:

> "Ha capito, Pulga Luciano? Su, svelto, sgomberi. Raccolga le sue brave masserizie, e si sposti accanto al *grande* Cattolica. Si sentirà onorato, immagino!"
>
> E mentre Luciano, carico dei suoi libri, si incrociava con me lungo il corridoio fra la seconda fila di banchi e la terza . . . un secco "*sst!*," sibilante e imperioso, si levò a stroncare sul nascere l'inizio di una nuova mormorazione. [p. 531]

> ("You understand, Pulga Luciano? Come on, hurry, collect your possessions, and advance. To the fourth desk, beside the great Cattolica. You must feel honored, I imagine!"
>
> And as Luciano, laden with his books, passed me in the aisle between the second and third rows of desks . . . a sharp "ssssh," hissing and imperious, was heard, to kill at birth a new murmur in the room.) [W:*D*, p. 128]

The chiasma they trace ("si incrociava con me" [we criss-crossed]) is a traditional symbol of inversion and completion or balance. The young boy who consciously re-places himself in the farthest possible corner of the classroom secures by that act the possibility of his return to the center. The author who writes the boy's story thus traces for himself the possibility of an achievement of power and, at the same time, the actuality of that achievement by his very creation and valorization of a wicked antagonist, Luciano Pulga, outside the fold. Luciano and his family represent vulgar Fascism and festering anti-Semitism; Carlo Cattolica represents their cultivated counterpart. Although the schoolboy protagonist separates himself from both, he remains impotent in self-loathing, fit only for a painful second place: "I was right," a schoolmate reports upon reading the posted final grades: "Cattolica's first, and you're second" (W:*D*, p. 132). Second place is equivalent to last or no place. The charge of homosexuality leveled against the narrator by Luciano, in a conversation with Carlo (and reported in the first person by the narrator), conjoins the narrator's feeling of impotence, shame, and disease: "Ma sì. Ero di sicuro un 'finocchio,' sia pure allo stato potenziale: un 'busone' in attesa soltanto di 'saltare il fosso,' e tuttavia ignaro (questo, il tragico!) della bella carriera che mi stava davanti, inevitabile" [p. 527] (Of course, I was surely a "pansy," though still only potentially; a "fairy," only waiting to become one, to become one really, and at the same time unaware—that was the tragic thing!—of the fine career that was before me, inevitably [W:*D*, p. 121]).

Bassani juxtaposes the narrative of Luciano Pulga with that of Micòl Finzi-Contini, the former one following the latter chronologically and compositionally within the *Romanzo*. This ugly, pale, devious, and sickly boy is the very antithesis of the beautiful, vibrant, mysterious, and healthy Micòl. The *Giardino*, which culminates in the narrating subject's artistic ripening and the writing of the novel, immediately precedes the publication of *Porta*, which silences its narrating subject in utter self-loathing and spiritual aridity. Whereas Micòl's apotheosized femininity symbolizes love and creativity, Luciano's diminished masculinity symbolizes self-love, social infertility, and waste—the charge Luciano lays on his putative school friend (the narrator) when he labels him a homosexual. Micòl's home, that is, her spatial identification, is at Ferrara's periphery, the classical locus of pure potentiality and transformation to a higher order of being. Luciano's home is far beyond the city walls; beyond, that is, the collective social body and Micòl's redeeming grasp, beyond the moral possibility of communal identification, that is, of participation in city life of which the Finzi-Continis (Micòl most of all) are the highest embodiment.

The literary portrait of the narrative persona that constitutes the major subject matter of *Porta* images defeat and waste, as the story's opening passage (to cite once again) nakedly proclaims: "The years that have passed since then have, after all, done no good." The pain, the "secret wound" Luciano opens, seems incurable. Bassani's demonic figures of destruction, such as Luciano and Sciagura, are utterly virulent. Thus the spiritual sacrifice inflicted by Sciagura and his Fascist cohorts upon their fellow citizens sadistically shot, remain fundamentally without issue, without redemptive potential within the framework of the narratives. Only at the extratextual level of the reader is communal regeneration imaginable, and only at the intratextual level of the writing subject (*Odore* rewriting *Porta*) does authorial regeneration materialize. But absolute death, that is, the absence of (fertile) love, is a constant condition of the social collectivity of the *Romanzo* and an almost constant imminence for its protean persona. Equivalent to a severe moral judgment, its symbolic reification is located "outside the walls."

Chapter 4
Sexual Identity and Political Persecution

l'amore, quando è puro, cioè totalmente disinteressato, è sempre anor-
male, asociale, eccetera . . .

Il giardino dei Finzi-Contini

Homosexuality

In the Bassani narratives homosexuality signals moral weakness, both personal
and social. It represents an impotence or infertility that blocks all potential for
social health. In its initial expression in "Una notte del '43," the "sick" association
between the pharmacist Pino Barilari and the Fascist Sciagura determines the
negative coordinates of the social forces that will operate in one way or another
throughout Bassani's fiction. The social consequences of the hinted homosexuality in this story animate an important literary and ideological position developed
in numerous texts of the *Romanzo*. The intense and sadistic power of Sciagura
over Pino is implicitly homosexual. Bassani has stressed this element in the bond
between the two men by pointing to Pino's almost certainly unconsummated
marriage as one indicator and the plot's logic of homosexuality as another.[1] Inso-
far as the bond functions to prohibit the purpose of justice, that is, the conviction
of Sciagura as a war criminal, it is antisocial. In the courtroom Pino refuses to
testify against Sciagura, not only because he is transfixed by the Fascist's imperi-
ous gaze, but also beause he is protecting his own person. Pino's self-respect is

88

at stake in his testimony: admission of his witness would lead to revelation of his cuckoldry.

Sciagura actively imposes violence and terror on Ferrara; Pino passively objectifies disease and alienation. Sciagura and Pino's comportment contaminates their compatriots, who respond to the respective brutality and banality of the pair with cowardice and condescension, postures that require the dismissal of moral will. The implications of homosexuality as a metaphor of social infertility and decay are nowhere in the fiction more dramatically rendered than in the consummately orchestrated trial scene of "Notte": the community, yearning for justice and self-justification, is totally defeated, whereas Sciagura, the personification of social disorder, triumphs. This scene is Bassani's most merciless expression of moral disdain for his society's feebleness in its historical moment of extreme testing.

Once written into his fiction, the idea of homosexuality takes possession of the author. Whether elegant and sensitive or pathetic and dull-witted, the homosexual becomes a metaphor of the diseased social body. Individual relations, such as Sciagura's and Pino's, are inevitably poisonous to the pair; thus they become metonyms of Ferrarese society under Fascism and—most important—metonyms of that society in relation to the smaller one of the Ferrarese Jews.

The narrative following "Notte," the short novel *Gli occhiali d'oro*, centers on a homosexual. Doctor Athos Fadigati is, in fact, the only overtly homosexual character in the *Romanzo*. He is also more elaborated than any of the other characters created to channel a "homosexual" network of textual meaning. Hence *Occhiali* is the author's best text for understanding the narrative implications of the subject.

The text of "Notte" does not state explicitly that Pino Barilari is a homosexual. It verifies only that as a sexually innocent teenager he was fearful of prostitutes and that his marriage at age thirty-two to a seventeen-year-old *femme fatale* is incomprehensible, virtually an act of communal betrayal: Anna Repetto was "una ragazza troppo in vista e vistosa, insomma, perché a farsela soffiare sotto il naso da uno come Pino Barilari non si sentissero defraudati, traditi un po' tutti" [p. 138] (too obvious, too glamorous, altogether too important a girl for a nonentity like Pino Barilari to catch her without everyone feeling a bit defrauded, even betrayed [Q:*P*, p. 183]). Furthermore, within two years the pharmacist's paralysis forces him to abandon his marital bed for a cot in a room of his own. If Pino's history, including his wife's infidelity, does not confirm his homosexuality, it certainly conveys his homoeroticism (or latent homosexuality), which is only a small scale of difference within the textual logic of homosexuality.

Pino's relation to Sciagura is patently that of slave to master. A similar relation exists between Dr. Fadigati and Eraldo Deliliers (*Occhiali*). Sciagura and

Eraldo are profligate womanizers of sadistic and commanding demeanor, the one awesome for reasons of power, the other for reasons of beauty. Whether their flaunted erotic dalliances mask or display their true sexual natures is irrelevant; for each the most important relationship, from both the personal and the textual point of view, is with a man. Moreover, Sciagura's penchant for prostitutes and Eraldo's for conspicuous flirtations underscore a lack of substantial relationships with women. Eraldo becomes identified with an admitted homosexual; Sciagura, with a likely one. Both relations lead to catastrophe: the one, personal—Fadigati's suicide—the other, social—Ferrara's shame. Fadigati's suicide also lays responsibility on the Ferrarese who condemn and ostracize him. By having the death conclude the novel, Bassani ensures that the possibility of communal expiation, materially beyond textual reach, is left unrealizable. Public proclamation of the incipient persecution of the Jews, juxtaposed in the novel with Fadigati's complete loss of community toleration, is an event similarly deprived of potential moral redemption.

Doctor Athos Fadigati, twenty-nine years old, arrives in Ferrara from his native Venice in 1919—a time of intense political violence, precipitated by the unemployment, inflation, and general instability of the postwar period. It is also the inaugural year of the Fascist movement, in which Ferrara participates by forming its first *fascio di combattimento*.[2] By late 1937, when the local newspaper—"in the style of the time"—announces Dr. Fadigati's suicide as an accident, the Fascist press is unleashing its suicidal anti-Jewish campaign and the narration of *Occhiali* comes to a close. The book's epigraph—an eleven-line cry of despair uttered by Sophocles' Philoctetes, who begs to have his poisoned, intolerably painful foot cut off at the cost of death if necessary—emblematizes the desperate condition of the Italian body politic and the Ferrarese community's refusal to risk mortal injury: a refusal that secures for the community an insufferable affliction of *moral* injury.

Because of the conspicuous, intimidating Socialist activity in its streets and because of the "feverish, agitated atmosphere" (W:S, p. 84) following the Great War, provincial Ferrara takes comfort in welcoming the refined, courteous, pleasantly portly Athos Fadigati. The young doctor's gold-rimmed eyeglasses seem to verify his reassuring respectability. Within a few years the Venetian becomes director of the ear, nose, and throat division of Ferrara's principal hospital (the historical *Ospedale Sant'Anna*, where Tasso was a patient); in his office at home, he enjoys a thriving private practice: his modern, spacious, well-furnished clinic greatly appeals to the city's upper classes, who delight in the De Chirico and De Pisis paintings gracing the walls. By now, Fadigati is a distinguished citizen accepted as one of the community's own. Indeed, he seems a perfected image of the Ferrarese. His high status defines a standard by which the entire community as well as the homosexual doctor must be measured. In the end, Ferrara obliterates Fadigati's assimilation (as it will the local Jews'), and reidentifies him as an outsider and an outcast. The fact that Ferrara rejects those it formerly embraced entails self-rejection, a self-inflicted social violence, which can issue only in collective shame. Specular and nonsacrificial, this type of victimization is practiced without reference to the public good—indeed, contrary to it. Thus it is necessarily unproductive (infertile), even suicidal. While the shame kindled in the exquisitely refined Fadigati, as in the crude Pino Barilari, marks a loss of social value, their ostracism, beyond marking a privation of society, reveals the aridity of communal life.

The story of Athos Fadigati is a parable of Fascist persecution and Jewish homelessness. The doctor leaves his native Venice to escape the painful atmosphere ("atmosfera angosciosa") of a home in which, within a brief period, both parents and a deeply loved sister have died. In other words, tragedy and sudden rootlessness, rather than pursuit of fortune or adventure, impel the young man's displacement to Ferrara. Within a few years the foreigner gains a new homeland and a sterling reputation. Analogously the Italian Jews, regarded before 1860 as foreigners in their own land, were granted the rights and privileges of citizens in the Kingdom of Italy and subsequently achieved high professional and civic standing. But the spirit of tolerance is easily subdued. Fadigati's homosexuality overtakes his respectability; his "disease" withers his social worth. Pino's paralysis, a moral as well as physiological disease, manifests his social unfitness.

In Bassani's fictive universe, social unfitness implies homosexuality and vice versa. In the case of Pino Barilari, the "condition" of homosexuality is visible in his sick body, his childless marriage, and even his father's membership in the bourgeois-liberal Masonic Order. Fascism, by contrast, glorified the athletic male body, encouraged large families, and persecuted and imprisoned homosexuals, Jews, and Masons.[3] Ferrara's regime, in Bassani's fictionalization, views Pino's paralysis as politically offensive and provocative: "Nel suo ostentare senza pudore una malattia indecorosa non era mica da vedersi, per caso, un'intenzione sottilmente offensiva e provocatoria?" [p. 140] (Wasn't there something subtly offensive and provocative about the way he flaunted his indecent disease so shamelessly? [Q:P, p. 187]). Pino's father, a widower "from time immemorial" who dies in 1936, held a very high Masonic grade but originally felt some sympathy for Fascism.[4]

The senior Barilari's Masonry, notwithstanding his slight support of Fascism, suffices to mark him as profoundly unpatriotic in the Fascist view, a heritage passed on to his son. The political taint is reinforced by the son's physical resemblance to his father: (" 'Non sarai mica il figlio del dottor Barilari?' qualcuno gli aveva subito chiesto" [p. 142] ("You wouldn't happen to be Dr. Barilari's son, would you?" someone had asked him right away). Fascism, furthermore, linked Masonry and the Jews by using each to disparage the other. Bassani appropriates the quintessential Fascist *bête noire*, homosexuality, as a logical metaphor of the

Jewish condition during the *ventennio*. The association is explicit in *Occhiali*. Fundamental to the relation of Fadigati and the narrating Jewish youth—and highly appreciated by the novel's commentators and readers—this theme plumbs many waters. The intricate crossflowing of Jewishness and other attributes of various repugnant, respectable, and narrating characters will be discussed in detail in chapter 5 as components of the author's complex representation of his persona. Ineluctably, in working out each of the narratives and their interrelations, the reader assembles pieces of a composite persona masking Giorgio Bassani.

The obverse of Fadigati's victimization by Deliliers is his own self-loathing, which becomes evident after his scandalous fall from respectability before the eyes of Ferrarese vacationers in the drawing room of the Grand Hotel at Riccione. Fadigati literally falls to the floor from Eraldo's blow to his face: the young lover's response to the older man's whispered reproach. Until the time of his association with Eraldo, the doctor maintains a comportment of discretion and conformity. He is admired by Ferrara's "piccole società per bene" [p. 170] (small, respectable societies) for his good taste, gracious manners, meticulous daily routine, and professional position. Although (in his own words) he is "apolitical by nature" (p. 172), he joins Ferrara's *Fascio* upon the personal urging of its secretary. He also holds memberships in the principal social clubs of the city. By these expressions of identification with the ruling class, Fadigati mirrors the narrator's father (as portrayed in other narratives as well), who himself symbolizes Ferrarese Jewry.

The doctor's curious "spirito di *bohème*" (p. 171) and lack of interest in taking a wife raise eyebrows, but they are rationalized by his adoptive countryfolk. It takes more than ten years for rumors of the "vice" to circulate and for the doctor's daily habits to take on a mythopoeic "daytime" and "nighttime" character. The townspeople conduct themselves accordingly: "Di giorno, alla luce del sole, fargli tanto di cappello; la sera, anche a essere spinti ventre contro ventre dalla calca di via San Romano, mostrare di non conoscerlo" [p. 174] (During the day, in the light of the sun, show him every respect; after dark, even when they were pressed, belly to belly, in the crowd of Via San Romano, they should give no sign of recognition [W:S, p. 94]). For his part, Fadigati maintains an "unexceptionable conduct" (p. 176), carrying out his professional duties during the day and spending late evenings either wandering through the city or watching films. It is in the "night" world of darkened theaters that the eyes of the public assiduously—voyeuristically—peep at him:

> Ficcando gli sguardi nelle *tenebre*, oltre la balaustrata della galleria, lo cercavano là, *in basso*, lungo le *sordide* pareti laterali, presso le porte delle uscite di sicurezza e delle *latrine*, senza trovar requie finché non avessero colto il tipico luccichio che i suoi occhiali d'oro mandavano ogni tanto attraverso il *fumo* e *l'oscurità*. [p. 175; emphasis added]

(Peering into the shadows, over the railing of the balcony, they would look for him down there, along the sordid side walls, near the emergency exits and the doors of the toilets. They couldn't understand his behavior. For this very reason, perhaps, they could find no peace until they had caught the characteristic glint from his gold-rimmed eyeglasses every now and then, through the smoke and the darkness.) [W:S, p. 94]

Darkness and sordidness become one and the same for the Ferrarese as they track Fadigati's whereabouts. Although his other publicly known night habit—listening to music in the early hours of the morning—evokes a "particular atmosphere" (p. 177), and passersby take for granted that the lighted shuttered apartment protects one of the doctor's working-class male lovers. The text calculatedly associates the music—"Wagner, above all" (ibid.)—with Wagner's illicit lovers, Tristan and Isolde. This famous pair embodies Freud's interconnected concepts of the amorous (Eros) and destructive (Thanatos) impulses inherent in the human psyche. More broadly, the combined, contrary impulses give names to the self-destructive and inextricably sexual passions of the omnipresent persona, of whom the frail Dr. Fadigati is one pale reflection. As we shall see, Eros-Thanatos undoes the young Bruno Lattes, the major personification (in the third person) of the narrating subject. The legendary Tristan and Isolde, acting out their high drama of uncontrollable passion, analogically give wry testimony to the bourgeois doctor, whose uncontrollable passion does not exceed paltriness and pathos and whose Isolde never materializes.

The reader of *Occhiali* finds Fadigati discussing the *Tristan und Isolde* two pages before his music-filled apartment is described. His appreciation of a *Tristan* performance lingers especially for the second act's (in the doctor's words) "long love lament" (p. 176). The bench—the "transparent symbol of the nuptial bed" (ibid.)—and the lovers' "notte di voluttà eterna come la morte" [ibid.] (night of sensual delight as eternal as death) enthrall Fadigati. Erotic violence in the Bassanian oeuvre is a metaphor of social violence. Fadigati's fascination with the *Tristan* (and with Wagner in general) foreshadows his self-punishment by suicide and adds sinister meaning to his mimetic attachment to Wagner's impulsive lovers. On another level, the Wagnerian association adds a decadent intellectual Germanic strain to the Venetian doctor and invokes the Austro-Hungarian Empire, of which Venice was once part. A more direct Austro-Hungarian presence enters the text of "Una corsa ad Abbazia," which also recounts the moral and existential disintegration of its primary character, Bruno Lattes; decadence and the "Germanic principle" seem to go hand in hand.[5]

Isolde and Tristan's tragic and illicit night/love offers Fadigati at first a mystifying vehicle to displace and idealize his erotic passion. Bassani sets the doctor's erotic fantasies voyeuristically against a backdrop of suggestive light, seen from outside the music lover's apartment in the hours before dawn. In recalling the "everlasting" night of love, Fadigati half-closes his eyes "dietro le lenti, sorridendo rapito" [p. 176] (behind his glasses, with a rapt smile [W:S, p. 96]). This gesture of false security mocks the doctor's own ephemeral erotic relation, and the house he believes shut to the outside is, like his eyelids, only half-shut. Like a suggestive film in a darkened theater, the curtained house titillates unseen spectators on the dark streets. Originally a sign to others of his social credentials, the gold-rimmed eyeglasses have become a shade behind which the doctor's half-closed eyes can no longer fully shut out the others. Darkness and ecstacy are about to transfuse into simple sordidness.

Retuned and reduced, the social opposition delineated by the two lives of the doctor reappears in *Dietro la Porta*. This time a respectable schoolboy (also the story's narrator) becomes an intimate friend of a self-serving new classmate, Luciano Pulga. The former perceives the moral descent wrought by his friendship as a diseased "night" world of talk in contrast to the healthy "day" world of soccer games. The narrator's self-loathing is a fruitless but not absolutely self-destructive emotion that persists throughout and beyond the telling and writing of his story. A far more ingratiating character than the schoolboy, Dr. Fadigati suffers an extreme degree of ostracism: rejection, ridicule, and robbery by his handsome young lover; severance from his profession; scorn from his scandalized compatriots; and suicide: "Ma era possibile durare indefinitamente a vivere così, nella solitudine più assoluta, circondato dall'ostilità generale?" [p. 233] (But was it possible to continue, indefinitely, living like this, in the most absolute solitude, surrounded by general hostility? [W:S, p. 176]).

One relaxed day before the fatal event, Fadigati describes to some student acquaintances a fictional character who, like himself once, was a "solitary" student in Padua: "Come me, vive in una stanza d'affitto che dà su un orto vastissimo, pieno di alberi velenosi" [p. 188] (Like me, he lived in a furnished room over a huge garden, filled with poisonous trees [W:S, p. 113]). Although a peasant family who tended arable land near Fadigati's window often invited him to dinner (a gesture suggesting the attitude of the narrator and his family toward the doctor), the unsettling presence of the poisonous trees dominates the account. Fadigati's isolation, at first self-imposed, becomes forced and diseased by the poison of the community. The rented room of his story emblematizes his own status of stranger, of *meteco*, in Ferrara. (See chapter 1, where this term is used to disparage Luciano Pulga.) Eraldo Deliliers too is an outsider, at least partially (his father, now dead, was not *ferrarese*, and Eraldo has not been in Ferrara long). Neither he nor Luciano has any desire to be assimilated. On the contrary, they are fundamentally alien. Thus they sow their hostile acts against a native son and then leave town: Luciano returns to Bologna, and Eraldo goes off to Paris. The latter, like the alluring Carlo Cattolica of *Porta*, is "un bellissimo ragazzo, alto un metro e ottanta e con un volto e un corpo da statua greca, un reuccio locale vero e proprio" [p. 192] (a very handsome boy, six feet tall, with the face and body of a Greek statue . . . a proper little local monarch [W:*S*, p. 119]). It is not hard to associate the noble, young Grecian with Thomas Mann's statuesque youth loved homoerotically by an old, refined gentleman, but Fadigati's attraction to Eraldo is less aesthetic than it is masochistic. The masochism, however, is less psychological than it is symbolic of (homosexual) social impotence. In the volcanic political period during which the novella unfolds, Eraldo comes to represent perfected (politicized) erotico-violent power. Handsome and seductive, he wins the favor not only of the homosexual Fadigati, but also of almost everyone else. On the beach at Riccione his graceful, nearly nude body is admired "dalla maggior parte degli astanti, dagli uomini come dalle donne" [p. 198] (by most of those present, men and women alike [W:*S*, p. 128]). Because of their admiration," toccava poi a Fadigati scontare in qualche modo l'indulgenza che il settore ferrarese della spiaggia di Riccione riservava a Deliliers" [ibid.] (Fadigati, as a reaction, had to pay somehow for the indulgence that the Ferrara sector of the Riccione beach granted Deliliers [W:*S*, p. 128]). Although he resembles a Greek statue and his heritage is French, Eraldo personifies the dream of unfettered, youthful, Aryan dominion, as much sexual as political. The important Bassanian motif of envious erotic desire finds its fullest expression in the several Bruno Lattes fictions, which will be discussed later. In the context of *Occhiali*, the Greek-named Athos Fadigati seems a failed and rejected model of the "Grecian" Eraldo, who, like the "Aryan" Nazis, is beautiful only on the outside. Fadigati, on the other hand, is beautiful only on the inside. The gold frames of his eyeglasses can make him no match for the fully "gilded" Eraldo. Not only does the motif of victimization that pairs these two turn a homosexual doctor into a symbol of oppressed Jewry about to be grotesquely yoked by anti-Jewish laws, but it also makes homosexuality equivalent to tabooed and impotent erotic desire. Thus, as the (non-Jewish) Ferrarese sunbathers fuel their sexual fantasies by gazing upon Eraldo's androgynous physique, they look to the tarnished Fadigati ("guilty" for being neither beautiful nor heterosexual nor Aryan) to expiate their own and Eraldo's (erotic) guilt. Fadigati indeed safeguards their "innocence"; by denouncing (sacrificing) the scapegoated doctor, the Ferrarese, in their own eyes, cleanse their lustful souls.

Fadigati accepts without question the guilt placed upon him. He shares his feelings with the story's narrator: "Dopo ciò che è accaduto l'estate scorsa non mi riesce più di tollerarmi. Non posso più, non debbo. Ci crede che certe volte non sopporto di farmi la barba davanti allo specchio? Potessi almeno vestirmi in un altro modo!" [p. 234] (After what happened last summer, I can't tolerate myself any more. I can't; I mustn't. Will you believe me, if I tell you that sometimes I can't bear shaving, facing myself in the mirror? If I could at least dress in another way! [W:*S*, p. 178]). The narrator judges the unfortunate pair of lovers without mercy: "uno carnefice, l'altro vittima. La vittima al solito perdonava, consentiva al carnefice" [pp. 234–35] (one, an executioner; the other, the victim. The victim, as usual, forgave, agreed with his executioner [W:S, p. 178]). Fadigati's assumption of guilt acknowledges his weakness, his self-loathing that leads to self-destruction. Motivated by public shame, his suicide is a sign of social failure, as inevitable as Ferrara's moral and political impotence following the wartime execution of eleven citizens ("Notte").

By enmeshing homosexuality into the sociopolitical context of Ferrara, Pino Barilari and Athos Fadigati force into relief the inevitablity of moral collapse for the entire community. The homosexual "message" is also encoded within the smallest social unit of the family; specifically in the family privileged above all others, the Finzi-Continis. The social behavior of Alberto Finzi-Contini aligns him with other male characters who may be classified as latent homosexuals, or, in Bassani's word, "cryptohomosexuals." Within this alignment their sexual practice evidences social sterility rather than sexual aberrance.

Whereas the figure of Micòl dominates the family garden—the acres of trees, plants, and pathways surrounding the house—the figure of Alberto emblematizes disease within the garden, the acreage of wasteland within it. Alberto's name and Micòl's, like their lives and even their speech, invariably coalesce in the early parts of the narrative, so that the brother and sister may be said to have a single nature, Alberto representing the negative image of Micòl. Their various attributes inevitably contrast: her blond hair, his brown; her success in college, his failure; her love of nature, his love of technology; her love of memory, his love of things; her activity, his passivity; her health, his sickliness. Alberto's most serious shortcoming is social: he is indifferent to others and to life in general. The narrator recalls that during a visit, Alberto "mi considerava con la strana espressione di simpatia distaccata, oggettiva, che in lui, lo sapevo, era il segno del massimo interesse per gli altri del quale fosse capace" [p. 349] (considered me with the curious expression of detached friendliness, an objective look I knew meant he was as interested as he possibly could be in somebody else [Q:G, p. 150]). Talking about his phonograph records, the host lists "nomi e titoli, cortese ed equanime come d'abitudine ma con indifferenza: né più né meno che se mi desse da scegliere in una lista di vivande che lui, per parte sua, si sarebbe guardato bene dall'assaggiare" [ibid.] (names and titles, polite and equable as ever, but indifferently: neither more nor less than if he were asking me to choose from a list of dishes, which he personally would be very careful not to taste [Q:G, p. 151]).

Micòl describes her brother as "più passivo di un *punching ball* . . . sempre amico di tutti e di nessuno" [p. 336] (more passive than a punching ball . . . everyone's friend and no one's). The only thing that elicits some response from Alberto is his superb phonograph equipment: the mechanical perfection of a manufactured—that is, lifeless—object. Diseased in spirit, indifferent to the life cycle of nature—hence the opposite of Micòl—Alberto predictably succumbs to bodily disease. His remains are buried in the garish ancestral family tomb. In contrast, the life-authenticating *magna domus* (the Finzi-Contini mansion) functions as a symbolic, Etruscan-style home-tomb for Micòl, her parents, and her grandmother, whose actual graves remain unknown. Alberto dies a year before the family's deportation to Germany. Having refused to share their (healthy) humanity during his life, in death he is excluded from participating in their moment of final sacrifice.

Insight into the family roles of the Finzi-Continis, and especially of Micòl and her brother, may be found in the metaphors of health and disease analyzed by the philosopher Philip Wheelwright. On the subject of vegetation religion in his book about the language of symbolism, Wheelwright explains:

> Good is life, vitality, propagation, health; evil is death, impotence, disease. Of these several terms *health* and *disease* are the most important and most comprehensive. Death is but an interim evil; it occurs periodically, but there is the assurance of new life ever springing up to take its place. . . . Disease and blight, however, interrupt the cycle; they are the real destroyers; and health is the good most highly to be prized.[6]

Bassani's texts suggest that the opposite of health is homosexuality and that the form of health (the good) most highly to be prized is a form of heterosexuality. Sexuality is sociality, and human relations—whether personal or public—require both a male and a female component for the "assurance of new life ever springing up." Alberto's most intimate relation is with his Communist friend from Milan, Giampiero Malnate. "Giampi," whom the narrator and Micòl find "portly and oppressive" and who assumes an air of ideological superiority toward his bourgeois-liberal Ferrarese friends, is one more rendering of the dominant and antagonistic partner in a typical Bassanian male relation. The narrator compares Alberto's comportment before his favorite friend to that of a frightened bird (p. 363), a figure equally applicable to Pino Barilari, Athos Fadigati, and even the *liceo* pupil-narrator of *Porta*, whose counterpart to Giampiero, Luciano Pulga, defames his putative friend by calling him a latent homosexual ("un 'finocchio,' sia pure allo stato potenziale" [p. 527] (a "pansy," though still only potentially [W:*D*, p. 121]). The virginal friend (the narrator) himself confirms the *symbolic* value of the charge—that is, his relational status among his peers—less by his befriending "una compagnia tutta di maschi" [p. 540] (a group of boys only) than by his justification of sexual abstinence because of his "diseased" state: "Se anche ne avessi pescata qualcuna, i foruncoli che mi deturpavano la faccia mi avrebbero di sicuro impedito di essere preso in considerazione" [ibid.] (If I did encounter any woman, the pimples all over my face would surely prevent her from taking me into consideration [W:*D*, p. 145]).

Malnate's domination of Alberto extends even to abuse of Alberto's family. In reaction to the Communist's depiction of all Finzi-Continis as "degli sporchi agrari, dei biechi latifondisti, e degli aristocratici, per giunta, ovviamente nostalgici del feudalesimo medioevale [che dovrebbero pagare] in qualche maniera il fio dei privilegi da loro goduti fino a questo momento" (dirty land-owners, the evil exploiters of undercultivated estates, and aristocrats, what's more, harking back nostalgically to medieval feudalism [who should pay] the penalty a bit for the privileges they'd so long enjoyed [Q:G, p. 162]), Alberto laughs until he cries, nodding his head up and down in sign of agreement: "Sì, lui per conto proprio avrebbe pagato più che volentieri" [p. 357] (Yes, as far as he was concerned, he would be most glad to pay [ibid.]). His amused concord with Giampiero's censure—a foretaste of the family's slaying by the Nazis—is a further sign of the indifferent youth's refusal of social engagement and his lack of moral opposition. The episode is juxtaposed with Malnate's reminiscence of Alberto's refusal of a young woman's sexual invitations ("una ballerina del Lirico . . . disinteressata, convenientement puttana" [p. 358] (a music-hall dancer at the Lirico . . . not after anything, and a convenient hooker) and the older friend's insinuation of Alberto's homosexuality ("Vogliamo finalmente metterle, le carte in tavola?" [ibid.] (Shall we finally put our cards on the table?). Social violence, sexual violation, and disease sound a three-note discord at one extreme of Bassani's narrative register.

The diseased Alberto contaminates even the superbly furnished bedroom of which he is so proud and which alone arouses in him an impassioned defense (p. 351). He calls his room a studio and keeps a large drawing table in it. Like Fadigati's medical studio, Alberto's bedroom-studio is "rational, functional, and modern" (p. 350) and features a De Pisis on the wall—a "nudino maschile" [p. 349] (a little male nude). When the narrator asks whether he designed the furni-ture himself, Alberto replies no, that he merely copied the designs from a num-ber of architectural magazines and had the furniture made by a local carpenter (pp. 350–51). Alberto's copying (imitation) is equivalent to his homosexuality (sexual self-imitation). Specularity and homosexuality are aspects of a single condition that is antithetical to creativity and heterosexuality. In a context related to sexuality, the Giardino opposes both the false, or sterile, artist (Alberto) and the true, or creative, one (the narrator).

Between Alberto's indifferent itemization of his record collection and his re-mark about copying furniture designs, an episode occurs that suggests what Al-berto is not. As noted earlier, he represents the opposite of his sister. On the occasion of the narrator's visit, Micòl is away in Venice. Another young woman, a servant, makes a momentary appearance: "Bionda e riccia, con le guance ar-rossate delle venete delle Prealpi, la figlia di Perotti preparò in silenzio e a ciglia abbassate le tazze, le posò sul tavolino, quindi si ritirò. Nell'aria della stanza rimase un buon odore di sapone e di borotalco" [p. 350] (Fair and curly-haired, with the rosy cheeks you find in Venetians from the foothills of the Alps, and downcast eyes, Perotti's daughter silently arranged the cups on the small table and left. A pleasant smell of soap and talcum powder hung about the room [Q:G, p. 152]). The shy, sweet-smelling, blond wholesomeness of the girl, whose appearance irritates Alberto, is a soft-spoken textual intimation of the nature of (healthy, female) otherness in respect to Alberto and to males in general. Her clean *bodily* presence, in contrast to Alberto's antiseptic attachment to objects, also connotes a sexual aroma. The Bassanian trope of fragrant aromas gently signals the presence of an animating power in Alberto's room (in this case, an innocent erotic power), of which the characters in the scene nevertheless remain unaware.

The primary expression of differentiation in Bassani's texts is sexual. The attribute of homoeroticism and homosexuality, as numerous male characters demonstrate, allegorizes failed socialization and sterile survival. To this category we may add heterosexuality *manqué*. Heterosexual impotence and homosexuality are the recto and verso of a social or spiritual lack that distresses most of Bassani's male characters, who are invariably victims although few of them die (an important distinction, to which we shall return). The character whose story most fully revolves around "failed" heterosexuality does die, a suicide. He is the protagonist of Bassani's last novel, *L'airone*.

Before examining the allegorical nature of *Airone*—which involves the construction of the authorial persona—let us consider the novel for its illustration of the qualities and functions of the "failed lover" type, whose extreme example is the forty-five year-old Edgardo Limentani.

Suicidal Heterosexuality

Nowhere else in Bassani's works are the erotic and the phallic as crucial for plot development and as rich in symbolism as in the novel *L'airone*. Sexually "coarse" language and acts—markers of transgression and violence—retrospectively violate the subdued treatment of erotic matter in the preceding texts of the *Romanzo*. To the erotic should be added the biological, which in Edgardo's case is inseparable from the former. When he sits alone in a hotel restaurant, disgusted by the food he eats, and watches a tableful of hunters enjoying a meal together, he physically manifests his inability to unite with others. His sexual impotence and his distaste for eating—especially his distaste for eating with others—are signs of his "exile" from all forms of social intercourse. The satisfied bodies of the ("virile") hunters renew, through the sharing of food, the bonds of civilization; Edgardo is but an onlooker. The objectivity of his dysfunctioning sexual and biological processes—indigestion, constipation, lack of desire for food and for sexual intercourse—diagrams social and moral principles.

Edgardo's story begins at the negative extremity of violence—nonarousal (with connotations of both sleep and sex)—and it ends in the ultimate violence of suicide. The story covers one Sunday in December of 1947, shortly before

Figure 8. On route to Codigoro (about 40 kms east of Ferrara) Edgardo Limentani hopes to relax "when in the uncertain light of twilight" he discerns shapes of "low, deserted terrain" separated by "broad expanses of water apparently stagnant yet really flowing" (*L'airone*).

Christmas, from the time Edgardo wakes up and gets ready for a duck-shooting trip in the marshland outside Ferrara to the time he returns home, after dark, and prepares his suicide. The character's existential condition in the novel's post-war present of 1947 reflects the considerable political power just achieved in Ferrara by the Communist party. No longer a respected and feared *padrone*, Edgardo has become instead a figure of impotence and derision: "I tempi dei sorrisi, delle scappellate, degli inchini, erano finiti. Per tutti: ex perseguitati politici e razziali compresi" [p. 551] (The times of smiles, hat-tipping and bows were over. For everyone – including former victims of political and religious persecution). Edgardo's Jewishness, as well as his sociopolitical status, is a major factor in his deadened sense of self.

The anti-Jewish legislation of 1938 impels Edgardo to marry the Catholic Nives Pimpinati, a "donnino di paese" [p. 555] (commonplace villager) of long acquaintance, so that in her name he can continue to control his considerable property.[7] All of it – more than a thousand acres of agricultural land and some urban real estate – passes from the late father's ownership to the daughter-in-law's, becoming "definitivamente roba altrui" [p. 551] (property belonging definitively to someone else). Almost a decade before the beginning of institutionalized persecution, Edgardo buys his lover a "villetta (venduta, poi, all'epoca delle leggi razziali), dove . . . per anni era entrato da padrone" [p. 574] (little villa [sold later, at the time of the racial laws] where . . . for years he had entered as lord and master [W:*H*, p. 41]). Edgardo's diminished status and lowered self-esteem reflect all the consequences—existential, erotic, familial, communal—of his marriage, which separates his former power from his present impotence. The marriage union is, paradoxically, a ritualistic assertion of self-division: an alienation of the self from itself, which issues forth from the fetid seedbed of the anti-Jewish legislation and which asserts itself in the bodily form of Nives, a monstrous "twin" usurper of Edgardo's power. By the end of the day, his impotence finds the effective weapon of suicide.

Recurrent images of male and female sexuality translate Edgardo's suicidal drama into a predominantly erotic discourse. Several times in the narrative, he recalls the historical year of 1938. The marriage provoked by the anti-Jewish decrees almost immediately consumes his claim to authority, as the simple sight of his familial bed shows:

> Ed ecco, avvicinandosi al grande letto matrimoniale di legno scolpito, rossastro, dove lui, figlio unico, era stato concepito, e dove, dal '39 in poi, aveva dormito così di rado con sua moglie, per la seconda volta in quella mattina si sentì invadere da uno strano senso di assurdità. (p. 554)

> (And then, as he approached the great double bed with its carved headboard of reddish wood, where he, an only child, had been conceived, and where, since '39, he had slept so rarely with his wife, for the second time that morning he felt himself overcome by a strange feeling of absurdity.) [W:*H*, p. 13]

The bridal bed, the bed of (Edgardo's) conception, has been falsely claimed: it is actually a bed of sexual aridity. Its positive association with a woman's place of birth-giving yields to a negative female image, the well, which the novel's opening sentence introduces: "Non subito, ma risalendo con una certa fatica dal *pozzo senza fondo* dell'incoscienza, Edgardo Limentani sporse il braccio destro in direzione del comodino" [p. 547; emphasis added] (Not immediately, but climbing with some effort up from the bottomless pit of unconsciousness, Edgardo Limentani stretched his right arm toward the bedside table [W:*H*, p. 3]).

In *Airone* the female image of the well is a symbol of death: a tomb in which "mother" earth buries her children. The image develops textually in opposition to the phallic tower, the preeminent male image personified mainly by Edgardo's cousin but also by some lesser characters. Edgardo's wife is a contemporary embodiment of the mythical devouring or emasculating female. Behind his back, Edgardo imagines, his wife probably satisfies her erotic desire with one of Edgardo's own employees. Furthermore, the narrative suggests, the indifferent and passive Edgardo, utterly without passion, has an emasculated or female nature; his sexual failure seems imaged in the symbolic female forms of bottomless pits.

In an interview in the French newspaper *L'Express*, Bassani explained the suicide of Dr. Fadigati (*Occhiali*) in terms of passion: "He commits suicide because passion always dies." The author also related passion to politics and art, both of which, like Fadigati, are doomed to fail:

> La défaite de la Résistance a symbolisé pour moi la défaite de toutes les résistances. La résistance politique au fascisme a son analogie dans la passion amoureuse, qui est une résistance à la vie ordinaire, ou dans la poésie, qui est une résistance au langage courant. Eh bien, selon moi, toutes les résistances sont vouées à l'échec, la vie ordinaire et le langage courant reprennent toujours le dessus.[8]

> (The defeat of the Resistance symbolized for me the defeat of every resistance. Political resistance to Fascism has its analogy in amorous passion, which is a resistance to ordinary life, or poetry, which is a resistance to everyday speech. In my opinion, every resistance is doomed to failure; ordinary life and everyday speech always recover the advantage.)

Edgardo Limentani embodies the author's belief in the failure of resistance/passion. The political disfigurement of the province of Ferrara wrought by the postwar Socialist-Communist "tide" (p. 549) parallels Edgardo's physical and social malfunctioning. His sexual dysfunction, epitomized in his "lifeless" penis, connotes his religious estrangement. Urinating, he glances at his organ

> con una curiosità, una sorpresa, e un'amarezza mai provate prima d'allora. . . . "Toh," sogghignò. Grigio, misero, da niente, con quel segno della circoncisione, così familiare e insieme così assurdo . . . Non si trattava che di un oggetto, in fondo, di un puro e semplice oggetto come tanti altri. [p. 620]

> (with a curiosity, a surprise, and a bitterness never experienced before. . . . "Ha," he sneered. Gray, wretched, pathetic: with that mark of his circumcision, so familiar and, at the same time, so absurd . . . It was no more than an object, after all, a mere object like so many others.) [W:*H*, p. 110]

Later, while sleeping, Edgardo dreams that Bellagamba's hotel is filled with men and prostitutes having sex. The prostitute he actually saw earlier in the hotel restaurant approaches him in his dream, smiling, "molto più giovane, ora, all'apparenza, molto più ragazza" [p. 628] (much younger now, apparently much more girlish [W:*H*, p. 121]). The day itself is rejuvenated in the dream: the sky is intensely blue and sunny instead of foggy and dark, the time is midafternoon instead of dusk, the season is late spring instead of winter. In this atmosphere charged with radiant hope, the sleeper rebukes the provocative sexual gestures of the prostitute (who, as the day darkens, assumes the coarse manners and fea-

tures of an aging kitchen scullion). Her final gesture is to acknowledge his impotence: " 'Sei proprio a terra,' mormorava allora lei. . . . 'Sei proprio senza' "
[p. 630] ("You're really in bad shape," she murmured then. . . . "You've got
nothing at all" [W:*H*, p. 124]). The woman *cannot* arouse him; he is "dead,"
without passion, an aging survivor past his time. A woman once again images
his self-perception; in this case, his decaying ugliness.

In a different episode, Edgardo's expectation of a good lunch is quashed as
he bites into a sandwich bought in a village grocery filled with enticing aromas.
The bread of the sandwich turns out to be the wrong kind, and the *mortadella*
is greasy:

> Unta era unta, puah, niente da dire. Però di grana grossa. E con un fondo
> di rancido, nel sapore, da ricordargli il '42, il '43, le tessere annonarie,
> i tempi in cui, faticosamente quanto volonterosamente, aveva tentato di
> fare il marito, il buon marito: gli anni peggiori della sua vita, in sostanza.
> [p. 596]

> (It was greasy, all right, ugh, no doubt about that. But tough; and with a
> rancid aftertaste that reminded him of '42, '43, ration cards, the times
> when, laboriously, though willingly, he had tried to act the husband, the
> good husband: the worst years of his life, in fact.) [W:*H*, p. 75]

The food that fails, the wife that fails, the body that fails: all are signs of Edgardo's estrangement from the world and from himself. It is no wonder that this
failed hunter, contemplating the face reflected back to him in a shop window,
sees over his features "the dust of years and years" (p. 652).

Edgardo is a dusty still life—a *natura morta*, in the more stark Italian term
that was the original title of *Airone*.[9] He is effectively a carcass, an embarrassing
and disgusting burden ("carico" [p. 612], like the heron and the other dead birds
filling his car trunk, all shot by the young guide, Gavino. Edgardo's consequent
identification with the "perfected" (stuffed) heron is an identification with his
own *natura morta*. Ultimately the wealthy landowner's "still life" condition is *socially* determined as his gaze fixes on groups of people in common endeavors,
namely, cardplayers and hunters. These people rouse his admiration but also his
sense of unalterable estrangement; he is incapable of comradely (male) pleasures. The men playing cards at a café window seem "talmente estranei e irraggiungibili" (so alien and unreachable):

> Nella stanza non una sola seggiola libera. Ogni persona, ogni cosa, rispon-
> devano a un loro compito ben preciso. Gli pareva di trovarsi davanti a un
> quadro in cornice. Impossibile entrarci dentro. Non c'era posto, spazio
> sufficiente. [p. 646]

> (There wasn't a free chair in the room. Each person, each object, cor-
> responded to a precise function. He felt as if he were standing before a

picture in a frame. It was impossible to enter. There was no place, no room for him.) [W:*H*, p. 150]

The living (male) world has no room for Edgardo, and the female world is beyond his reach. He is a survivor: excessive. The receptive social space of pre-1938 is irretrievable; *he*—his former person, his position of power—is irretrievable. Only the community of *natura morta*—stuffed birds, foxes, squirrels—seems truly alive to him: these creatures "più vive che se fossero vive" [p. 650] (more alive than if they were alive) are perfected by their "bellezza *finale e non deperibile*" [p. 651; emphasis added] (*ultimate and nonperishable* beauty).

An abandoned and irreparable Venetian-style palazzo in Codigoro (where Bellagamba's hotel is located) and already-faded street names honoring Resistance heroes spell out the decay and death of Edgardo's values. So do the tantalizing aromas, warmth, and wrinkled faces of people inside a village grocery where he stops to buy some sandwich meat: "Come sarebbe stato bene lì dentro se avesse avuto modo di rimanerci!" [p. 591] (How happy he would have been, here, if he could have stayed! [W:*H*, p. 68]). But the meat turns out to be rancid; the store thus represents an even more putrid picture of decay—and Edgardo is part of it.

Cousin Ulderico Cavaglieri weaves in and out of Edgardo's thoughts like a paradoxical ghost in the real world. Ulderico is the very antithesis of Edgardo. Most telling is the cousins' contrasting adaptability to the political and social forces that have radically changed their lives. Their destinies, "così uguali e così diversi" [p. 575] (so similar and so different) in Edgardo's recollection, kept them "inseparable" friends for the "first good two-thirds" of Edgardo's life (p. 574)—that is, until 1932, when they drew apart. In that year, Ulderico marries the Catholic Cesarina, a trousers maker with whom he has publicly been linked for a long time. He is baptized on his wedding day and moves permanently from Ferrara to Codigoro, his wife's hometown. Although Cesarina and Edgardo's wife, Nives, share many characteristics, only Ulderico has an integrative marriage. He becomes fully assimilated to his small, new community, helped by a wife from the area, a flock of children, "everything." He muses, "Chiunque, in simili circostanze, finisce con l'assimilarsi all'ambiente, anche il meno disposto" [p. 580] (Anyone, under these circumstances, ends by becoming assimilated into his surroundings. Even the least predisposed [W:*H*, pp. 50–51]). The least disposed is, of course, Edgardo, projecting his own assimilation: the possibility of living instead of merely surviving. Edgardo is an Ulderico *manqué*. Motivated by the hunting trip, he decides to revive their friendship by telephoning his cousin to locate a local guide for him. Once in Codigoro, Edgardo calls again, but this time he reaches only the maid. While she calls Cesarina (Ulderico is out), Edgardo, receiver pressed to his ear, eavesdrops on the noisy, irritating sounds of Ulderico's six children "con una specie di ansiosa, combattuta avidità" [p. 582] (with a kind of anxious and confused greediness). Earlier he had mused how Ulderico's large, Catholic family protected his cousin and how Ulderico paid no attention to the Communists now, just as he had paid no attention to the *repubblichini* and Nazi SS troopers and had outwitted the Fascists by keeping his guns even when it was against the law for Jews to carry arms (p. 550). Edgardo's ruminations about his cousin sketch a portrait of masculine authority and success entirely lacking in his own life. In the context of his lack and Ulderico's boldness, even Edgardo's wartime escape to Switzerland acquires a negative value of passivity.

The male and female images associated with the cousins reflect their antithetical sexual qualities. The annihilating psychic movement embodied in the well image propels Edgardo toward a specular and antinomal tower image, whose most alluring form to him is the "alto, massiccio, incombente" (high, heavy, and threatening) ten-story apartment building in Codigoro where cousin Ulderico lives (p. 639). The actual Codigoro building upon which this fictive one is modeled is only three stories high, a difference that illustrates the role of factual distortion in Bassani's production of symbols.[10] For Edgardo the phallic image is a negative power. Ulderico, who is completely absent (negative) from the reader's view, is a brilliant representation of Edgardo's "missing" self. The negative specularity of the cousins is generalized concisely by Ulderico's capacity for productive socialization in the very community that has no "sufficient space" for Edgardo.[11]

Other phallic symbols are Edgardo's guns. The new, never-used Browning and the old Krupp Edgardo takes on the hunting trip delineate, respectively, the negative and positive limits of his masculinity. The apprehensive hunter, crouched in the blind and unwilling to shoot, lends the Browning to his guide, Gavino, who promptly downs some forty birds. The weapon Edgardo selects for his suicide is the Krupp, like its owner (by his own judgment) a "survivor." The Browning, which will remain unused by Edgardo, is thus bequeathed symbolically to the Gavinos of the new Italy.

Edgardo believes, or likes to believe, that Gavino may be Ulderico's illegitimate son. Together the older cousin and the young guide represent the major forces of contemporary Italian life impinging on and threatening Edgardo's existence: politically, the Christian Democratic and Communist parties, and socially, the prosperous middle class and rising working class.

While driving to the blind, Edgardo finds some new reasons for discontent and regret: Gavino's exhuberant hunting dog, who fills the car with his "obsession" and his "life," and Gavino himself, a former "combat partisan," whose composure oppresses Edgardo. What most unnerves (and also attracts) him is Gavino's "masculine" strength, of a kind with Ulderico's but experienced as a physical (sexual) *presence*. Gavino's hand alone poses a threat to Edgardo:

Gli guardava la mano destra, appoggiata alla gomma verdastra dello stiva-
lone da valle poco più su del ginocchio. Era una mano grande, bruna, più
da sportivo che da operaio, con le unghie appena sciupate e ricoperta da
ciuffi di peli rossicci. E ogni volta, a guardargliela, tornava a ricordarsi
con crescente imbarazzo e fastidio di Ulderico. [p. 592; emphasis added]

(Every now and then he looked at Gavino's right hand, resting on the
greenish rubber boot, just above the knee. It was a large, long hand, a
sportsman's more than a worker's [the original erroneously inverts the two
terms compared]: a dark hand . . . its nails only slightly cracked, and
it was covered with clumps of reddish hairs; and every time, as he looked
at it, he recalled, with mounting embarrassment and annoyance, Ulderico.) [W:*H*, p. 70]

The *signore* in Gavino comes out through physiognomy and, threateningly,
through manner: "Ma quella vaga aria di scherno che gli circolava attorno agli
zigomi ossuti non era forse più eloquente e deprimente di qualsiasi discorso?"
[p. 593] (But the vaguely contemptuous expression that played over Gavino's
bony cheeks: wasn't it, perhaps, far more eloquent, and depressing, than any
words? [W:*H*, p. 70]). The guide and his "master" are now, *by the older man's
actions*, "legati insieme. A filo doppio" [ibid.] (bound together. Inseparably).
They are as one, yet, because of this, all the more different from each other.
Gavino oppresses Edgardo, as does Ulderico, but because Gavino intrudes physically into Edgardo's inert solipsism, the enactment of Edgardo's existential fate
is thrust upon him before his very eyes, in the form of a parable of the hunt that
stages his social and corporeal drift to death.

The novel's central episode (and structural midpoint) is the slow slaughter of
the heron. The actors are four: on one side, Edgardo and the dying bird (the victims), and on the other, Gavino and his female hunting dog (the executioners):

Niente più [a Edgardo] appariva come reale. Gavino, sul suo isolotto, la
fronte corrugata e il Browning scottante nelle mani, attento a scrutare in
alto, in giro, per non farsi cogliere di sorpresa. La cagna accucciata ai suoi
piedi, ma pronta, dopo ogni sparatoria, a balzare in acqua per riportare
al padrone, tenendoli ben stretti e alti nella bocca grondante, nuovi uccelli
da aggiungere al mucchio dei morti o degli agonizzanti. Lui stesso, seduto
in botte col fucile in mano come Gavino, però inerte, incapace, di un solo
gesto... [p. 604]

(Nothing, any longer, appeared real to him. Gavino, on his sandbar, his
forehead wrinkled and the Browning scorching his hands, carefully peering up, around, so as not to be taken by surprise; the dog, crouched at his
feet, but ready, after each round of shooting, to spring into the water and
bring back to her master, holding them tight and high in her dripping

mouth, more birds to add to the pile of dead or dying; he, himself, seated in the hogshead with the gun in his hand like Gavino, but inert, incapable of a single movement . . .) [W:*H*, p. 85]

The heron becomes Gavino's next target. The dismayed Edgardo imagines rescuing the wounded creature and bringing it home, and then he imagines his wife's disgruntled reaction: "Figuriamoci le sue grida, le proteste, i piagnistei" [p. 608] (He could imagine her shouts, her protests, her whining [W:*H*, p. 90]). The next words of the text are "La cagna," meaning not only the dog from whom the bleeding heron, Edgardo imagines, is trying to hide, but also Nives. In fact, the dog shortly flushes out the heron, and Nives has already "caught" Edgardo.

Edgardo offers Gavino the weapon of the heron's (Edgardo's symbolic) destruction in a gesture analogous to his conferment upon Nives of the weapon of proprietorship. In effect, Edgardo surrenders his power (masculinity) to an archetypal heroic male (Gavino) and an archetypal predatory female (Nives). Nives's countenance even resembles that of a predatory creature. Edgardo, taking leave of his wife that morning, notices with special interest her "naso corto e adunco come il becco d'un rapace" [p. 555] (short, hooked nose, like the beak of a rapacious bird). The *sopravvissuto* landowner perceives not only his wife, but the world in general, as predatory and himself as threatened and helpless, sinking into an abyss. Sexual categories express Edgardo's victimage and subtend religious categories that embrace his Jewishness. The hunt, the actual goal of the single day in which the novel transpires, is an allegorical recitation of force and victimization in which the chief actor, the reluctant hunter Edgardo Limentani, is also—indeed primarily—the object of the hunt. The once-welcomed and respected proprietor, while getting ready for his day of hunting (the beginning of the narrative), recalls a recent "nasty mishap" in which he was trapped like an animal:

> Rivedeva ancora una volta se stesso in mezzo ai campi sterminati, seduto sul ciglio di un fosso con attorno una trentina di braccianti (facce note, la maggior parte, e magari da anni e anni . . .), i quali, le zappe alzate, pronti a sbattergliele giù sul cranio, gli chiedevano la revisione immediata dei patti di compartecipazione. [p. 551][12]

> (He could still see himself, seated on the edge of a ditch, alone in the midst of the endless fields, with at least thirty farm workers around him (familiar faces, most of them, known perhaps for years and years!), their hoes raised, ready to be brought down on his skull, as the men asked him for an immediate revision of the crop-sharing agreement.) [W:*H*, p. 9]

In the same context of the hunt, Edgardo fastens mentally upon 1939, when his patrimony passed into the hands of his wife:

Siccome dal '39 l'intestataria dell'intero patrimonio agricolo e immobiliare del fu Leone Limentani era diventata la nuora Nives, Pimpinati Nives, cattolica, ariana, e a quel tempo incinta di otto mesi, il figlio Edgardo e la vedova Erminia Calabresi, suoi eredi in linea diretta, dovevano ormai considerare i quattrocento e passa ettari della tenuta . . . definitivamente roba altrui. [ibid.]

(Since 1939, the whole property, agricultural and urban real estate, of the late Leone Limentani was in the name of his daughter-in-law Nives Limentani, née Pimpinati, Catholic, Aryan, and at that time eight months pregnant, so the son Edgardo and the late Leone's widow Erminia Calabresi Limentani, the direct heirs, had to consider the thousand or so acres of the estate . . . definitively the property of another.) [W:*H*, pp. 9–10]

The reversal of hunter into hunted involves betrayal as well as force, as in the case of the betrayal of the Jews by the Italian government and the final betrayal by the Nazis with their widespread net of collaborators leading to the extermination camps. Italy's anti-Jewish legislation is explicit in Edgardo's memory, and the trace of the death camps, through linguistic inference, is no more distant than the "campi sterminati" (endless fields) from the "campi di sterminio" (extermination camps), and the edge of a "fosso" (ditch) from a "fossa" (grave), or the "cranio" (skull) of a living man from a death's head. The threatened Jew, Edgardo, looks up into faces of violent assailants. The violence barely held in check traces a circular configuration ("con attorno" [around him]) of ritualized slaughter in which the victim at the center of the closed circle—an exploitive landowner, in the eyes of the laborers—is figured as the symbolic surrogate of all the death-camp Jews. Here is a trace of unspeakable matter: the unparalleled, limit case within Bassani's entire writings on estrangement, persecution, and betrayal. When Edgardo gazes upon the "object" that is his penis, the only particularity he notices is its ethnic identifying mark: "with that *sign* of circumcision, so familiar and at the same time so absurd" [p. 620; emphasis added]. The sign—the wound—of circumcision marks the socially wounded Edgardo indelibly and "absurdly" as a Jew, an outcast, a foreigner.[13] When the power of the landlord begins to be challenged in postwar northern Italy by an energized Communist party, Edgardo interprets the menace in the modality most devastating to his person, that of a victimized Jew.

Edgardo was spared the concentration camp. His successful flight to Switzerland is an event acknowledged incidentally and indirectly on the novel's first page: "certo è che la camera da letto dove, a parte un breve periodo subito dopo sposato, e a parte, poi, naturalmente, l'anno e mezzo di Svizzera, aveva dormito fino da ragazzo" [p. 547] (in any case, this bedroom where he had slept since childhood, except for a brief period just after his marriage and then, naturally, the year and a half in Switzerland [W:*H*, pp. 3–4]). The brutal *un*naturalness

Figure 9. A Fascist parade in Codigoro in May of 1926.

of the Jews' flight from Italy in the frantic weeks following the Nazi occupation in September of 1943 is ironically understated by the "naturally" that precedes the veiled allusion to the period of Edgardo's forced exodus: the one and a half years from the start of the Nazi-Fascist regime to the Liberation on April 25, 1945. This very early, apparently casual memory of the worst period of political and religious persecution of our age is the novel's first signal and approximation of the unspeakability of that experience.

When Edgardo stops in the town of Codigoro, where he has not been "since 1938," he remembers the ex-Fascist Gino Bellagamba, now a hotel owner. In "those years" (1938 and 1939), Bellagamba, dressed in his Fascist militia uniform, would look at Edgardo—menacingly and with scorn—"as a 'Jew', as a

Figure 10. Coming out of Codigoro's church, Edgardo Limentani beholds the square "in all its vastness," turns right noticing the "gloomy" facade of the ex-Fascist headquarters, then in the middle of the square sees the World War I monument to fallen soldiers "in every detail" (*L'airone*).

'nonpolitical', and as a landowner," every time that Edgardo, who was occasionally obliged for business reasons to pass through Codigoro, was "unlucky enough to come within his range" (p. 567). Bellagamba, who in the same passage is described as a bull, a mastiff, and a watchdog, epitomizes the brute Fascist power that subjugated and humiliated the Italian Jews. Shortly after his recollection, Edgardo reads a newspaper scrap left as toilet paper in the hotel bathroom. It announces anew the threat of Jewish persecution:

> A dar retta all'autore dell'articolo c'era da credere che nella Polonia rossa del 1947 le persecuzioni contro gli ebrei continuassero non meno crudeli e sanguinose che in quella del *Gauleiter* Frank, il fiduciario di Hitler per gli affari polacchi. Possibile? [p. 573]

> (According to the author of the article, one was to believe that in Red Poland, in 1947, the persecution of the Jews continued and was no less cruel and bloody than in the brownshirt Poland of Gauleiter Frank, Hitler's governor general. Was it possible?) [W:*H*, p. 39]

Shortly before Edgardo left his house that morning, he had coffee with the old family servants, Romeo and Imelde, who told him about their pregnant daughter and her "good-for-nothing" husband, who slept all day and sometimes beat her. "Era vero. Glielo garantivano che fosse vero la faccia di lui, livida di rancore a stento contenuto, e quella di lei, anche di più, *con quei suoi occhi da vittima predestinata e forse consenziente*" [p. 563; emphasis added] (It was true. They swore to him it was true, Romeo's face, livid with ill-repressed bitterness, and hers, even more, with those eyes, like the eyes of a foreordained victim, perhaps a willing one [W:*H*, p. 26]). Moments before, Edgardo had yearned to remain there, hidden and secure, with the old people in their kitchen. But the face of the "predestined and perhaps consenting victim" and the family's inability to ease the daughter-victim's suffering made the kitchen immediately unbearable, "un posto anche questo da cui bisognava sloggiare. E subito" [ibid.] (this, too, a place from which he had to clear out. And at once [W:*H*, p. 27]). Imelde's face assumes the look of the immemorial Jew as stereotyped by the Christian world. Edgardo, arch consenting victim, needs to flee from his own image. Ironically, when he is face-to-face with Bellagamba, the latter behaves not as a sadistic bully, but as a welcoming servant; he speaks "con quel tono, insinuante e insieme umile (lo stesso col quale avrebbe potuto rivolgerglisi un contadino delle sue terre prima del '38" [p. 569] (in that tone, insinuating and humble at the same time—the same tone that, until [1938], would have been used, in addressing him, by a peasant on his lands [W:*H*, p. 35]). The ex-Fascist with a phallic name (Beautiful Leg) now runs a successful hotel and restaurant patronized by wealthy industrialists and pleasure-seeking hunters who enjoy his obsequious attention. He has deftly reversed his post-Fascist role to become prosperous as a servant of the presently powerful; unlike Edgardo, Bellagamba is a fertile survivor. His bull-like physique is a testament to his durability.

Edgardo, on the other hand, is a sterile survivor, one whose only self-protective act is to commit suicide. A spectator and a voyeur (sometimes even of himself), he is capable only of being acted upon. As the novel opens, he peers at himself in his bathroom mirror and sees a face that seems not to belong to him. Crouched in the duck blind, he watched Gavino shoot, refusing himself to become a participant in the slaughter. When he listens to the sounds of his cousin's family at the other end of their telephone line—"voyeuristically" participating in Ulderico and Cesarina's private life—he gives free rein to his sexual imagination. In Bellagamba's restaurant he sits alone, watching groups of men enjoy dinner and each other's company. Walking along the streets, he peers through a window at men playing cards together. His greatest spectator satisfaction derives from stuffed creatures behind a display window.

Sterile survival is a state of nonidentity. As a result of the incidental telephone conversation he has with Cesarina, Edgardo gains full consciousness of being a nonperson. Her talk conjures for him a fatal image of a predatory, promiscuous woman who wishes to lure him, her husband's cousin, to bed (p. 640). This fantasy in turn summons up a youthful memory of himself in the company of his cousin, being stricken by nausea and dragged uphill by others, out of control of his own destiny (p. 641). Edgardo concludes that his whole day has been one of delirium, but the delirium gives way to self-questioning: "Con una lucidità repentina si sorprese a chiedersi: ma lui, lui stesso, vestito da caccia, col berretto di pelo in testa, a quell'ora, sotto quei portici, ma lui chi era, veramente?" [p. 642] (With a sudden lucidity, he surprised himself by wondering: he, he himself, in his hunting clothes, with the fur cap on his head, at that hour, under those arcades, who was he, who, really? [W:*H*, pp. 143–44]). In his imagination he turns into a sexual object for the wife-prostitute Cesarina, who is "Grande, grassa, calma. E puttana, specialmente" [p. 641] (Big, heavy, calm. And whorish, above all [W:*H*, p. 142]), then into the sexual equivalent of his cousin. "Rico e lui non erano forse stati grandi amici, da giovani, addirittura inseparabili, al punto che fino al momento che [Cesarina] era diventata la sua amante, di Rico, la sua mantenuta, avevano l'abitudine di andare assieme anche a donne e spesso di scambiarsele?" [ibid.] (Hadn't they been great friends, he and Rico, as young men, actually inseparable, so much so that until [Cesarina] had become his mistress, Rico's, his kept woman, they had been accustomed to go whoring about together, and often, to trading their women? [W:*H*, p. 142]). Finally Edgardo recognizes the sham of his pose as a hunter, which is equivalent to acknowledging his lack of any true identity. His hunter's clothes mock his actual existence of impotence and passivity and cast him in a demystifying and self-devastating light.

The Other he sees in the taxidermy shop is his own perfected potentiality. Earlier in the day, his mirror projected a wretched, unpleasant self that resembled a weak, female Other. All but one of the mirrored facial details correspond to Bassani's own features (a receding hairline, pale blue eyes, a strong, "aristocratic" nose). A striking exception is the shape of Edgardo's lips: "grosse, sporgenti, un po' da donna" [p. 549] (thick, protruding, a bit womanish); the author's are thin. The full, "feminine" lips seem to betray a weakness in Edgardo, a flaw in his masculinity, the quality possibly of the "predestined and perhaps consenting victim." Edgardo *volunteers* for defeat; he hands over his new shotgun to a muscular sharpshooter, and the keys of his home to a "rapacious" bride. The womanish lips bespeak a victim's lips, even a concentration-camp victim's lips; that is, those of a Jew. In this novel, "Jew" encodes weakness and impotence; "Catholic," strength and power. The meanings are justified by and dated in 1938, when Jewish citizenship was repudiated and Jewish oppression legalized. Edgardo's Catholic wife can usurp the Limentani family patrimony *because* she is Catholic; the text registers her appropriation of the Jewish family's home by the picture she keeps next to the (Limentani) parental matrimonial bed that she alone now occupies: a picture of Mary Mediatrix, to whom Codigoro's principal church is dedicated. Other signs of assumption of entitlement are the photographs of *her* parents that Nives places in the bedroom and an assortment of *her* sewing materials (p. 557). Nives's religion and gender (for Edgardo, specifically) are textual markers of predatory power. Ulderico's conversion to Catholicism *before* the era of Jewish persecution, his large Catholic family, and his high standing in the community of Codigoro delineate nonexploitive, assimilative, "healthy" male power, which is beyond Edgardo's grasp. The wife native to Codigoro and the cousin resettled in Codigoro represent, respectively, the negative (female) and positive (male) poles of power as Bassani sketches them. Codigoro is, for Edgardo, a desert of trial and temptation (the locus of his fatal conversion to death) and, for Ulderico, a garden of terrestrial delight (the locus of his fruitful conversion to life). By placing Ulderico's success story against Edgardo's defeat story, Bassani does not, of course, intend to valorize the choice and condition of Catholicism over that of Judaism; rather, he means to use the two religions—as also the two cities of Ferrara and Codigoro—to thematize the social dynamics of individual and community. Within that arena, Bassani works out critical notions of scapegoatism, (self-)victimization, and sacrificial crisis, employing the essential (if not always obvious) agency of sexual symbolism.

Female Sexuality

The threatening social spasms that thrust Edgardo Limentani toward suicide are adumbrated in the person of his wife. Her social background, religion, personality, and lack of matrimonial love constitute a kind of checklist of the more general societal sources of Edgardo's sense of estrangement from himself and from the world. The reader is introduced to Nives in the first pages of the novel as Edgardo, dressed to go hunting, attempts to slip out of the house unnoticed. When Nives hears his footsteps, he is distressed for two reasons: he expects she will sneer at his costly new shotgun; and he dreads that she will propose he stay for sexual intercourse. These two fears mirror Nives's principal passions: money and sex. Next, Nives's role is established as usurper of her husband's heritage, not only of his wealth, but also of his religion and his lineage: she is pictured lying in the Limentani bed, with the photographs of her hometown church and parents close by. Then, "lazily," she lifts a "naked" arm and covers her yawning mouth with the back of her hand: "Mezzo sepolto nella carne grassa e cerea del palmo, il cerchietto d'oro della fede quasi non si distingueva" [p. 554] (Half buried in the fat, waxy flesh of her palm, the narrow gold wedding ring could hardly be discerned [W:*H*, p. 13]).

Sleepy sensuality is here incarnate—in the ironic pose of a reclining Venus beckoning to bed her husband-warrior, Mars. In this case, however, the carnal act points to a betrayal of the marriage vow: the fleshly eclipse of the gold ring that symbolizes marital fidelity. Later in the story, Edgardo convinces himself that in fact Nives is unfaithful to him. Seductive, predatory, vulgar, she is seen to bear much of the blame for Edgardo's existential crisis. All seductive women are blameworthy in Bassani's tales, whether wives or prostitutes. The sign of failed masculinity in these narratives is literal and metaphoric impotence, a male "nature" that is passive.

Passivity in a woman, on the other hand, is tantamount to the nonpresence of lust, endowing the woman with a certain radiance and beauty. Edgardo's mother is exemplary. Pictured like Nives lying in bed—upright, however, with her head resting against two pillows, "i soffici capelli di bambagia appena più bianchi della fragile cartapecora del viso" [p. 663] (the soft cottony hair hardly whiter than the frail parchment of her face [W:*H*, p. 175])—she seems to her son "beautiful, very beautiful. Perfect." The old mother, whose exalted presence in bed concludes the novel, contrasts with the young wife, who in an initial episode is a sullied presence in bed.

The mystification and defamation of female sexuality are coordinates by which Bassani plots and penetrates the fundamentally male drama of his fiction, ultimately that of the persona who propels the texts from within. The women who reflect the male image and struggle fall into two principal categories: the nonseductive and the sexually provocative. In the first category are a number of mothers and rejected women, as well as the youthful, enigmatic, and singular Micòl Finzi-Contini. In the second category are prostitutes and unfaithful or unloving wives. The sexual factor, either by emphasis or by absence, directs the narrative function of nearly every female character. The seductive women are always secondary characters, even when instrumental to the progress of the plot. Anna Repetto of "Notte" and Nives Pimpinati of *Airone* stand out among the characters in that group; scattered among several stories in only an episode or two are prostitutes and flirtatious young women who also highlight and contribute to the fashioning of a more important male character. The characters in the nonseductive category are more complex and varied than the others, operating in a mythic or symbolic modality that transcends their narrative roles. The major exemplars are Micòl Finzi-Contini (who, without peer, is the most highly valorized character, male or female, in the total corpus) and Clelia Trotti ("Anni"). Minor figures include the narrator's mother (*Occhiali, Porta, Airone*) and women whose role as mother is crucial to their stories, such as Lida Mantovani ("Lida") and Egle Levi-Minzi ("Necessità").

The sexuality of Nives Pimpinati, as already observed, is coupled with the usurpation of her husband's social status. Her various gestures thematize an act of betrayal—a concept that underpins all these texts. The figure of young Anna Repetto is drawn according to the same model and similarly seeks the reader's condemnation for an act of marital betrayal. Yet Anna's textual role is more complex than Nives's, and judgment of her less clear-cut. Unlike Nives, Anna is subjected, internally to the text, to the judgment of her compatriots. *Their* judgment in turn becomes subject to the reader's judgment, which then becomes a factor in the final assessment of Anna. The question of betrayal strikes more deeply than the marriage vow; it encompasses the violation of an innocent partner, that is, the violation of an intimate and morally inviolable social contract. Thus the theme of sexual (marital) betrayal symbolizes a theme pivotal to the comprehensive text of Ferrara: the theme of collective (social, religious, political) as well as personal betrayal of human bonds. The story of Anna Repetto joins the social to the personal act in the large narrative arena of a public, political trial. Her story thus postulates the implications of sexual license in a way that Nives's does not. It stands to reason, then, that Anna's sexual character is more subdued than Nives's.

Both women are married to men much older than they. And each woman motivates her husband's supreme act of self-defeat which transforms into an act of self-redemption. Nives's motivation is more emblematic than actual. Edgardo's marriage to her signifies his self-effacing accommodation to society's betrayal of the Jews in 1938. This is the double-edged decision that transforms Limentani from a ruler (*padrone*) into a victim. From his condition of victimage he descends farther into a state of nonidentity, until he persuades himself that death by suicide will reaffirm and revalidate his life. Anna Repetto, an essential, if minor, character, stands in relation not only to her husband, but also to the Ferrarese community, which her presence exposes as a collection of smallminded gossipers. Anna stands out in this predominantly male story for her "enticing" female sexuality.

Bassani links the theme of Fascist violence to sexual violence. The behavior of the promiscuous women in Bassani's narratives usually mirrors male impotence, which is more temperamental, finally, than sexual. The uniqueness of Anna Repetto is that her role in establishing Pino's "impotence" implicates the moral weakness of the whole Ferrarese community. Most important, she is pivotal in revealing the communal voice of gossip as the voice of the morally corrupt citizenry. "Gossip" (conventionally in the female gender) has a central function as a feckless, contaminated force murmuring in acquiescence beside the thundering violence of Fascist power. Anna is a victim of the circumstances orchestrated by that power. As a young girl she reveals her own incantatory power: "Si trattava di un tipo piuttosto sfrenato, perennemente a zonzo in bicicletta o a ballare nei Circoli Rionali, e sempre seguita, oltre che da folti codazzi di coetanei, dagli sguardi di parecchi non coetanei fissi ad ammirarne di lontano le evoluzioni" [p. 138] (She was a wild sort of creature, who had already dazzled the high-school boys, always on the go on a bike or out dancing, with a train of youths her own age behind her wherever she went, and older eyes staring too, from a distance [Q:*P*, p. 183]). Fantasies flourish in which powerful men succumb to her sexual magnetism: "Avendola notata su una spiaggia della vicina Riviera Adriatica, un pezzo grosso di fuori se ne innamorava di colpo e la sposava; un produttore cinematografo, anche lui stregato dalle sue grazie, se la portava dietro a Roma per farne una diva di primo piano" [ibid.] (Some big noise from somewhere would see her in a bathing suit on the beach at Rimini or Riccione, fall in love with her at first sight and marry her. A film producer [similarly bewitched by her charms] would take her to Rome and turn her into a star [ibid.]). This stock fantasy-drama taps out the rhythm of an awesome real-life drama of guilt, shame, and betrayal that will defile Anna's sexual power and bewitch Ferrara for years following the executions. In the real drama, the impersonal figure of the male collectivity jealous of Pino Barilari takes the specific shape of Carlo Aretusa, the leading Ferrarese ex-Fascist accused after the war of mortally betraying some of his compatriots. Known as "Sciagura" (Calamity), he is the smiling embodiment of evil and Pino's negative alter ego. As inseparable elements of Ferrara's drama of guilt, the two men are bonded by an erotic incident predating by fourteen years Pino's marriage to the seventeen-year-old Anna. The incident takes place in a brothel during a stopover in Bologna on the long train ride back from the march on Rome in 1922. Under the tyrannical gaze and poised revolver of Sciagura, the teenaged and timid Pino is deflowered by a prostitute and infected with the syphilis that will spawn his paralysis seventeen years later, three years after his marriage. At the very moment of the time written into history by Mussolini's ludicrous yet ominous march on Rome, the personal relation of Pino and Sciagura engenders the silence that will smother Ferrara's grasping voice of vengeance at Sciagura's trial in 1946 for his part in the wartime murders.

Until the final (fifth) chapter of "Notte," the reader knows Anna only through the eyes of others. In that chapter the viewpoint shifts to her own. Retrospectively the collective fascination with Anna emerges as a component of Sciagura's trial. The broken marriage, Pino's broken mind, and Anna's broken spirit are by-products of the tragic night of political murder; their personal entanglement is a miniature enactment of the social guilt and dissolution of which they are both representatives and victims. Bassani uses the community's early interest in Anna's seductiveness and its resentment of her marriage to establish a case for the primary criminality of the community rather than of Sciagura. In 1950, when Pino is forty-five, Anna angrily blurts out her version of their life together. In effect he never grew up, she charges, and she adds that she nursed him loyally during his incurable illness. The narrative verifies his immaturity, sexual and social, through references to his high-pitched, boyish voice, his childish delight in reading horror and adventure stories and solving crossword puzzles, his virginity (notwithstanding the night in Bologna), his terror of sexual contact with prostitutes, and his postparalysis retreat to the small bedroom he occupied as a child. When Pino showed up at the train station to participate in the march on Rome, Sciagura found his childishness amusing: " 'Ma lo sa, il papà, che vieni via con noi?' E lui adesso faceva di no, guardandoli [i fascisti] nel mentre con quei suoi occhi da bambino che sta vivendo un film di avventure" [p. 142] ("But does your Dad know you're here with us?" And then he shook his head and looked from one to the next as he did so, with the eyes of a child living in an adventure film [Q:*P*, p. 190]). Although Pino was seventeen, "era peggio che se fosse stato un bambino" [ibid.] (it was worse than having a child about [ibid.]).

Anna recalls the once-mutual contentedness of the pair in a mother-son relationship; she also recalls her discretion in seeking sexual partners. Pino presumably has experienced only the one-time sexual encounter forced on him by Sciagura. Bassani has called his frail character a homosexual;[14] his text postulates a perennially immature boy: the depictions are of course compatible. Pino's relation to Anna (son to mother) finds completion in his relation to Sciagura (son to father). It is hard to ignore the Oedipal triangle drawn by these interactions and the implied homosexuality at the base of the bond between the two men. It should be remembered that Sciagura, always in command with "quella sua voce pesante e sgradevole da vecchio padrone" [p. 157] (his loud disagreeable top-dog's voice [Q:*P*, p. 211]) and often encircled by solicitous (male) subordinates (p. 140), still – with a patronizing, paternal smile – defends the "unfit" Pino from Fascist ire as late as 1939. In a smug rodomontade he recalls with sadistic pleasure the day he permitted Pino to join the trainload of Fascists headed for Rome: "In fondo era risultato lui, il ragazzo, l'unico, autentico divertimento di tutto il viaggio. A ripensarci, la Marcia su Roma era stato proprio lui che l'aveva salvata" [p. 142] (The fact was he was the only amusing thing about the whole trip. Now he came to think of it, Calamity felt it was the boy who actually saved the March on Rome [Q:*P*, p. 189]).

The light shed on Anna at the trial resulting from the 1943 massacre publicly proves her husband to be a cuckold, despite his own attempts to hide the fact. Pino's only way to protect his wife's role as mother is to pretend he did not see her return home before dawn from a lovers' tryst. But when this private drama becomes public at the trial, Pino's denial of witness ("I was sleeping") protects merely his delusion of a normal marriage. Sciagura, observed by Pino at the very moment of the predawn executions, is the only one of the three to act guiltless and confident. His power over the boy-man is unassailable. Profoundly in awe of the ex-Fascist leader who once forced him into sexual initiation, Pino remains in spellbound silence in court two decades later; that silence culminates their relationship. It also aggrandizes Sciagura, formerly the chief embodiment of violent authority in Ferrara and currently the masterful manipulator of that society. The Ferrarese come to court to purge themselves but succeed only in condemning Anna and Pino. Just as the gossipy townspeople, with their erotic desire of Anna and their envious resentment of Pino, had earlier stamped the marriage into their own malicious mold of infidelity, they now, after the unsuccessful trial, bend and inflate the ancient rumors with their attempts to reconstruct Pino and Anna's activities on the fateful night. Reality outstrips their imagination when Anna boisterously begins to play out their whispered accusations. Within two years of the trial, she files for a legal separation and moves into an apartment near the city walls (the logical move of an "outsider"). Now nearly thirty years old, Anna is a caricature of her former self: she has resumed her youthful habit of bicycling through town, has added weight and cosmetics, and looks older than her age.[15] Agitated, publicly promiscuous, and nearly obsessed by the night of infamy, Anna continually recounts bits of her memory of the episode. Pino has withdrawn into a fantasy life and become a permanent "sleeper" who, after the trial, has need of no one:

> In apparenza non era cambiato niente, nei loro rapporti. Tranne che da allora in poi, essendogli venuta la mania del cannocchiale, consumava le giornate così, sorvegliando il marciapiede di fronte, e senza più chiamarla di sopra come una volta, per mostrarle come era bravo a risolvere i cruciverba e i rebus a frase. [p. 163]

> (Outwardly nothing had changed in their relationship. Except that from then onwards after the trial, he became crazy about field-glasses, and spent the days like that, watching the pavement opposite . . . but without calling her up as he used to, to show her how clever he was at crosswords and puzzles.) [Q:*P*, pp. 219–20]

Pino now holds court from his apartment window, his eyes hidden and transformed behind binoculars, a self-consecrated witness and protector of the city's "sacred" space. His madness has the power to cow the community, to keep consciences alert. Sciagura vanishes from the text, his person inviolable, his last words a lingering condemnation of the community. Anna, fully vulnerable and fully innocent, is the only one at the trial over whom the gossipers can exert their power, which debases her to sexual animality and social marginality. Alone and frantic, entrapped in Ferrara, she becomes a creature pursued, a scapegoated screen for a guilty, still lustful society. Anna's promiscuity and hysteria are the visible forms of the society's own furies.

Micòl Finzi-Contini

At the other extremity of Bassani's textual arch of female sexuality is Micòl Finzi-Contini. The principal heroine of the collected prose volume, she has the attributes of a goddess: blond hair, blue eyes, youth, vitality, intelligence, grace, majesty, mystery, mischief, untouchability. In keeping with her special qualities, she contains contradictions and paradoxes and means more than she is. But however clearly her beauty and commanding presence "rationalize" her textual preeminence, it is the author's naming of her that transcribes his act of primary sacralization. As wife of the Hebraic King David, "Micòl" signifies sacred and regal Jewish history. Furthermore, she belongs to a sacred cultural tradition of Italian letters: she is one of a mere handful of Biblical Jewish women—vastly outnumbered by classical and Christian ones—to warrant a place in the *Divine Comedy*.[16] While the name Micòl synthesizes the two cultural histories most important to Bassani, it bears additional meaning as an emblem of the author's struggle with his art. The "humble Psalmist"—David— of Dante's poem, "more and less than king," is a ready synecdoche for the author; under the name David (Bassani's earliest textual embodiment in the *Romanzo*), the author engenders a relation with Micòl that, across an intertextual expanse, posits the Biblical/Dantean/Bassanian majestic, vexed, and scornful young woman as a self-reflecting and self-contradictory image of his creative/amorous (un)success.

Perhaps Micòl's most salient characteristic is her clearmindedness; her penchant for irony is an expression of true vision, that is, of "divine" distance from ordinary acts and encounters. Of all the characters in the *Romanzo*, only she exercises self-irony and, more, self-demystification. Just such an operation— inconceivable to her story's narrator—is cleverly invoked by the author, behind the shield of his narrating double. The scene is thus: Micòl is back from Venice; her relationship with the narrator is past its peak; her reply to his question about boyfriends is affirmative; he accuses her of lying:

> "Quante bugie. Sei anche tu come tutte le altre, va' là."
> Scosse il capo, non so se per compatire me o se stessa.
> "Nemmeno i *flirts*, anche quelli piccoli, sono cose che si imbastiscono con degli amici," disse malinconica; "e perciò, a parlarti, di amici, devi riconoscere che ti mentivo fino a un certo punto. Però hai ragione. Sono anche io come tutte le altre: bugiarda, traditora, *infedele . . . . . .* "
> Aveva detto "infedele" spiccando al solito le sillabe, ma con in più una specie di amaro orgoglio. Proseguendo, aggiunse che se io avevo avuto un torto era sempre stato *quello di sopravvalutarla un po' troppo. . . .* Tuttavia lei aveva sempre letto nei miei occhi tanto "idealismo" da sentirsi in qualche modo *forzata ad apparire migliore di quanto non fosse in realtà.* [pp. 402–3; last two emphases added]

> ("What lies. Your're just like all the others, that's what you are."
> She shook her head, whether pitying me or herself, I couldn't tell.
> "Not even *flirts*, however small they are, can be mixed up with friendship," she said sadly; "and so, when I spoke to you about friendships, you must realize I was only half lying to you. But you're right. I *am* like other girls:—liar, [traitor], *unfaithful. . . .* "
> When she said "unfaithful" she separated the syllables, with a kind of bitter pride. Then she went on to say that if I'd been wrong it was rating her rather too high. . . . But it was a fact: she'd always seen such "idealism" in my eyes that she felt somehow forced to seem better than she actually was.) [Q:*G*, pp. 227–28]

If the chaffing exchange between the novel's two principal players seems to betray a rare authorial moment of self-irony, the narrative soon reinstates Micòl to an exalted status. Speaking metatextually for the author some few pages later, the narrator equates Micòl with truth itself:

> Ma Micòl non discese per questo dal piedistallo di purezza e di superiorità morale su cui, da quando ero partito per l'esilio, l'avevo collocata. Lei continuò a rimanerci, lassù. Ed io mi consideravo fortunato di poter continuare ad ammirarne l'immagine lontana, bella di dentro non meno di fuori. *"Come la verità / come essa triste e bella . . . "*: questi due primi versi di una poesia che non finii mai, sebbene scritti molto più tardi, a Roma, subito dopo la guerra, si riferiscono alla Micòl dell'agosto del '39, a come la vedevo allora. [p. 414]

> (But this didn't bring Micòl down from off the pedestal of purity and moral superiority I had placed her on since I went into exile. She stayed right on it, up there. And as far as I was concerned I thought myself lucky to be let in to admire the distant image, no less lovely within than without. . . . *"Like the truth—and like it sad and lovely . . . "*: these two lines of a poem I never finished, although written much later [in Rome], immediately after the war, referred to Micòl in August '39, to the way I then saw her.) [Q:G, p. 243]

The truncated poetry embedded in the prose—a condensation of Dickinson's poem translated by Micòl—represents a *complete* Micòl, that is, Micòl truncated by death, and a cryptic condensation of the entire narrative to its kernel of "truth": "August of 1939"—signaling the narrator's last sight of Micòl before her deportation, also a sign of impending Jewish death; "right after the war"—signaling the writing of the unfinished (never-ending) poem, also a sign of never-ending Jewish survival. In the simpler time of childhood, Micòl's clarifying irony already operated to soothe and instruct the schoolboy narrating "I," whom she then barely knew. A dream the narrator has—almost at the precise midpoint of the text—assimilates the grown and the pubescent Micòl in an image of extraordinary, indeed awesome, beauty:

> Della bambina di dieci anni prima . . . che cosa era rimasto in questa Micòl di ventidue anni? . . . Sì—confrontavo—: ecco là della bambina i capelli biondi e leggeri, striati di ciocche quasi canute, le iridi celesti, quasi scandinave, la pelle color del miele, e sul petto, balenando ogni tanto fuori dallo scollo della maglietta, il piccolo disco d'oro dello *sciaddài*. [p. 338]

> (What was left of the child of ten years ago . . . in this twenty-two-year-old Micòl? . . . Yes—I thought, comparing them—there was still the child's fair, floating hair with streaks that were almost white, and blue Scandinavian eyes, and honey-coloured skin, and on her breast, occasion-

ally bouncing out of the neck of her shirt, the small gold disc of the *schiaddai*.) [Q:*G*, pp. 135–36]

The detailed description connotes Micòl's uniqueness; she is set apart from her Italian peers by a beauty more Nordic than Latin, and she irradiates a more than human beauty with her talismanic necklace, honey-colored skin, blonder-than-blond hair, bluer-than-blue eyes. Similar to Petrarch's blond and blue-eyed beloved, Micòl is apotheosized — not seated in quiet dignity under a gentle spray of flowers, but playing tennis:

> [La guardavo] mentre giocava a tennis con Alberto. . . . Tornavo a dirmi che era splendida, così sudata e rossa, con quella ruga d'impegno e di decisione quasi feroce che le divideva verticalmente la fronte, tutta tesa come era nello sforzo di sconfiggere il sorridente, un po' fiacco e annoiato fratello maggiore. [ibid.]

> (I was watching her play tennis with Alberto. . . . Again I kept telling myself that she was splendid, that I liked her all rosy and sweating like that, with a line down the middle of her forehead of almost ferocious keenness and determination, all strung up as she was in the effort of beating her smiling, rather slack and bored elder brother.) [Q:*G*, p. 135]

Micòl is an athletic beauty more energetic, more sad, more individualized than Petrarch's Laura, but still sister to the "dolce mia guerrera" (sweet warrior) who refuses a proferred love and retains the perfection of a "divin portamento" (divine bearing).[17] Micòl's poetic biography, like Laura's, outlines a woman-goddess, an enigmatic mixture of earth and heaven. Micòl's heavenly blue eyes ("iridi celesti") are like the rainbow the Italian "iride" equally denotes, connecting earth to sky.[18] Her golden disk, a religious medallion in the shape of the mystical symbol of perfection, flashes upon her breast like heaven's lightning ("balenando" in its figurative as well as its literal meaning).

In the dream sequence cited above, Micòl's sense of freedom is the greatest of her qualities: "questa Micòl dall'aria così libera, sportiva, moderna (libera soprattutto!)" [p. 338; exclamation point is new in this volume] (this Micòl who seemed so free, so sporty, so modern [free above all] [Q:*G*, pp. 135–36]). Later, during a discussion of Melville's *Bartleby*, Micòl "si era messa a esaltare in Bartleby l'inalienabile diritto di ogni essere umano alla non-collaborazione,' cioè alla libertà" [p. 395] (had taken to exalting in Bartleby the "inalienable right of every human being to non-collaboration," that is to freedom [Q:*G*, p. 216]). Her own noncollaboration extends from the ostentatious eating of ham (taboo in orthodox Judaism) and the childish disobedience of her mother's rules to the rejection of the narrator as a suitor and her brusque refusal to play the conventional role of a courted young woman in love.

The motif of freedom is essential to the Bassanian oeuvre; it originates in the collective historical experience of Fascism, which voided Jewish social and economic rights and imprisoned the author for his anti-Fascist acts. After the war, Bassani repossessed his sense of liberty at great cost. Rupture with the past was one requirement, as may be recalled by his own words cited extensively in chapter 1 of this text. Micòl, to whom I now return, symbolizes both authorial loss (the "paradisiacal" past) and vitality (renewed creativity).

Micòl's sense of freedom, unbound by ancient fetters such as those that suffocated her author, attaches to her life in a paradisiacal garden-home. Her fate to die in a concentration camp is sacral, scapegoated "compensation" for her energetic love of life and the present moment. Micòl is the very symbol of life, and if she enjoys an exceptional power of vision and liberation, she remains nonetheless a mortal woman of stunning sexual power. Even when they were both children of thirteen, Micòl held much fascination for the narrator. He remembers how by chance (fatefully) she saw him alone one day, lying on the grass by her garden wall.

The "ragazetto . . . molto borghese e molto vanitoso" [p. 280] (very bourgeois and very vain little boy) is in a dark mood, the result of a failing grade in mathematics. Although she knows him from temple services, they have never before talked or been alone together. Deep in morbid fantasies, he is startled when she calls to him: "Guardavo, cercavo, succhiudendo gli occhi al riverbero. Ai miei piedi (soltanto adesso me ne rendevo conto), le chiome dei nobili alberi gonfie di luce meridiana come quelle di una foresta tropicale, si stendeva il Barchetto del Duca" [p. 277] (I gazed about, searching, and half-shut my eyes against the glare. At my feet (it was only then I noticed) the foliage of its noble trees filled with midday light, like that of a tropical forest, Barchetto del Duca was spread before me [Q:G, p. 48]). Before the desperate boy notices Micòl, he sees the garden—the sunlit "hair" of the lush trees. By means of a verb in the simple past tense surrounded by numerous other verbs in the imperfect, the narrative stages a mystical moment of revelation: "Per via dei capelli biondi, di quel biondo particolare striato di ciocche nordiche, da *fille aux cheveux de lin*, che non apparteneva che a lei, *riconobbi subito* Micòl Finzi-Contini" [p. 277; last emphasis added] (From the blonde hair, that special streaky Nordic-looking blonde of the *fille aux cheveux di lin*, which was hers alone, I immediately recognized Micòl Finzi-Contini [ibid.]). Micòl flashes into recognition as an extension of the noble trees, both of them creatures of nature glowing under a brilliant midday sun.[19] The humorously childish scene prepares and anticipates the narrator's eventual passage into the garden, but now, despite Micòl's earnest efforts to help him reach her, the hesitant boy fails to cross over the wall, that is, to "grow up," to sexualize their relation. Indeed, because at this time he can only dream of their erotic union, the boy-narrator "loses" Micòl.

The subterranean *cunicolo* (a female-shaped large chamber, "round, with a

dome vault" [p. 285]), where Micòl advises her unexpected guest to hide his bicycle, inspires a sexual fantasy: "E ogni giorno ci saremmo baciati, al buio:
perché io ero il suo uomo, e lei la mia donna" [p. 286] (And every day we'd
kiss, in the dark: because I was her man, and she was my woman [Q:G, p. 60].
By the time he emerges, Micòl has been ordered back from the wall. Although
for the moment the "vert paradis des amours enfantines"[20] remains beyond the
boy's reach, from its threshold Micòl has already begun to guide him; her ironic
belittling of his poor grade has already relieved his misery and increased his self-
awareness: "D'un tratto mi ero accorto che la questione della bocciatura era
diventata secondaria, una faccenda bambinesca che si sarebbe sistemata da sé"
[p. 279] (Suddenly I realized that this business of my failure had slipped into
second place, a childish matter that would settle itself [Q:G, p. 50]). In short,
Micòl has started him on his way to manhood. Her intelligence is clear, even
at this young age, and her later behavior, though it will perplex and disappoint
the young suitor, will be an expression of her enduring wisdom. Micòl is a
knower—in her father's words, an "angelo tutelare" (p. 347)—and her principal
service, at least from the point of view of the novel's writer, is to educate the
young hero.[21]

Ten years later, another fortuitous occasion—rain—brings the now-adult pair
into a second private and erotically charged confrontation. Again a symbolically
female refuge—the old horse-drawn carriage belonging to the Finzi-Continis—
provides the setting. The narrator follows Micòl into the carriage, which is
stored in the huge garage, and the carriage door closes "da solo con uno schiocco
secco e preciso da tagliola" [p. 326] (by itself with a sharp, definite slam, like
a trap). A trap for the narrator, for Micòl the carriage represents a lie: in the
"semiobscurity" of the garage it seems "miraculously" new, but "outside, in the
natural light" it shows itself to be a "pitiful piece of wreckage" (p. 327). The
scene immediately following this one, juxtaposed across a temporal and major
narrative divide, translates Micòl's demystifying and unsentimental angle of vision and the narrator's metaphoric entrapment (impotence) into a cryptic
presagement of erotic failure:

> Infinite volte nel corso dell'inverno, della primavera, e dell'estate che
> seguirono, tornai indietro a ciò che tra Micòl e me era accaduto (o meglio,
> non accaduto) dentro la carrozza prediletta dal vecchio Perotti. . . . E
> dimenticavo di chiedermi l'essenziale: se in quel momento supremo,
> unico, irrevocabile—un momento che, forse, aveva deciso della mia e
> della sua vita—io fossi stato davvero in grado di tentare un gesto, una pa-
> rola qualsiasi. Lo sapevo già, allora, per esempio, di essermi innamorato
> *veramente*? [p. 329]

(Endlessly, during the winter, spring and summer that followed, I turned
back to what had happened (or rather hadn't happened) between Micòl and

me in old Perotti's beloved carriage. . . . And I forgot to ask myself the essential question: whether, in that supreme, single, irrevocable moment—a moment that perhaps had decided my life and hers—I was really capable of trying to do or say anything at all. Did I, for instance, already know that I was *really* in love?) [Q:*G*, p. 123]

Hindsight, for both the narrator and the reader, makes it clear that the former is still immature and that Micòl feels no erotic passion for him. Six months after the "nonevent" the two play out *in extremis* their parts of uncontainable lover and unresponding beloved: the narrator, seeing Micòl after her long absence from Ferrara, impetuously kisses her on her mouth. She simply looks into his eyes, "e il suo sguardo entrava in me dritto, sicuro, duro: con la limpida inesorabilità di una spada" [p. 377] (and her look went straight inside me, sure and hard: clear and inexorable as a sword [Q:*G*, p. 190]). Micòl's metaphoric knifing stops time for the "mortally" wounded narrator: "Quella notte non sarebbe finita mai" [p. 383] (That night would never end), banishing him suddenly from his *vert paradis* into arid solitude: gone are the expectant days of their already "*antichi rapporti*" (p. 385; emphasis added). Micòl's adamant refusal of her would-be lover's kiss is not, however, a gesture of dislike; on the contrary, she has much affection for him. For an "angelo tutelare" erotic passion is inadmissible. When, later, she explains her lack of passionate desire for him, she appeals to their "familial" bond: they are so alike, she insists, as if to be sister and brother. In other words, an erotic relation for them would be incestuous. Micòl and the narrator are, in fact, twinlike: they were born in the same year, they have grown up together in the Jewish community, and they have similar dispositions and outlooks; in Micòl's words, they are "equals" (p. 400). Thus they are free to enter into a relation of spiritual intimacy, in which Micòl can alter the narrator's life profoundly yet remain "uncontaminated" by sexual intimacy. In this regard, Micòl is to Bassani as Beatrice is to Dante and Laura to Petrarch. But only Micòl has historical and physical life to rival that of the male narrative subject. As his idealized object, the female participates in a relation of similarity (that in its extreme reaches "incest" or self-love). But the male-female union is also one of difference. In Bassani's *Romanzo*, difference invariably represents conflict, or lack of (male) self-harmony. The best example of this is the self-destructive, erotic relation between Bruno Lattes and Adriana Trentini, depicted in several texts. The relation is doomed less for personal than for religious difference; specifically, for the so-called racial separation of Jew and "Aryan" in the Fascist era. Its turbulent quality signifies Jewish self-hatred, stemming from the exclusion of Jews from society.

Blond, blue-eyes Aryans are textual markers of Jewish humiliation; they raise Bassanian difference to the limit of nonidentity. Thomas Mann's dark-complexioned Tonio Kröger speaks for the similarly dark Bruno when he states that his "deepest and secretest love belongs to the blond and the blue-eyes."[22] Difference, or alterity, finds universal expression in the opposition of male and female. In Bassani erotic passion guarantees difference with a vengeance; creative passion feeds on the absence of difference. To the extent that Micòl and the narrator are equals, Micòl functions as her author's symbol of artistic inspiration; thus she remains chaste and mystified. Her banishment of the narrator is required for her ideal image to be preserved intact. An erotically permeated dream offers an interesting variation on the theme of chastity. It has the "desperate" narrator relive slightly altered snatches of his unfulfilled meetings with Micòl, who retains her slightly mocking and disavowing attitude toward him. In the most surreal part of the dream, the narrator observes endless rows of *làttimi* (glass objects) that Micòl keeps (in dream and in fact) in her bedroom. In the dream the objects have changed into bottle-shaped, oozing ("stillanti") small cheeses (the word *làttimi* evokes milk). A smiling Micòl invites her guest to taste one "of the best ones," but "stared at" by Micòl's dog and "anguished" about a rising tide of water surrounding the house, he declines. This explicit symbolization of sexual intercourse has Micòl (the threatening "female" water)—in apt proximity to her bed—proposing sex (the oozing "male" cheese); but the exposed and imperiled narrator, longing for the protection of an "outside," a non-Finzi-Continian space (pp. 338–40), refuses her offer. The dreamworld projection of a sexually available Micòl reins in its own desire *in order to protect the narrator*, whose creative "oozing" must depend on his pen and not his penis. The two parts played out, in which sameness is a primary factor, are interchangeable. Thus, when the narrator urges Micòl to tryst away from home, she refuses: "con me fuori di casa e del giardino non ci sarebbe venuta mai" [p. 340] (she'd never come outside the house and garden with me [Q:*G*, p. 137]). In her "enchanted" garden, Micòl's purity, notwithstanding her temporary role as temptress, is unassailable. The image of a seductive Micòl is merely the verso of the recto image of rectitude (a common male fantasy of woman). Protection—or, better, nonprofanation—of the narrating persona is inextricable from the nonprofanation of Micòl.

During her childhood, Micòl's dispassion reveals itself at the first threshold meeting at the garden wall. Before the bewildered and tearful pupil who has failed a course, Micòl is "tranquilla come se il nostro non fosse stato un incontro casuale, assolutamente fortuito" [p. 278] (as calm as if ours were not a casual, absolutely chance meeting [Q:*G*, p. 50]). From the outset she seems to be in possession of arcane knowledge. This special gift may account also for her sadness, her bittersweet response to life. Even her tastebuds favor the bittersweet. When she was small, she especially liked the "brogn serbi" (p. 321; dialect for "sour plums") produced by the great old plum tree in the garden; at sixteen, she develops a taste for chocolates, "bitter chocolate, however, only the bitter kind!" (ibid.). Micòl herself appears bittersweet, "sad and beautiful" (p. 414), as her devotee describes her in a poem, and "half tender, half scornful," in a facial expression that seems to capture what "her heart suggested" (p. 321). Seldom leaving the grounds of her home (dream and reality are compatible here), Micòl watches over the growing and dying of both vegetation and animal life. As a figure of creative productivity, she finds nature's bounty a primary source of pleasure. When, ten years after the conversation at the garden wall, the narrator is at last admitted inside, Micòl delights in acquainting him with the vast garden's many trees and plants: elms, limes, oaks, planes, rare and exotic plants; in short, "every tree that is pleasant to the sight and good for food" (Genesis, 2). By pointed contrast, the initiate has no botanical knowledge: "Le sembrava assurdo, a lei, che esistesse al mondo un tipo come me, il quale non nutrisse per gli alberi, 'i grandi, i quieti, i forti, i pensierosi', gli stessi suoi sentimenti di appassionata ammirazione. Come facevo a non *capire*, mio Dio, a non *sentire*?" [p. 320] (It seemed absurd to her that someone like me should exist in the world, someone who wholly lacked her own feeling of passionate admiration for trees, "great, strong, and thoughtful trees." How could I fail to *understand*? How could I go on living without *feeling*? [Q:*G*, p. 108]).

Micòl's intensity of feeling for trees is not unlike her regard for people. But her passionate joys do not yield to erotic ones. Her innocent intimacy with the natural world circumscribes the limits of her more-than-ascetic yet less-than-seductive sexuality. This "earth goddess" often speaks of the trees in dialect, a language she otherwise reserves for the Perotti family, the old and faithful servants who live in a farmhouse on the grounds. Textual rhetoric transforms the couple into creatures of the earth. Another garden creature is the decrepit Great Dane, Jor, who is often at Micòl's heels. Jor's huge, sculptural appearance suggests mythology rather than reality, and his impassive, two-toned eyes ("cold, expressionless eyes, one dark and one sky-blue") encompass the colors of heaven and earth, the contradictory and superhuman qualities of Micòl. Perotti, the "animalesque" servant and family *portinaio* who exhibits "rabbiosa fedeltà da vecchio animale domestico" [p. 391] (fierce loyalty, like that of an old pet), functions as a threshold guardian (p. 282). He and his wife are chthonian attendants of the earth divinity Micòl, whose tower-apartment is reached by an elevator with the color and sharp smell of fermented wine. Suggestive of the pleasures of the body, and therefore of Micòl's (natural) sensuosity, these earthen products are mythic signs of the narrator's crossing of a psychic threshold. His extreme sensitivity to the elevator's smells and strange attraction, when he visits the tower, represents his heightened and inspirited sense of well-being—as does each suspended (timeless) infinitive verb:

Varcare la soglia della cabina, che era un antidiluviano scatolone tutto lucidi legni color vino . . . essere preso alla gola dall'odore pungente, un po' soffocante, tra di muffa e d'acqua ragia, che impregnava l'aria racchiusa in quell'angusto spazio, e avvertire d'un tratto un immotivato senso di calma, di tranquillità fatalistica, di distacco addirittura ironico, fu una cosa sola. [p. 390]

([To cross over into the cabin,] which was an antediluvian box all of gleaming wine-coloured woods . . . [to be seized by] a pungent, faintly suffocating smell, compounded of mold and turpentine, a smell that impregnated the stuffy air in that enclosed space; and [to feel] an unmotivated sense of calm, of fatalistic tranquillity, of positively ironic detachment, [happened] all in the space of a moment.) [Q:*G*, pp. 210–11]

Another authorial figure, Bruno Lattes, is also revitalized and becalmed by one of nature's aromas, the smell of hay. The olfactory trope of reanimating earth smells, associated with a tiny constellation of dynamic male figures as well as with Micòl, productively complements the author's more dominant visual imagination.

Each of the four principal parts of the *Giardino* ends in a climaxing scene involving Micòl, casting her into increasingly significant ritual functions, which also forecast her destiny of death. By the end of part one, the boy-narrator's heart is opened to the smiling girl who has invited him inside her garden. By the end of part two, already welcomed as a favored household guest and with the elation of a lover, the grown youth enjoys Micòl's habitual companionship. Part three opens with a lament to the end of the "luminous" Indian summer, and Micòl, like the autumn, begins to "die." In a process of gradual disembodiment, she recedes from her lover—becoming first a voice on the telephone (chapter 1), then printed words in letters from Venice (chapter 4), then immaterial spirit sensed as a presence in her home by her young lover there with her family (chapter 5). The final chapter of part three limns the family apotheosis that celebrates Micòl's actual reappearance (rebirth) at the Passover meal. Part four marks the breakdown of the suitor's romantic passion: Micòl becomes irritated with his juvenile and embarrassing behavior, that is, his "sostanziale aridità" (p. 412). She subsequently exiles him from the paradisial garden, and his loss propels him farther ahead on his journey toward self-adequacy. As the chapters progress, the figure of Micòl recedes more and more, until the narrator's world becomes male-dominated, Micòl outgrown. Through her exuberance and her femininity, Micòl stands for the creative imagination. The narrator's erotic desire translates finally into the act of writing: the narrating subject becomes a writer on the level of plot, inscribing as well the figure of the book's actual author.

At the farthest extremity from the pole of feminine creativity, as calibrated across the entire range of Bassani's writing, is masculine infertility—the state of "aridity" that, for an angry Micòl, describes the intrusive, self-absorbed youth who would be her lover. This pole is occupied also by the solipsistic suicide, Edgardo Limentani, and the treacherous transient, Luciano Pulga (see the earlier

Figure 11. The dining room of Bassani's home in Ferrara. "Aside from the glow that burst
forth from the burning logs . . . the great upside-down corolla of the chandelier poured out
a real cataract of light" (*Il giardino dei Finzi-Contini*).

part of this chapter). The positive charges that energize Bassani's fiction are explicitly female. Although various male characters—Geo Josz, Pino Barilari,
even Edgardo Limentani, as well as some unnamed first-person characters—
ultimately become implied, if not proclaimed, sources of social and personal
renewal and thus indirect positive forces, only a female—Micòl—enjoys positive
value without first having to undergo a humiliating psychic descent.

In a minor modality, the nine-year-old Giannina of the frame-prologue of the
Giardino represents the same kind of inspiring vitality as Micòl. It is Giannina,
aglow with sparkling dark eyes and cheeks warm from playing, who, according
to the narrator, conveys to the grown-ups with her at Cerveteri an appreciation
of the living humanity of the long-dead Etruscans; this awareness propels the
narrator to preserve in writing the living humanity of the Finzi-Continis, especially of Micòl. A boy-child could not have played the role assigned to Giannina.
Like the ancient Muses, femininity uncontaminated is the predictable source of
male inspiration—and Bassani is not an exception in tapping that source. Femininity contaminated (think of Nives Pampinati and Anna Repetto) is the equally
predictable source of male degeneration. Between the two extremes lies a maternal femininity that bears in its idealized representation of a mature, indulgent,

and protective mother a stain that sullies her relation with her son and that fosters or confirms the son's inner transformation. Mothers of daughters have different roles to play in Bassani's texts. Of these, the mother of Lida Mantovani is the most notable. In Zolaesque fashion she "explains" the daughter's impoverished dependency, victimized fate, and stubborn survival. Sons with idealized or insignificant mothers are always figures of the author. In this category are the mothers of Edgardo Limentani and the narrator of *Porta*, as well as the paler figure of the narrator's mother in the *Giardino*.

Maternal Sexuality

The sole truly instrumental maternal figure is the one in *Porta*, who functions primarily as an unwitting and defiled agent of her young son's shame and subsequent isolation. Her idealized motherhood, briefly illumined before the novella's close, is reduced to a pinpoint by another boy's contradictive befoulment of her image. Two highly mythicized portraits of her are constructed toward the end of the narrative. In the first, her son sees her in the garden of their home:

Al centro del suo reame, del suo teatro, circondata dalle sue "sante bestie," la barboncina Lulù, i due gatti persiani color fumo, la tartaruga Filomena, mi guardava e sorrideva. Stava ricamando l'orlo di un lenzuolo o di una tovaglia. L'ago le scintillava in grembo. Il giardino fiammeggiava attorno, rigoglioso come una piccola giungla. [p. 536]

(Seated at the center of her kingdom, of her theater, and surrounded by her "holy creatures," the tiny poodle Lulù, the two smoke-colored Persian cats, and the turtle Filomena, she looked up at me and smiled. She was embroidering the hem of a sheet or a tablecloth. The needle sparkled on her lap. The garden was blazing all around her, like a little luxuriant jungle.)

A few lines later, the son sees her as a young woman in a photograph:

Poco prima, mentre attraversavo un salotto, mi ero fermato a osservare una vecchia fotografia. . . . Ritraeva me e mia madre nel '18, durante l'ultima estate di guerra. Magra come una ragazza, vestita di bianco, la mamma appariva inginocchiata accanto a me sullo sfondo luminoso dell'orto della casa di campagna dei nonni. . . . E mentre mi stringeva appassionatamente al seno, rivolgeva in direzione dell'obiettivo un sorriso gioioso, intensamente felice. [ibid.]

(Shortly before, while I was walking through the parlor, I had stopped to look at an old photograph. . . . It was of my mother and me in 1918, in the last summer of the war. As thin as a girl and dressed in white, Mother was kneeling down next to me, against the luminous background of the orchard in my grandparents' country home. . . . And while she clutched me lovingly to her breast, she turned toward the camera a joyful, intensely happy smile.)

These two sparkling images, redolent of Micòl in the florid Finzi-Contini garden, in fact for the adolescent son transform the mature, maternal figure he sees, in contained sensuality, into the sexually vibrant young wife of the photograph, whose joy is flamed not by the child she embraces, but by the photographer, her soldier-husband home on leave: "Ma soltanto qualche minuto fa, guardandola, avevo compreso il reale significato di quel sorriso della mamma, sposa da appena tre anni: ciò che prometteva, ciò che offriva, e *a chi*..." [pp. 536–37] (But only a few minutes ago, while I was looking at her, did I understand the real significance of that smile belonging to a bride of just three years: what it promised, what it was offering, and *to whom* . . .) The image of the woman seen in the garden, bereft entirely of bodily attributes and formed instead of a restful pose, a glance, and a smile, depicts a maternity dependent on her son's remaining a boy—too young to gauge her sexuality. The scene is artful, strangely static and unreal, like an old-fashioned photograph. It seems a conscious, nostalgic effort of the viewer (the young son) to preserve a fading picture of a private and comfortable family universe. More accurate and truthful to him now is the real photograph, whose primary viewer is a grown man (his father) and whose primary message is sensuality: the girl-woman's smile is not abstract, as in the garden scene, but "joyful, intensely happy," and her impassioned embrace of the child she "clutches to her breast" sensualizes the sacred Christian theme of the Madonna and Child. The backdrop further heightens the sensuality. The open fields suggest a natural, that is, wild landscape—the passion of a bride rather than a mother. And even the small, cultivated garden space enclosed by the urban home bursts imagistically into a flaming, jungle landscape, bestial and erotic, that denies its presumable function of maternal seclusion and repose.

If this textual discourse inscribes doubled, contradictory readings of the two maternal scenes, the son's newly altered and conflictive perception of his mother is the immediate consequence of remarks made by Luciano Pulga, an outsider from Bologna who becomes the boy's unsavory school friend.

A short time before the episodes cited, Luciano, unaware that his narrator-friend is eavesdropping "behind a door," ebulliently maligns the latter's mother to a few classmates:

Era una signora sui trentatré, trentacinque anni—proseguì [Luciano]—magari un po' "sfasciata" come sono sempre le ebree, ma però con una bocca tale, con certi occhioni "*marron*," e con certe occhiate, specialmente . . .

Certo è che l'estate al mare . . . una donna così doveva combinarne di tutti i colori al marito anzianotto le settimane che lui, rientrato in città per stare dietro ai suoi affari, la lasciava nella villa d'affitto senza altra compagnia all'infuori di quella delle serve e dei bambini! Con quella bocca larga, "ingorda," con quegli occhi languidi mezzo nascosti dai capelli (il petto le aveva un po' basso, d'accordo, ma la "carrozzeria" meritava forse un viaggio apposta), impossibile che, presentandosi l'occasione, se la lasciasse scappare. [pp. 526-27]

(She was a woman about thirty-three, thirty-five years old, continued [Luciano], maybe a little "flabby" as Jewesses always are, but with what a mouth, what big brown eyes and, especially, what intense looks.

But surely in the summer, at the shore . . . a woman like her must have played all sorts of tricks on her elderly husband, during the weeks when, having gone back to work in the city, he left her alone in the rented villa with only the servants and the children! With that wide, "greedy" mouth, with those languid eyes half hidden by her hair (her breasts sagged a bit, to be sure, but the "body work" maybe was worth a special trip), it was impossible that when the opportunity came, she would let it slip by.)

Luciano refers twice to the mother's mouth, as opposed to the son's (repeated) use of the word "smile" – recalling Dante's careful distinction of the two terms when referring, respectively, to the passionate Francesa and the idealized Guinevere.

The narrator-son, sixteen years old, can no longer look upon his mother except in sexual terms; he surrenders his childish love to Luciano's sexually sullying demystification of her: her lost innocence is his lost innocence.

His resultant self-loathing and her tainted person mark the first stations of the son's journey to manhood. The young wife's exhuberant expression, captured in the old photograph, seemingly in harmony with her slender body, her white dress, and the luminous orchard of the country house before which she poses, becomes a besmirched sign of erotic passion following the son's discovery of "libidinous" maternal sexuality: "Guardavo lei, ora, mia madre non più così giovane, così ragazza, e sentivo che il cuore tornava a riempirmisi di ribrezzo e di rancore. . . . Oh, andarmene via, fuggire! Non vedere più nessuno, e soprattutto non essere veduto più da nessuno!" [p. 537] (I looked at my mother now, no longer young or girlish, and I felt my heart fill up again with disgust and bitterness. . . . Oh, to go away, to flee! To see no one any more, and especially, to be seen by no one!). The despair felt by the boy-narrator expresses the "death" of his childish self-contentment and pride, and seeds the potentiality of an adult "birth." His gaze upon the serene, sentimental pose of his mother in the garden evokes both nostalgia for a lost purity and certainty and feelings of betrayal by a fallen idol. The sight of her also arouses a tabooed erotic desire. Textually, that sexual prohibition is very lightly inscribed but nonetheless visible in Bassani's final version of the story (1980). It originates in a preceding episode, Carlo Cattolica's resolute unmasking of Luciano's snide pretense of friendship with the ingenuous subject of the tale (pp. 504-7). Two momentary circumstances prepare the erotic eruption. First the narrator looks out from his bedroom window to the garden below. Remembering his mother's glad news that her turtle had finally come out of its winter hibernation, he calls to the creature. And then he undresses: "Mi spogliai adagio, e . . . mi stesi supino sul letto. . . . Ero completamente nudo. Su dal giardino veniva un profumo intenso di piante, di erba" [p. 508] (I slowly undressed, and facing up, stretched out on the bed. . . . I was completely naked. From the garden rose an intense perfume of flowers and grass). The unmistakable erotic pattern woven of these acts and words does not jog the bourgeois code of sexual repression of maternal love, but it conveys nonetheless the tabooed desire. In the 1974 edition, the paragraph immediately following the scenes quoted above edges venturously toward stating the boy's desire:

> Mi vedevo con l'immaginazione picchiare [Luciano] senza pietà: e il membro, frattanto, mi si era indurito come quando, da bambino, attraverso la porta socchiusa di cucina, spiavo non visto la cuoca (Ines, si chiamava: un pacifico donnone di campagna, *dall'aria materna*) sventrare un pollo. [1974, p. 557; emphasis added]

> (In my mind I saw myself pitilessly beating Luciano; and my penis meanwhile became hardened, like when I was a child and through the half-open kitchen door peeked at the cook [Ines was her name—a mild, maternal kind of big country woman] who was eviscerating a chicken.)

It is a pity, in a way, that Bassani expunged this deft and allusive network of meaning from the definitive version of his *Romanzo*. The little scene is a marvelous compaction of the violence and sex of the climactic scene in which a lacerated son truly hides behind a closed door and spies on Luciano, who—in the language of sexual abuse—is violating the narrator's mother. Yet the author's rejection of the original episode rests on solid ground. The rationale is implicit in the following declaration, which formulates Bassani's poetics:

> Ricordo che Fortini mi rimproverava di non aver esaurito tutto il potenziale erotico che poteva scaturire dai rapporti tra Alberto, l'io scrivente, Micòl e Malnate: tutto un coacervo di implicazioni erotiche da me non elaborate. Ma io lo sapevo benissimo che c'erano, queste implicazioni, eccome se lo sapevo! Senonché non erano esse la materia del mio romanzo. Se avessi impalcato su quella base di incontrovertibile verità storica un castello romanzesco di rapporti sessuali ipotetici o ipotizzati sullo sfondo di Buchenwald avrei prodotto un *monstrum* artistico.[23]

> (I remember that Fortini reproached me for not making the most of the erotic potential resulting from the relations between Alberto, the narrating "I," Micòl and Malnate: an accumulation of erotic implications that I did

not elaborate. Of course I knew that those implications were there! But they were not the subject of my novel. If on my base of incontrovertible historical truth I had built a romantic castle of dubious or conjectured sexual relations against a background of Buchenwald, I would have produced an artistic monster.)

The author's example of the *Giardino* is both the most and the least likely source of erotic potentiality in his narratives, for the very reasons he gives. Later texts, specifically *Porta* and the subsequent *Airone*, explore erotic moments in bolder imagery and language. Significantly, the male subject of desire in these two texts locates the female object in insignificant, lower-class women, such as the servant Ines (*Porta*) and the real and fantasized prostitutes of *Airone*. The mother in *Porta* is only indirectly an object of desire. Her very abuse by Luciano safeguards her inherent purity. Indeed, as we shall see in a moment, this victimized woman also stands before "the backdrop of Buchenwald."

For Bassani (as for many other male writers), the hero's psychic death is entwined with female lust and sirenic attraction. Only in the confessional tale of *Porta*—even more tortured and hopeless than *Airone*, the story of a suicide—does Bassani introduce the Oedipal limit of sexual transgression. To be sure, the mother-son relation is sexual only in the son's imagination, sparked by a wicked friend's erotic conjurations. The boy's sense of self-loathing and shame, unmistakable evidence of his trespassing of sexual bounds, draws upon an ancient, patriarchal view of female sexuality as demonic and destructive, in opposition to conventional maternal asexuality, the mother as a paradigm of virtue and charitable love. But the most compelling Oedipal evidence can be found in the imagery and events of the episode discussed above that mediate the boy's erotic desire. Another male figure, constructed solely to plumb the consequences of sexual transgression, is—at least in his nostalgic memory— also the son of a virtuous, that is, unsexual mother. The son, Dr. Fadigati (*Occhiali*), recalls:

A Venezia . . . lui aveva la casa, il papà e la mamma, soprattutto la mamma: gli "affetti" più sacri, insomma.
Come l'aveva adorata—sospirava—la sua povera mamma! Intelligente, colta, bella, pia: in lei si assommavano tutte le virtù. [p. 187]

(In Venice . . . he had his home, Mamma and Papa, and especially Mamma: the most sacred affections, in other words.
How he had worshiped her—he sighed—his poor Mamma! Intelligent, cultivated, beautiful, devout: she was the summation of every virtue.) [W:*D*, p. 112]

Adored mothers in these texts are invariably counterbalanced by sons who are self-hating and self-destructive: Dr. Fadigati is driven to suicide by his notorious homosexual liaisons; the narrating schoolboy of *Porta* sinks into self-destructive shame; an apathetic Edgardo Limentani shoots himself.

In *Porta* Bassani cleverly protects in *fact* the mother's purity while reaping the narrative harvest of the son's need to know sorrow and despair, to experience the destruction of the self. As recounted in the third person by the narrator, Luciano pronounces on the mother's diabolical nature: "Per convincerlo a trattenersi a cena e magari a dormire, d'un tratto si era messa a fissarlo occhi negli occhi con una forza tale da impaurire non dico lui, che ci voleva poco, ma il diavolo in persona" [p. 526]. (To persuade him to stay for supper, and perhaps to sleep there, she had taken to staring at him for a while, looking him straight in the eye, with such insistence . . . that she would have frightened not only him, which didn't take much, but the devil himself [W:*D*, p. 120]). Furthermore: "Accomiatandosi, non mancava mai di lanciare attraverso la fessura della porta un bel sorriso accompagnato da un'occhiata 'mezzo materna e mezzo assassina' " [ibid.] (She never forgot . . . saying good-by, to fire from the open door a beautiful smile with a glance "partly maternal and partly tormenting" [ibid.]). The word "assassina" also connotes seduction. The mother's smile described by her son's new studymate is, then, the deadly guile of a temptress.

Luciano's violent and treacherous verbal aggression against the mother foreshadows a similar but material violence against the public body (the beginning of the anti-Jewish laws in 1938) only nine years removed from the narrative present of 1929, which itself marks the beginning of Fascism's bloom, soon to be withered by Mussolini's pacts with Nazi Germany and his acquiescence to anti-Semitism. Luciano's initial description of the mother combines anti-Jewish caricaturing with an objectification (devaluation) of the mother's body: "She was . . . a little 'flabby,' as Jewesses always are." This brief remark sullies more than an individual mother. It conjoins female sexuality and religion in a classic evocation of the Jewish woman as erotic, and it extends the ancient stereotype to envelop the unique Nazi brand of death-camp violation of female Jewish bodies for sadistic sexual entertainment, a phenomenon hovering just beyond Bassani's textual limit. The mere use of the adjective "flabby" (the Italian term "sfasciata" refers especially to females, often those "flabby" from childbirth) is sexually abusive of the narrator's mother; the juxtaposition of stereotyped Jewishness sharpens the remark into the cruelest possible statement that could be made in a Bassani fiction. It is a terrifying intimation—all the more so because apparently off-hand, in a jesting tone, possibly even missed by the reader—of the approaching Nazi success at Jewish victimization. In this light the narrator's mother prefigures, if at an almost subliminal textual level, the wanton suffering of the Jews just a few years away, and in particular the fate of Micòl, whose experience in a concentration camp Bassani keeps silent. The narrator of *Porta*, whose story is a grim descent into humiliation, experiences the shame directed at his mother. In that experience he effectively *becomes* his mother; he assumes the shame for an offense of which she is completely unaware and presumably innocent. He suffers doubly thereby for her and for his own loss of her immaculate motherhood. A pair of subdued oxymorons conveys the son's bewildered disenchantment and complicitous deprecation of his mother and himself: "Immersa nell'*ombra soleggiata* . . . era non più che una *macchia chiara*, lontana" [p. 535; emphasis added] (immersed in the sun-streaked shade . . . she was no more than a bright, distant spot [W:*D*, p. 135]). The distant "macchia chiara" signifies both a bright spot and a dirty spot. The son's perception of maternal blemish distances irrevocably the no-longer-resplendent mother while, paradoxically, her stained image fixes itself permanently – and unbearably – upon his mind. Inextricably bound to the defilement of both mother and son is their Jewishness, especially as it becomes fascistically stigmatized. Although the novella recounts a personal story, the certain direction of the Italian political future is implied in the slight but conspicuous anti-Jewish and pro-Fascist remarks made by Luciano Pulga and his father. Speaking about his Jewish classmate, Luciano "certainly" finds in him "quali scarti di carattere ci si possa aspettare da un ebreo" [p. 523] (the sort of quirks you could expect from a Jew [W:*D*, p. 114]). The Fascist-inclined Dr. Pulga has a "red 'cyanotic' face" and "green, bulging 'Basedow' eyes" that suggest deformity and disease, as do the blackheads that spot Luciano's "waxy-skinned face" and the "callosità giallastre che gli ispessivano stranamente i palmi delle mani, grandi, magre, un po' da gobbo" [p. 481] (yellow calluses that strangely hardened his large, thin hands, somewhat like a hunchback's [W:*D*, p. 46]). Dr. Pulga has a taste for the defamatory that offends the narrator's father. The slanderous tongue ("linguaccia") of the former, for example, strikes at a highly esteemed Bolognese surgeon with whom he, Dr. Pulga, professes friendship: "Ecco una bella mostruosità" [p. 481] (It was monstrous, it really was! [W:*D*, p. 46]) is the speaker's retort. Like son, like father; the Pulgas' shared, most notorious attribute is violent verbal aggression against others, of a treacherous cast. Its monstrosity, we have seen, foreshadows political violence. From the narrator's and the reader's temporal vantage point, the father's indignation at Dr. Pulga's malevolent and self-aggrandizing discourse seems a pitiful expression of ineffectuality: the impotence of the victim-to-be.

If the Pulgas represent the crassest kind of Fascist, the Cattolica family represents its most sophisticated version. Carlo Cattolica, another classmate of the narrator's, is on the surface, the antithesis of Luciano. The latter is short, devious (a trait deftly caught in the "secco spostamento laterale che, pronunciando la zeta, imprimeva alla mandibola" [p. 481] (sharp, sideways movement of his jaw when he pronounced the letter "z" [W:*D*, p. 46]), a weak student, self-deprecating, poor. Carlo is tall, forthright, a superior student, self-righteous, affluent. It is he who is responsible for opening the narrator's eyes to Luciano's malicious ways, though Carlo's motivation is no more altruistic than Luciano's.

The narrator, about to agree to Carlo's eavesdropping scheme, is not under any illusions: "Pallido, magro, mi scrutava coi suoi occhi neri, ardenti di fanatismo in fondo alle orbite come quelli di un monaco medievale. Capivo bene che a muoverlo era solo la voglia di umiliarmi" [p. 509] (Pale, thin, he stared at me with his black eyes, glowing fanatically in their sockets: the eyes, I thought, of a medieval monk. I realized he was driven only by a desire to humiliate me [W:D, p. 88]). Carlo is the purified equivalent of the narrator, the rival who cruelly reflects back to him his own inferiority. Too refined (or perhaps simply too cautious) to make overt anti-Jewish remarks, Carlo is nonetheless not beyond condescension. In an earlier conversation, when the two seemed on the verge of friendship, Carlo posed questions about Jewish beliefs:

> Ci eravamo messi a discorrere di religioni in generale, ma lui mi chiedeva se era vero che noi "israeliti" non credevamo nella Madonna, se era vero che secondo noi Gesù Cristo non era il figlio di Dio, se era vero che aspettavamo ancora il Messia, se era vero che "in chiesa" noi tenevamo il cappello, eccetera. E io a rispondergli punto per punto più che di buon grado, sentendo a un tratto dentro di me che la sua curiosità generica, volgare, per non dire insolente, anziché offendermi mi piaceva, mi liberava. [p. 471]

> (What did we talk about? Religions, naturally. He asked me if it was true that we "Israelites" didn't believe in the Madonna, if it was true that, in our belief, Jesus Christ wasn't the son of God, if it was true that we were still waiting for the Messiah, if it was true that "in church" we kept our hats on, and so forth. And I answered him, point by point, with feverish, exaggerated enthusiasm, not even noticing how elementary his questions were, how generic and vulgar, not to say insolent, his curiosity was.) [W:D, p. 31]

The narrator's "enthusiasm" is an early sign of his impulse toward self-destructiveness, which materializes in full in the friendship he soon cultivates with Luciano. Carlo's insolence inflames in his interlocutor a momentary fantasy of friendship, softly ironized in the final scene of this episode (and chapter), when the two boys are walking together to their classroom "like close, affectionate friends" (p. 472). The word "like" betrays the friendship as illusory. Just prior to the walk, the conversation took a turn by which the narrator, suggesting that the name Cattolica might be of Jewish origin, seemed intent on leaving no chance for friendship:

> "Scusa," avevo detto, "ma voi... intendo la tua famiglia... siete sempre stati cattolici?"
> Aveva stirato le labbra in un breve sorriso orgoglioso.
> "Penserei di sì. Perché?"

"Mah, non so. Cattolica è un paese, un paese di mare vicino a Riccione... fra Riccione e Pesaro..., e gli ebrei, come sai, hanno tutti cognomi di città e paesi."
Si era irrigidito.
"Qui ti sbagli," aveva ribattuto seccamente. [pp. 471–72]

("Tell me," I said, "have you . . . I mean your family . . . always been Catholics?"
"I should say so," he answered, with a brief, proud smile. "Why?"
"Oh, I don't know. Cattolica is the name of a town, a town on the coast near Riccione . . . between Riccione and Pesaro . . . and Italian Jews, as you know, all have the names of towns and cities."
He stiffened.
"In the first place, that's not correct," he replied at once.) [W:D, p. 31]

More than displaying Carlo's negative feelings about Jews, the narrator's question betrays his own effort to equate the celebrated classmate with himself—an act largely of sadomasochistic motivation that will find its full satisfaction in the boy's relationship with Luciano. His question is a challenge to Carlo, an implied threat to the Catholic boy's very identity, a pale proleptic trace of the Nazi pursuit of "impure" Aryan blood. How fiercely ironical is the encounter, in which the Jewish boy plays the part of the Nazi inquisitioner!

The above dialogue takes place at Christmastime, after a conversation between the narrator and a longtime friend, Otello Forti, who has come home from *collegio* and is now about to depart again. The juxtaposed encounters, filling the entire short chapter, constitute what may be Bassani's most potent parable of historical Jewish ostracism and persecution. Both meetings of the schoolboys are dominated by notations of exclusion: For the first time in ten years none of Otello's siblings has invited the narrator to help construct the *presepio*; Otello refuses his friend's offer to help pack his baggage; neither has written the other for some time; and Otello has a new friend—a sign of the narrator's displacement (pp. 467–69). Compositionally this lost friendship—unrelated to differences of religion—gives way immediately to a lacking friendship—for reasons vaguely infused with religious content, including Carlo Cattolica's name.

The author punctuates the two encounters with references to christological sculptures. The first, in Otello's home, is a representation of Christ's birth in a "great, resplendent crèche" (p. 467). The second, in a church next to school, is a representation of Christ's death, an "atrocious scene": "il corpo livido e misero del Cristo morto, disteso sulla nuda terra, con attorno, impietriti in muti gesti, in mute smorfie, in lacrime che non avrebbero mai avuto né termine né sfogo di grida, i parenti e gli amici accorsi" [p. 470] (the livid, wretched body of the dead Christ, lying on the bare earth, and around it, petrified in their grief, with mute gestures, grimaces, tears that would never end or bring solace, the friends and relatives who had gathered [W:*D*, p. 29]). What emerges in the friend's house as a sign of personal rejection assumes greater precision, in the church, as a sign of religious violence. The victimage of Christ, with its primary cause in politico-religious persecution and its communal effect of unending, inconsolable grief, embodies also the coming in history of Christian intoleration and Nazi extermination of Jews, and the inconsolable grief of the Jewish survivors— numbering, of course, Giorgio Bassani. The auspicious, "refulgent" birth of the infant Jesus is immediately, that is, violently, blackened out by the "utterly atrocious" death of the sacrificed God. Bassani takes care to present the two sculptures as social events. In the manger scene, the narrative ignores the joyful entourage beholding the newborn child, highlighting instead the viewer's (narrator's) absence of admiration for the nativity representation, caused by his exclusion from its construction:

> Mi aveva subito portato ad ammirare il grande, fulgido Presepio, collocato come sempre nel salotto a pianterreno, ma alla cui messa in opera, quell'-anno, per la prima volta dopo almeno dieci anni, nessuno dei suoi fratelli si era ricordato di invitarmi a collaborare. [p. 467]

> (He took me at once to admire the great, resplendent crèche, set up, as always, in the living room on the ground floor. . . . That year, for the first time in at least ten years, none of his brothers had remembered to invite me to help arrange it.) [W:*D*, p. 24]

The description of the *Pietà* highlights the pious, mourning relatives and friends—the Madonna, St. John, Joseph of Arimathea, Simon, the Magdalen, two holy women—(p. 470)—in their everlasting posture of grief.

As he looks upon the sculptured figures, the narrator remembers his aunt Malvina, "the only Catholic aunt I had." Then the narrator sees Carlo kneeling behind a pew. The latter shows interest in hearing about the Catholic aunt (actually, a great-aunt—the Catholic link is thin indeed), especially about her "passione fondamentale": visiting all the churches of Ferrara (p. 471). For the first time in many years together in school, the two boys engage in extended conversation. The possibility of a deeply desired friendship advances, thanks to the narrator's part-Catholic ancestry: Catholic blood is good. But when the Jew wonders whether Carlo may have any Jewish ancestry, the Catholic stiffens, denying the possibility, and the conversation ends: Jewish blood is bad. In this book so little conditioned by historical Jewish persecution and tightly held within the context of schoolboy rivalries almost a decade before official anti-Semitism, the critical thematics of friendship and betrayal raise a specter of persecution that manages to infiltrate the schoolroom and bourgeois familial bounds. The humiliation that induces a sense of unredeeming despair in the narrator links textually with Christ's humiliation on the cross, not in terms of the individuals persecuted, but of the religious groups they represent and the extremity of persecution to which each was subjected.

The narrator's mother, a figure of the innocent victim (unlike the son, whose character marks him with culpability), embodies persecution in a sensual and Jewish framework. Another female character, drawn from history and given the major female part in the homonymously titled short story "Gli ultimi anni di Clelia Trotti," embodies persecution in terms of political dissent. Her sexuality, too, thematizes political repression; it operates not sensually or promiscuously, however, but sentimentally to express the outmoded, turn-of-the-century ideology to which she is still wed. Clelia is at once heroic and pathetic, an idealistic and courageous former Socialist leader either imprisoned, in forced political exile, or under surveillance most of her adult life. Her last years, underscored somewhat ambiguously in the story's title, have at least two reference points: the period in which Bruno Lattes befriends her (1939 to 1943, with emphasis on the time of major narrative interest, 1939–40) and the period of Bruno's flight to America (1943 to 1946, with narrative attention restricted primarily to the scene of Clelia's funeral in 1946). Chronologically an epilogue, the funeral scene in "Anni" opens the narrative. Its subject proper is Bruno's acquaintance with Clelia and their numerous secret meetings to talk about her past and his future; she is in her sixties when they meet, he in his twenties. Bassani's technique of a prelude-epilogue, which he will use later in the *Giardino*, immediately discloses the destinies of the major characters. In this case, Clelia's Communist-organized funeral, tantamount to a political resurrection, instructs the reader on her legendary Socialist past, which in turn becomes the touchstone of her helplessness in the remaining three-fourths of the (retrospective) narrative. Similarly but inversely, foreknowledge of Bruno's safe flight and eventual good fortune lightens the stifling air of Jewish repression in the Ferrara of 1939–40 that menaces his life and those of his compatriots. Bruno's successful escape from the invading Germans in 1943, his emigration to the United States, his budding academic career and greatly desired ("sospiratissima") American citizenship (p. 109) are textual rewards I shall turn to again in the next chapter, in the context of the authorial construct.

Politics is the ironized subject of the opening chapter of "Anni." A large crowd of spectators in the Piazza della Certosa, which borders the vast municipal cemetery, watches a funeral cortege of bearded ex-partisans and peasant women in hammer-and-sickle-patterned red tunics escorting a casket, at its head the distinguished members of the ex-Committee of National Liberation: a seeming reexperience of the "excitement of the Liberation," a "magical return to the climate of 1945" (p.99). The anonymous narrative voice, clearly Ferrarese, ironizes this carefully staged production that deploys a "forest" of red banners, scores of eulogizing signs ("Socialist Martyr," "Heroic Guide of the Working

Class"), and red roses and carnations in the hands of the peasant "priestesses of Socialism" (p. 100). The lightly ironic narration, in fact, creates its own carefully staged production of the postwar "tide" of Communist political power that in another context will play a part in the suicidal death of Edgardo Limentani (*Airone*). Here, however, the narrative's male hero, Bruno Lattes, is successful and only temporarily returned to Ferrara: the restrained irony is an indirect assertion of his commanding textual position.

The political theatrics that spotlight Clelia Trotti in hope of eternalizing the recent Communist accession to power are dimmed and extended by another dimension of the scene, the cemetery itself, which the narrator takes time to explain to the uninformed reader in the story's opening paragraph:

> A definire il vasto complesso architettonico del Camposanto Comunale di Ferrara come bello . . . c'è rischio anche da noi di far nascere in giro le solite risate. . . . Ciò nondimeno . . . la veduta improvvisa della piazza della Certosa e dell'adiacente cimitero dà sempre, inutile negarlo, un'impressione lieta, quasi di festa. [p. 97]

> (If you call the huge architectual complex of Ferrara's city cemetery beautiful . . . there's a risk, even among us, that people will start laughing at you. . . . Nonetheless . . . the sudden sight of Piazza della Certosa and the neighboring cemetery [there's no sense denying it] leaves you with a happy, almost festive, feeling.)

The terracotta angels along the edges of the colonnade, although posed as if to blast their long, bronze trumpets of Judgment Day, are entirely unawesome: "non hanno nulla di tremendo" [ibid.] (there is nothing fearsome about them). They appear instead, with their features of big and robust local types ("ragazzoni robusti"), like boys eager to play (pp. 97–98). Far from instilling a sense of desolation in the bystander, the tranquil and solitary place has always been a meeting place for lovers (p. 98). Within the aura of eternity, the bombed bell tower of the adjacent church—looking like a bloody stump ("sanguigno troncone")—proclaims the illusoriness of every guarantee of eternity; the message of hope that radiates from the unscarred colonnade is just "un inganno, un trucco, una menzogna bella e buona" [ibid.] (a fraud, a trick, an out-and-out lie).

Bassani's baroque portrait of the cemetery and the funeral blends images of deception, illusion, and paradox in a theatrical flourish for which one of the players, Bruno, has a particular appreciation. Observing the familiar anti-Fascists assembled to honor Clelia, Bruno marvels at the lack of change in their appearance, as if they were wax figures playing the part of their former selves. The thematic of illusion pervading this text gathers into its empty embrace an authentic demon of imprisonment, whose victims include Clelia Trotti first of all, but also Bruno's father, Clelia's jailer-sister, even the honorable former deputy Mauro Bottecchiari, and, finally, all the Ferrarese. The archvictim Clelia be-

comes the agent of Bruno's salvation; without her, he would likely have numbered among the many victims (and did, for a time) for his persistent discounting
of his father's advice to flee the country. Clelia's desperate self-deceit is a mirror
that cracks Bruno's naive expectations and convinces him, when the opportunity
miraculously arises with the fall of Mussolini in 1943, to abandon rather than
battle his country. Clelia is a chiasmic center of trajectories that point Bruno and
Ferrara toward opposite destinies: the young man toward liberation and the community toward putrefaction.

Clelia's last years are also the last (narrativized) years of Bruno, a period
(1943–46) of her distintegration in prison and his freedom and self-fulfillment.
Historically the years span the period of Nazi terror in northern Italy. Bruno
thinks of this time as he hears the emotional voice of the venerable Bottecchiari
eulogizing Clelia's life; he thinks particularly of the "beginning of that final and
ferocious three-year period" when his parents were deported and when successful flight spared him their fate or else probable death in the November 1943 massacre of Jewish and anti-Fascist citizens (p. 104). "Gli ultimi tre anni contavano
insomma come una intera vita" [p. 105] (The last three years, after all, added
up to a whole life), he concludes: his life and the life of the city reached the limit
of mortality. Death, to Bruno, still seems to oppress Ferrara: the city and his
acquaintances are even ossifying his own memories. Bent over and shabby now,
the old guard of the Committee of National Liberation seems a worthless little
gang ("piccola squadra di nullità" [p. 101]). Clelia's funeral thus stands for the
burial of all Ferrara and justifies Bruno's own decision to expatriate. This perspective in the opening narrative prevalorizes Bruno in the way the preface of
the *Giardino* prevalorizes Micòl. The young woman is an idealized specular image of the mystery and joy of creation; the mature Bruno of the first pages of
"Anni" represents a moral and social strength remarkably different from the
other Bruno and first-person figures that inhabit the *Romanzo*. Micòl dies a
sacrificial victim of a persecuting regime, but Bruno survives—a war and an
earlier self—to transcend and judge harshly the ossified remnants of Ferrarese
moral leadership. Both celebrated figures stand as direct (Bruno) or indirect
(Micòl) critics of their society.

Bruno's desire to meet Clelia is related to the growing persecution of the
Jews: "Nel tardo autunno del 1939, quando pressappoco a un anno di distanza
dalla promulgazione delle leggi razziali, decise di muovere alla ricerca di Clelia
Trotti, di lei Bruno Lattes non sapeva ancora quasi niente" [p. 106] (In late autumn of 1939 when he decided to track down Clelia Trotti—which was about
a year after the anti-Jewish laws had been proclaimed—Bruno Lattes knew almost nothing about her). Of all Bassani's fiction, this narrative is most dominated by the presence and immediate effect of the anti-Jewish laws. If these laws
engraved on disbelieving minds a sense of profound betrayal of Jewish Italians
by their national kin, they did not spare the Jewish population a sense also of

self-betrayal. That task of conscience in "Anni" is assigned to the longtime anti-Fascist lawyer Mauro Bottecchiari, "il capo riconosciuto e indiscusso dell'-antifascismo cittadino" [p. 101] (the recognized and indisputable leader of local anti-Fascism), who dared to walk along Ferrara's main street, Corso Giovecca, "sventolando spavaldamente in distanza la zazzera bianchissima, addirittura luminosa, in faccia ai pochi amici e ai molti avversari" [p. 109] (with his snow-white, absolutely luminous great mane of hair fluttering defiantly in the distance, facing his few friends and his many enemies). When Bruno goes to Bottecchiari's office to inquire about Clelia's address, he grasps the old lawyer's unspoken condemnation of him and his coreligionists:

> "Eh già," dicevano nel frattempo i suoi occhi azzurri, pieni di rosse venuzze, lampeggianti di ironico trionfo, "eh già! Per vent'anni mi avete guardato con sospetto, evitato e spregiato *anche voi* come antifascista, come sovversivo, come avversario del Regime, e adesso che il *vostro* bel Regime vi butta fuori, adesso eccovi a Canossa con tanto di orecchie basse e di coda fra le gambe!" [p. 107][24]

> ("Oh yes!" his blue eyes said, meantime, his blue red-veined eyes, flashing with ironical triumph, "Oh yes! For twenty years now you've been looking suspiciously at me, avoiding me, despising me as an anti-Fascist, as a subversive, an enemy of the Regime, and now this same precious Regime of yours has kicked you out, look at you, here you are [in Canossa, with your ears hanging down and your tail between your legs!]") [Q:*P*, p. 137]

The fiery lawyer, unlike the equally outspoken Clelia, is able to remain free during all the years of Fascist rule. No doubt Bruno prefers to meet Clelia rather than join forces with Mauro because she is one of the persecuted. Just as important—or, perhaps, more so—Clelia is a woman and a stranger. Her formidable history of militant leadership in the Socialist party before and after the First World War and her long years of persecution by the Fascists are common knowledge. Bruno believes—because (as it turns out) he does not know the real person—that she will be able to help him who is now, like her, one of the persecuted. Bruno's first steps toward a "new life" begin literally with his first steps in search of Clelia's residence. As the narrative describes his walk, it brusquely interjects the information that Bruno is still a "prisoner of love": "Ancora invischiata dalla passione che fino all'agosto di quello stesso anno lo aveva reso schiavo di una delle più brillanti e corteggiate ragazze di Ferrara, l'Adriana Trentini" [p. 109] (Still entrapped by a passion that until August of this year had kept him a slave of one of the most brilliant and courted young women of Ferrara, Adriana Trentini).

From other stories in which she appears, the reader knows that Adriana is very young, very beautiful, blond, statuesque, and Catholic; in this story, knowledge of the character is limited to the remarks just quoted. The failed romance between her and Bruno, as recounted even in its brevity, connects the onerous period of the anti-Jewish laws with an aching erotic void in Bruno, as if the two phenomena are one and the same. The Jewish youth projects his anger at Adriana's rejection of him, and indeed his own self-loathing, on the elegant prototypes of his former lover passing by. His interest in Clelia is an attempt to reenergize himself, to substitute his very young and much-courted lover with an old and long-ostracized utopian idealist: thus erotic passion translates into political passion.

Bruno's quest of Clelia is imbued with unreal and supernatural expectations, arising first in the narrative's prologized consecration of her in the scene of the funeral procession and again in the plotted obstacles that both inflame the young pursuer's (and the reader's) desire and slow his face-to-face meeting with her. Clelia finally appears in person at the precise midpoint of the narrative (on the eighteenth of thirty-six pages); the chapter keeps account of the stages of Bruno's disenchantment, a process that occurs in the actual and emblematic winter of the year filled with anti-Jewish decrees. Bruno comes face to face with political reality: the global imprisonment that is soon to be the only future available to the Jews. As Clelia nostalgically reminisces about her past incarcerations and idly envisages a new socialist future incarnated in Bruno, he quickly sees her as a figure of imprisonment and delusion. A snowfall closes the chapter, as if suffocating the future of Bruno and everyone else. With war imminent and permission to leave the country about to become impossible (despite Bruno's father's privileged status as a first-hour Fascist), the only road to follow is "evidentemente quella che portava tutti, nessuno escluso, incontro a un futuro vuoto di speranza" [p. 122] (clearly the one that was carrying everyone, with no exceptions, toward a future devoid of hope). All Bruno can do is to be a part, "non fosse altro che per pietà e umiltà, alle fantasticherie solitarie, ai disperati passatempi, ai poveri, miserabili deliri da ergastolani onanisti dei propri compagni di viaggio" [p. 122] (if only out of pity and humility, of the lonely daydreams, the desperate amusements, the wretched and empty wild dreams such as impotent life-term convicts might have about their own traveling companions). This startling *de profundis* lamentation for those—including Bruno—who are about to die ineffectually, like life-term prisoners, is a slow, dark wail repeated by the nightlong, thick-falling snow that Bruno predicts will shortly spread over "tutta la città, prigione e ghetto comune, il suo silenzio opprimente" [p. 122] (the entire city, at once prison and ghetto, its oppressive silence). These words, like the blankness of the remaining page, picture the expiration of life: in Bruno, in Clelia, in Bruno's father, who so resembles the aged revolutionary, and in Ferrara itself. Although the reader already knows that death is not Bruno's fate, the character's identification with and compassion for the dead ("non fosse altro che per pietà e umiltà") is a form of participation in their collective death. This act of participation images the textualized persona, a writer who, like Emily Dickinson, poises himself to recount his vision from an uncanny point beyond the grave. Bruno's *pietà* for the persecuted, like the short story itself, is a tribute less to Clelia than to the Jews of Ferrara, whom Clelia emblematizes. Bassani's interfusion of Clelia's "prison" and Bruno's father's "ghetto" constitutes all of Ferrara under oppression. For Bruno, Clelia and his father are dying dreamers: the one dreams of a rebirth of Socialism; the other, of his son's brilliant career in America or Palestine.

The elder Lattes represents the mass of middle-class Italian Jews, including volunteer soldiers decorated in the First World War, who with a keen sense of patriotism and an equal fear of Socialism backed and joined the Fascist party at its founding a year after the war. They maintained their support up to the proclamation of the anti-Jewish decrees; Ferrara had a Jewish Fascist mayor for many years until the decrees banned Jews from public service.

Clelia represents the bright-eyed, if confused, brand of reformist Socialism that organized thousands of abused agrarian workers and accomplished early miracles in the Po Valley at the turn of the century until violence, strikes, and the Russian Revolution harnessed support all over Italy for the fledgling Fascist party and its club-swinging *squadristi d'azione*, who promised to wipe out the Socialist blight. Alda Costa, upon whom Clelia Trotti is modeled, was a schoolteacher in Ferrara for many years — until she was fired in 1926 for refusing to salute her superiors in the required Fascist-Roman style. At that time or earlier, she was secretary of the Socialist federation in the province of Ferrara and a major contributor to the Socialist newspapers *La Bandiera Socialista* and *La Scintilla*. Soon after losing her job, she spent five years in political confinement in southern Italy and a total of several months of imprisonment in Ferrara. Costa was taken to the nearby town of Copparo for her final imprisonment. She died there in 1944. The following year, after the Liberation, on the anniversary of the 1943 massacre at the Este castle — when, along with many others, Costa was arrested and detained for possible execution by the Salò Fascists — her body was transferred "through the sunny streets of Ferrara, in that autumn of hope" to the Church of the Certosa in Ferrara's municipal cemetery, where she was buried close to other anti-Fascist "illustrious citizens."[25]

Bassani's Clelia dies in Codigoro, the town in which Edgardo Limentani rests, eats, and looks into a display window that inspires him to take his life. Edgardo recalls Clelia's fate when he notices several faded street signs honoring illustrious Communists (Marx, Engels, Stalin, Gramsci — and Clelia Trotti); Edgardo remembers Clelia as the "famosa maestra elementare, socialista, morta di stenti durante l'inverno del '44 proprio a Codigoro, nelle carceri locali" [*Airone*, p. 645] (famous elementary-school teacher, a socialist, who died of privations during the winter of '44 right here in Codigoro, in the local prison [W:*H*, p. 148]).[26] Clelia's manner of death emphasizes her isolation and neglect (as the prematurely faded street sign conveys). Alda Costa died of bronchopneumonia in the *spring* of 1944 (April 30) in the hospital at Copparo.[27] Bassani's preference for death by disregard and death in winter, as well as his preference for Clelia's post-Liberation burial in nonconsecrated ground, heightens the figure's loneliness and marginality. In a Bassanian text, these traits are signs of dignity and potential grace. For the protagonist of *Airone*, Codigoro functions symbolically as a city of otherness, an extraneous place of personal trial and self-discovery. For Clelia, Codigoro seems to represent a communal locus of sacrificial separation, a Fascist attempt to prevent her "contagion" from spreading within Ferrara, a precondition that intensifies her jubilant reentry and apotheosis, after death, to her native home. The town of Copparo undoubtedly functioned symbolically this way in the real historical drama of Alda Costa, but it plays no role in Bassani's texts; such historical faithfulness would result in a diminished signifier. Codigoro resonates with carefully programmed intertextual significance.

In addition to Alda Costa, Bassani uses the prominent Ferrarese lawyer Mario Cavallari, who had close Socialist party ties with Costa, as the model for Mauro Bottecchiari. In "Anni," Clelia and Mauro are known to have been close associates in their youth; "it was whispered" that they had been lovers, "at least until the First World War broke out" (p. 106). This rumor, reported early in the text, promptly introduces the sexual factor into the legend of Clelia as a humanitarian reformer. Mauro seems to confirm the rumor to Bruno with a wink of presumed understanding:

> Ebbene, che cosa aveva voluto significare, l'onorevole Bottecchiari, con quell'ammicco di intesa? . . . non aveva voluto magari alludere al legame che un tempo lo aveva unito, e forse, chissà, tuttora lo univa in segreto, all'antica compagna di partito: allusione questa sufficiente, era chiaro, a togliere anche al poco già detto qualsiasi peso *politico*? Infatti era proprio così che ci si comportava di solito a Ferrara, quando, un po' vantandosene e un po' vergognandosene, ci si confidava da uomo a uomo (ma tra borghesi, soprattutto!) una relazione con una ragazza del popolo. [p. 108]

> (What on earth did [the Honorable Bottecchiari] mean by that understanding wink of his? . . . was it, perhaps, . . . meant to refer tactfully to the way he had once been bound, and who knows might still secretly be bound, to his old political girl-friend: which would obviously be quite enough to remove every sort of *political* indiscretion from even the small amount he had said? And anyway, wasn't it exactly the way people were in the habit of behaving in Ferrara . . . when "respectable" people, half bragging, half abashed, and with man-to-man winks, confessed to an affair with a working-class girl?) [Q:*P*, p. 139]

Mauro's wink reduces the extraordinary personhood of Clelia to her humble class origins and her sex. She is a sexual victim as well as a political one. No wonder that the wink turns Bruno's thoughts to the honorable attorney's incapacity to remain entirely untouched by the pervasive immorality of the times. It is "closed within these thoughts" (p. 109) that Bruno's erotic relationship with Adriana flashes into his mind.

Bruno, like Clelia, if on a smaller scale, is also a sexual as well as political victim. When the young Jewish man and the old working-class woman first meet, they each reach out for a person who is not the one before them. Bruno's first response, born of despair, is entirely, if self-consciously, fanciful: he sees a fairytale princess come to life in the place of the wicked witch or monster (Clelia's sister), who on countless prior occasions had barred Bruno's entry into the house:

> Doveva succedere. In qualsiasi favola che si rispetti . . . è raro che la vicenda non si concluda con la sparizione del Mostro o con la sua metamorfosi. D'un tratto l'incantesimo si era spezzato, la signora Codecà era scomparsa. . . . [In sua vece appare] la donnetta risecchita e trasandata, la specie di beghina di cui parlava la gente! Per sincerarsene bastava guardarle gli occhi. Erano tuttora gli occhi stupendi della libera, ardita fanciulla . . . eroina della classe operaia. [p. 115]

> (It had to happen. In any fairy tale you admire . . . you rarely find that the story does not conclude with the monster's disappearance or metamorphosis. Suddenly the spell was broken, Mrs. Codecà disappeared. . . . [In her place stood] the withered, shabby, sort of pious church-going little woman people talked about! You only had to look at her eyes to be convinced. They were still the stupendous eyes of the liberated and daring girl . . . the heroine of the working class.)

The spell of the monster is broken imediately, and once over the threshold the spell of the princess is also broken. Clelia leads Bruno to a sitting room—her place, or, rather, her prison—in which "tutto parlava a Bruno di noia, di accidia, di lunghi anni di gretta, ingloriosa segregazione e di oblio" [p. 117] (everything spoke to Bruno of boredom, indolence, and long years of shabby and inglorious seclusion and oblivion). And although Clelia, unlike even Honorable Bottecchiari, has remained "most pure in soul," now (Bruno realizes) she is a piece of wreckage, an impotent and pathetic relic: "La guardava, la patetica perseguitata antifascista, la pietosa prigioniera. . . . Quale specie di aiuto—pensava, continuando a fissare quel povero collo mal lavato—poteva lui attendersi da Clelia Trotti, da Rovigatti, e dalla cerchia chissà poi se davvero esistente dei loro umili amici?" [p. 117] (He looked at her, such a pathetic persecuted anti-Fascist, such a pitiful prisoner. . . . What sort of help, he thought—still staring at her poor, badly washed neck—could he expect from Clelia Trotti, from Rovigatti, from the circle, if it really still existed, of their humble friends). The new life Bruno anticipates as a result of knowing Clelia is born nonetheless precisely from her demystification, which convinces Bruno to cease their "colloquio grottesco" (grotesque discussions) and heed instead his father's advice to get out of the country (ibid.). As we know from the opening chapter, however, it takes Bruno almost four years to act. In the meantime he meets with Clelia, who views him as the promise of a renewed future. Despite the obstacles of a frightened guardian-sister and increased surveillance by the dreaded secret police, Clelia and Bruno meet frequently in different places: her home, the Jewish school where Bruno teaches, his home, and, finally, in Piazza della Certosa.

When Clelia arrives unexpectedly at the Jewish school after Bruno's many unsuccessful attempts to get past her sister, the old Socialist—who, when Bruno first met her, looked like a *beghina* (a person of religious devotion)—appears before her young friend "assettata con cura, la cipria se l'era data perfino sul collo" [p. 125] (trim and tidy, and powdered right down to her neck). The earlier *Romanzo* follows this description with the blatant "aveva voluto farsi bella per lui!" [1974, p. 142] (she had wanted to make herself beautiful for him!). But the more subdued version is clear enough: winter has turned to spring, for Clelia as for the climate. Her excitation blurs the distinctions between her reawakened ideological ambitions and her personal rejuvenation. Reminiscent of the time when her impassioned political activism and her romantic liaison with Mauro were fused, Clelia waxes ecstatic over Italy's declaration of war in June of 1940, because she believes that Fascism has decreed its own ruination *and* that Bruno—unlike the young Mauro in 1915, who used Italy's entry into war as an excuse to get rid of her—must now remain in Ferrara. Before long, Clelia and Bruno are meeting frequently after dinner, in Bruno's study. A feeling of playfulness develops between them that takes on, for Bruno, an "aria di sotterfugio erotico" [p. 127] (air of erotic subterfuge), fueled by the uncertainty of the moment of Clelia's arrival and his eagerness to see her.

Bruno and Clelia's final narrated meeting, which occurs three years before their actual final meeting, takes place in the Piazza della Certosa, a favorite lovers' glade, as the first chapter points out. They meet here to avoid the increased police surveillance, but their encounters are charged with the erotic intimations characteristic of the area. What is more, the jealous cobbler Rovigatti, Clelia's friend since elementary school days and reluctant Gallehault of the clandestine appointments, intensifies the subplot of erotico-political intrigue. Clelia tells Bruno about her long acquaintance with the cobbler, looking at him "non senza ironia, più che mai giovane" [p. 129] (not without irony, and seemingly young). For Bassani the hallowed square of Ferrara's cemetery on the city's boundary stands with the encircling ramparts as historical spaces of politicized eroticism. The city walls, concretizing the might of the Este *polis*, gradually assume erotico-political significance. In the opening tale of the *Romanzo* ("Lida"), Lida and David make carnal but affective love on the ramparts; and the still-unmarried Elia and Gemma ("Passeggiata") seal their unhappy bond there. The falsehearted romances of these earlier stories heighten the more complex passions of Clelia and Bruno. Of particular significance during the last evening recounted in "Anni" is Bruno's fascination with a young "Aryan" couple in the piazza. He is there with Clelia. Up to this moment, her talk has dominated their meetings: the blackshirts' rough treatment of her in the twenties; the self-knowledge that imprisonment teaches; her (impossible) desire to be buried among the "illustri sia pure eretici" (illustrious if heretical) deceased in the beautiful piazza (p. 129). In this lover's glen Clelia's mind remains fixed on her own political beliefs and Bruno's political future. By contrast, on the evening of the conversation that closes the text, Bruno's mind attaches to the sentimental sexual scene before him, which appears to show a healthy bond between a tall blond boy and a girl who runs to meet him, "anche lei bionda e molto bella" [p. 132] (she, too, blond and very beautiful). As at his very first sight of Clelia, the sight of the affectionate pair enchants Bruno: "Bruno non si saziava di guardarli. . . . Più che belli gli apparivano meravigliosi, irraggiungibili" [p. 133] (Bruno couldn't look at them enough. . . . More than beautiful, they seemed marvelous, unreachable).[28] Hardly hearing Clelia's words through his rapture, Bruno "with a desperate love and hate" fixes his gaze upon them: "Eccoli dunque là i campioni, i prototipi della razza!" [ibid.] (Look at them there, the champions, the racial prototypes!). With Clelia beside him, Bruno has followed the pair to the adjacent ramparts, the common city sanctum for lovemaking that the narrative draws to the reader's immediate attention. Bruno's vision of unstained normal love (a resentful envy of mainstream religious affiliation that haunts Bassani's texts) hurls back at him his own isolation and impotence as well as Clelia's, whose real world is her mind's fantasy of the past. "Perduta come sempre nel suo solitario, eterno vaneggiamento da reclusa" [ibid.] (Lost as always in her lonely, endless raving, the result of her reclusive life), the old revolutionary has taken no notice of the young couple. Bruno's notice—and its privileged narrative positioning to climax and conclude the short story—suggests that his salvation (his successful escape and eventual expatriation) originates in the vision and self-knowledge he achieves at sunset on the ramparts. The *possibility* of his self-knowledge stems from an erotic factor that traces back to his relationship with Adriana Trentini and climaxes in his displaced erotic attachment to Clelia. His attainment of knowledge is of a kind with the episode in the *Giardino*, where the young protagonist, in despair over a failing grade, is healed by the thirteen-year-old (that is, blossoming womanhood of) Micòl. Each of these sexual relations is either a preliminary or an impure form of the fully liberating erotic (though not fully sexual) relation with the twenty-two-year old Micòl that concludes the *Giardino*. In "Anni," Bruno's liberation is followed — to under-score this event as the climactic narrative moment — by three years that pass on the narrative margin, even though his continued meetings with Clelia and his escape occur in those years.

The scene of the "Aryan" lovers represents the final — and the only successful — interpenetration of the erotic and the political in "Anni." Clelia's victimization by Mauro is rooted in her social and sexual status; her victimization by Bruno, in her captive and erotic-surrogate status. Bruno's abuse of Clelia stems from his need for *self*-sustenance; his bad faith is spelled out in the text's 1974 epigraph (expunged in the 1980 volume) that cites a Svevian moribund who "non accettò neppur di parlare con delle persone che lo amavano perché *egli aveva fatto creder loro* di amarle" [1974, p. 111; emphasis added] (refused to speak even to people who loved him because he had made them think he loved them). Bruno's need of Clelia retrocedes to Adriana's sexual rejection of him, which in turn retrocedes to the anti-Jewish laws: Bruno's sexual unsuccess is equivalent to his social impotence. Like his father self-incarcerated at home ad formally excluded from social organizations, and like Clelia formally and informally excluded from virtually all social intercourse, Bruno sees himself as helpless — impotent and sterile — before the burgeoning Fascist restrictions on Jewish Ferrara. Following the early reminder of his failed romance with Adriana, the narrative, in its temporal sweep of seven years, is silent on Bruno's relations with women except for Clelia. The culminating scene of the blond, happy teenagers projects in sexual imagery Bruno's desire of full participation in society.

In the narrative context of Jewish deportation to Germany, Bruno's choice to escape rather than to join the Resistance movement is implicitly justified at the outset of "Anni," with his postwar return to Ferrara:

All'inizio di quell'ultimo, atroce triennio, i suoi genitori, che mai avevano creduto di dover fuggire, mai avevano accettato di fornirsi di carte false, erano stati portati via dai tedeschi, e i loro due nomi adesso figuravano insieme con quasi duecento altri nella lapide che la Comunità israelitica aveva fatto porre sulla facciata del Tempio, in via Mazzini. E lui? Lui, al contrario, da Ferrara era scappato. Se ne era allontanato al momento giusto *per non subire la stessa sorte di suo padre e di sua madre, oppure, magari, per non farsi fucilare nel dicembre successivo da quelli di Salò.* [pp. 104–5; emphasis added]

(At the beginning of those terrifying last three years, his parents — who had never thought they would have to flee, never tried to get false papers — were taken away by the Germans. Their names were now inscribed — along with almost two hundred others — on the plaque the Jewish community put on the outside of the temple on Via Mazzini. And he? He, on the other hand, escaped from Ferrara. He got away at the right time, thus avoiding his father and mother's fate and even, possibly, the fate of being shot the following December by the Salò Fascists.)

Both mortal dangers avoided by Bruno implicate his Jewishness. The second one is an elliptical reference to the oft-cited massacre at the center of "Notte."

The narrative makes no claims for Bruno as a Resistance fighter; its political focus is solely upon his grave fears regarding Jewish persecution. Bassani, on the other hand, was a founding member of the highly respected anti-Fascist *Partito d'Azione* and spent three months in prison in Ferrara. The author's exclusion of political activity on the part of Bruno in this tale (which is otherwise dense with autobiographical data), as well as his invention of Bruno's (nonautobiographical) flight to the United States, allows his character as an *outsider* to recognize the political travesties of the postwar administration. More important, Bruno's nonactivism isolates his Jewishness during the "atroce triennio" (horrible three years), as well as the issue of Jewish status at all times, while political alliances and struggles are always, to some extent, mutable and extrinsic. Jewish identity, from the anti-Jewish laws to the end of the war, is at best a political state of nonexistence (Bruno's father immobile in his study) and at worst, extinction (Bruno's father in a concentration camp). Bassani magnifies his thematics of Jewish extermination by a radical autobiographical untruth: his parents' political naiveté and consequent death-camp destiny. In fact, both parents fled to safety with false passports shortly after their son reached Florence.

Bruno's return to his liberated homeland is the occasion of a startling political lesson. His memory of the "Aryan" youths leaps to mind during Clelia's funeral as he sights a very blond girl and boy who, "it was clear," were in the Piazza della Certosa for a lovers' appointment (p. 103). These later models of amorous and racial perfection, aggressively indifferent to the funeral ceremony "come se uscissero, *teenagers*, ignari di tutto, dalle pagine di una rivista illustrata americana" [p. 104] (as if these teenagers, unaware of everything, had stepped right out of the pages of an American picture magazine), represent a political and historical blankness that effectively—and with lacerating irony—buries Clelia out of reach of the "new" Italy, sealing her in a coffin with no trace, silencing a graveside reach to new "pupils" who might safeguard the future. Like the chrome-plated motor scooter the girl rides, with its special gadget to increase the noise of the engine exhaust, these teenagers seem intent on drawing attention only to themselves. Their lack of historical awareness similarly threatens to eradicate, for future generations, any moral lessons regarding anti-Semitism; and thus this young pair threatens the very story in which they participate, while the author attempts with words to combat the blank pages of their minds.

Although Clelia's wish to be buried near the "heretical" illustrious deceased in the nonconsecrated Piazza della Certosa is eventually granted, the narrative dedicated to her undermines the promises fulfilled in liberation, much as the statues of playful angels on the piazza colonnade diminish the awe of the Judgment Day they wait to trumpet. And yet, in death, Clelia succeeds in possessing the love-consecrated piazza, which was her far-fetched "pio desiderio" in life (p. 129). The site suffices to symbolize Clelia's high ideological sentiment but also, if only metaphorically, her sexual solitude.

Chapter 5
The Act of Self-Inscription

. . . finché visse, Lida Mantovani ricordò con emozione l'evento del
parto . . .

"Lida Mantovani"

Bassani: Quando cominciai a scriverlo [*L'airone*] mi trovavo in uno stato
d'animo particolare. Ero amareggiato, stanco: ogni rapporto con le persone
e con la vita era divenuto *arido*, non aveva più ragione. Mi pareva di vivere
in una specie di *vuoto*, mi mancavano gli interessi. Per la prima volta
sperimentavo una condizione terribile: quella della *sterilità*, del
non-amore. . . .
Cancogni: E quando hai finito, ti sei liberato dall'indifferenza mortale che ti op-
primeva?
Bassani: Sì, è la parola giusta: è stata una *liberazione*. Ho provato una *felicità*
immensa. *D'un colpo* mi sono liberato da due mali: la *fatica* provata a realiz-
zare il mio progetto (nessun libro, prima, m'era costato tanto) e *l'impassibilità*
davanti alle cose che m'aveva fatto dubitare di me stesso[1] [emphasis added].

Bassani: When I began to write it, I knew I was in a very special state of mind.
I was bitter and tired; my contact with people and life had become arid and
no longer had any meaning for me. I seemed to be living in a kind of void;
nothing interested me. For the first time, I felt in a terrible state of sterility
and nonlove. . . .
Cancogni: And when it was over, did you feel liberated from the lethal indifference that oppressed you?

Bassani: Yes, that's the right word; it was a liberation. I experienced enormous joy. I was instantly liberated from two painful problems: the effort expended on finishing my project (no book had ever cost me so much before) and the apathy I felt toward everything that made me doubt myself.)

The pattern of Bassani's life is consistent with the pattern of his fiction: renewal (joy, self-liberation, writing) deriving from emptiness (aridity, nonlove, a sense of imprisonment). This pattern of psychic and artistic processes, reflecting a natural cycle of life that is followed by death and rebirth, also constitutes a temporal and spatial configuration akin to the biblical history and topography of Exodus: The Egyptian land of suffering is both Ferrara after the anti-Jewish laws and the narrative persona in a state of psychic sterility; the central desert wilderness is political, communal, and personal trial resulting in the failure of the many and the triumph of the few; the promised land of plenty is the finished text, the narrative subject's liberation, the potential of a restored society. Bassani's narrativized Ferrara, like the biblical event, suggests a spatial symbolism of outside, periphery, and inside, as well as authorial voices that speak from these spaces. One marginal voice, omniscient and prophetic, utters historical "truth" and decries a sinful populace; another — a subjective, poetic voice — forges and inspects, in "intimate solitude," its self-created icon. This glittering icon — the text — is incarnate in the golden personhood of Micòl Finzi-Contini, who also represents an irretrievable social golden age, when landlords — including Jewish landlords — could count on servants' smiles and bows. The retrospective, reverent narration, retrieved across a temporal canyon, conjures a nostalgic memory of love through "deceptive and desperate words" less characteristic of Micòl than of Giorgio Bassani: words that "treat shades as solid things" ("trattando l'ombre come cosa salda": the Dantean epigraph to the 1974 edition of the *Romanzo*). The full poetic line could be a declaration of Bassani's artistic devotion to Micòl, his poetic invention: "Ed ei surgendo: 'Or puoi la quantitate / comprender de l'amor ch'a te mi scalda, / quand'io dismento nostra vanitate, / trattando l'ombre come cosa salda' " [Purg. 21, 11. 133–36] (And he, rising, "Now you may comprehend the measure of the love that burns in me for you, when I forget our emptiness and treat shades as solid things" [Singleton, Purg., p. 233]). Let us examine some of the autobiographical representations and authorial images and metaphors that inscribe the making of the writer and the writer's making of a social world.

Pain, Humiliation, and Childbirth

Most of the dramatic action of the *Romanzo* can be related to the first two actions of the Exodus typology: political infliction upon a foreign population and private despair. Two very different male figures in the first two of the *Cinque storie* illustrate aspects of self-inadequacy and nonlove and cast faint shadows of the authorial persona. Both narratives – "Lida" and "Passeggiata" – tell of silence and lack. The first presents the unpitiable David Camaioli and the central figure, Lida; the second one, the pathetic Elia Corcos and his shadowy and peripheral wife. The two male figures bespeak self-defeat and sterile sexual relations: they are signs of death. The composite male protagonist who doubles for the author gradually descends from these opening texts through the subsequent ones to a state of utter humiliation and despair. Yet "Lida" also speaks an allegorical language of presence and affirmation, in which the birth of both author and text is announced in an imagistic discourse that unites the end of the *Romanzo* with its beginning.

We shall return to the subject of this productive circular movement after noting that the journey to rebirth proceeds from the pain of apathy and humiliation. The debilitated figures of David and Elia foreshadow the greater suffering and growing political persecution that will find their literal expression in intratextual figurations of Bruno Lattes. David Camaioli never appears in the "Lida" narrative itself; he is presented only in Lida's thoughts. The text builds on backward vision, or wishful dreams, that establish a present time of impoverished existence. Lida's perennial sense of want declares itself when, as a penniless, abandoned, unmarried new mother, she recalls her own mother's absurd attempt to glamorize an illegitimate daughter born into poverty by insisting she spell her name with a "y" (probably after the silent film star Lyda Borelli): "E come ci tenevi quando andavo a scuola [grida alla madre] che lo scrivessi sul quaderno con tanto di i lungo! Cos'è mai che ti sognavi che diventassi, da grande: una del varietà?" [p. 12] (How you wanted me to spell it with a y when I went to school! What did you think I'd grow up into: a [cabaret] star? [Q:*P*, p. 11]). The small difference in spelling is a slash that registers both the condemnation of Lida to an unglamorous life and the plaintive, more general narrative sign of an inadequate self. David, through Lida, creates a make-believe life to replace the "boring and hypocritical" one of studies and family (p. 22). For the upper-class university student, Lida represents a glamorized poverty. He lives with her in a lower-class apartment building long enough for her to become hopeful and pregnant and for him to become morose and rejective.

The ideals of love, marriage, and childbirth strike false notes in the separate substories of Lida and David, Lida and Oreste Benelli (a diligent bookbinder who marries Lida), Lida's mother and the forsaking lover of her youth, and even in the concordat between the Catholic church and the Fascist state. Beyond the content of the plot, a muted dialogue ensues between the author and his text that retrospectively speaks with full voice to announce the single fruitful birth embedded in the text: that of the writer himself. The theme of procreation brackets the narrative, which opens with the birth of Lida's son, Ireneo, and closes with Oreste's forlorn hope of fathering his own son: a hope extinguished by his sudden death. Nor does the birth of Ireneo augur life's flowering. Frail, diseased, and spiritless, the visible reminder of Lida's wasted and misdirected adolescent passion seems to live on the periphery of life, to iterate incessantly by abject example the dullness of his mother's existence and the fruitlessness of her dreams. Like his father, David, Ireneo figures absence and lack. Bassani's six-page essay that ends the *Romanzo* begins with a short paragraph dedicated to the volume's opening selection: "*Lida Mantovani* ebbe una gestazione estremamente laboriosa. La abbozzai nel '37, ventunenne, ma negli anni successivi la rifeci non meno di quattro volte: nel '39, nel '48, nel '53, e infine nel '55. È questo il lavoro su cui sono stato più a lungo. Quasi vent'anni" [p. 729] ("Lida Mantovani" had a very difficult gestation. I drafted it in 1937, when I was twenty-one, but in the following years I rewrote it at least four times: in 1939, 1948, 1953, and for the last time in 1955. I spent more time on this piece than on anything else. Almost twenty years).

The metaphors of pregnancy and birth that dominate this passage encircle the more than seven hundred pages of this definitive volume: in the joining of the last pages to the beginning ones, "Lida" becomes a metaphor of the painful process of writing. Like the central character, the writing itself suffered labor pains. Contrary to Lida's, Bassani's pains (of almost twenty years!) bore a healthy offspring, whose long gestation finds permanent duration in this volume and whose arrival signals both the birth of the author and the end of his narrative cycle – as punctuated by the volume's final essay. The publication of *Odore* and its climaxing/epilogic place in the *Romanzo* are both logical and rhetorical decisions of supreme importance to the textual evolution of the Bassanian persona. That persona is born with the birth of the short story "Lida" and Lida's child (on the first page of the text).

Hope for an energizing new life characterizes the four adults of "Lida": the title character, her mother, David, Oreste. The latter is the only one to actualize his desire – a good Catholic marriage – but even that remains seriously deficient in not producing an offspring. Lida, like her mother, suffers the despair of abandonment while carrying the child of the man she has expected to marry. David's quest for a new life is inherently self-defeating: it is a negative desire to diverge from the bourgeois values of his family. It results in his abuse of Lida, sexually, affectively, and morally. In the throes of "noia" and "insofferenza," he suddenly suggests to Lida that they set up house together,

"come una coppia di operai qualsiasi." . . . Si era deciso a rompere definitivamente coi suoi – aveva aggiunto – e questo per farsi "una nuova esistenza." Avrebbero abitato in una "mansarda," una "bella, poetica mansarda all'ultimo piano." [p. 31]

("like an ordinary working-class couple." . . . He had decided to break off definitively with his family, he added, so he could make a "new life" for himself. They would live in a mansard, a beautiful, poetic mansard on the top floor.)

David's pretentious plan to become a laborer, his disdain for marriage ("una delle più tipiche e nauseanti 'pagliacciate borghesi' " [p. 32] [one of the most typical and sickening examples of "bourgeois buffoonery"]), his fabrication of a " 'relazione sentimentale' con una signorina della migliore società" [p. 25] ("relationship" with a young woman of high society), his refusal to meet Lida's mother, and his withdrawal from Lida's life all mark his "nonexistence" and self-isolation: "Ma lui, chi era? – si chiedeva adesso [Lida], dopo tanti anni" [p. 31] ("But who *was* he?" she was asking herself now, after so many years). This insistent question begs for the response "no one." Even David's ability to father a child seems mocked by the apathy and weak will of his son. David is worse than nonexistent; he contaminates.

Scattered dates in the text enable the reader to situate the main action of "*Lida*" in the first decade of Fascism. The birth of Ireneo can be traced to 1921, when the fledgling Fascist party was on the brink of assuming national power. The signing of the Lateran Pacts in February of 1929, acknowledged textually through the exuberance of the former seminary pupil Oreste, caps the glory of the entrenched regime: "La primavera già in arrivo avrebbe veduto aprirsi l'era della pace e della gioia perpetue, rinnovarsi la mitica età dell'oro" [p. 38] (The spring, which was now beginning, would see the start too of an era of peace and joy, the mythical golden age [Q:*P*, p. 42]).

There is no textual evidence that would allow the blame for David's malaise to be traced to the political order, which at the time of David's drama was generally supported by the Italians, Jews and non-Jews alike. But if we recall that the original writing of this story was done in the late thirties, during the crisis of the Hitlerian influence leading to the anti-Jewish laws, and if we remember that Bassani needed to hide his Jewish identity under a false name in order to publish the story, then its thematics of nonexistence, delusion, and self-hatred assume an obvious political hue. By comparing the first version of "Lida" (entitled "Storia di Dèbora") with the revisions written after the demise of Fascism, the political coloring becomes clear, if not pronounced. Crucial refinements of the original text, for example, specify the date of Oreste's death and elaborate the period of the reintegration of Church and (Fascist) State. This latter occurrence backgrounds the marriage of the devout Oreste and the "sinful" Lida, who, as the years pass, develops from a thin and vulnerable girl into a fine and florid Catholic wife. It is in the context of this episode that Bassani inserts parenthetically the news of Oreste's coming death: "Gli anni che seguirono, laboriosi, tranquilli, sostanzialmente felici, non dettero luogo ad avvenimenti di rilievo. Perfino gli inverni – diceva Oreste, il quale morì però molto presto, nella primavera del '38 – sembravano aver messo giudizio per sempre" [p. 40] (The years that followed, hard-working and peaceful, and substantially happy, did not give rise to any noteworthy events. "Even the winters," said Oreste, who died soon after, in the spring of 1938, "seemed to have calmed down for good").

The year 1938, we know, is a signifier of tremendous impact; Bassani's selecting it as Oreste's year of death (which effectively closes the narrative action) inserts the entire period of Nazi-Fascist Jewish persecution as a powerful presence at the near edge of the text. This hovering presence acts as an immediate interpretant of the story to which it attaches: it comments on the "promising" first decade of Fascist rule and on the *political* nature of the authorial anxiety concealed within the fictive subterfuge of a melancholy sexual attachment between two misfitted young loves. The mood of "Storia di Dèbora," maintained in its later form as "Lida," reflects a then-current literary strategy of opposition to the grandiloquent rhetoric promoted by Fascism, an opposition exemplified – frequently – by Montale's verses of negative protest: " . . . ciò che *non* siamo, ciò che *non* vogliamo" (what we are *not*, what we do *not* want).[2] Bassani's cry of protest, however, is directed not diffusely against the style of the regime, but pointedly (and angrily) against the Fascist state's betrayal of its Jewish citizens. Whereas the young Bassani – like the young Montale and many other writers of that time – could not express his aversions explicitly, the older Bassani, as soon as Fascist repression ceased, asserted the historical horrors of the authoritarian State in his rewriting of "Dèbora," by the elliptical simplicity of a date: 1938. Through the simpleminded Oreste, devoted to the familial and religious values of both Church and State, Bassani (in the 1956 edition) ironizes the misbegotten faith in early Fascism, which in hindsight every postwar reader can recognize: along with Oreste's death in the "spring of 1938," just months prior to the promulgation of the anti-Jewish laws, credulity in the "spring" of Fascism is buried. These events occur in the penultimate chapter of "Lida."[3] The very brief final chapter puts to rest as well Oreste's apparent serenity in marriage. Given the happy and interfused 1929 events of matrimony and concordat, the bookbinder's quiet torment over his childless union (revealed in the last chapter) foreshadows and symbolizes the political desperation that will soon overcome all his countrypeople. In the final words of the text:

> Per tornare a parlare di quell'età dell'oro della quale nel febbraio del '29 aveva predetto il ritorno, non aspettava evidentemente che di sentirle dire:
> "Sono incinta."
> Era chiaro però, con altrettanta evidenza, che la morte, cogliendolo di sorpresa, aveva prevenuto l'insorgere in lui di qualsiasi principio di disperazione. [p. 43]

> (To go back to the golden age whose return he had predicted in February '29, all he needed was to hear her say:
> "I am pregnant."

And yet with the same certainty, taking him by surprise, death had come and forestalled even the beginnings of despair.) [Q:*P*, p. 48]

Oreste's embrace of the sociopolitical order is the antithesis of David's disdain for bourgeois conventions. The former's anticipation of the future contrasts with the latter's atemporal withdrawal into himself and his estrangement from daily realities. Both Oreste's belief in the future and David's indifference to all time are temporal stances implicitly rebuked by Micòl's (and the narrator-author's) privileging of past and present time and distrust of the future. David figures the author in a state of social and creative impotence, a state of "extinguished passion," which the epigraph to the short story (1974 edition), dedicated in the first place to Lida, links obliquely to David and, by extension, to the authorial persona.[4]

Patriarchs with Hebrew Names

A state of estrangement and diminished productivity also characterizes the protagonist of Bassani's second narrative, "La passeggiata prima di sera." Like David, Dr. Elia Corcos is a Jewish *signore* who has an affair with a poor, unschooled, Catholic teenager who becomes pregnant. Against his better judgment, the thirty-year-old Elia marries her. In contrast to David's story, which is only faintly sketched, Elia's is foregrounded.

The matrimonial decision burdens Elia's eventual renown and intimates his ultimate fate as a victim. By contrast, David's abandonment of Lida establishes his fate as a victimizer—but also as a willful nonpresence, that is, a self-victimizer: a victim. Elia's marriage, too, is an act of self-victimage:

Diceva quel suo volto pieno di paura (il profluvio di parole che intanto seguitava a uscirgli di bocca non contava, non aveva la minima importanza):

"Per qual motivo mi trovo qui, a chiedere, come ho chiesto un attimo fa, al vecchio ubriacone la figlia infermiera in isposa? A che scopo, in nome di Dio, sto rovinandomi con le mie stesse mani? Soltanto per riparare a una gravidanza? E nemmeno accertata, per giunta?" [p. 56]

(His face showed how frightened he was [the rush of words that kept coming out of his mouth didn't mean anything, didn't have the slightest importance]:

"For what reason am I here, asking the old drunkard as I did a minute ago for the hand of his nurse's-aide daughter? To what end, in God's name, am I ruining myself with my own hands? Just to make good on a pregnancy? And no less for one that isn't even certain?")

Figure 12. View from the eastern section of the city walls. Corso Giovecca, "the city's main artery," is visible through the arches. "Having reached the height of the *Prospettiva* . . . [Gemma Brondi] automatically raised her eyes toward the three supporting arches of the architectural interruption" and suddenly heard a voice greet her ("La passeggiata prima di cena").

The marriage raises questions about Elia's religious background and his splendid career. Rather than the wholeness and fulfillment wanting in the unmarried state, Gemma reflects to her husband a stifling image of otherness. The Brondi family as well—in particular "the four males at home"—immediately recognize in the young stranger, Elia, someone "appartenente alla classe dei signori, e perciò diverso, fondamentalmente estraneo" [p. 53] (who belongs to the bourgeoisie, and is therefore different, fundamentally alien). The house Elia buys twelve years after the marriage—like the marriage, a primary symbol of (familial) unity—from the start has a character of divisiveness: Gemma's relatives approach it from the back door, where its orchard abuts the city's walls, ancient ramparts that provide an earthen path along which her urban-peasant family feels comfortable walking; Elia's visitors approach the house from the paved street, where the main entrance displays a brass plate inscribed with the words "Dr. Elia Corcos, Physician-Surgeon." Elia becomes the director (*primario*) of the women's division of Ferrara's St. Anne Hospital, earning himself local eminence. History alone—in choosing to develop Bologna over

Ferrara—restricts Elia's renown within the bounds of his native city.[5] Elia himself chooses to restrict his private life effectively within the bounds of his own person. The dark, rustic kitchen of the Brondi house, where Elia in one action offers marriage and seals himself into "defeat and sacrifice," seems to reshape itself within a dark corner of his home, where the now-prominent doctor sits absorbed at his desk, withdrawn from society as well as from family in pursuit of private reveries. The gaze he focuses "fuori, di là dall'orto, di là dal muro di cinta che separava l'orto dai bastioni, di là dai bastioni medesimi" [p. 61-62] (outside, beyond the garden, beyond the city wall that separates the garden from the ramparts, beyod the ramparts themselves), as far as the sky toward Bologna, seems to seek the adventure of which his life in Ferrara is barren. Gemma's sister, Ausilia, is persuaded that "neppure a Gemma, benché moglie e padrona, era mai riuscito di oltrepassare il muro invisibile dietro il quale Elia si estraniava da tutto quanto lo circondasse" [p. 62] (not even Gemma, his wife and mistress of the house, managed to step across the invisible wall behind which Elia withdrew from everything around him). Elia's posture recreates the classic image of the writer isolated at his desk, seeking the inventiveness of his own imagination to picture the world. But Elia's sense of estrangement ("si estraniava") and encirclement ("da tutto quanto lo circondasse") wrenches his posture as writer or contemplator into one of a menaced prisoner, or a victim—an Edgardo Limentani surrounded by hostile workers (chapter 4).

Whether factual or fabricated by gossipers, Elia's affair with the chic and influential Duchess Costabili compensates for the void in his personal and married life. Dr. Corcos's desire of the duchess corresponds to the reach for the "perfected feminine" that allegorizes the male writer's yearning for perfected imagination, as played out metatextually in the *Giardino* through the narrator's desire of Micòl.

In the matter of fidelity to Judaism, the "eccentric" and "bizarre" doctor's public and personal actions are open and, for him, in concord. Refusing to mask his lack of faith, he categorically declines to help finance religious instruction; as a believer in ritual practices, he circumcises his sons and buries one, an eight-year-old, in the Jewish cemetery. Elia's eccentricity is a feature of his authority: his social place is literally "away from the center"—on the margin of community norms—as much as it is central. Not surprisingly, Elia is the object of both reverence and spiteful gossip.

The coexistence of insider and outsider in one individual is a dilemma common to many Bassanian characters, and all such figures double the author. By Bassani's own statement, Elia represents an aspect of himself. The writer who created the prominent Ferrarese doctor is surely—even more than his character—"una specie di istituzione, di simbolo municipale" [p. 54] (a kind of institution or municipal symbol) and the object equally of Ferrarese reverence and malice.

Among the fictive males who stand for the author, only one death is reported, that of Elia. Even Edgardo Limentani, whose whole story builds to his suicide, takes his life beyond the narrative confine: it is not his death, but the signs of his dying and his will to die, that are recorded. Elia represents Bassani's lineage and public renown. Other fictional males who embody personal traits of the author enact the death of the spirit, but never the death of the body. Set earlier in time than any of the other narratives (Elia's engagement takes place in 1888), "Passeggiata" constitutes a kind of prelude or pre-text to authorial presence (state of *being*), situated in an always-present time, demarcated by the subsequent stories of the *Romanzo* up to the concluding *Odore*. "Lida," too, functions as an autobiographical pre-text (David figuring the state of nonbeing), its chronology and the character of the bookbinder Oreste Benetti underscoring the dated and irrecoverable twenties ideology as it is overwhelmed by the political violence of the thirties and forties. By means of a different literary technique, *Odore* functions as a post-text to Bassani's narrativized portrait of his progress toward artistic maturity that culminates in *L'airone*.

"Lida" and "Passeggiata," the two opening stories of the original *Cinque storie*, are not only preludes to the main matter of the *Romanzo* but also previews of it: with the textual incision of the death of Oreste in 1938 and the deportation of Elia in 1943, the two most important dates of Bassani's history enter the narrative as actors in their own right, appropriating the personal events as signifiers of the social implications of the political foundation. The year 1938 (to repeat) proclaims the end of Italy's delusionary trust in Fascism and the beginning of violent, institutionalized betrayal. The Catholic Oreste and the Jewish Elia represent the opportunities of Ferrarese society in the dawn of the century and the destabilization about to threaten its bourgeois values and assumptions. The dates 1938 and 1943 sweep the two "picturesque," "provincial," "pre-textual" tales into the narrative mainstream as the historical preconditions of a runaway social (dis)order. Commonly perceived as stylish examples of the literary hermeticism and taste for the ineffable in vogue during the first decades of the century, Bassani's early tales come to be less private and more political in their final versions and appear even more so alongside his subsequent work. The two dates are iterative instruments that interweave all the narratives; they function like many of Bassani's fictive characters, including the bodied and the disembodied narrative voices that orient the texts. The two early texts adumbrate essential features of the authorial persona, who is both "behind" the text (directing the narrative point of view) and within it (as the characters David and Elia): they trace the masks of the writing subject, who achieves full authority and presence by the end of the writing, and of the aggregate character-object written partially and self-critically into each narrative.

Bruno Lattes and Politico-Erotic Failure

The fourth of the *Cinque storie*, "Gli ultimi anni di Clelia Trotti," introduces the character Bruno Lattes; he will reappear in the *Giardino* and again in the triad of stories in *Odore* grouped under the title (as if an update — in fact, a late and different confession of sorrows) *Altre notizie su Bruno Lattes*. No other named character in this oeuvre is a central character in more than one text. From the first, Bruno bears a heavy autobiographical responsibility — the only third-person character to do so. Even though Bassani abandons third-person narration after *Cinque storie*, having found a better voice in the first person (beginning with *Occhiali*),[6] at the end of the *Romanzo* he inscribes himself as the third-person Bruno a final time. This happens immediately before the series of first-person autobiographical recollections that conclude the book.

In the sonnet preceding the Bruno stories in the 1972 edition of *Odore*, the author confesses that he has spent his life spirit on poetry and consequently is himself "dead": "Per te, o Poesia, così consumandomi vissi: / così, Vita, mia povera vita, mai t'ho vissuta" [p. 29] (For you, oh Poetry, I lived, consuming myself: / and so, Life, my poor life, I have never lived you). In Bassani's writings, the paradox of death-in-life and life-in-death is primarily a metaphor of personal, social, and artistic states of being. The linear organization of *Odore* and its quality of discourse as memory (to which we shall return) blazon the work as a "dying" utterance. Let us here recall the author's own words: "Ho riscritto il *Romanzo di Ferrara* dalla prima riga all'ultima, perché sono alla fine del mio lavoro" (I rewrote the *Romanzo di Ferrara* from the first line to the last, because I am at the end of my work). *Odore* is the self-conscious conclusion of the author's lifework, that is, of his creative writing. It is both a summation and an end, "une belle mort" that once and for all establishes the victory of authorial presence over victimage and extinction. It proclaims the definitive completion of its author's "story/history" of Ferrara, a completion that is a return to the beginning, a journey of the self. The figure of Bruno Lattes, standing at both edges of the *Romanzo*, emblematizes the (interior) return to the beginning. He is also a critical compositional element in the construction of the authorial figure.[7]

In all his appearances, Bruno is linked sexually to Adriana ("ariana") Trentini; his identity and his narrative function are inseparable from his relation to her. The Bruno-Adriana pair is, in a sense, the germ of the central relation of the entire *Romanzo*: that of the narrator and Micòl Finzi-Contini. This relation, in turn, flowers into the superstructural, symbolic one of the author and his text.

The first Bruno ("Anni") seeks female companionship in Clelia Trotti, a woman of great reputation in Ferrara among the anti-Fascist population. In a deeply disturbed state of mind that intertwines personal, political, social, and sexual anguish, Bruno embarks on his search for Clelia's house:

Bruno risalì lentamente via Mazzini e via Saraceno. "Che schifo!" sibilava ogni tanto fra i denti. Guardava con odio le vetrine sfavillanti, la gente ferma di fronte ai cristalli a osservare la merce esposta, i commercianti che si facevano sulle soglie delle loro botteghe e dei loro negozi, abbastanza simili negli atteggiamenti – si diceva – alle megere che vigilavano, sempre mezze dentro e mezze fuori, le porte dei casini di via Colomba, via Sacca e dintorni. Ancora invischiato dalla passione che fino all'agosto di quello stesso anno lo aveva reso schiavo di una delle più brillanti e corteggiate ragazze di Ferrara, l'Adriana Trentini, specialmente le donne che venivano avanti in senso contrario al suo e lo sfioravano senza notarlo (le belle, le bionde, e le eleganti in particolare) gli sembrava che in tutto il loro modo di essere e di fare, insieme adorabile e detestabile, portassero impresso il marchio mal dissimulato della depravazione. "Che marciume, che vergogna!" continuava a ripetere furibondo, nemmeno tanto sottovoce. [p. 109]

(Bruno walked slowly up Via Mazzini and Via Saraceno. "How disgusting!" he muttered to himself every now and then. He looked with repugnance at the sparkling shop windows and the people there, looking at the merchandise displayed, and at the shopkeepers standing in the doorways of their shops and stores, resembling the old battleaxes who, half inside and half outside, kept watch over the brothel doors on Via Colomba, Via Sacca, and other nearby streets. Still enmeshed in his passion that since the preceding August had made him a slave of one of the most glittering and courted girls of Ferrara, Adriana Trentini, the women who were walking ahead from the opposite direction and brushing against him without noticing him [particularly the beautiful, blond and elegant ones] seemed to him, in their very way of being and doing, which was both lovable and detestable, to be branded with a mark of depravity. "What rot, what shame!" he kept furiously saying, and not very quietly.)

Bruno's walk through the serpentine streets of medieval Ferrara encompasses the topography of the former Jewish ghetto (Via Mazzini and Via Saraceno), bringing to his mind the nearby bordellos (Via Colomba and Via Sacca). As if likening them, the narration blends shrewish old women ("*megere*," after the name of one of the Furies) and elegant female passersby. The two contiguous but distinct neighborhoods, conflated by Bruno as one and the same, function in Bassani's narratives as major social signifiers. The ancient ghetto is visible testimony of Jewish ostracism; the red-light district is the principal locus of male shame and degradation. Thus, for example, when the homosexuality of the formerly respected Dr. Fadigati (*Occhiali*) becomes the object of gossip, the narrative and the townspeople take note of the doctor's habit of walking in the neighborhood where sex is sold. Bruno's passage through the former ghetto traces his demoralized and stigmatized state of being: the ghetto streets reflect the public degradation of Jews since the issuance of the anti-Jewish laws, while his own sense of self-degradation is imaged in the attractive but "vile" bourgeois women passing by, all of whom figure Adriana. Now in his twenties and about to graduate from the University of Bologna (Bassani's alma mater), Bruno abruptly finds himself to be an outcast, his future seized. The "shame" and "rottenness" imprinted upon the women is a *marchio* (stain, brand, "trademark") that also marks the lowest depths of Bruno's self-loathing—his *own* sense of shame and rottenness—precipitated by the Fascist laws against the Jews. Like a prostitute, the cast-off Jew has become a cheap, dilapidated commodity.

Both the failure of Bruno's relation with Adriana and his interest in meeting Clelia stem from the institution of the anti-Jewish laws. That legislation is a notable insert in the opening sentence of the second chapter, which in the form of a flashback introduces the central narrative action—Bruno's pursuit of, and friendship with, Clelia: "Nel tardo autunno del 1939 . . . pressapoco a un anno di distanza dalla promulgazione delle leggi razziali" [p. 106] (In late autumn of 1939 . . . about a year after the promulgation of the anti-Jewish laws). The specification of time also establishes, elliptically, Bruno's still-smoldering sexual desire for Adriana, which had rendered him her "slave" until August of "the same year," that is, the year just dated in terms of the anti-Jewish legislation. The *marchio* that brands the well-dressed women is a sign—like Hester Prynne's scarlet letter—denoting moral wrong.[8] An indelible *marchio* made, for example, with a red-hot brand to identify cattle and other goods, suggests the Nazi way of identifying ("naming") death camp inmates, whose skin they scarred with numbers. In less brutal days, it will be remembered, the Nazis marked Jews as outcasts by requiring the Star of David to be displayed on their clothing.

The word *marchio* turns up again in "La ragazza dei fucili," a Bruno story in *Odore* set in the "fatal" year of 1938, just after the anti-Jewish laws were announced (p. 683). In rage over Adriana's decision not to see him for a while, and tormented by fantasies about her, Bruno seeks diversion in Ferrara's seedy little Luna Park. There he is attracted to a young, sensuous woman from Tuscany, "animalesque" and "wicked," who runs a shooting gallery. When, after several visits, Bruno finds the booth closed and the woman gone, he is seized by a flash of insight, which ends the narrative:

> E di colpo capì due cose: che soltanto a cominciare da quel momento avrebbe saputo ciò che davvero volesse dire la parola "sofferenza"; e che il ricordo della smorfia della ragazza dei fucili (una smorfia che la sera prima lo aveva riempito improvvisamente di felicità, di gelosia, e di un oscuro senso di abbiezione) gli sarebbe rimasto impresso dentro per molti

anni a venire, chissà mai quanti. Come un piccolo marchio: minimo ma indelebile. [p. 685]

(And, abruptly, he understood two things: that only now, from this moment on, would he know the meaning, the real meaning, of the word "suffering"; and that the memory of the rifle girl's pout [a grimace which, the night before, had suddenly filled him with happiness, jealousy, and an obscure feeling of degradation] would remain impressed on his mind for many years to come, no knowing how many. Like a little brand: tiny, but indelible.) [W:S, p. 27]

The strange combination of happiness, jealousy, and degradation indelibly engraved on Bruno marks the unerasable self-loathing and intense moral suffering of a consenting victim. The alluring young woman of the shooting gallery is a sirenic "foreign" figure, sadistic and powerful, who both seduces and shames her lover/victim; victimage falls to this Jew *because he is a Jew*. Bruno's easy sexual entrapment is a transparent replay of his entrapment—or, better, betrayal—by Adriana, which for him is inseparable from the anti-Jewish laws. With perhaps not altogether mocking self-pity, the rejected and worn-out Bruno imagines Adriana coming back and feeling sorry for him: "Era così smagrito e sciupato, lui, c'era nei suoi occhi tanta sofferenza, le leggi razziali lo avevano reso talmente degno di compassione, che l'Adriana non avrebbe resistito" [p. 683] (He was so thin and worn, there was such suffering in his eyes, the anti-Semitic laws had made him so deserving of pity, that Adriana would be unable to resist [W:S, p. 24]). Recalling the Bruno of "Anni," this Bruno, with particular deliberation, walks through the small streets of the bordello neighborhood and wherever else he finds squalor, including Luna Park (p. 684). Although he remarks that between the shooting-booth attendant and Adriana "there was absolutely nothing in common," the very observation is an act of *linking* the two young women. Bruno finds the other woman, like Adriana, irresistible: "Se gli riusciva di incrociare i propri sguardi con quelli di lei, sentiva il cuore dare un sussulto. Ne ricavava un piacere amaro, una specie di gioia vendicativa" [p. 685] (If he managed to catch her gaze, he felt his heart leap. He derived a bitter pleasure from it, a kind of vindictive joy [W:S, p. 26]). The low-class, vulgar "temptress" of Luna Park is an apt agency for Bruno's expression of rage ("gioia vendicativa") against Adriana, which is ultimately a rage against himself. Bruno's defiled sense of self—his sense of defilement as a Jew—politicizes the "innocent" Luna Park flirtation and invests the deep ("indelible") *sofferenza* with a specific signification that otherwise would seem undecipherable, or at least grossly exaggerated. The rifle-smart *toscana* (that is, outsider) who "brands" Bruno emblematizes violent and degrading sensuality, which is itself a metaphor for Jewish victimization, specifically of the Nazi "brand."

Following his failure as Adriana's lover, the Bruno of this narrative remains in a state of pained isolation and self-contempt. A year later, in "Anni," he reflects upon Adriana as a past, if still disturbing, experience, his hope for self-renewal turned in the direction of political passion. Clelia serves him well as an authentic guide, although not in the way she fancied. She becomes for Bruno a mirror of decadence, a sign of both the impossibility of fruitful personal commitment and the danger of moral contamination within the bounds of Fascist Italy. Bruno's salvation requires that he shed his identity, that he *escape*—which he does in 1943. He escapes across an ocean of purifying waters to the United States, where his future is safeguarded and where he will become (post-textually) an American citizen. By pinpointing the year 1943, Bassani has Bruno's escape occur during the first frenzied moment in Italy of Nazi deportation. His extraordinary safe flight to the United States at the very time his co-religionists (including his parents) are being herded off to the death camps is an authorial sign of especial grace for this character, a declaration of his *need* to survive. The narration of Bruno's postwar visit back to Ferrara, recounted in the first chapter, portrays a matured man who is morally distanced from his still self-serving compatriots and compassionate toward the now-dead Clelia. Bruno is also alone: it is significant that there is no textual reference to women in his new life. The Americanized Bruno is a calm, righteous, and productive person (he teaches at an American university) beyond sexual—which is also to say communal—bondage. Gone is his erotic "enslavement" by Adriana and his Oedipalesque "seduction" by Clelia; gone, in other words, is his despairing self-loathing as a Jew, a lover, and a political. Bruno has escaped becoming the prisoner of his own delusions, unlike Clelia, who imprisoned herself in her fantasies even more than the Fascists contained her within her sister's shabby home. Back in Ferrara, Bruno becomes a seer, rightly sizing up the self-interested theatricality of Clelia's Communist-organized funeral commemoration. He becomes a wise, asexual (dispassionate, "pure") figure whose narrative function is to remember. He is, in brief, a figure of the author bearing witness: the insider who has become an outsider—to his own past and to his society's present, and for that reason, the just and truthful recorder of both.

The main action of all the Bruno narratives (including his brief appearance in the *Giardino*) is set in the period 1938–39, with the single exception of *Odore*, which is set in 1933. In all cases the chronology is consistent in the details of the character's age and his relationship with Adriana, which lasts for three years. Bruno meets Adriana when he is eighteen and she is fourteen. Their relationship effectively ends right after the anti-Jewish decrees are announced, in the fall of 1938. In the *Giardino*, Bassani doubles his persona to include Bruno as well as the narrator. Playing the minor role this time, Bruno is assigned a younger age (by two years), the difference making the narrator the same age as the Brunos of the other stories.

The composite Bruno-figure constructed in "Anni" and "Ragazza" personifies death and rebirth. His "death" is public defilement and spiritual aridity; his "rebirth," self-renewal in a distant land. The Brunos in the remaining narratives, *Giardino*, "Odore," and "Abbazia," refine the pattern of death. Their lives are played out strictly within the epoch of the anti-Jewish laws. The narration of the youngest (eighteen-year-old) Bruno stops even before then, looking backward from 1933 (the time of the narrative present) to his early childhood ("Odore"). "Anni," which introduces Bruno, is the only narrative to propel the character forward, that is, to locate a remote, even nontextual, space of self-awareness and to inscribe in it authorial presence. That space requires the achieved non-presence of Adriana, a symbolic reflection of Bruno's (masculine) inadequacy. Right at the beginning of "Anni"—and only in that tale—Adriana is reduced to a brief recollection. The later three texts, which, in reference to narrative chronology, precede the action of "Anni," cast Adriana as a major character. She represents, in general, an impossible and forbidden dream of desire. Her presence signifies Bruno's self-damnation.

In the *Giardino*, Bruno and Adriana enter the narrative together as protagonists in an unexpected incident that becomes the principal subject of one of the novel's chapters (pp. 298–302). They are among six of Micòl and Alberto's acquaintances who are waiting for the gate (*portone*) in the walled Finzi-Contini estate to be opened. They have been invited to play tennis on the family court because local officials, in response to the new anti-Jewish laws, have forbidden Jews access to the *Eleonora d'Este*, the city's private tennis club. Just a few days earlier, the final match of a tennis tournament in which Bruno and Adriana were competing (and winning) as partners was abruptly suspended. That incident becomes the topic of the group's conversation as they wait. By this time, the novel's narrator—its central male character—has already supplied the reader with important information about the minor figure of Bruno, especially in relation to himself. The last to join the waiting group, the narrator immediately notices Bruno, who seems eager to be recognized. These two young men, of slight acquaintance, are functional doubles: both are enrolled at the University of Bologna, both are students of literature, both are tennis players, both are Jews. The other males present (as the narrator observes) are distinctly different from them.[9] Although they are practically strangers, the narrator and Bruno share an unspoken understanding: "Passò rapida tra me e lui l'inevitabile occhiata di ebraica connivenza che, mezzo ansioso e mezzo disgustato, già prevedevo" [p. 299] (The inevitable flicker of Jewish understanding passed between us, quickly; as, half anxious and half revolted, I had already foreseen it would [Q:G, p. 80]). The narrator's "disgust" with the Jewish characteristic of group commiseration is primarily self-directed, a recognition that the "dark" Bruno is his own true image. A preposterous metonym of touching bicycle tires becomes a precise index of the narrator's identification with the younger, "unattractive" boy:

e guardavo infine Bruno, lì davanti, sempre più alto e secco, sempre più simile, di carnagione scura come era, a un giovane negro vibrante e apprensivo, e in preda anche quel giorno a una tale agitazione nervosa da riuscire a trasmettermela attraverso il lieve contatto delle gomme anteriori delle nostre due biciclette. [p. 299]

(and lastly [I saw] Bruno, there in front of me, taller and [thinner] than ever, and, with his dark skin, more than ever like a young, vibrant, worried Negro: in such a state of nervous excitement, even that day, that he managed to transmit it to me through the light contact between the front tyres of our bikes.) [Q:G, pp. 79–80]

Although Bassani's nameless narrator has the major responsibility for orienting the text, the double, Bruno, challenges him, in a sense, as a composite of contradictions. Bruno's difference is inscribed in his physique: his tall, thin body and swarthy complexion oppose him to the short, solid, fair-skinned narrating persona, who is given the author's salient feature of clear-blue eyes. As his name attests, Bruno is a figure of darkness, an embodiment of the author's young and desolate manhood that climaxes in the historical years 1938–39. With the important exception of the postwar Bruno ("Anni"), a wise observer and commentator on life who represents achievement, the normative Bruno, an agitated participant in life who represents failure, develops fully in the years 1938–39 and then vanishes.

In contrast to Bruno, Adriana radiates Aryan beauty, as the *Giardino's* narrator observes: "Guardavo l'Adriana Trentini, i suoi bei capelli biondissimi, le sue gambe lunghe, affusolate: magnifiche, senza dubbio, ma dalla pelle troppo bianca sparsa delle strane chiazze rosse che sempre le venivano quando era accaldata" [pp. 298–99] ([I looked at] Adriana Trentini, fine coppery [author's note: original "biondissimi" means "very blond"] hair loose on her shoulders, long and admittedly marvellous legs, but an over-white skin curiously splotched with red, as always happened when she was hot" [Q:G, p. 79]). Adriana's maculate beauty ("chiazze rosse"), which dazzles Bruno as it does most other young men, cannot compete with the equally blond but immaculate beauty of Micòl Finzi-Contini. Particularly in ths novel, Adriana and Bruno reflect partial and inferior images of Micòl and the narrator.

It is mainly Adriana who tells the narrator about the tennis incident. In the telling, her moral and rational deficiencies are revealed to exceed even those of the Fascist officials, who claimed they were canceling the match because of growing darkness rather than growing anti-Semitism. Adriana's fervid indignation fastens on the Fascist *style* of discrimination and her own petty vanity:

E lei, Adriana, era rimasta talmente disgustata e indignata da tutta questa faccenda, che aveva giurato di non metterci più piede, all'*Eleonora d'Este*: almeno per un pezzo. Avevano qualcosa contro Bruno? Se ce l'avevano, potevano benissimo vietargli di iscriversi al torneo. Dirgli onestamente: "Siccome le cose stanno così e così, spiacenti, non possiamo accettare la tua iscrizione." Ma a torneo cominciato, anzi quasi finito, e a un pelo, per giunta, che lui vincesse una delle gare, non dovevano in nessun modo comportarsi come si erano comportati. Quattro a due. Che porcheria! Una maniera di trattare del genere era roba da zulù, non da persone beneducate e civili! [pp. 300–301][10]

(And she, Adriana, had been so disgusted by the whole business, so outraged . . . that she'd sworn never to set foot in the *Eleonora d'Este* club again: [at least for a while]. Suppose they'd got something against Bruno, well, they could have forbidden him to take part in the tournament; said frankly: "Things being the way they are, we're terribly sorry, but we can't accept you for it." But once the tournament had started, in fact was nearly over and he was within a hair's breadth of winning one of the matches, they just shouldn't have behaved the way they did. Four-two! What pigs! The sort of piggery you might expect from Zulus, not from anyone supposed to be educated and civilized!) [Q:*G*, p. 82]

Adriana's shallowness ("abituale sventatezza" [p. 299]) redounds to Bruno and underscores her inferiority to Micòl. Bruno's inferiority to the narrator is made apparent in the latter's announcement that he ceased frequenting the tennis club at least the year before, "sicuro che un giorno o l'altro sarei stato buttato fuori lo stesso. Difatti non mi sbagliavo" [p. 299] (sure I'd be chucked out sooner or later whatever I did. And I wasn't mistaken [Q:*G*, p. 80]).

The episode of exclusion from tennis is a threshold experience Adriana depletes of significance; her story, which draws attention primarily to herself, reduces it all to an ill-mannered and ultimately inconsequential snub. Bruno, instead, focuses on the interplay of the culprits: the sniveling Fascist opportunist Cariani—"una 'mezza cartuccia' . . . un verme" [p. 301] (a "half pint" . . . a worm)—and the vice-president and secretary of the *Eleonora d'Este*, the "distinguished" but cowardly Marquis Barbicinti. Bruno's rendition responds to the tactics of intimidation by which subaltern, vulgar Fascists coerce individuals against the Jews. Bruno imagines Cariani saying, "E domani? Ha pensato a domani sera, marchese, quando il Federale verrà qui, per la festa da ballo, e si troverà a dover premiare un...Lattes con tanto di coppa d'argento e relativo saluto romano. . . . grane, grane a non finire" [pp. 301–2] (And what about tomorrow? Have you thought of tomorrow evening, marchese, when the Federal Secretary will be coming here for the ball, and he's got to give the silver cup and the Roman salute and the rest of it to a . . . Lattes? . . . trouble; endless trouble [Q:*G*, pp. 83–84]).

The group of tennis players at the Finzi-Contini wall emblematically stand at the threshold separating the secure, non-Jewish middle-class community (incarnate in the *Circolo del Tennis*) from the excluded Jewish community (incarnate in the Finzi-Continis). For Bruno, the devastating consequences of the anti-

Jewish laws unfold in a different textual space. On center stage in this novel is the narrator, for whom the tennis incident signals an exquisite opportunity: access to the hitherto exclusive Finzi-Continis. For him, the laws become an avenue to personal and artistic growth, of which Micòl is the principal instrument. The Finzi-Continis, by virtue of their *chosen* exclusivity, are untouched by the social exclusion forced upon the other Jews of Ferrara. They do not escape Nazi persecution and death, but they nonetheless—indeed, therefore—represent proud Jewish resistance and immunity to the moral contamination spread in Ferrara by the Nazi-Fascist regime. The difference between Bruno and Adriana, the narrator and Micòl, and the future relations of each pair can be identified by their responses to the anti-Jewish decrees. For the former pair, the laws expose the moral weaknesses in each partner; for the latter, they unite two kindred souls, although in both cases the promise of marriage is shattered. The superimposition of the two couples is a clever literary stratagem of doubled vision that projects simultaneously the most passive and the most productive limits of the writing persona.

The scene at the *portone* traces a moment of finality and disjunction—a premonition of the death-camp gate?—and entry into the estate coincides with the chapter's close. By means of an electric intercommunication system installed soon afterward, which permits immediate access for visitors (p. 304), the narrative draws retrospective attention to the singular initial staging of the scene: the spatial topology that maps an exceptional threshold situation. Once the socially charged electrical system operates, passage becomes simple—even routine—for the tennis players. Nonetheless, the Finzi-Contini garden is not a gentle point of arrival; it is a space of trial and promise, particularly for the narrator, but for others present too, including the host family.

With the first appearance of Micòl's parents after many afternoons of tennis, Bruno's function as the narrator's double again affirms itself; Micòl introduces the two university students to her father as virtually a couple:

> Aveva cominciato *con me e con Bruno Lattes*, parlando *sia dell'uno sia dell'altro* in modo distaccato, marcatamente oggettivo: come per trattenere in quella particolare circostanza il padre da qualche possibile segno di speciale riconoscimento e preferenza. Eravamo "*i due letterati* della combriccola," "tipi bravissimi." [p. 310; emphasis added]

> (She started with me and Bruno Lattes, speaking of us both in a remote, noticeably objective tone: as if to stop her father, in those special circumstances, from showing the least sign of special friendships and preferences. We were the two "literary ones in the gang," two "really bright ones.") [Q:*G*, p. 95]

If Micòl has her reasons for pairing the two young men, the author has reasons even more compelling. Much later, when Micòl and the narrator have become good friends, Bruno and Adriana reenter the narrative arena. Micòl, in a telephone conversation, points out to the unaware narrator the sexual nature of their friends' relationship; she claims that Adriana is flirtatious and treats Bruno "like a slave." Micòl paints a sympathetic, if slightly chaffing, portrait of Bruno, notable for its biographical resemblance to both Bassani and the novel's narrator. Her remarks seem to embed an *authorial* critical commentary that poses the Bruno-Adriana coupling as a bad or else too-true copy of the narrator and Micòl. There is a parallel, for example, between Micòl's observation of Adriana and Bruno kissing one evening in the *Hütte* near the tennis court—"lei li aveva visti mezzi stesi sul divano, che si baciavano a tutt'andare" [p. 334] (she had seen them half lying on the sofa, kissing away for all they were worth [Q:*G*, p. 131])—and two other scenes in which the narrator kisses a resisting Micòl, first in the *Hütte* and another time in her bedroom.[11] During the telephone conversation, the narrator admonishes Micòl with an abrupt "Fai il paio con l'Adriana" [p. 335] (You're just like Adriana). He is responding to her "disgusting cynicism" ("cinismo ributtante" [ibid.]) although his words apply also to the common physical attributes of the two women—their blond hair, athleticism, exceptional beauty—and to their similar social and cultural backgrounds. The pairing accentuates Micòl's superiority. She has more of the positive qualities and fewer of the negative ones; in other words, she excels physically, socially, and morally, she is less sirenic and flighty as a lover. Micòl's ensuing defense of Adriana bespeaks her own high degree of self-awareness: "L'Adriana è un angelo innocente. Capricciosa, magari, ma innocente. . . . Mentre Micòl è buona . . . e sa sempre quello che fa, ricòrdatelo" [ibid.] (Adriana's an innocent angel. Capricious, maybe, but innocent. . . . Whereas Micòl's good . . . and *always* knows what she's up to, don't forget [Q:*G*, p. 133]).

Adriana's innocence is that of a fool, while Micòl's perspicacity is that of a seer. In common, however, is the attachment of each to an erotic partner, which is essential to their narrative functions. Enmeshed in their erotic power is their ethnic identity: Catholic versus Jew. The Catholic Adriana, like Nives in *Airone* and even like the passive Gemma in "Passeggiata," is a negative influence on— and, even more, a negative mirror of—the principal partner in the relation, always a Jewish man (Edgardo, Elia, Bruno). Only Adriana among Bassani's sexually significant female characters strongly resembles Micòl. The author directly juxtaposes her and Micòl, staging the lesser tale of Adriana and Bruno as an enactment of the greater tale of Micòl and the narrator *as it might have gone wrong*: as a dead-end, second-rate, unproductive effort to love. From the opposite perspective, *her* perspective, Micòl suggests that the lesser relation might have gone *right*: "Alta quasi quanto Bruno, bionda, con quella splendida pelle alla Carole Lombard che aveva, in altri momenti sarebbe magari stata proprio la ragazza che ci voleva, per Bruno, al quale, si vede, piaceva il genere 'molto ariano' " [pp. 334–35] (Nearly as tall as Bruno, blonde, with that marvellous Carole Lombard skin of hers, at any other time she might have been just the girl for Bruno, who obviously liked "real Arians" [Q:G, p. 131]). In *another* time, Jewish assimilation, including mixed marriages, was an ordinary, or at least unprovocative, social phenomenon. In the narrative present – the winter of 1938-39 – history, that is, the anti-Jewish legislation, prevents Bruno from committing (in Micòl's words) "la sciocchezza più grossa: quella di fidanzarsi" [p. 335] (the stupidest thing of all: getting engaged [Q:G, p. 132]). The same history aids the narrator, through Micòl, through his *not* becoming engaged to her, to achieve self-knowledge and poetic expression. Thus the structures of the two romances posit the second as the "right" denouement of the first. Bruno's character, especially as Micòl describes it in the same episode, is very close to the author's; her statement therefore takes on the quality of an authorial confession: a condemnation of youthful weaknesses (a delicate sensibility, a moralistic bent, an attraction to Aryan women) and an "aspiration" to suffer (p. 335). Bruno's pitiable relationship with Adriana is a parable of psychic and moral descent. By contrast, the despair that the narrator subsequently experiences because of a thwarted romance initiates a moment of movement. That despair, in its wake, accumulates the power of creative ascent, of which the final success coincides with his writing. Bruno, as Micòl remarks to the narrator, is "like you, a literary person, someone who *wants* to write" ("*tira* a scrivere" [ibid.; emphasis added to highlight aim rather than attainment of writing]). But unlike the narrator, Bruno is fixed in his desolation, without a narrative future, incarnate of an early and self-destructive authorial stage.

The clearest sign of Bruno's inevitable textual death (erasure, inconclusion) is his Aryan object of desire. Micòl, the only Jewish woman in all Bassani's narratives to have a major erotic role, is also the only woman to influence the narrator and reflect him positively. As observed earlier, she enjoys a privileged status as a figure of art and thus of love.[12] For her to be the narrator's object of desire is to project and therefore ensure his (textual) life. From the perspective of the totalized narrating subject, Micòl's Jewishness symbolizes sameness. She represents sameness idealized: the perfected (female) form of specularity. Thus, paradoxically, she must recede from the persona-narrator's possession (to avoid contamination as a mere person) in order to figure more purely the persona's quest (object of desire): the work of art, the finished (perfected) book, the act of love. The supremacy of this act of love requires the purification of Micòl in her narrative role as an object of erotic desire: she evokes passion but does not partake of it.

The narrator cannot possess Micòl any more than Ariosto's Orlando can possess Angelica, although both women are exceedingly desirable and almost within grasp. Because Micòl is not "possessed" sexually, desire for her can find satisfaction only through her suitor's allegorization of her. Adriana, on the other hand, becomes Bruno's lover. In the final Bruno texts, Bassani foregrounds the character's erotic desperation. The narration of Bruno's psychic sundering is the author's final and condemnatory thematization of the imprisoning, self-defeating lack of (male) will; erotic Aryan temptation and destructiveness are the instruments that interlock poetico-erotic failure and political persecution. The texts in question are "La ragazza dei fucili" and "Una corsa ad Abbazia" in the volume *L'odore del fieno*. The assorted fables, short stories, and autobiographical recollections of this volume may at first seem the stuff of a minor collection of miscellanea grouped with no particular design under one cover. They may even strike the reader as an anticlimactic close to the series of powerfully plotted narratives preceding them. But these diverse pieces are both interrelated and essential to Bassani's aesthetic rendering of a definitive ending for the collected fiction. *Odore*, both epilogue and endpoint of the *Romanzo*, effects the retrospective transformation of all the narratives into a consummately structured — doubled, specular, and unified — text of a city and a self.

The contents of *Odore* are divided into five parts: *Due fiabe* (two pieces); *Altre notizie su Bruno Lattes* (three pieces); "Ravenna" (a single piece and the pivotal textual point, structurally and thematically); *Les neiges d'antan* (two pieces); and *Tre apologhi* (three pieces), followed by the essay "Laggiù, in fondo al corridoio." Three very short stories complete the Bruno cycle: the first one depicts a teenaged Bruno not yet acquainted with Adriana and takes him back in memory to the age of three; the latter two elaborate the final parting of Bruno and Adriana. Thus the additional news about Bruno lengthens his textual life in disparate, yet equally extreme, temporal directions: the first news ("Odore") reaches back in time to his earliest childhood, while the other two texts ("Ragazza" and "Abbazia") anchor him *within* the time of his disintegrating romance with Adriana, that is, *in extremis amori*. These narrative addenda effectively complete Bruno's life story, from virtual birth to virtual death. Yet the abrupt return to Bruno Lattes late in the *Romanzo* has another kind of effect — an openendedness about him suggestive of inconclusiveness, which in a Bassanian literary universe is equivalent to moral collapse. The further news of Bruno condemns him to nonexistence. We shall soon discover how the later news of Bruno brings him to the brink of apocalypse.

In its place within the linear narrative chain that constitutes the *Romanzo*, Bruno's "biography" precedes and prefigures the subsequent "autobiography" of the writer that completes the entire volume. These three final narratives frame Bruno in an ambience of estrangement and war. The temporal trajectory of the first narrative, which gives its title to the volume, takes Bruno farther back in time than does any other Bruno sequence: to the period of the First World War. The remaining two texts, set in the late thirties, present a spiritless, "funereal" Bruno in the context of the Second World War about to begin. The last one, "Abbazia," whose title names a resort town near the Yugoslavian border, executes a peripheral spatial dislocation that anonymizes Bruno. By contrast, "Odore" places him at the deepest center of his customary milieu: the Jewish cemetery of the Jewish community of Ferrara. This circumambient topography is at once spatial and social and, by mythic definition, protected.

In the text's opening words, the expansive cemetery is "delimitato torno torno da un vecchio muro perimetrale alto circa tre metri" [p. 677] (completely surrounded by an outside wall about three yards high [W:S, p. 14]) and very close, on the eastern side, to the city wall: self-contained but also joined to a larger whole.[13] In the second paragraph it becomes "our" cemetery: a space that acknowledges family and, in the same instant, the danger inherent in communal identification: "Durante i mesi estivi, l'erba nel nostro cimetero è sempre cresciuta con forza selvaggia. Attualmente non so. Certo è che attorno al '38, all'-epoca delle leggi razziali . . . " [p. 677] (In the summer months, the grass in our cemetery has always grown with savage force. I wouldn't know how it is today, but certainly until 1938, at least—till the time of the anti-Semitic laws in Italy . . . [W:S, p. 14]). The parenthetical reference to the anti-Jewish decrees brusquely reminds the reader that a well-defined minority community, such as the Jewish one of Ferrara, can easily become a highly visible target for persecution. But the vigorous grass emblematizes the survival of the dead; the survival, concretely, of the Jews and, by implication, of the author. The aroma of the newly cut grass (the "aroma" of the title) has reanimating power. This power is material for the weary funeral attendants of the story; once past the cemetery entrance, "un odore acuto di fieno tagliato sopraggiunse a rianimare il corteo oppresso dal caldo. Che sollievo. E che pace" [p. 678] (a sharp smell, the smell of newly mown hay, would come to animate the procession, oppressed by the heat. What relief. And what peace [W:S, p. 15]). In its place as the title of the final prose collection of the *Romanzo*, the aroma signifies a reanimating afflatus for the author, whose Great Work, like a literary Holy Spirit, moves him past desire for a suicidal death, a subject thematized in the work immediately preceding this one, the novel *L'airone*. This metanarrative glance, however, anticipates a reading that depends on the final pieces of *Odore*. To return to the text in question, we note that the narrative present is datable to 1933; Bruno's age is eighteen; two years must pass before he meets Adriana.

An earlier (1946) version of "Odore" (entitled "Il muro di cinta") interlocks with the prewar "Lida" through the family name Camaioli. David Camaioli, of "Lida," is followed by Girolamo Camaioli (Bruno's counterpart) and his uncle, Celio, whose funeral service is performed in "Muro." In the later "Odore," the central character and his dead uncle are both surnamed Lattes. Thus the sign "Bruno" reinscribes this tale as an integral part of the Bruno narrative continuum, while the erased Girolamo Camaioli vests David Camaioli as a Bruno-figure, a shadow to a "Bruno" body. As noted, David functions even *within* the "Lida" text as a shadow, an absence in the narrative present but also a marker of the allegorical birth of a generative authorial figure; this birth occurs in the breach created by Bruno's incapacity to love and his biological capacity to seed a (sickly) child (semiotize a [healthy] authorial birth).

Images of Nazi Persecution

The texts of "Odore" and "Anni" delimit the cardinal points of Bruno's biography — cognitive "birth" and maturity — in a historical context crucial to the entire *Romanzo*, that is, the years of the anti-Jewish laws. Bassani's own increasing sense of the narrative centrality of this epoch can be apprehended by his addition of a phrase in the opening lines of the second version of the cemetery story: "Certo è che attorno al '38, all'epoca delle leggi razziali" [p. 677] (certainly until 1938, at least — till the time of the anti-Semitic laws in Italy [W:S, p. 14]). In contrast to the first writing of "Lida" (that is, "Dèbora"), written under a pseudonym during the very period of the laws and thus at a time when any reference to them would have been unthinkable, "Muro" was written *after* the war, when Bassani was at liberty to write anything he wished but before he had conceived most of what he was to write. The author required some passing of time, and considerably more writing, to think through the overall conception of his work. In the twelve years between the publishing of "Muro" and the publishing of "Odore," he decided to add a direct reference to the period of the anti-Jewish laws. In its revised, postwar shape, "Lida" too contained a significant, if indirect, reference to that epoch, underscoring its essentiality to Bassani's literary organization of reality and truth.

Some key revisions in "Odore" convert the original "Muro" into a fit endpiece (a story of return) for the *Romanzo* and for the substructure of the Bruno construct. The common structure of the twice-written story allows this "single" narrative to both anticipate and echo "Anni," allowing the latter, as we shall see, to "reread" the former.

The historical infiltrates into the brief, private story of "Odore" in critical ways. Bruno's agitation at the funeral reminds him of the earlier funeral of his grandfather in 1924, when Bruno was nine. The chronology establishes the present time as 1933: the year Bruno turns eighteen and Hitler becomes chancellor of Germany. The leitmotiv of Celio's funeral is cancer: (p. 678) "Cancer is not forgiving" chants Bruno's father; cancer is "the family sickness" (p. 679). The disease takes on a metaphoric social identity against which Bruno rails: "Che il cancro potesse diventare assillo quotidiano, pensiero dominante da alimentare e coccolare dentro, fra paura e delizia, per anni e anni? Schifo! Questo al cancro non glielo avrebbe mai permesso. Mai e poi mai" [p. 679] (Should cancer be allowed to become a daily nightmare, an obsession, to be fed and cherished, privately, between fear and delight, for years and years? Disgusting! He would never allow cancer this satisfaction. Never, never [W:S, p. 17]). A correlation builds between the moment of Bruno's uncle's death by disease and the ascent of Hitler to (cancerous) power. Although Celio dies of nephritis, not cancer (as Bruno clarifies), the grandfather *is* struck down by cancer after two years of "inenarrabili sofferenze" (ibid.). The semiotic constellation of "family disease," "1933," and "unspeakable suffering" turns this religious burial rite into a premonitory parable of the unutterable suffering to be inflicted upon the Jewish people, by Hitlerian Germany.

Opening the text of "Odore" is an image of the high-walled Jewish cemetery, its vitality evidenced by the quantity and vigor of the plants with which it merges. Without the plant life the image would remain stark, connoting a barred, imprisoning space, more like the "campo recintato" that describes the same cemetery in "Muro" (p. 7). We can visualize that denuded space as the sign of death camp confinement. The very titles of the two texts signify the difference between the "sterile" earlier tale—"Il muro di cinta"—and the "fertile" later one—"L'odore del fieno."

Bruno's first trip to the cemetery is occasioned by his grandfather's funeral, which the youth now remembers for the swarms of mosquitoes that in his childish imagination resembled warplanes he had actually seen from his grandfather's home years before, during the First World War. Despite the presence of past and future world wars in this brief narrative of death, and even despite the superimposed tracing of the death camp over the burial field, what prevails in "Odore" is life. The cemetery grass, Bruno recalls, was newly cut at his grandfather's funeral "just as now." The trimmed turf—this fiction's sign of animation—impels the nine-year-old Bruno to run in play. Falling, he scrapes his knee. The trivial accident reanimates Bruno's weary mother, who after devoting months to her dying father, now turns to the affectionate nurturing of her son. Her motherly act and her smiling face close the narrative in a small sign of life's dominion over death.

"Odore" may be read as a commentary on "Anni." Both texts open with an extended description of the cemetery in which a funeral procession is about to take place. The names of the dead—Celio and Clelia—are almost the male and female forms of the same name; the processions are slowed by the traffic of peasants returning home at the end of the day; noisemaking disrupts the funeral orations, angering the mourners; Bruno thinks about or sees embracing lovers; war, erotic love, and Bruno's state of sexual solitude are thematically interwoven. The immense communal cemetery, with its prescription of non-Catholics (like Clelia) to burial at its outside bounds (Piazza della Certosa), is an image of social exclusion but also of youthful love, for it is in this square that the city's couples (including Bruno and sixty-year-old Clelia) arrange their rendezvous. Because of these reasons, the *camposanto* always leaves "un'impressione lieta, quasi di festa" [p. 97] (a happy impression, almost a festive one). For Clelia and Bruno the piazza is also a clandestine corner of Ferrara where, as individuals persecuted by the State, they seek "illicit" and partially erotic comfort in each other. The earlier edition of the story emphasizes their emargination as a condition of privilege; many "illustrious non-Catholics of the previous century" are buried outside consecrated soil: "a few Masons, a Jewish freethinker, two or three Protestants" (1955, p. 14). Evoking spirits from Mazzini to Keats, the grand "non-Catholics" of the nineteenth century represent Risorgimental love and defense of liberty, nation, and human rights. The old Socialist Clelia Trotti and the Jew Bruno Lattes, defiled as traitors by the current State, are bruised patriots, and the idealistic Masons and Jews of the last century represent to them a nostalgic time of naive political calm before the Fascist storm.[14] Bruno escapes the storm in 1943, and after the war he returns to Ferrara as a critical observer at Clelia's funeral. The Bruno of "Odore" feels similarly detached from the mourners at his uncle's funeral. Both the post- and the pre-Adriana Brunos occupy a sealed and secure, primarily mental space of critical witness: an embryonic writer's space.

A quiet spectator in a large crowd, the older Bruno, reacting to Clelia's funeral rites, transforms the ceremonies into an ironic social commentary on the political situation of postwar Italy. The younger Bruno, regarding himself as completely different from the blood and ethnic kin standing with him in the Jewish cemetery, poses the sectarian social dilemma of Italian Jewish place. His thoughts are worth quoting at length:

> Che cosa c'era di comune—tornava a domandarsi—fra lui, da una parte, e suo padre coi relativi suoi parenti e affini dall'altra? Lui era alto, secco, scuro di pelle e di capelli, mentre il papà, e dietro al papà l'interminabile sfilata dei Camaioli, dei Bonfiglioli, degli Hanau, degli Josz, degli Ottolenghi, dei Minerbi, dei Bassani, eccetera, costituenti tutti assieme la cosidetta "tribù Lattes," erano in larga prevalenza bassi, tarchiati, forniti di occhi azzurri, di un celeste slavato . . . e di certi speciali menti molli e rotondi, inconfondibili. E moralmente? Ebbene, anche dal lato carattere nessuna somiglianza fra lui e *loro*, grazie a Dio, nemmeno la più piccola. Niente di instabile, di eccitabile, di morboso, in lui, niente di così tipicamente ebraico. Il suo carattere era molto più vicino, così almeno gli sembrava, a quello forte e schietto di tanti suoi amici cattolici, e non per nulla la mamma, nata cattolica, cattolicissima, si chiamava Marchi. [pp. 678-79]

(What was there in common—he asked himself again—between him, on the one hand, and his father with all the complement of kith and kin, on the other? He was tall, slender, with dark skin and hair, while Papa, and with him the endless array of relations named Camaioli, Bonfiglio [*sic*], Hanau, Josz, Ottolenghi, Minerbi, Bassani, etc., who, all together made up the so-called "Lattes tribe," were for the most part short, stocky, with blue eyes, a watery blue . . . and with weak, round chins, unmistakable.

And spiritually? Even when it came to character, there was no resemblance between him and *them*, thank God, not the slightest. Nothing flighty, excitable, morbid in him, nothing so typically Jewish. His character—at least, so it seemed to him—was much closer to the strong, straightforward nature of his many Catholic friends, and it was no accident that his mother had been born a Catholic, into a devout family. Her maiden name had been Marchi!) [W:*S*, pp. 16–17]

The eighteen-year-old protagonist of "Odore" is even ready to take on the family cancer demon: "Che venisse pure, un giorno o l'altro, se avesse avuto voglia di venire! Avanti. Si accomodasse" [p. 679] (Let cancer strike him, one of these days, if strike it must! Let it come, make itself right at home [W:*S*, p. 17]). This Bruno aggressively dissociates himself from his Jewish paternal lineage, aligning himself unequivocally with his Catholic friends and his "happy," "simple," and "natural" mother. This Bruno alone is decisively Catholic. What is particularly striking about his attitude—and his physiognomy—is that it exists in this form only in the text's revised versions (1972; 1974; 1980). Also of note is the text's shifting compositional placement: it first appears (as "Muro") at the beginning of *Storie* (1960), preceding the five narratives of *Cinque storie*. The later "Odore," in the homonymously titled *Odore* (1972), both follows the major works of fiction, from *Cinque storie* to *Airone*, and heads the sequence "Altre notizie su Bruno Lattes." In this context, the reanimating aroma of the grass gains potency as a response to the preceding narrative gesture, Edgardo Limentani's plan of suicide: reinvigoration prevails over death.

The Bruno of "Odore" has little in common with the Girolamo of "Muro":

Più o meno, i Camaioli si assomigliavano tutti—pensava Girolamo. . . . Ogni volta che gli capitava di guardarsi allo specchio, era sempre con disappunto che ritrovava nel proprio volto qualche tratto della fisionomia comune alla famiglia. Anche il suo volto, si diceva allora, come quello di suo padre e di tutti gli altri, era pieno di difetti. Anche lui aveva occhi d'un azzurro scialbo, una fronte dalla linea incerta, un mento rotondo e molle. E il suo carattere, come era? Oh, il suo carattere non era diverso da quello tipico della famiglia. Instabile, morboso, eccitabile: troppo *inferiore* al carattere di tanti suoi amici cattolici, così semplice e forte, invece. [*Storie*, p. 8]

(The Camaiolis pretty much all looked alike, thought Girolamo. . . . Each time he happened to look into the mirror, he was always disappointed to find in his own face some feature that was common to the family. His face, too, he would then say to himself, like his father's and the rest of them, had plenty of defects. He, too, had pale-blue eyes, a not very strong forehead, and a soft, round chin. And what was his character like? Well, his character was no different from the rest of the family's: unstable, morose, and excitable. Really *inferior* to most of his Catholic friends, who, on the contrary, were simple and strong.)

In the later version, Bruno sheds the very traits that denote his sense of inferiority to his Catholic friends and that mark what is "so typically Jewish" in him; traits, furthermore, that are recognizable not only in the Camaioli clan, the sole family named in "Muro," but also in the "interminable" succession of Jewish families named in "Odore." In the latter, names of fictive families mix with others of real families and finally, with the author's own name. The "defective," "inferior," and very Jewish "Bruno" (Girolamo) of the 1960 "Muro" undergoes a metamorphosis into the belligerent, "Catholicized," even anti-Semitic, Bruno of "Odore."[15] This Bruno resembles his counterpart in the *Giardino*, whose "abnormal" appearance and behavior have already been noted (see chapter 1). Bruno's affection for the "decidedly Aryan" species embodied in Adriana begins to suggest a desire to eradicate his Jewish identity by displacing it with an Aryan lover. The self-hatred that generates his ethnic disownment finds its (abject) expression in his (failed) attempt to engage in clandestine political activity (in "Anni"). With merciless logic the narrative's closing scene posits a "hollow" Bruno feeding his existential pain, that is, his insatiable desire to be an Other, by riveting his gaze on a fine-looking young blond couple—the "racial champions" of the day—frolicking on the grass (p. 133). This degree of ethnic self-loathing is matched in the *Romanzo* only by the first-person protagonist of *Porta*, whose self-disgust does not, however, hinge on his Jewishness.

In brief, then, the factor of Jewishness becomes more intense as "Muro" is rewritten into "Odore." From his earlier depiction as a "soft," "deficient," unremarkable, and "characteristic" Jew, Bruno-Girolamo, in the year of Hitler's ascension to power, evolves into an aggressive, scornful, self-confident anti-Jew, ripe at eighteen for an erotic liaison with a Catholic girl. His liaison with Adriana (developed in other texts) materializes two years later and collapses in 1939, in the wake of a gathering war.

"Anni" carries Bruno from the breakup of his erotic relation to his return to Ferrara after the war as a mature and much changed thirty-one-year-old man whose future (in a symbolically valorized America) is open and promising. His earlier turmoil as an outcast Jew and an outcast lover spurs him to cultivate his relation with Clelia, which reaches fruition, finally, in the distant seedbed of America. The archetypal progress from psychic despair and estrangement to self-realization and (creative) strength is of course the grand structural pattern of the *Romanzo*. The imagistic rhetoric of vigor and survival, as in the "reanimating" aroma of the grass and the *calce viva* (quicklime) scattered over the remains of the dead ("Odore"), competes with the textualized historical facts—of rising Nazism and the German occupation of Italy—that invade the narrative present of "Odore" and the narrative climax of "Anni."

Clelia Trotti dies of political persecution: the national disease; Celio Lattes dies of cancerous waste: the family disease. The older Bruno's recollection ("Anni") of his agitated relation with Clelia parallels the younger Bruno's recollection ("Odore") of a childhood moment "perduto in fondo a una lontananza quasi infinita" [p. 680] (lost at the end of an almost infinite distance) when his mother left him with his grandfather while she spent time near the war zone with his father, on military leave. Both instances are encased in erotic anger and loneliness: Bruno's present condition of sexual solitude. The global thematics of the *Romanzo*—psychic death and rebirth—are inextricably attached to relations of sexual suffering.

Unlike the narrating subject of the *Giardino*, who achieves artistic and personal liberation, the composite Bruno counterpart "dies" an empty figure by the end of the three short tales collectively entitled *Altre notizie su Bruno Lattes* (*Odore*). The increasingly "dark" Bruno may be a Bassanian voodoo that exorcizes the worst embodiment of his autobiographical persona in order to clear space for the new embodiment of his persona, the first-person narrators and the metanarrative authorial image born and empowered simultaneously at the close of the extended narrative corpus. Bruno's ethnic estrangement followed by sexual defeat prepares the authorial way of artistic success and power in a context that cleverly foregrounds the textually crucial historical period 1938–39 as the *background* of Bruno's sexual impotence.

By now, the temporal information of early winter 1938 ("Ragazza") and late summer 1939 ("Abbazia") is an instantly recognizable leitmotiv of Jewish humiliation and fear. The final texts to narrativize this period, "Ragazza" and "Abbazia" chant a *de profundis* lamentation for the name-defined dark/dying Bruno, the autobiographical shadow from which our author must liberate himself: "Out of the depths have I cried unto thee, O lord. / Lord, hear my voice: let thine ears be attentive to the voice of my supplications" (Psalms 130:1–2). Bassani's secularized voice, also crying out for moral righteousness and victory, hurls condemnation upon "sinners," including the oppressed as well as the oppressors. Bruno, his sharpest reflexive self, is at once his most unredeemed victim and his most cherished victim: a fallow creature not deprived of authorial grace.

The last texts to center on Bruno zero in at extremely close range on his definitive self-effacement. "Ragazza," opening on his threatened romance with Adriana, lays bare the lovers' fall into grave disaffection; "Abbazia" lays bare their final dissolution. When these episodes conclude, Bruno dissolves as a textual entity, displaced by a firmer alter ego, the writing "I" cunningly constructed in the very last part of the segmented *Odore*. In respect to the total narrative chronology, "Ragazza" and "Abbazia" take place during and after the previously remarked tennis socials of 1938–39 on the grounds of the Finzi-Contini estate. This is the time when marriage between a Jew and a non-Jew (Bruno and Adriana's apparent intention) is outlawed and just before the lovers' breakup leads

Bruno to seek out Clelia Trotti. In other words, Bassani isolates the narrative of the crisis of separation from the narrative continuum and retells it at the outer edge of the *Romanzo*, in a violent language of erotic passion and servitude. "Ragazza" opens in rage: Bruno asking angry questions ("rabbiose, insistenti") and Adriana responding with her habitual and threatening silence (p. 682). Her manner re-evokes Bruno's entire three-year-long relationship with her: "Anche quando ci dava più dentro con le sue famose girandole di chiacchiere spiritose, divertenti, mondane, anche allora dell'Adriana non c'era per niente da fidarsi. In realtà stava lì ad ascoltare in silenzio, minacciosa. Come un muro, non so, o un albero..." [p. 682] (Even when he was at the height of his famous turns of witty chatter, his amusing gossip, even then there was no trusting Adriana. In reality, she sat there and listened: silent, threatening. Like a wall, or, what? like a tree... [W:*S*, p. 22]). Two qualities stand out in Bruno's memory of Adriana: her untrustworthiness and her posture of threat—the very qualities now characteristic of the new political turn to Jewish repression. Bruno's intense desire for (sexual) union with Adriana is a trope of the Italian Jew's desire for (social) union with the (Aryan) nation.

Silence, isolation, and the yearning to recuperate Adriana's sexual favor characterize the Bruno of his last two narratives. In "Ragazza," places of isolation—the room in Adriana's home where Bruno is forced to accept his youthful lover's inclination to be "alone for a while" and the study in Bruno's home where he shuts himself off from his family—reinscribe the self-imprisonment of another authorial surrogate, Elia Corcos ("Passeggiata"), and of Bruno's own father ("Anni"). The first man, a respected doctor, gazes in self-absorption upon open countryside from a home that topographically retraces Adriana's; the second man, a haggard lawyer, "con dolorosa voluttà" [p. 121] (with sorrowful pleasure) seals himself in his "ghetto" home after being expelled from a professional association for being a Jew. Elia's complete surrender to isolation follows from an ill-suited love affair; the father's, from ethnic persecution. Once again the themes of erotic love and Jewish persecution are joined to the theme of self-imprisonment. Bruno's own state reflects an amalgam of eros and ostracism. In solitude and self-pity, he reenvisages Adriana's room, which "lui di notte era potuto penetrare tante volte. Stesa sul letto l'Adriana fumava" [p. 683] (he had been able to enter so many times at night. Lying on her bed now, Adriana would be smoking [W:*S*, p. 24]). Bruno interrupts his "immobilità accidiosa" (p. 684) to roam the streets at night, deliberately avoiding the (bourgeois) center of town and wandering instead among the winding streets of the medieval quarter with its wretched bars. Bruno's peregrination of social and psychic humiliation leads to "that desert . . . that squalor" (p. 684) that names the shrill shrine of Luna Park—the *locus "amarus"* of the "rifle girl." Bruno's is a liminal journey into self-reduction at the lowest degree. His nostalgic fantasy of Adriana in bed, awaiting his "penetration," carefully places his erotic paradise in a nostalgic time of relative political innocence: January to June of 1938, the period immediately preceding the anti-Jewish decrees. "Ragazza" ends with the extreme suffering and degradation of Bruno; his denial of Eden leaves him "branded" with pain.

A long sentence that constitutes a paragraph rich in infinitive and participial verb forms opens "Abbazia" like an echoing of Bruno's state of suspended animation. Its first words slowly trace the passing of the seasons of political and erotic exclusion that have deepened his mortification: "Dopo un inverno, una primavera e una estate trascorsi a macerare in solitudine" [p. 686] (after a winter, a spring, and a summer spent wasting away in solitude). The last words of the sentence initiate the final episode of Bruno's textual history: "Verso la fine d'agosto del '39 Bruno Lattes cominciò a considerare seriamente l'opportunità di rivedere ancora una volta l'Adriana Trentini" [ibid.] (Toward the end of August of 1939 Bruno Lattes began seriously to consider the wisdom of seeing Adriana Trentini one more time). That year is marked by heightening persecution against the Jews: "le leggi razziali che di giorno in giorno si facevano sempre più rigide e opprimenti (pochi scherzi: a farsi beccare, c'era da finire lei in questura come una puttana da marciapiede, e lui al confino)" [ibid.] (the anti-Semitic laws becoming harsher, more oppressive every day [it was no joke; if the two of them were caught, she would end up at Police Headquarters like a common streetwalker, and he would be sent into forced residence somewhere] [W:S, p. 28]. Yet Bruno is determined to make love with Adriana one last time. Only in this way, he believes, will he "liberate himself," shake off his "yoke of servitude," "turn a new page," begin once again to "live" (ibid.). These swift linguistic brushstrokes suffice to polarize erotic bondage and artistic liberation. The political state of extreme risk in August of 1939 is analogous to Bruno's sexual state of extreme servitude. As "Anni" informs us, the definitive end of his "bondage" to Adriana leads to thoughts of political activism: Clelia becomes a substitute (political) "temptress" who offers hope of spiritual liberation.

The desire to "live" again motivates Bruno's impetuous, daylong journey to the city of Abbazia, near the Yugoslavian border, where Adriana and her family are vacationing. In the course of his travel, Bruno is preoccupied equally by visions of Adriana in bed with him and the likelihood of imminent political convulsions: "D'accordo, di Austria e Cecoslovacchia Hitler aveva fatto due soli bocconi. Era davvero pensabile, tuttavia, che a questo punto gli lasciassero inghiottire anche la Polonia? E l'Italia? E gli ebrei italiani?" [p. 687] (True, Hitler had gobbled up Austria and Czechoslovakia in two mouthfuls. Was it conceivable, still, that they would now let him swallow Poland as well? And what about Italy? And the Italian Jews? [W:S, p. 307]). The intensification of the political crisis, as structured in Bruno's thoughts, focuses finally on himself as a Jew. His fear of war is coupled with intensified erotic fantasies of Adriana:

C'era per altro una immagine suscitata dalla sua fantasia che tornava ogni tanto a riempirlo di un paralizzante senso di sfiducia, di incredulità: la grande immagine biondo-rosea dell'Adriana a letto, nuda, la sua pelle liscia e dorata, la sua bocca carnosa da *vamp* americana, i suoi capelli così chiari da sembrare ossigenati al platino, il suo seno, il suo ventre, le sue cosce, il suo odore. [p. 689]

(But there was a vision produced by his imagination, which returned every now and then to fill him with a paralyzing lack of confidence, a feeling of incredulity: the image of Adriana, pink and blond, in bed, naked, [her smooth, golden skin, her full mouth like an American vamp's], her hair so pale it seemed bleached platinum, her breasts, her abdomen, her thighs, her smell.) [W:*S*, p. 32]

The erotic discourse in this narrative is unique within the Bassanian opus for its explicit attention to the sensuous particulars of the female body. Adriana's body is the awesome but potentially liberating "sacred space" toward which Bruno journeys. The entire brief narrative plots a structure of ritual quest: the grail the pilgrim seeks is sexual possession. The liminal space in which Bassani locates Adriana — the "remotissimo" peninsular corner of Istria, near Fiume, isolated from the Ferrarese — allows Bruno the anonymity to defy with probable impunity, "with almost total freedom," in his words (p. 657) the Fascist interdict against Jewish and Aryan socializing. But by placing Adriana in one of the prime hotels of Abbazia, the old Hapsburg Victoria Hotel, Bassani selects an environment that boldly aggrandizes Adriana's Aryan place among the ruling class and her position of irreducible difference with respect to Bruno. Her surname "Trentino" ("from the city of Trent") further intensifies the logic of her "place" within the Austro-Hungarian Empire.

From the start of Bruno's trainride early on the morning of Tuesday, August 29, 1939, through the next two days — Wednesday, the thirtieth, and Thursday, the thirty-first, when at sunset the narrative closes — narrative time conspicuously secures textual prominence. The unusual temporal specificity acts as a magnifying lens surveying in dramatic slow motion not only the psychic death-blow that Adriana delivers to Bruno, but also the conclusive hours before Germany's invasion of Poland on September 1, 1939, which launches the beginning of the Second World War. Bruno's journey transpires in a narrative discourse alternating between intense living and intense dying, with the latter increasingly overwhelming the former. The topos of the journey, utilized in this apparently slight tale, traces the controlling pattern of the *Romanzo* on a microscopic scale rendered grand by means of temporal inertia and the impetus of history. The death of a self (Bruno) and a society (war-ravaged Italy — and Europe) registered by this text is the precondition of the authorial birth and rebirth that is subse-

Figure 13. Abbazia, now the Yugoslavian city of Opatija, on the Adriatic sea. A lovelorn Bruno Lattes rushes to the splendid resort in "Una corsa ad Abbazia."

quently narrativized; this sequence brings the macroscopic journey of the *Romanzo* to a close.

During the busride that carries him into the city, Bruno's fantasy of finding Adriana and himself in Abbazia, leisurely strolling together in public, gives way to a real landscape of thin woods and "sassi, dovunque cumuli di sassi bianchi come ossa" [p. 687] (stones, everywhere heaps of stones as white as bones). These mounds of stones, redolent of the skeletal remains of concentration camp corpses, impose Thanatos upon Eros even before Bruno arrives in the purgatorial seaside (desert shore) of Abbazia, his stomach empty and his mind drifting (ibid.). The biologically, spiritually, and sexually hungry Bruno remembers the "decine e decine di notti" (dozens of nights) of lovemaking in Adriana's bedroom over the course of almost a year. Bruno's recalling the early days of their frequent lovers' rendezvous in Ferrara and the naturalness of their being together anywhere in public is an effort to recuperate that past, to go dancing again, for example, *out in the open* (p. 688), as in the "normal" pre-1938 days. Bruno's need to rightfully reclaim a public space — to liberate himself (p. 686) — seeks its resolution in sex. His vision of dancing "cheek to cheek" with Adriana passes rapidly to one of her returning with him to a rented room, in Abbazia or nearby Fiume, "a seaport and border city". Bruno's attraction to a marginal place — the frontier city within the frontier zone — spatializes his internal tension as an individual ostracized from society and seeking a foothold where social structure cannot reach. But the image of sensuous, nude Adriana lying in bed inflicts itself on Bruno's mind as unrealizable desire and fills him with a "paralizzante senso di sfiducia" [p. 689] (paralyzing sense of distrust). Thus the desired woman offers only denial and, worse, betrayal. As reality replaces fantasy, this semblance of Adriana accrues greater meaning, more concrete and more threatening.

In response to his telephone call, a surprised but "calmissima" Adriana (p. 689) invites Bruno to join her and her family the next morning at the beach. Bruno spends two days in their company, never alone with Adriana and steadily intimidated by her. A remarkable passage that capitalizes on contrasting physiological and spatial particulars encapsulates the relation of oppressor and (willing) victim that now defines the estranged pair:

> Era grande, l'Adriana, abbronzata, pacifica, potente. Mentre lui, nervoso, magro-scheletrico, sbiadito di pelle, non poteva non fare la figura del tipo per tanti motivi sgradevole (pessimo nuotatore, fra l'altro!), da piantare quasi subito là, accoccolato nell'acqua a pochi metri dall'asciutto, in paziente attesa che lei, la *vamp* americana e ariana, dopo essersi allontanata a pigre bracciate verso il largo . . . si degnasse infine di restituirsi alla terra. [pp. 689–90]

> (She was a big girl, Adriana, tanned, tranquil, strong. Whereas, nervous, thin as a skeleton, his skin colorless and not only his skin, he couldn't help looking like somebody who was, for many reasons, unpleasant (a terrible swimmer, into the bargain!), somebody to be left behind almost at once, as he crouched in the water a few yards from the beach, patiently waiting for her, the Aryan, the American vamp, to swim lazily out to sea . . . and then, finally, to condescend to restore herself to the land.) [W:*S*, p. 33]

The figure of the calm and powerful young woman juxtaposed with that of the nervous and skeletal young man evokes, like other variously masked images of Bassanian victimage, the recurrent textual presence of the Nazi-Fascist ("Aryan") oppressor and the Jewish victim. With Adriana's mother, Bruno engages in barely restrained opinions about the likelihood of war, insisting against her belief that Italy will indeed be caught up in a widespread massacre. Throughout their charged exchange, Adriana and her younger sister concentrate their attention on the culinary manners of their little brother Cesarino, creating of themselves a jeering, composite figure of youthful aggression. The scene is followed by Adriana's total withdrawal from Bruno and the latter's withdrawal into himself, alone in his *pensione* room with his fantasy of Adriana's reawakened interest. At this point, the narrative again conflates war and sexual desire: "Tra pochi giorni, forse tra poche ore, la guerra sarebbe scoppiata: oramai lui lo sapeva con certezza. E siccome nel baratro della guerra sarebbe finito tutto,

tutto, perché vietarsi già da adesso di sperare nell'assurdo e non attendere [la telefonata di Adriana] un altro poco?" [p. 691] (In a few days, perhaps in a few hours, the war would break out [it wasn't a presentiment now; he knew it for certain]. And since, in the abyss of the war, everything would end up, *everything*, why forbid himself already to hope for the absurd and to wait [for Adriana's call] a little longer? [W:S, p. 35]).

Imminence of a military holocaust, coupled with failure in amorous expression, like an explosive chemical admixture, transforms Bruno into a consenting victim. The last episode of the story yanks this posture into that of the nonconsenting victim. At sunset Bruno looks across the "silky" Adriatic toward Fiume and sees an elegant white ship, all of its lights on, crossing the gulf "majestically" in the direction of the open sea. This seductive image of beautiful, liberating movement[16] gives way to a jolting greeting from Adriana's little brother, who is riding by on his bicycle. Cesarino, in the "rossa, cupa luce del crepuscolo faceva pensare a uno scugnizzo napoletano in cerca di clienti. Oppure al demonio" [p. 692] (dark red light of sunset, he made one think of a Neapolitan urchin on the lookout for customers. Or else, of a demon). Hanging from his beautiful, new bicycle is a triangular cloth — "una specie di lingua vermiglia, color sangue" (a kind of bright-red tongue, the color of blood) — that, when unfolded, displays a swastika. With a smile that bares his "denti forti e bianchissimi da cane giovane" (strong and very white teeth, like a young dog), Cesarino explains to Bruno that the banner is there "Così, per bellezza" [ibid.] (just because it's pretty). The child's brief and "demoniac" explanation closes the text, leaving a blank space the reader quickly fills.

Cesarino is the little Caesar of the future, a seemingly innocent child who will mature into a powerful and violent demon, a Nazi. The seductive ship, a female image suggestive of Bruno's desire for Adriana, vanishes before the seductive banner, a male image of menace that spells the hopelessness of Bruno's desire. The boy-child who carries the banner is the not-yet-ripe sign of Nazi persecution in Italy, particularly persecution of the Italian Jews. The swastika has the last word in this story. Offering no challenge to the smiling child, Bruno is brought to silence, reduced to a nonexistence that marks his absolute fall into despair: the Neapolitan urchin has effectively found his customer-victim. The definitive casting-out of Bruno is enacted through a textual process that amalgamates personal (erotic) repudiation and political aggression. Neither action is privileged over the other: they are one and the same; or, more accurate, each is a metaphor of the other. A global note of defeat and imminent catastrophe tolls Bruno's slide into the abyss and the end of the tale.

Fables of Death and Survival

The two short narratives that open *Odore* are bracketed under the prescriptive title *Due fiabe*. The first one, "La necessità è il velo di Dio," is dominated by a theme of birth and mothering: a Jewish woman, Egle Levi-Minzi, "non brutta, né povera, né sciocca, né matura—non specialmente appetibile, se vogliamo, però neanche da buttar via" [p. 669] (neither ugly nor poor nor foolish nor old—not especially appetizing, so to speak, but neither worth throwing away), *finally*, in her middle thirties, has a child. Her taut story, which begins in 1935, is a mythico-historical affirmation of Jewish life that turns on a pivotal character, her young son—"vivace, intelligente, prepotente, bellissimo" (lively, intelligent, domineering, and very handsome)—who survives the war and becomes an inspiring example of vitality to the Jewish community of Ferrara (p. 672).

Egle Levi-Minzi is in certain ways cut of the same cloth as Micòl Finzi-Contini, from their rhyming, hyphenated surnames and Sephardic Jewish origins to their prosperous, elderly fathers and, most important, to their willful decision (as both narratives take care to point out) not to marry during the expected marrying years of young female adulthood. In Egle's case, the text is strangely and ambiguously silent on the question of marriage to her child's father, as if to emphasize that the union matters only for the child that is born. A robust, mythopoeic figure of fertility—real and metaphoric, as is Micòl—Egle symbolizes through her child the divinely protected survival of the Jewish people; Micòl, through the novel-"document" of her would-be husband, the novel's narrator, symbolizes the artistically protected survival of personal and moral witness.

Egle's beautifully crafted fable of procreative blessing in "Necessità" is a palinode of "Lida," the opening piece of the *Romanzo*. The poor and Catholic Lida bears an unhealthy child, "di una natura un po' fiacca, un po' svogliata" [p. 28] (whose nature is a bit weak and listless). The child, Ireneo, resembles his Jewish father, David, who abandons Lida and is, throughout the narrative-present, no more than a perplexing memory. This first birth *of* (not only in) the *Romanzo* "miscarries," that is, promises nothing. But it informs from the start the thematic of (female) birthgiving and (male) maturation that retrospectively assumes a major intranarrative role in the project of authorial "birth." The end of the *Romanzo*, as we shall soon see, recapitulates this theme in allegorical discourse, within which the author's self-as-text, in the form of the pronoun "I," is *finally* (the long time required for this birth is analogous to the late motherhood of Egle) born.

The Ashkenazic Jew Yuri Rotstein, who fathers Egle's child, reaches Ferrara from the Ukraine with his dignified and religious "old world" parents on an east-to-west migration (the traditional movement of progress) that was to conclude in Palestine but instead concludes in a German death camp. The childlike, poor, and homeless Yuri is a "Lohengrin" whose halted wandering shortly before death secures, symbolically, the survival of the Jewish people—Eastern and Western, Ashkenazi and Sephardi—in the being of the singular child he and Egle conceive. Yuri's fortuitous presence in Ferrara cannot be attributed to the usual good work of the Jewish community, which, through its network of contacts, ensures a proper husband for a needy woman. As the text informs: "Non c'era mai da disperare. Quando a produrre uno sposo non fosse bastata la piazza, eccolo, Lohengrin, sopraggiungere di lontano: a vedere, a farsi vedere, e quasi sempre a concludere" [p. 669] (No situation was ever desperate. When our own city failed to produce a bridegroom, lo, some Lohengrin would arrive from afar: to see, to be seen, and almost always to conclude the transaction [W:S, pp. 3–4]). But in this case the presence of the distant stranger only passing through must be attributed to "necessity": the "veiled" act of God, not of human beings, to which the title alludes. Yuri and Egle's son, a virtual miracle of contingency, is a sign of Jewish indestructibility despite great trial. The "really exceptional" child – named after his father – seemed "ai pochi di noi che scamparono ai campi di sterminio e al resto . . . la personificazione stessa della vita che in eterno finisce e ricomincia" [p. 672] (to the few of us who escaped the Lagers and the rest . . . the very personification of life that eternally ends and eternally begins again [W:S, p. 7]). The young Yuri and his mother live "still" and "forever" in their large house in Ferrara (ibid.); the child's paternal heritage lives too, stamped boldly in the slanted blue eyes and high cheekbones inherited from his father and his father's father: God's visible sign of Jewish continuity and destiny.

The difference between the offspring Ireneo and Yuri is the difference between the author's prewar vision of social entrapment and hopelessness and his postwar vision of social outrage and self-righteousness; in other words, the difference between impotence and power. The self-defeating, introspective David, who fathers a listless son, yields in time and narrative space to the magnificent, Lohengrinesque Yuri of the "smiling" and "wild" blue eyes (p. 671), who fathers a timeless child of life. So too Lida's stifling backward gaze yields to Egle's strong and forward-looking ("everlasting") vision: *her* gestures valorize history.

Egle's desire for sexual intercourse is motivated by maternal, rather than erotic, interest: "Ebbene, perché non averlo appunto con quel giovane, un figlio? – si era detta a un tratto Egle Levi-Minzi come risvegliandosi da un lungo torpore" [p. 671] (Well, why should she not have a son by that very young man? Egle Levi-Minzi had asked herself abruptly, as if waking from a long slumber [W:S, p. 7]). The distinction is significant, for the erotic in woman (by Bassanian depictions) always has its dark side; female sexual desire is, simply, "impure" – but Egle is eminently otherwise. Bassani's eroticized Jewish women are totally different from his Catholic ones; for example, Nives Pimpinati (*Airone*) or Adriana Trentini ("Ragazza" et al.). The latter women are endowed with "negative" attributes, such as flirtatiousness, mediocre intelligence, insensitivity; but the Jewish women – Micòl, Egle, the mother in *Porta* – are strong-minded, upper-class exemplars of untainted womanhood.

Micòl and the mother in *Porta*, both apotheosized rulers of a garden, are Jewish women who arouse erotic desire; the reader, however, is given no textual indication that either is sexually active. The eroticism forced upon the mother of *Porta* is a necessary humiliation *of the son* in its particular place within the narrative structure of the *Romanzo*. Within the novella, the son's humiliation (which closes the story) is a point of truncation, an unfruitful self-alienation. In the context of the entire *Romanzo*, it becomes a narrative moment that will be surpassed—or, better, a moment that will, from the viewpoint of subsequent texts, assume positive signification.

"Ai tempi della Resistenza," the second of the two fables that open *Odore* (the book that constitutes the last chapter of the *Romanzo*), again embeds the historical in the ahistorical, this time through the modality of dream discourse. "Resistenza" is set on a late night in December, in Ferrara's Hotel Tripoli—"now" destroyed, the narrator points out (p. 673). (In another text [*Porta*], this lowest-quality hotel, once the temporary home of the Pulga family, implied the family's lowest possible status as human beings.) The "Resistance" plot places a weary Mr. Buda, of southern speech, in this exceedingly unclean and inhospitable space. Buda seems to be a traveling salesperson but is really (or does he only dream it?) a militant anti-Fascist with a suitcase full of clandestine printed matter. After considerable insistence, the stranger in town succeeds in claiming the last available room in the hotel. Once in it, he repeats out loud the familiar saying Life is a dream: "La vita è un sogno."[17] This literary topos speaks freshly in this narrative to the equation (or fusion) of life and dream. At the base of the traveler's vision is the implied "unreality" of Italian life created by the Fascist assumption of power. Bassani translates Buda's sensation of unreality into anamorphic distortions: oblique views (a door that opens into a corner, a closet mirror that reflects an angled section of Buda's room) and obscure views (across fog and humidity; and dark and dirty garments that conceal the stranger's face) that intimate the "darkest epoch of Fascism" (p. 673), in which this fable is set.

One would ordinarily ascribe Fascism's darkest moment to the period of the Nazi-Fascist Salò regime of 1943–45, and the narrative's title seems to confirm this, for Italian resistance properly begins with the German occupation of Italy in late 1943. Textual chronology, however, locates the Hotel Tripoli near the Este castle *before the war* (that is, before May of 1940), "about forty years ago" (p. 673). Thus (assuming the author's usual attention to historical and autobiographical veracity) the story would unfold, with respect to the narrative present, in the immediate prewar period, that is, in the late thirties, the time of the anti-Jewish laws. Before this, Fascism was still enjoying the so-called years of consensus. (When Bassani affronts historical accuracy, as in his bold redating of the November 14 massacre in Ferrara [see "Notte"], the reader must assume that narrative needs, not carelessness, dictate any falsification.) In "Resistenza" the historical conflation of 1943–45 and 1938–39 effectively superimposes the Nazi-Fascist persecution of Resistance fighters on the Fascist persecution of Jews. Thus the lone Mr. Buda, a "Calabrian or Sicilian," becomes a figure of the persecuted Ferrarese Jew. Both the persecuted Jew and the southerner find themselves in danger and easily recognizable: the Jew, by membership in the Jewish community; the southerner, by his "foreign" speech and his anti-Fascist pamphlets. Both are considered traitors to the State: the Jew, by ethnic definition; the southerner, for his anti-Fascism. Both are homeless in Ferrara: the Jew, as a disenfranchised citizen; the southerner, as a *forestiero*. In the "foreign" city of Ferrara, each becomes suspect and risks mortal punishment. In his "dream within a dream," Buda sees himself in a mirror:

> E alla vista del corpo, del *proprio* corpo, anziché meravigliarsene faceva col capo un cenno d'assenso. Bene. Molto bene. Completamente nudo, le bianche gengive scoperte, ridotto a quel puro fantoccio e basta che *doveva* essere, sedeva appoggiando la lunga guancia nera di barba alle ginocchia rannicchiate. [p. 676]

> (And at the sight of the body, of his own body, instead of being amazed, he gave a nod of assent. Good. Very good. Completely naked, white gums bared, reduced to that mere puppet and nothing else, the puppet he *had* to be, he was seated with his long cheek, black with beard, resting on his huddled knees.) [W:S, p. 12]

Persecution is dehumanization: the person become puppet, the self negated, the face distorted ("white gums bared"), the body exposed and vulnerable (naked and in a fetal position), the victim, the Jew. The victim in this fiction, however, escapes: he reaches the train station as a locomotive pulls in. Or *does* he escape? – for Buda does not depart. In any case, where would the train take him: to safety? to a death camp? In contrast to the fable of assured survival with which it is paired, "Resistenza" internalizes the uncertain survival of the victim as an eerie psychic journey into a dislocated (anamorphic) reality. Reality is the familiar world of work, affection, and routine. Mr. Buda's self-conscious dream within a dream is a wrenching, disjunctive experience of placelessness. The author Primo Levi's *La tregua* (*Reawakening*), a novelized record of Levi's experience under the wardship of the Russian Army after his liberation from Auschwitz and until his repatriation to Italy, provides in its final words a paradigm for Mr. Buda's dreamworld:

> Giunsi a Torino il 19 di ottobre [del 1946]. . . . Ma solo dopo molti mesi svanì in me l'abitudine di camminare con lo sguardo fisso al suolo, come per cercarvi qualcosa da mangiare o da intascare presto e vendere per pane; e non ha cessato di visitarmi, ad intervalli ora fitti, ora radi, un sogno pieno di spavento.
> È un sogno entro un altro sogno, vario nei particolari, unico nella sostanza. Sono a tavola con la famiglia, o con amici, o al lavoro, o in una campagna verde: in un ambiente insomma placido e disteso, apparen-

temente privo di tensione e di pena. . . . al procedere del sogno . . . tutto cade e si disfà intorno a me, lo scenario, le pareti, le persone, e l'angoscia si fa più intensa e più precisa. Tutto è ora volto in caos: sono solo al centro di un nulla grigio e torbido, ed ecco, io *so* che cosa questo significa, ed anche so di averlo sempre saputo: sono di nuovo in Lager, e nulla era vero all'infuori del Lager. Il resto era breve vacanza, o inganno dei sensi, sogno: la famiglia, la natura in fiore, la casa. Ora questo sogno interno, il sogno di pace, è finito, e nel sogno esterno, che prosegue gelido, odo risuonare una voce, ben nota; una sola parola, non imperiosa, anzi breve e sommessa. È il comando dell'alba in Auschwitz, una parola straniera, temuta e attesa: alzarsi, "Wstawac."[18]

I arrived in Turin on October 19 [of 1946]. . . . But only after several months did I lose the habit of walking with my eyes fixed on the ground, as if I were searching for something to eat or to put quickly into my pocket to sell for some bread; and a frightening dream never stopped coming back to me, sometimes very frequently, sometimes only occasionally.

It's a dream within a dream, changing in the particulars, but the substance is always the same. I'm sitting at the table with my family or friends, or at work, or in a green countryside: in a quiet, relaxed place, in short, apparently devoid of any tension or pain. . . . as the dream goes on . . . everything around me falls and disintegrates: the scenery, the walls, the people; and my anxiety becomes more intense and more precise. Everything has now become chaos. I am alone at the center of a gray and murky nothingness, and suddenly I *know* what it means, and I also know that I have always known it: I am once again in the concentration camp, and nothing was real beyond the concentration camp. The rest was a brief vacation or deception of the senses, a dream: family, nature in bloom, home. Now this internal dream, the dream of peace, is over, and in the external dream, which continues icily, I hear a very familiar voice calling out a single word; not arrogantly however, but in a quick, subdued way. It's the command at dawn in Auschwitz, a foreign, feared, and expected word: get up, "Wstawac.")

Mr. Buda's dream within a dream also structures anguished helplessness. He dreams he is asleep and then that he is awake. In this state of dreamed wakefulness, he starts to fulfill his political mission, but he lacks its substance, the anti-Fascist literature. When he actually wakes up and realizes that his failure and fruitless self-exposure were mere dream figments, he is left only "amaramente" (painfully) comforted, for the outer dream to which he returns is the Fascist reality, the topsy-turvy world of chaos, threat, and reduction to puppetry. The resister (to repeat Levi's words) is "alone at the center of a gray and murky nothingness." Levi's camp victim and Bassani's Resistance victim respond to similar structures of dislocation and isolation. The lost reality of normal family and so-cial life – the "brief vacation" of full-class citizenry – comes to a precipitous end in Bassani's texts with the advent of the anti-Jewish laws. Coextensive with the broad, narrative unfolding of his fiction is the Jewish shame under those laws, its reduction (to use his own metaphors) to the "lowest category," that is, to "nu-dity."[19] Historically, Jewish anti-Fascist activity rallied in response to the anti-Jewish laws. This was true specifically for Bassani. Thus the author interrelates and interchanges anti-Fascism and Jewish oppression as figures of each other. Less easily was he able to represent the Auschwitzes of Europe, whose direct experience fortune spared him. Bassani's literary solution to his personal inex-perience lies less in the brief declarations of deportations interspersed in his texts than in the allusive imagery and rhetorical circumlocutions that assert with quiet power the invisible presence of that unspeakable reality. The exposed stranger, Buda, enclosed in a disorienting hotel room; the threatened Edgardo Limentani encircled by angry workers; the mother maligned as a "Jewess" and a sex object by a young proto-Nazi; and the periphrastic naming of the period of deportation all illustrate Bassani's techniques of expressing what he did not witness and therefore could not narrativize. The intermittent discourse of allusion does not constitute an incidental narrative statement about the Holocaust. Rather, the ex-emplary veiled imagery fashions exclamatory punctuation within the fiction's predominant discourse of memory and moral castigation. Bassani's texts are poetic sermons to the immorality of the many during and immediately after the Fascist and Nazi-Fascist epochs. The orientation of the texts places them in a lamentational literary tradition reaching back to the Old Testament.[20] Death and survival are Bassani's great themes; his desire to invent a metaphor for those themes finds its supreme object in the 1938 anti-Jewish legislation and its after-math, the 1943–45 exterminations. Egle Levi-Minzi and her extraordinary child embody survival – the survival of Jewish survival despite Draconian persecu-tion; Mr. Buda embodies the dreamlike unreality of "naked" impotence before pitless violence. Bassani's global persona strives to overcome mortal and metaphoric death across the several texts of the *Romanzo*; the historical origin of his literary pursuit of death and survivorship must be located, I believe, in the Hitlerian enactment of the so-called final solution. It is Bassani's necessary literary task to send beloved characters like Micòl Finzi-Contini and Doctor Elias Corcos to death in concentration camps, but those deaths are eventually compensated by the hard-won survival of the (recording) persona, the registrar of their lives.

Ravenna: The Turning Point

The theme of survival in the two fables just discussed yields to that of death in the three Bruno Lattes stories that follow (grouped under "Notizie"). Then, from the "death" of Bassani's most representative third-person persona (in "Abbazia") rises the first-person autobiographical narrator of "Ravenna"; this text (structurally central in *Odore* and thematically central in *Romanzo*) lays the groundwork for the emergence of a self-possessed and victorious writerly "I."

The title "Ravenna" is more an ideological than a geographical term; the earlier edition of the *Romanzo* (but not the 1980 one) spells this out in the first paragraph: "Si era, insomma, con ogni probabilità, tra il '21 e il '22, durante quel periodo di agitazioni e di violenza, in Emilia-Romagna più gravi, forse, che in qualsiasi altra regione d'Italia, che condusse alla Marcia su Roma e al resto" [1974, p. 765] (In all likelihood it was sometime between 1921 and 1922, during that period of strikes and violence, perhaps more serious in Emilia-Romagna than in any other region of Italy, which then led to the March on Rome and the rest [W:*S*, p. 38]). As the capital of Romagna, Ravenna encapsulates the extreme political violence of the 1920s that nurtured the rise of Fascism. Mussolini himself was *romagnolo*. By late 1920 and early 1921, the contiguous regions of Romagna and Emilia (which includes Ferrara) were strongholds of organized and terroristic Fascism; they were, in fact, the very center of its agrarian formation.[21] As a point of passage for a vacationing boy (who later writes down this narrative of summertime family trips), Ravenna functions as a *personally* significant city. The narrative interlaces a portrait-montage of political events and representative individuals in Emilia-Romagna between post-World War I and mid-World War II with an autobiographical portrait that extends from childhood to marriage. Traces of earlier texts define the work ultimately as the writer's testament to his own literary history. The minimal strokes that sketch the youth's progress to adulthood simultaneously sketch his literary maturity. By juxtaposing various swatches of intertexts, the narrative forcefully detaches itself from the earlier third and first-person personae demarcating a new, liberating space for a new model of the writing subject.

The first of "Ravenna's" six segments is dense in intertextual markers: the narrator's father as a military officer, World War I warplanes, Uncle Giacomo, a farm worker's sickle ("falce"), a field of fresh grass ("l'erba fresca, dura, del prato" [p. 693]). This constellation of images resonates to the specific text of "Odore"; the one exception is Uncle Giacomo, who appears in the text's prior form, entitled "Il muro di cinta." Both versions, it will be recalled, narrate Bruno Lattes's recollection of youthful incidents—a literary form adopted in some respects by "Ravenna." The mowing ("falciatura") that in "Odore" symbolizes renewed spiritual vitality is politicized in "Ravenna" and split into two concrete, demystifying signs: violent "Bolshevik" farm workers carrying (of course) sickles ("falci") and bellicose Fascist war aces gathered on a runway of grass— fresh grass that animates in *this* text a celebration of violence. The structural similarities of the texts, plus Bassani's expropriation of his earlier tropes and flagrant deformation of their original meaning, effect a usurpation and transvaluation of Bruno's space for another voice: a new first-person voice that only now can surpass the exhausted/expired third-person Bruno-image of the creator.[22] This achievement occurs in the first segment; the remaining five, as if to assist the authorial lunge forward, continue in a less structured, more intense way to interpose among their own events citations from earlier narratives. Because each of the segments is very short and discontinuous, the reader feels assaulted by a rapid sequence of images that carry her or him simultaneously backward — to narratives already read — and forward — toward the writing persona about to claim a personal space.

The narrator begins "Ravenna" with a recollection of himself as a child of six. The year, 1922 (if we use information in the 1974 text), is autobiographically accurate, but it also signals a monumental political fact: Mussolini's installation as prime minister. In the 1980 text, the muted autobiographical specificity of the author's birthdate and the expunged allusion to Ravenna's infamous standing as the cradle of agrarian Fascism enhance the contingent and experiential over the fixed historical. The narrative structure of six distinct tableaux separated graphically by asterisks spatializes the factor of temporal discontinuity that accentuates the ritualistic function of the narrated events. The intertextual resonances extend the semantic power of this four-page text still farther, to metanarrative.

The second tableau's constellation of the narrator (at age "ten or eleven"), his family, and various seaside summer resorts in Romagna (Rimini, Cattolica, Cesenatico, and so forth) retraces the context and the slightly older protagonists of *Porta* and *Occhiali*. The hot July sun at its zenith, the crowd of hefty, "bronzed," "feverish-looking" Ravennese men, and the family's habitual stop at the central café en route to the sea invest the anecdotal scene with a mythic quality. The year is 1926 or 1927 and the men are the "famous" *squadristi* of Ravenna (p. 695), whose brutal and vandalistic history, as the text notes, goes back to the earliest Fascist combat bands of 1919. The next episode, disengaged momentarily from the gnarled thread of Fascism's progress that binds these "Ravenna" tableaux, is a study in serenity set some time after 1930 (when the narrator is about fourteen). This third episode excludes all society except the narrator and his family, and it shifts their usual summer stopover from the city (Ravenna) to the open countryside (Sant'Apollinare), where the sea breezes, the coolness of the cathedral, and the family's affectionate race to Sant'Apollinare — some go by bicycle, some by car — function utopistically to preserve the prelapsarian Jewish state of social parity that Fascism, like a roaring tornado, will soon shatter. This idealized third episode will echo darkly in the sixth (and last) one, which is dedicated to the narrator's marriage and honeymoon. The intervening parts return to the political situation and age the narrator to nineteen. The fourth episode stages another beach scene exemplary of "the dramatic intensity of contrasts" that the narrator finds characteristic of Ravenna. The drama here consists of the explosive "ardore segreto, la cupa, ribollente lava interiore" [ibid.] (secret ardor, the dark, fermenting, interior lava [W:*S*, p. 43]) felt by some children of anti-Fascist Anarchists and members of the Catholic *Partito popolare* whom the narrator befriends; their political consciousness responds to the end of Italian parliamentary government and the Fascist entrenchment. The penultimate episode takes place in 1935 (a still-innocent time) and centers on a "bella casa in mezzo alla pineta con annesso campo di tennis" [p. 697] (beautiful house among the pines with its own tennis court [W:*S*, p. 43]), where a group of youngsters arrive, "tutti in bicicletta e vestiti da tennis" [ibid.] (all on bicycles, in tennis clothes [W:*S*, p. 44]): this staging is an obvious invocation of the *Giardino*. The unfamiliar elements in the "Ravenna" text, however, reduce the rarefied Finzi-Continian matter to a narrative of brute power and sadistic humiliation. Most pointed is the "magnifica ragazza . . . una brunona formidabile" [ibid.] (magnificent young woman . . . a splendid, large brunette), who cuckolds her bemused and spineless literary aspirant of a husband with Ravenna's *squadristi*. The effect of the nearly symmetrical composition is textual dislocation, which highlights not the heroine Micòl on the tennis courts, but a secondary female character of the *Giardino*, Adriana Trentini, another tennis player. A form of Adriana reemerges in the "brunona" of "Ravenna," who betrays her legitimate (marital) sexual partner; the husband's analogue in the *Giardino* is an illegitimate (rejected) sexual partner, Bruno. The ironic intertextual play evidences the "new" persona's self-irony—and therefore success—in "killing off" the old Bruno-persona.

The final episode reaches the historically critical moment of the short-lived Badoglio liberation and represents a critical textual crossroad. The spare opening sentence (paragraph) is dense with contradictory implications: "Ci sposammo nell'agosto del '43, durante il periodo badogliano" [p. 697] (We were married in August of 1943, during the period of the Badoglio government). Each of the sentence's three constituent parts expresses a *rite de passage*: the transformation of a nineteen-year-old youth into a twenty-seven-year-old husband ("ci sposammo"); the end of the Fascist regime and the outlawing of the Fascist party ("nell'agosto del '43"); the reinstitution of parliamentary government ("durante il periodo badogliano"), which is, however, about to distintegrate under the Nazi occupation and the "second coming" of Fascism under the name of the *Repubblica sociale italiana*. The first transformation, the ritual of marriage, pales before the political rupture and national upheaval that are tersely inscribed in the remainder of the same short sentence.

The topos of marriage is traditionally reserved for the final act of a literary text (as it is here), to circumscribe halcyon and productive closure. But the newlyweds of "Ravenna" remain suspended between two worlds: a daytime world of pleasurable boating and bathing in waters near Ravenna and a nighttime world of political discussion inside the oppressive quarters of a Socialist butcher (p. 698). Italy's "daytime" hope for armistice and peace in August of 1943 darkens under the renewed sound of war that beats a rhythm of September of 1943 and cataclysmic subjugation. This narrative on catastrophe's edge concludes at the edge of day. Against the picturesque backdrop of a falling sun behind woods edging a shore, warplanes at practice preannounce the coming disaster while retracing a circular literary trail that reinvokes the eighteen-year-old Bruno Lattes in the act of remembering himself as a three-year-old child who saw distant fighter planes as mosquitoes. The narrator-husband, a closer approximation than the Bruno figures of the "life-size" author-creator, observes life-size planes practically grazing his head. Yet, the infantile joy of the child Bruno is still implanted in the adult arena of sadness and death, where the narrative reaches silence: "Piccoli, argentei aeroplani da caccia facevano evoluzioni di prova. . . . E il loro rombo lacerante, quando sfrecciavano sulle nostre teste accostate, ci riempiva di un'allegria infantile, alla quale, in me, seguiva una segreta tristezza tutta intrisa d'addio" [p. 698] (Tiny, silvery pursuit planes swarmed, on maneuvers. . . . And their piercing roar, when they whipped over our joined heads, filled us with a childish joy, followed, in me, by a secret sadness, all steeped in farewell [W:S, pp. 45–46]). In one sense, the new husband's "allegria infantile" (infantile happiness) is an "allegoria infantile" (infantile allegory) that offers a nostalgic homage to the Bruno-child, a homage ameliorating the prior "slaughter" of the Bruno-young adult. The full-scale airplanes that image the impending war and the presence of the narrator-husband also contrast with the absence of Bruno, now only a shadow.

The narrator assumes still greater life-size proportions in the definitive *Romanzo* (in contrast to the earlier edition): the bride's name is no longer Vittoria, but "Val," short for Valeria. The change is a corrective unmasking of the earlier, now truly fictive name, for the name of the woman Bassani married in August of 1943 is Valeria. Thus the writer moves his textual self closer to his phenomenal self, in an act parallel to the conversion of "infantile joy" into "secret sadness, saturated [*intrisa*; also "soiled"] with good-byes." The "soiled" joy and secret sadness bid a retrospective good-bye to the simple pleasures of a long-ago family outing to Sant'Apollinare. That brief vacation relived has retrospective metaphoric value similar to the one about which Primo Levi has written. The narrator of "Ravenna" does not share his sadness with his wife: "In *me*," he notes, a secret sadness followed. This small gesture of privacy reaffirms at the narrative's terminus the singularity of the writing persona, the generation of a writing "I" that *from now on* will claim unmediated textual life and power: "Ravenna" is the originating moment of the vengeance of the once self-destructive and victimized (as a Jew and as an anti-Fascist under Fascism) autobiographical persona.

The narrative's placement at the pivotal center of *Odore* is underscored by the two fables following it: "Cuoio grasso" and "Pelandra," whose collective title is *Les neiges d'antan*. Compositionally these narratives correspond to the opening *Due fiabe* of the same book. The structural symmetry suggests that the second pair of fables announces a second textual beginning. In contradistinction to the first half of the book's contents, which concludes in Bruno Lattes's spiritual and textual death ("Ragazza" and "Abbazia"), this beginning concludes with a form of authorial birth. The parallel structure *and* the dissimilar contents informing it are equally productive of reciprocal meaning. As if in antiphonal response to the themes of Jewish and Resistance survival in extreme danger ("Necessità" and "Resistenza," respectively), "Neiges" thematizes the contrary movement of (Aryan) youthful promise suffocated. Each of its texts focuses on a young Ferrarese man who associates with a circle of crude, self-indulgent *sfatti* (wasters; good-for-nothings). The relation of diametric opposition between these stories and those of Egle Levi-Minzi and Buda (*Due fiabe*) derives from their temporal spans (preceding and postdating Fascist persecution versus existing with it), from their sociopolitical situations (privatized family dramas with no political content versus representative political dramas of persecution), and from their stylistic modalities (naturalistic versus allegorical). These distinctions create an instrumental difference between the two sets of texts: the realistic participation of a self-naming authorial "I" as a character within the fiction *in the second group alone*.

The narrator of "Cuoio" is writing "now" in Rome: "In ogni caso mi sono dato da fare, come dicono qui a Roma, lavorando, faticando, vivendo" [p. 700] (In any case, I kept busy, as they say here in Rome, working, toiling, living [W:*S*, p. 49]). This interpolation of the writing subject *in the act of writing*, that is, participating in a doubled narrative time—past and present—is unprecedented in the Bassanian oeuvre. Until the texts of "Neiges," the narrating voice has functioned as a recorder of the past. As recently as the text of "Ravenna," that perspective has remained intact: "Il ricordo più lontano che ho di Ravenna è dei tempi immediatamente successivi alla prima guerra mondiale" [p. 693] (My most distant memory of Ravenna belongs to the years just after the First World War [W:*S*, p. 38]). The present-tense "che *ho* di Ravenna" functions exclusively to put distance between the writer and the experience he is recording. The first sentence of "Cuoio," without any reference to present time, appears even more typical of the narrator's reflection solely upon past time: "C'è sempre stato qualcosa che mi ha impedito di diventare amico di Marco Giori, di diventarlo veramente" [p. 699] (Something always prevented me from becoming Marco Giori's friend, a real friend [W:*S*, p. 47]). Having in the first paragraphs firmly established the narrative action in the distant past—the narrator a boy of fourteen, the year 1930—the unexpected entry of the narrating "I" in present time and presently occupied space ("here in Rome") creates the illusion of doubled temporality: the narrator's contemplation *in* writing of past experience and his self-reflexive writing *of* writing. Memory and experience conflate to produce the (illusory) process of the writing as a narrative event that inscribes the narrator-author as a textual "presence."

Bassani's awareness of self-inscription may be discerned by the changes he made in the original version of "Cuoio," entitled "In esilio" (in *Storie*). Revisions of the text occur significantly in the two key paragraphs that insert the first-person, autobiographical, *authorial* voice into the text. The original reads: "Dopo mi sono sposato, ho avuto dei figli, sono andato via da Ferrara, sono ritornato, sono ripartito di nuovo. Non è che nella vita io presuma di aver combinato molto. Comunque mi sono dato da fare, come dicono qui a Roma, ho lavorato, ho vissuto" [p. 322] (After I was married and had children, I left Ferrara, then returned, and then left again. I really don't think I put much together in my life. Nonetheless I kept myself busy, as they say here in Rome, working and living). In the revised version, Bassani adds critical specificity—about his writing profession and his relocation away from Ferrara: "Dopo mi sono sposato, sono andato via da Ferrara, ho messo radici altrove, ho avuto dei figli, ho scritto e pubblicato dei libri: coi molteplici contraccolpi in bene e in male che da tutto ciò è derivato. In ogni caso mi sono dato da fare, come dicono qui a Roma, lavorando, faticando, vivendo" [p. 700] (Afterward, I married and left Ferrara, I put down roots elsewhere, I had children, I wrote and published books: with the many results, good and bad, that derive from all those things. . . . In any case, I kept busy, as they say here in Rome, working, toiling, living [W:*S*, p. 49]). In addition to abandoning rhetorical modesty regarding his standing as a writer (he had already won a literary prize for *Cinque storie* four years before *Storie*, and the *Giardino* was in a late writing stage), Bassani underscores the continuing process and immediacy of his writing by changing the present-perfect verbal forms of "Esilio" into present participles in both *Romanzo* collections: "lavorando, faticando, vivendo" (working, toiling, living). The addition of "faticando"—the effort of doing—underscores still more the continuing (and implicitly painstaking) task of writing: a Pavesian "lavorare stanca."[23] Chronological updating in the rewritten text also underscores the narrative's intention of autobiographical veracity: Marco's father buys him a car "twenty-five years ago" in "Esilio" (p. 322), "some thirty years ago" in "Cuoio" (p. 700). Similarly, "fino a pochi mesi fa" [*Storie*, p. 323] (until a few months ago) becomes "fino a qualche anno fa" [p. 701] (until a few years ago).

In noting his "present" comfortable position as an established writer, husband, and father now living in Rome, the narrating "I" draws the measure of his success against the story he is unfolding: that of an elegant, affluent, and popular youth, Marco Giori, with whom the pubescent narrator has long and unsuccessfully coveted friendship. Marco (although the text does not state it overtly) is an example of the prototypical Aryan envied by the prototypical Jewish first- or third-person protagonist of Bassani's fiction. The teenaged narrating "I," in contrast to Marco, reckons himself "non soltanto diverso, ma inferiore. Era chiaro, la mia presenza non contava un centesimo" [p. 700] (not only different, but inferior. It was clear: my presence counted for nothing [W:S, p. 48]). The twenty-one-year-old Marco, a paradigm of fashionable English dress and impatient to "clear out" of Ferrara and Italy altogether as soon as his land-owning father dies, in no way resembles his short, crude father with a neck like fatty hide, a man who wears old-fashioned country clothes and is content to limit his travels to the thirty-kilometer run between Ferrara and his hometown of Ambrogio. Some thirty years later and just "a few years ago" (p. 701), the narrator happens upon the father and son while passing through Ambrogio. Now past eighty and "più vivo e adusto che mai" [p. 703] (more lively and sun-baked than ever [W:S, p. 52]), the father seems to be standing next to his own, somewhat younger image: the now-fifty-year-old Marco, of slovenly, thickened appearance and with a neck exactly like fatty hide.

The narrator and Marco have reversed their expected destinies: the once-scorned narrator is now successful and lives in cosmopolitan Rome, whereas the once-envied Marco has been defeated and practically confined to his small-town childhood home. The exchange of social place is an act of authorial vengeance and a ceremony of victorious survival. As Elias Canetti has observed, "[The survivor] wants to strike [his enemy] down so that he can feel that he still stands while the other lies prostrate. But this other must not disappear completely; his physical presence as a corpse is indispensable for the feeling of triumph."[24] Marco's physiological fate expresses his psychic reduction to a state of paternal mimickry. Bassani exhibits his power as a writer "now" – the metatextual "now" of full writerly maturity – with this brief tale of male competition in which the Jewish subject vanquishes the Aryan antagonist. As a boy on the sidelines, the narrator had seen a youthful Marco "spiccare al centro di un crocchio di coetanei" [p. 699] (stand out in the center of a group of companions of his own age [W:S, p. 48]); as a man in the center of a comradely circle, the narrator introduces his Roman friends to a lonely Marco, a failed caricature of a man, a son limited to the company of his father and a priest. The tables are more than turned: Bassani's narrator disturbs even the dull space of those three darkened country figures, reinscribing himself there as the only enduring figure of authority. In a passing comment within a digressive description of himself, the narrator affirms the special (and autobiographical) status of the "man of letters" by a priestly example. The comment occurs in the extended passage that pitches the text from the 1930s into the much later time of the writing itself: "Bisogna tenere presente che Ferrara non è Bologna, dove la letteratura ci sta di casa. Da noi gli uomini di lettere vengono guardati un poco come i preti. Li si considera indubbiamente con rispetto, perfino con riverenza. Sempre, però, da una certa distanza" [p. 700] (Now you must bear in mind that Ferrara isn't Bologna, where literature is at home. In our city, literary men are regarded the way priests are, treated as they treat priests, more or less. Respected, even revered. But always from a certain distance [W:S, pp. 48–49]). The priest who accompanies Marco and his father materializes the narrator (a "man of letters"). "Now," the "true" priest – the writer – surveys from "a certain distance" his vanquished opponent.[25]

Similarly, the fable of "Pelandra" depicts the downfall of the once-envied insiders and the success of the once-lonely outsider – the narrating and authorial subject. The very structure of "Pelandra" exhibits the increasing rhetorical sophistication – that is, the *literary* victory – of the postwar persona. "Cuoio" employs a doubled-perspective structure in which the narrator observes himself both in the past and in his writing time; "Pelandra" expands and complicates the structure by embedding the principal story within a framing one. This mechanism gives the narrator a disinterested space of contemplation, a textualized space that narrativizes the enormous distance between the narrator and the numerous youths he knew long ago, in the "snows of yesteryear," such as Marco Giori, Pelandra, and the infamous Eraldo Deliliers (the same of *Occhiali*; see p. 704), all of whom number among the *sfatti* who flaunt their transgressions of Ferrara's social, and especially sexual, norms during the decade of the thirties. Bassani's "beautiful young men" replace François Villon's beautiful Roman courtesans and high-placed medieval ladies who loved illicitly. Through Villon's nostalgic discourse, which in fact masks "an allegory of poetic presence, history, and rejuvenation,"[26] Bassani indirectly becomes the narrative's principal subject and time's lone survivor. The fate of the ambitious Marco Giori, as we have seen, is to stagnate and rot; the symbolic soil of his putrefaction is not even Ferrara, but his hometown of Ambrogio, with its "gray" and "lifeless" (*spenta*) square "prossima a essere cancellata dal buio della notte" [p. 701] (about to be erased by the imminent darkness [W:S, p. 51]). The fate of Pelandra is to "evaporate": "Un giorno qualsiasi, un pomeriggio di domenica uguale identico a infiniti altri, [è] sparito da casa, da Ferrara, dall'Italia, forse dal mondo stesso dei vivi, senza lasciare niente, dietro di sé, niente di niente, neanche uno straccio di cadavere" [p. 708] (One ordinary day, a Sunday afternoon exactly like countless others, he vanished from his house, from Ferrara, from Italy, perhaps from the very world of the living, without leaving behind any trace, not even a lousy corpse [W:S, p. 60]). The fate of the narrator, whose resemblance grows ever closer to the prominent author of the 1950s and 1960s writing this fiction, is to outlive and surpass – professionally and morally – his former antagonists.

Pelandra's field of combat, like Marco's, is the family. Despite his playboy ambitions, Marco is incapable of breaking the paternal yoke. Pelandra (suggesting *pelandrone*: a "good-for-nothing") is an inauthentic *sfatto*: "Sembrava che . . . ogni passo gli costasse uno sforzo, ma più morale che fisico" [p. 704] (It seemed that . . . every step cost him an effort, but more spiritual than physical [W:S, p. 55]). He breaks the yoke of the *sfatti* in a sudden, purified moment of determination to marry into a sheltered Catholic family, "tutti casa e chiesa" [p. 705] (all home and church). For ten years he lives the model life of a husband, father, and son-in-law and then—in a sudden, depurified moment of determination—he quietly abandons his kin. The objective correlative of Pelandra's internal dissatisfaction, like Marco's, is his neglected body, become "grosso e corpulento" [p. 710] (big and fat).

The physical grossness of the older Marco and Pelandra, manifesting their psychic defeat, is anticipated by the moral grossness they manifest linguistically in their younger years. "Pelandra" is unique in Bassani's fiction for its quotations of street language. Although limited to a few expressions in the narrative's first paragraph, the vulgarisms suffice to mark this text with especial authorial contempt and self-contentment. They render a gesture of the victorious former victim self-righteously exposing the coarse pettiness of the vanquished. The only other textual occasion in which Bassani jolts his reader through transgressive language is in *Airone*. There his exposure of Edgardo Limentani's body—Edgardo's problems with defecating and urinating, his sexually inert penis—is a stratagem for manifesting the disgust the character feels with his reduction to a malfunctioning machine. This narrative "coarseness" culminates in a romantically conceived, redeeming suicide—for both character and author (see chapter 4). By contrast, the rhetoric of vulgarity in "Pelandra" serves only to slander the principal characters of the paired "Cuoio" and "Pelandra" (who appear in each other's stories and are friends). Unlike Edgardo, these characters are antithetical figures of the author, and their failures are absolute; "redemption" is reserved for the author. The author-narrator "authorizes" his self-portrait of success in the framing story of "Pelandra."

A Photographic Metaphor

Two characters occupy the space of the frame narrative: the narrator and Uller Tumaìni, a photographer nicknamed "al duterét" (dialect for "the little doctor"). A longtime acquaintance of the narrator and one who knows whereof he speaks, Uller is the perfect commentator of Pelandra's history. His accuracy in observing and recordng ("photographing") is as sure as an image forming from a properly treated negative; the "true picture" of Pelandra develops—logically enough—in the photographer's darkroom, which is his entire, always unlighted, small studio, "un bugigattolo tre metri per quattro, non di più. . . . Uller non accende la luce altro che in casi di stretta necessità (non l'ama, la luce: né quella elettrica, né quella naturale, tanto è vero che porta occhiali affumicati anche di sera)" [p. 708] (a kind of cubbyhole, nine feet by twelve, no larger. . . . Uller never turns on the light except in cases of strict necessity [he doesn't like light, electric or natural, and he wears tinted glasses even after sunset] [W:S, p. 60]). This modern "blind" seer is a construct of mythic material: the narrator neither knows nor cares to know whether Uller has a family; he is satisfied simply to find his friend, each time he visits Ferrara, "stazionante *in permanenza* sulla soglia dello 'studio' di via Garibaldi, e *immutato*. . . . Dopo tanti anni, non è miracoloso che lui abbia saputo *conservare intatta l'aria da vecchio giovanotto che aveva attorno al '37?*" [ibid.; emphasis added] (stationed permanently at the door of his "studio," and unchanged. . . . After so many years, isn't it a miracle that he has been able to maintain, intact, that same look, like an aged youth, that he had around 1937? [W:S, p. 59]). The depiction of the "buon Uller" (p. 704), concerned not with details but with the "caso umano" and the "caso morale" (p. 709), and being himself "una specie di immagine incarnata della fedeltà" [p. 708] (a kind of embodied image of trust), shifts the problem of truthtelling from the narrator to a demiurge, an unimpeachable authority. Freed from assuming responsibility for the facts, the narrator can slip into the role of spectator merely by being present in the posthistory (frame structure) of Pelandra's tale. The narrator does not innocently — that is, without his own textual history — enter Pelandra's narrative; before the first sentence of it is fully uttered, the reader learns that both the narrator and Uller were grown men living in Ferrara during 1937, when Pelandra hung out with the "prestigious constellation of the good-for-nothings." The year of reference is important: mentioned in the first sentence and again with reference to Uller, it is the only piece of historical, as opposed to "mythical," information in that sentence. In both instances the year indicates the temporal *beginning* of the tale to be told. Once it begins, the narrator and Uller fade out of the plot until, approximately thirty-five years later (the frame time), Uller reemerges "now" with the narrator to tell how Pelandra's tale *ends*. Since the anti-Jewish legislation took effect in 1938, 1937 stands also for the last year in which Italy's Jewish population continued to enjoy public commerce, that is, intermixed freely with Ferrara's non-Jewish citizens.

The narrator's sense that Uller looks exactly as he did in 1937 serves to compact that year into the narrative present (the frame time), as if all time between "then" and "now" were an irrelevant parenthesis. Thus the narrator's narrative value is attached on the one hand to his uncharted young manhood about to be threatened by the anti-Jewish laws and, on the other, to his present status as an occasional visitor to his native city of Ferrara. From "Cuoio" — the first chapter, so to speak, of "Pelandra" — the reader knows that the narrator has become a prominent writer who lives in Rome with his wife and children. This autobiographical as well as textual information dresses the first-person character boldly in the clothes of the living author, who is many years removed from his younger life of loneliness, persecution, struggle, and relative anonymity — many years removed, for example, from Bruno Lattes and the narrator of the *Giardino*, whose textual lives end about the same time as Pelandra's, in 1948. "Pelandra's" narrator effects his own apotheosis as an eternal seer by virtue of his proximity to the faultless Uller; both are "immortal" storytellers or, just as well, photographers of human acts. The narrating figure is both the victor (a successful man) among the then-favored contemporaries of his young years and the visionary (the writer). The latter reality is rendered "photographically" through images of light and darkness:

> Quando fuori, comincia a far buio, possiamo ritenere a buon diritto che dall'esterno nessuno di quanti passano lungo il marcipiede riesca a scorgerci. Strana sensazione, ad ogni modo! *Noi qui, invisibili, come fuori del tempo, come morti*. E là, richiamate ogni tanto dal *neon* sfolgorante della vetrina e dalle foto esposte, le ingenue, fidenti, inconsapevoli facce della vita, tutte scoperte e protese. [p. 708; clause emphasis added]

> (When, outside, it begins to grow dark, we can rightfully assume that none of the people going by on the sidewalk can discern us indoors. A strange sensation, in any case! We, here, invisible, as if outside of time, like the dead. And there, on the contrary, attracted now and then by the dazzling neon of the window and the displayed photographs, the ingenuous, trusting, unknowing faces of life, all open and thrust forward. [W:S, p. 60]

The merely living—the ingenuous pedestrians lacking awareness and vision—contrast ontologically with the deeply living—the all-knowing dead, who paradoxically are eternally alive: those who see but are not seen. The photography metaphor is probably Bassani's most powerful and positive rendering of the survivor-figure that shapes his persona: the survivor who survives death itself: "Noi qui, invisibili, come fuori del tempo, come morti" (We, here, invisible, as if outside of time, like the dead). The figure of the good little doctor with a foreign name is Bassani's idealized, nonautobiographical image; it has a touch of the foreigner in it, as befitting a writer's stance apart, and the sure vision that comes only from the grave—or from the darkroom. The Uller-Bassani construct has none of the existential anguish of the numerous autobiographical personae, and yet it depends for its vitality on total darkness, that is, death. Uller's "petto gracile" (frail chest) and "viso sempre ugualmente ossuto e cadaverico" (face bony and cadaverous as ever) are shrouded in a "camice bianco da dottore" [p. 708] (doctor's white coat)—a white burial cloth? Uller has neither home nor family because he is a skeletal corpse; in other words, he is Bassani's own prospering emblem, the emblem of a ghostly seer.

With this reading of *Les neiges d'antan*, we have considered three-fourths of the sixty-five-page *Odore*. My slow-paced reading of these pages responds to the concentrated character of the writing—the author's last words, as it were, on his story of Ferrara. Of greatest import is the need to document Bassani's quasi-photographic process of developing his definitive self-image. This process begins in the first paragraph of the first short story of the *Romanzo*. It then unceasingly refocuses partial autobiographical figurations through each of the individual texts of the volume and sharpens its image in the interweave of form and content of the unstable literary genre hovering between fiction and fact that constitutes *Odore*. Still to be considered in this polymorphous text is a quartet of "memoirs," which, in some twenty pages, reorients the story of Ferrara into the history of the writer, which, in turn, condenses into a kind of photographic close-up of the writer; this image is then further reduced metonymically to a word—"I"—that represents the here-and-now of textual existence.

In one perspective, *Odore* is a recapitulation of Bassani's opera omnia. The last four pieces, (*Tre apologhi* and "Laggiù"), continuing the volume's first-person narrations, whose principal character is the narrator, stand apart from the others in the collection. Originally listed (1974 edition) under separate titles, of which only the first was called "Apologo," the 1980 edition of the *Romanzo* groups the first three of the four texts (as numbers 1, 2, and 3) under the single title "Tre apologhi." The change emphasizes the accelerating forward movement of the author inside his texts, in the form of an allegorical act.

Allegories of Inscriptions

The first *apologo* is an anecdotal account of the narrator's automobile trip from Ferrara to Rome with his wife, Val, and their young children. The occasion is of a somewhat inconsequential personal nature. Thus its title seems odd at first, for the term "apologo" signals an allegorical fable intended to convey a moral. On second thought, however, recalling the fabulistic orientation of the preceding pieces of *Odore*, the title demands a serious, if ironic, reading of the three— indeed, all four—final pieces as a traditional *apologo* on behalf of the first-person narrator himself. The word *apologo* evokes also *apologia*, a statement in support of someone (the author himself?) or something, frequently of a religious or political doctrine (the fiction?). The collective "Apologhi" is, in short, a double-perspective cue to the allegorical meaning of Bassani's final discourse in the *Romanzo* and to the metanarrative content of the entire volume. The four concluding texts are not easily classified as fiction. They are, rather, anecdotal and occasional miscellanea of increasing *non*-fiction, whose function seems to be to snip the volume's characteristic *narrative* cloth in a final, definitive act of meditation, effected as unmediated ("lyrical") assertion of self. The two books that immediately follow the original *Romanzo*—both, collections of lyric poetry—verify the fiction's achievement of totalization: *Epitaffio*, an epitaphic, aesthetic end-punctuation and reaffirmation that Bassani's life work—that is, the "novel" of Ferrara—is done; and *In gran segreto*, a self-contradicting "secret"— *un*uttered speech—that implies a ghostly dialogue between the author and himself, a Dickinsonian post-mortem self-visitation. The subsequent publications of the *Romanzo* (1980), *In rima e senza* (1982), and *Di là dal cuore* (1984)— revised and collected works, respectively, of narrative, poetry, and essays— reinforce the sense of literary completion.

The first "Apologo" describes a family trip from Ferrara to Perugia, en route to Rome, and is datable to the 1950s. The opening paragraph prefaces the text proper by problematizing the significance of what is about to be recounted: "Accadde parecchi anni fa, prima dell'apertura delle grandi autostrade. Accadde? Beh, per modo di dire, giacché in realtà non accadde quasi niente" [p. 713] (It happened several years ago, before the big superhighways were opened. Happened? Well, in a manner of speaking, because in reality almost nothing happened [W:S, p. 65]). The reader is thus forewarned to seek the meaning of this memoir outside the "insignificant" reality of the actual narrative, presumably in the metanarrative or in allegorical interpretation.

The ride from Ferrara traces a southerly geographical "descent" matched by the narrator's dark and melancholy mood ("cupo, immalinconito"). He turns his melancholy against his wife, Val (again, the name of Bassani's wife), expressing irritation toward her and anguish toward Rome. After a while he finds relief in contemplating a stop for dinner at Todi or Narni – hilltowns wrapped in "their darkness" and "their silence" (p. 715). The writer's mood and his image of the hilltowns reproduce the particular qualities of Bruno Lattes's desperate flight to Abbazia ("Abbazia"). Further, the narrator's fantasy of being aboard a ship reproduces the beautiful steamship upon which Bruno gazes in that text. The resentful husband-narrator of the first apologue reflects:

> Pare di trovarsi a bordo di una piccola nave ultramoderna . . . ancorata soltanto per poco, in attesa come è di salpare, al limite delle acque portuali. . . . *ogni cosa, qui, sembra da principio non parlare che del futuro, di quell' "empio evo venturo"* pulito, funzionale, asettico, *che non vedremo e che ci dimenticherà.* [p. 716; emphasis added]

> (It's like being on board a small, ultramodern ship . . . anchored only temporarily at the edge of the harbor, waiting to sail. . . . everything here seems, at first, to speak only of the future, of that "evil time to come," clean, functional, ascetic, which we will not see and which will forget us.) [W:S, p. 69]

The ship that Bruno sees moves majestically, like a promise, toward the open sea. That promise is brutally and swiftly undone by the appearance of a boy (the young brother of Adriana, Bruno's former lover), who has decorated his bicycle with a banner bearing a swastika. The "ship" that the husband-narrator of "Apologo" sees is, in fact, a restaurant in Perugia, which turns out to be his road to Damascus: his spirit is forthwith becalmed by the local peasants who come to the restaurant and drink in silence their "usual, old, even ancient, drinks"; with them the narrator is enclosed by the "uniform darkness" of the city (ibid.). Tranquillity and affection impenetrate him; he takes his wife's hand; they walk off to their car; the narrative ends. The threat of the ultramodern ship of death – of *their* death, of *their* exclusion from the future – materializes not in this narrative, but in the margin of *Bruno's* narrative. "Apologo" (no. 1) deflects the threat by its promise of a homecoming: not to be conditioned by a disputed route to Rome, but by an existential *disponibilité* that assures the now-tender husband (and his wife) a carefree journey of return: "ventilati dalla brezza leggera, e ormai incuranti di dover varcare il famigerato ponte sul Tevere" [p. 716] (fanned by the light breeze, and now indifferent to the prospect of crossing the notorious bridge over the Tiber [W:*S*, p. 70]).

This textually *un*finished journey predicts authorial regeneration in the image of a communal agape performed by the silent peasants of the restaurant, in which the journeyer—silently—participates. Their mortal union in drink evokes the painting of the "peasant Christ" by Piero della Francesca, who, earlier in the text, was said to calm tourists' "restless frivolity" (p. 714). Within the frame of historical logic, the grim narrative set in Abbazia in 1939 is surpassed by a supposedly insignificant personal recollection of the 1950s. Within the frame of rhetorical logic, the mature persona of "Apologo" (no. 1) saves himself from the future—from the obliterating temporality of an "empio evo venturo" (wicked or ungodly future age)—by an act of *caritas*. The despairing spirit is quickened by recurring temporality—the (always past) time of ritual and remembrance and of the certainties of death: Micòl's "*pio* passato" (reverent or noble past).

The second apologue ("Topo") recounts a political trip from Rome to Naples that its narrator takes as a member of the anti-Fascist *Partito d'Azione* (which, it will be recalled, Bassani helped to found). The time is the Allied occupation, before the end of hostilities in northern Italy. Recalling the Roman winter of 1943–44 during the German occupation, which reduced him to "skin and bones," the narrator weaves his tale around the sudden abundance in Naples of American canned goods and cigarettes, a plenitude that fosters greed and gluttony among the newly influential, long-deprived anti-Fascists. Once again, details are pointedly autobiographical; in addition, the narrative voice employs the condemnatory discourse Bassani reserves for social and political injustice—in this case, the self-interest that grows during the restoration of democratic "normalcy" to Naples. This *apologo*, a variation on the first one, exchanges political for familial pain. Both texts, however, close with a ritual of food-sharing that involves the narrator in an act of human bonding. The first is a symbolic relation between a stranger and some peasants; the second, an actual relation between two old anti-Fascist college friends. The bonding in the second *apologo*—man to man—augments the familial bond already developed and here incorporated through a simple 'I wrote to Val almost every day" (p. 722). The narrator's renewed affection for his wife also results from *male* sodality (with the drinking peasants). As suggested previously, no woman in this body of work is an equal and fully valorized partner of a man.

The private family man of "Apologo" (no. 1) grows into a public (that is, political) person in the second *apologo* ("Topo"); in the third one ("Scarpe"), the figure is aggrandized as an artist: the mature and distinguished writer who represents Giorgio Bassani.

The first-person narrator of "Scarpe" lives a textual life entirely in the present tense. Thus, although the three short pieces follow an existential order of growth—family, country, art—rather than a chronological sequence, present time and artistic fullness overlap in the last of the self-defensive ("apologetic") series. The present tense of the narration undergirds the ongoing act of imagination that is the subject of this text. In the opening lines, the narrator's credentials as a prominent writer are immediately and modestly presented to the reader through a third party, a "giovane amica dalle calze rosse e dalla coda di cavallo, redattrice di un foglio della sera" [p. 724] (young friend with red stockings and a pony tail, on the editorial staff of an evening paper), who, in her words, is conducting a major research project involving writers (ibid.). The narrative time—judging from the editorial writer's hairstyle and large-framed eyeglasses and the abundance of leather worn by a motorcyclist who delivers some photographs to the writer—must be the 1960s. The indirect textual clue (to the writer's identity) in the first lines of the text is made precise in its last lines, with the citation of the narrator's books, *Gli occhiali d'oro* and *Dietro la porta* (the latter published in 1964). Thus the narrating "I" comes out of the shadow of his texts to assert his identity as Giorgio Bassani—or, more pointedly, as the "*autore* fra l'altro" [p. 727; emphasis added] (author, among other things) of the two works named.

In this brief text and in the subsequent ones, "Scarpe" and "Laggui," which conclude the *Romanzo*, Bassani claims an unusual space of his own within his epic "history/story" of Ferrara.[27] This space is both inside and outside Ferrara's textual walls. The first-person voice no longer pronounces moral judgment upon and from within a comunity in crisis (Fascist Ferrara). Rather, it reflects upon itself as the writing subject, now at ease and gracious, *beyond* crisis, respected and self-respected. By occupying a space within the bounded book of the *Romanzo*, the reinscribed author bridges the chasm between the fictional persona represented in innumerable guises and subjected to humiliation, unending trials, and self-defeat and the "liberated" writer, detached in time and place from the scene of struggle, a "voice-off" relative to all the narratives of the *Romanzo* through *Airone*. With *Odore*, the process of authorial self-liberation accelerates. Slowly, and from that text's very beginning, the narrating subject severs himself from his earlier representations, first by allegorical rewritings of the former representations, then by doubling narrative time to set off the phoenixlike emergence of a new, writerly "I," and finally, in the (barely veiled) name of Giorgio Bassini, by the explicit claim to an unshared textual space of dispassion, creation, and achieved power.

Using the pretext of a friendly request to select the most interesting among a group of photographs depicting recent newsworthy events such as passion crimes and candid shots of notorious celebrities, the narrator of the third apologue ("Scarpe") comes upon the picture of an old, undernourished vagrant dressed in threadbare clothes (p. 724). The writer "believes" that the snapshot portrays Riccardo T., a man under arrest for falsely declaring in public that he was a gold medalist, that is, a war hero. From the photograph, as from the postcard of "Passeggiata," the narrator generates a detailed story. The telling of the present story constitutes the narrative's main action. Fascinated by the photograph, the narrator shares with his reader the creative flow of imagination leading to the birth of a narrative:

> Guardo meglio, socchiudendo le palpebre: proprio come se, dinanzi, mi stesse non già un individuo reale, ma un personaggio di fantasia. L'operazione alla quale sto accingendomi, di mischiare il vero col falso, o, che è lo stesso, con l'immaginario, mi si preannuncia questa volta particolarmente arbitraria, empia. Ma che cosa importa? Oltre che intelligente (lo desumo dagli occhietti a capocchia di spillo che gli scintillano furbi attraverso le lenti), il signor Riccardo T. è senza dubbio persona gentile e comprensiva: più assai, in ogni caso, di tanti altri modelli presi dalla vita, ai quali, da quando scrivo novelle, racconti e romanzi, ho dovuto per forza rifarmi. Se gli accadrà di leggere queste linee da lui ispirate e a lui dedicate, sono sicuro che compatirà. [p. 725]

> (I look more closely, squinting my eyes: just as if, in front of me, there stood not a real person but a make-believe character. The operation for which I'm getting prepared, blending the real with the false, or, which is the same, with the imaginary, this time forewarns me of something particularly arbitrary and ungodly. But what does it matter? Not only intelligent (I infer that from his tiny pinpoint eyes that sparkle cunningly through his eyeglasses), Mr. Riccardo T. is undoubtedly a kind and understanding person: much more so, in any case, than so many other models taken from life who, ever since I've been writing novellas, short stories, and novels, I've had to remake. If he happens to read these lines inspired by him and dedicated to him, I'm sure he will forgive me.)

This deft description of the imagination at work, constructed in imaginative discourse, confirms the authority of this creative/creating writer in terms of experience ("ever since I've been writing novellas, short stories and novels") as well as talent (the text itself), while playfully confounding the reader with its merging layers of illusion and reality. The presence of the writer inside his narrative—itself inside another narrative (the third "Apologo")—is important for the writer to establish grandly. Having created a touching fiction of Mr. T's arrest, the author uses his authority to "erase" the police officer—by definition a person of limited comprehension—and to substitute himself for the sake of a better story:

"Non dice di più [il signor T.]: per motivi di ovvia prudenza, è chiaro. Eppure, supponendo che invece di un funzionario di polizia gli stesse di fronte un'altra persona qualsiasi (chi scrive, per esempio), figuriamoci se si fermerebbe qui" [p. 727] ([Mr. T.] says nothing more—clearly for reasons of obvious prudence. And yet, supposing that instead of a police officer there was another person in front of him [this writer, for example], you can imagine if he would stop here). Even during the questioning of the arrested man, the author evidences his own hand at work by keeping the dialogue in the third person, that is, as reported by a third person: the author. With the author's appropriation of the part of interlocutor, Mr. T. recognizes that he is now before one like himself:

> "Se lei, professore, quella sera . . . si fosse trovato nelle mie condizioni, forse che non l'avrebbe detta anche lei una piccola balla? E non la dirà, sia sincero, ogni qualvolta ne abbia bisogno... compreso... compreso quando scrive... quando"—e sogghigna—"compone? E poi, e poi: proprio da lei, autore fra l'altro degli *Occhiali d'oro* e di *Dietro la porta*, un poveraccio come me ha da sentirsi lesinare la comprensione?" [p. 727]

> ("If you, professor . . . had found yourself in my place that night, wouldn't you have told a little lie? And be sincere, wouldn't you lie every time you needed to— including— including when you write— when"—and he grinned—"you make something up? And furthermore, from an author like you, the author, among other things, of *Gli occhiali d'oro* and *Dietro la porta*, should a poor devil like me have to be begrudged some understanding?")

Mr. T.'s fib about the gold medal is both a harmless defense of his self-respect and a recognition of self-aggrandizing lying as a national habit (p. 728). The proud vagrant's last gesture, the "ghigno di vecchio, fraterno rottame della vita" [p. 728] (grin of an old, fraternal wreck of life), unites the celebrated storyteller and the censured one as partners in fantasy: The writer Bassani creates the narrator "Bassani," who creates the "old carcass" of Riccardo T., whose "surname is a truncated disyllable, and rather funny" (p. 725). The author's textual interest in photographs, beginning with the famous picture postcard that opens "Passeggiata," reaches a jovial climax in this apologue. In sharp contrast with the alienating image Edgardo Limentani scrutinizes in his bathroom mirror (*Airone*), the present photograph that is contemplated is a narcissistic mirroring of the joy of self-production. The retrograde series of authorial images illustrates Bassani's dexterous control of artistic form at the same time that he ironizes himself and his craft: the third apologue is a parable of the creative imagination.

The gradual development of the set of three apologues brings the author of the texts into increasingly sharp and almost exclusive textual focus. Bassani effectively claims at this point the entire range of the reader's field of vision. One more narrative effort—the final one, in which the entire impetus of narrative movement comes to rest—stops time altogether. "Laggiù, in fondo al corridoio" is both a straightforward essay on the generation and reception of each of the five Ferrarese stories that established Bassani's fame and an indirect autobiographical confession. This highly literary text gives new currency to the narrative "now" maintained in the present tense in the third apologue. The "now" of "Laggiù," along with the interspersed reflexive past tense, is internalized, thus becoming a metaphor of the duration of the writer's reflection on his past work and present self-inscription. This last enunciation—"Laggiù" is last in *Odore*, last in the *Romanzo*—takes place always, anywhere, in the metaphorical space of the writer's imagination, at the very edge or margin (*fondo*: edge and depth) of his being, in a condition of *fruitful* alienation. "Laggiù" brings to closure the apologues that increase the distance between the writer and his origin, Ferrara, until he arrives at the nondimensional space of writing; and it decreases the subjective time between the writer and his stages of social maturity, from marriage to the nontemporal moment of imaginative reflection, expressing "at the end of the corridor" the writer's most authentic and creative act of self-affirmation.

At the literal end of Bassani's textual corridor is an "I" ("io"), the pronoun and persona for which the entire narrative has been searching: "*Ancora adesso, scrivendo, incespico su ogni parola, a metà di ogni frase rischio di perdere la bussola. Faccio, cancello, rifaccio, cancello ancora. All'infinito*" [p. 729; emphasis added] (Still now, while I'm writing, I stumble over every word, in the middle of every sentence I risk losing my bearings. I write, erase, write again, erase another time. Endlessly). Here is the writer laboring to control his craft. Later he chooses linguistic metaphors to explain his absence ("in pratica non figuravo") (In effect I didn't figure) from the *Cinque storie*, or, more precisely, his hidden appearance "dietro gli schermi tra patetici e ironici della sintassi e della rettorica" [p. 734] (behind the partly pathetic and partly ironic screens of syntax and rhetoric). "Starting from now"—that is, beginning with his five stories (which he names one by one: the creator calling them into being)—and through the still-incomplete *Occhiali*, he seeks to liberate himself, to "uscire anche lui dalla sua, di tana" [ibid.] (come out, he too, from his hiding place) in order to "introduce"—that is, to name—himself: to dare to say "finalmente 'io' " [ibid.] (finally "I"). The liberation of "io" is achieved by his coming out ("uscire") of a hole ("tana")—in short, by being born. And moreover, like Venus, born as an adult. But in its textual position at the far edge of the *Romanzo*, this birth also encompasses and fuses with an ordinary one coterminous with the narrative's origin: the birth of Lida Mantovani's child.

"And the end of all our exploring will be to arrive where we started." The psychic pattern of encircling closure traced by this well-known line of T. S. Eliot (which Bassani used as an epigraph for "Laggiù," 1974 edition) becomes in the *Romanzo* a preeminently literary end and beginning. The title of the closing es-

Figure 14. Giorgio Bassani.

say redounds to the first page of "Lida"; Lida, about to give birth, has been bedridden for more than a month "in fondo a un corridoio" [p. 9] (at the end of a corridor): "*Lida Mantovani* [and Lida, and Bassani] ebbe una gestazione estremamente laboriosa" [p. 729] ("Lida Mantovani" had an extremely difficult gestation) is the opening sentence of "Laggiù". From the end of her corridor, Lida stares out a window at the leaves of a great magnolia tree "che sorgeva nel mezzo del giardino sottostante" [p. 9] (that rose in the middle of the garden below): "La magnolia che sta giusto nel mezzo / del giardino di casa nostra a Ferrara è proprio lei / la stessa che ritorna in pressoché tutti / i miei libri" ["Le leggi razziali" in *Epitaffio*] (The magnolia tree that is right in the middle / of the garden of our home in Ferrara is precisely / the one that comes back in almost all / my books). The first pages of "Lida" and "Laggiù" read in antiphony. Lida's recollection of the event of giving birth (p. 9) is answered by Bassani's recollection of the birth of his books: "Ed è vero altresì che ogni mia poesia, ogni mio racconto lungo o breve, ogni mio romanzo, perfino ogni mio saggio e, addirittura, ogni mio articolo d'occasione, nacquero sempre . . . come *Lida Mantovani*: con stento, e in gran parte per caso" [p. 729] (And it is just as true that each of my poems, each of my long and short stories, each of my novels, even each of my essays and occasional articles, was always born . . . like "Lida Mantovani": with difficulty, and mostly by chance).

Bassani's epigraph to the 1972 and 1974 editions of *Odore* was a passage from Simone Weil that foreshadows the book's intensive exploration of the narrating self: "On ne peut offrir que le moi. Sinon, tout ce qu'on nomme offrande n'est pas autre chose qu'une étiquette posée sur une revanche du moi" (One can offer only the self. Otherwise, everything we call an offering is nothing but a label attached to a vengeance of the self). The epigraph to "Laggiù" (the T. S. Eliot line cited above) proposes a circular route to self-knowledge, that leads (through Weil's proposal) to the gift of the self to others. The *Romanzo* is such a route.

The full-grown Bassanian "io" takes form only on the last page of "Laggiù." Here Bassani quotes his final "I"; quotes himself, that is, in the third person as author, as an "I" reflecting on itself. "Finalmente io" is a resonant and stunning conclusion to his magisterial literary corpus. It is hard to think of another literary closing that equals this terse, self-observing self-birth. The "I" goes back specifically to Bassani's decision to adopt a first-person narrator in *Occhiali*. But a part of this passage also suggests that the echo reaches farther back, at least to the last of *Cinque storie*, to the paralytic Pino Barilari of "Notte." The echo induces an adjustment in the reader, whereby the pathetic Pino retrospectively acquires the function of doubling the author. After recalling Pino in the little room ("cameretta") that he never leaves, Bassani refers to his own sheltered den ("tana"), which he determines to leave, however, in order to *qualificarsi* – to "introduce himself" (one meaning of the word) to the outside world and to "qualify" (second meaning) as a first-person narrator: the "I" who terminates the entire volume. The indirect conflation of Pino and the author implies a retrograde extension of the persona to the beginning of Bassani's writing, despite the third-person narration. In addition to the obvious autobiographical references and characters, such as the cultivated Bruno Lattes and David Camaioli, there are also the more subtle doubles like the obsessed Geo Josz and the contemptible Luciano Pulga. Throughout Bassani's fiction, narrative action turns on the confrontation and inversion of victim and victimizer, outsider and insider, outcast and leader. Incarnations of impotence and power are everywhere intermeshed in his texts, from the pitiful Pino and the Fascist brute Sciagura ("Notte") to the lonely Jewish schoolboy-narrator of *Porta* and his false friend, Luciano Pulga. In these examples, as in others, victim and victimizer inevitably exchange places, which is to say that they are one and the same.

Piece by piece, the last texts of *Odore* uncover more and more of the authorial "I," revealing the total composition of the *Romanzo* as an agonistic dialogue between writer and text that replicates the numerous antagonistic paired characters of the fiction, including the narrator-author and "Ferrara."

The individual books of the *Romanzo* iterate an insistent pattern of antagonisms that reduce to a relation of victim and victimizer. The pattern is at its simplest in the first two of the *Cinque storie*, where it traces erotic relationships between educated, upper-middle-class Jewish men and uneducated, lower-class Catholic women. The forms of aggression in the remaining three stories in this collection are at the extremities of social and political violence. They concern a Ferrarese Jew who, presumed dead, returns after the war to his native city from Buchenwald; an oldtime Socialist teacher and militant anti-Fascist abandoned by her friends during the Fascist regime; and eleven men massacred by Fascist blackshirts during the Nazi occupation of Italy. The faceless narrator raises doleful cries of guilt and shame to his compatriots. Next comes *Occhiali*, which makes kin of the rejected Jews and a homosexual doctor, each bearing the traits of the outsider who was once a productive and respected member of society. For the first time, the insider who becomes an outcast is a first-person narrator—what is more, a young, not-long-to-be innocent boy. In the *Giardino* the narrator/rejected lover achieves manhood and, at the story's close, becomes a full-fledged writer in a structure paralleling a Dantesque final union between the experiencing, ignorant character and the self-reflective, wise author. *Porta*, about growing boys, weaves a story of personal betrayal and self-discovery—essential, fundamentally self-reflexive Bassanian themes that also embody the broader themes of Fascism and social betrayal. *Airone* thematizes social betrayal through its subject of a suicidal retreat from the threatening, socially repressive atmosphere of the postwar era. The protagonist, Edgardo Limentani, enacts his private flight from alienation, but the novel also allegorizes the psychic retreat that precedes spiritual regeneration. According to Bassani's own testimony, the writing of *Airone* resulted in his personal, as well as imaginative, regeneration. In that novel the persona emerges through symbolism and allegory. The author's revitalization—his boon of victory for having defeated his deadened imagination—is itself symbolic of the reversal of the victim-victimizer relation. Martyrdom is not Bassani's measure: he survives victimage; but, like his character Geo Josz, survivor of a concentration camp, Bassani leaves his native city and its constrictive spaces. Resettled in Rome after the war, he seeks the inside of Ferrara from without, while needing to remain out in order to see within.

The futile trial of the Fascist Sciagura dramatizes Bassani's judgment of irreversible guilt upon the populace of his invented Ferrara. In all of his fiction, only one small space of possible redemption is open; it is the Finzi-Contini garden: the special space of Micòl, the female space of love and vitality. Micòl and her family are sacrificed; their home is ravaged; the garden trees are cut down. But the emptied space is a fertile one, in which the narrator-author writes down Micòl's story, *his* book. The narrator survives the war and persecution; the author survives the war and persecution; the book inscribes illimitable survival. Surviving sacrifice is a sacred act in Bassani's literary universe, as in his own life. The interaction of survival and sacrifice sparks the imaginative fires out of which a literary metal is forged, giving shape to a persona and the "sacred" fiction of Ferrara. By recording the wages of death of a certain time and place, the author breathes poetic life into the entwined forms of "Beauty" and "Truth," which, in the *Romanzo*, take the corporeal forms of Micòl Finzi-Contini and the narrating subject on whom her story depends. This is Bassani's final power.

Notes

Notes

Introduction

1. In Italy the term "racial" is used loosely. Italian newspapers have, for example, reported "racial" hatred between *veneti* and their southern compatriots now residing in the Veneto region. During Fascism the concept of an Aryan race was used to persecute Jews under so-called racial laws. Because it is, by definition, incorrect to equate a cultural, religious, or ethnic group with a race, I translate the Italian *leggi razziali* with quotation marks around the "racial" or — more commonly — rephrase the term as anti-Jewish.

2. Pier Paolo Pasolini, *Passione e ideologia*, p. 344.

3. Ibid.

4. Gian Carlo Ferretti insistently faults Bassani for lacking a "mature historical consciousness." He claims, in brief, that the author's original anti-Fascist ideals (and those of an entire generation of writers) have given way to a sentimental and nostalgic literature. Although Ferretti's interpretive categories are mistaken and simplistic, his book provides a useful overview of the cultural climate of postwar Italy. See his *Letteratura e ideologia* and his *La letteratura del rifiuto* (Milan: Mursia, 1968; enl. 1981). For a similar perspective but one more sensitive to Bassani's rhetorical power, see Giuliano Manacorda, *Storia della letteratura italiana contemporanea*, pp. 306–9.

5. For a good discussion of this confrontation see Nello Ajello's "Arriva l'avanguardia," pp. 133–86.

6. Trans. from "Postille a *Il nome della rosa*"; incl. in paperback ed. of novel (Milan: Bompiani, 1984), pp. 34 and 35. The English-language text, trans. by William Weaver, was published as a separate book entitled *Postscript to "The Name of the Rose"* (New York: Harcourt Brace Jovanovich, 1984).

7. Pasolini, *Passione*, p. 344.

Chapter 1. Death and Survival

1. Lietta Tornabuoni, Interview, p. 1.

For Bassani's "end of my work" comment in the preceding paragraph, see Carla Stampa, "Per scrivere ho bisogno del mare," p. 84.

The table of contents of the 1974 edition of the *Romanzo* lists individual book titles and their internal titles, or divisions. The table of contents of the 1980 edition, streamlined to show the unity of the "single" text, lists only book titles, prefaced as in classical literary texts by "First Book," "Second Book," and so forth, as if each of the six entries (books) were a chapter heading.

2. Giorgio Bàrberi Squarotti, "La poesia di Bassani e Ceronetti," after a hesitant start, agrees with my observation. In a review of *Segreto*, having described Bassani's poetic voice as "estremamente distaccato . . . quasi postumo" (extremely detached . . . almost posthumous), he goes on to assert, "Allo sguardo del protagonista poetico di Bassani tutto ha un valore e un significato definitivi perché egli proviene dalla morte, e le illusioni, allora, sono proprio impossibili" (In the eyes of Bassani's poetic protagonist everything has a definitive value and meaning because he comes from death, and illusions, then, are simply impossible).

As if to orchestrate the event of literary closure, the collection of narratives is followed by two additional collected works. The first, bounding together the earliest published poetry (1945) and the recent texts of *Epitaffio* and *Segreto*, appeared in 1982 as *In rima e senza*. The second, an expansion of *Le parole preparate* (1967), a book of essays, came out in 1984 as *Di là dal cuore*. Like an arpeggiated chord producing a triadic harmony of literary genres, these collected narratives, poems, and essays unite in a sound of unmistakable tonal resolution, fading to a silence that images authorial death.

3. Giorgio Bassani, *Le parole preparate*, p. 229; reprinted in *Di là dal cuore*, p. 211.

4. In Ferdinando Camon, *La moglie del tiranno*, p. 95. The same leitmotiv reappears in a much later interview, where Bassani speaks of the *Romanzo* as a book "che dice come tutti noi viventi uciamo da un evento terribile e in qualche modo sacro, da una esperienza fondamentale dell'umanità attraverso i secoli: dopo Buchenwald, non è più possibile pensare che gli uomini siano diversi uno dall'altro" [Tornabuoni, p. 1] (that tells how all of us alive come from a terrible and in some way sacred event, from a fundamental experience of humanity across the centuries: after Buchenwald, it is no longer possible to think that people are different from one another).

5. In Anna Dolfi, *Le forme del sentimento*, p. 82. This lengthy and lucid interview (monologue) (pp. 79-91) is as close to a formal declaration of poetics as we shall probably ever get from Bassani.

See also Antonio Russi, "Sei esemplari di narrativa contemporanea," pp. 411-28; this informative study includes a good bibliography. For Russi, Bassani's "symbolic homage" to the Jewish camp victims is also "un modo di giustificare a se stesso il quasi miracolo di essere scampato al massacro. È quindi una implicita rivendicazione di solidarietà con le vittime" [p. 420] (a way of justifying to himself the near miracle of having escaped the slaughter. It is thus an implicit claim of solidarity with the victims).

6. From the poem "Lettere" in *Epitaffio*.

7. Renzo De Felice, *Storia degli ebrei italiani sotto il fascismo*, pp. 319, 321.

A related work in English is H. Stuart Hughes's *Prisoners of Hope*, which focuses on the fiction of six prominent modern Italian Jewish writers, including Bassani. Despite Hughes's tendency to accept fictional representation as pure autobiography, and despite his occasionally unconvincing (to me) generalizations regarding Jewish traits, I highly recommend this book for its interesting and animated historical overview.

The anti-Jewish laws were repugnant even to some prominent Fascists, such as the Ferrarese Italo Balbo, who sat on Mussolini's Grand Council. Primo Levi, a writer of consummate narratives deriving from his experience as a former internee of Auschwitz, believes that "Italian anti-Semitism does not have Italian roots. We are a singular, privileged nation hardly aware of what a Jew is. . . . I have never had, not even during the "racial" laws, the sensation of being identified as an outsider ("estraneo"), of being pointed out with scorn" (*Epoca*, 10 October 1981, p. 111). Levi's fiction is eloquent on the subject. In the novel *Se non ora, quando?* a man named Chàim, a member of the Palestinian Brigade of the English army, travels through Italy to Brenner, Austria, right after the end of World War II in order to aid the Jewish refugees. Coming upon a small band of Polish and Russian Jewish partisans, Chàim engages them in conversation:

"L'Italia è un paese strano," disse Chàim. "Ci vuole tempo per capire gli italiani, e neanche noi, che abbiamo risalito tutta l'Italia da Brindisi alle Alpi, siamo ancora riusciti a capirli bene; ma una cosa è certa, in Italia gli stranieri non sono nemici. . . . Ma . . . vi devo dire la cosa più strana di tutte: gli italiani si sono mostrati amichevoli con tutti gli stranieri, ma con nessuno si sono mostrati amichevoli come con noi della Brigata Palestinese."
    "Forse non si sono accorti che eravate ebrei," disse Mendel.
    "Se ne sono accorti sicuro, e del resto noi non lo abbiamo tenuto nascosto. Ci hanno aiutati non *benché* fossimo ebrei, ma *perché* lo eravamo. Hanno aiutato anche i loro ebrei; quando hanno occupato l'Italia, i tedeschi hanno fatto tutti gli sforzi che potevano per catturarli, ma ne hanno preso ed ucciso solo un quinto; tutti gli altri hanno trovato rifugio nelle case dei cristiani, e non solo gli ebrei italiani, ma molti ebrei stranieri che si erano rifugiati in Italia. . . . Una cosa . . . dovete saperla: gli ebrei italiani sono strani come i cattolici. Non parlano jiddisch. . . . Parlano solo italiano; anzi, gli ebrei di Roma parlano romano, gli ebrei di Venezia veneziano, e cosí via. Si vestono come gli altri, hanno le stesse facce degli altri . . ."
    "E allora, come si distinguono dai cristiani quando passano per la strada?"
    "Appunto, non si distinguono. Non è un paese singolare?" [pp. 241–42]

("Italy is a strange country," said Chàim. "You need time to understand the Italians, and not even we, who have ascended all of Italy from Brindisi to the Alps, have been able to understand them well; but one thing is certain, in Italy foreigners are not enemies. . . . But . . . I must tell you the strangest thing of all: the Italians have shown themselves to be friendly with all the foreigners, but with no one have they shown themselves as friendly as with us of the Palestinian Brigade."
    "Perhaps they didn't realize you were Jews," said Mendel.
    "They certainly realized it, and moreover we didn't keep it hidden. They helped us not *in spite of* the fact that we were Jews, but *because* we were. They also helped their own Jews; when they occupied Italy, the Germans made every effort to capture them, but they caught and killed only a fifth of them; all the others found refuge in Christian houses, and not only Jewish Italians but many foreign Jews who had taken refuge in Italy. . . . One thing . . . you must know: Italian Jews are as strange as Catholics. They don't speak Yiddish. . . . They speak only Italian; in fact, Roman Jews speak Roman, Venetian Jews speak Venetian, and so on. They dress like the others, they have the same faces as the others . . ."
    "So how do they distinguish themselves from Christians when they walk along the street?"
    "That's the point; they don't distinguish themselves. Isn't it a singular country?")

8. Massimo Grillandi, *Invito alla lettura di Bassani*, p. 22.
9. From the notebooks of Henry James, inserted epigraphically in the title story of *La passeggiata prima di cena*.
10. John Freccero, "Medusa: The Letter and the Spirit," pp. 7–8, says, "From the ancient *Physiologus* through the mythographers to Boccaccio, the Medusa represented a sensual fascination, a *pulchritudo* so excessive that it turned men to stone."
11. The term *meteco* named the alien resident of ancient Greece, who was granted very limited civil rights and was viewed with hostility by the native population. The similar status of the Jew during the seven years of anti-Jewish legislation is obvious. Charles Maurras posited an "anti-France" governed by four estates: Jews, Protestants, Freemasons and other anticlericals, and *métèques*.

12. By the time (1974) of *Epitaffio*, whose very title suggests elegy, the longing for a home becomes desperate but also tempered by the fatigue and sadness of long life: "Qualunque casa a questo / punto della mia vita mi piace qualsiasi / tana minimo-borghese è capace / di tentarmi di riempirmi / d'invidia e di gelosia / Dovunque ormai vorrei vivere / adesso tranne che a casa / mia" ["Villino tricamere," pp. 79–80] (Any house at this / point of my life pleases me any / minimal-bourgeois hole is capable / of tempting me of filling me / with envy and jealousy / Anywhere at this time I would like to live / now except in my own / house ["Three-Room Cottage"]).

13. *L'alba ai vetri*, p. 86.

14. "Mi piaceva soltanto la sera, soltanto la luce del tramonto" (I used to like only the evening, only the light of sunset), the poet recalls (*Alba*, p. 86). The verses of *Alba* are characterized by images of transmutation: fog, mist, twilight, shadows, autumn, the moon, the seashore, a moving train, the "disappearance" of the poet into his verses. The title of the volume immediately projects an ephemeral time (dawn) and hampered vision (windowpanes—seeing through a glass, darkly) that seek stabilization in an unearthly world.

15. Dolfi, *Sentimento*, p. 86. A terse poetic utterance sums up the same argument: "l'amore . . . quando è vero / non può essere che . . . nemico della vita" ["4 marzo '73" in *Epitaffio*] (love . . . when it is true / cannot be but . . . an enemy of life ["March 4, 1973"]).

16. Luigi Bàccolo, "Bassani dentro la sua Ferrara, città dei morti," *Gazzetta del Popolo*, 21 January 1975.

Mario Boselli frames the posthumous authorial figure in this description of Bassani's literary language: "I paesaggi di Bassani, le case e le strade di Ferrara, sono narrati con lo scrupolo di un urbanista, ma *collocati in uno spazio fuori del tempo*, perché la sistemazione degli oggetti e delle persone avviene con la coscienza del loro appartenere *ad un mondo finito*" ["Ambiguità di Bassani," p. 11; emphasis added] (Bassani's landscapes, and the houses and streets of Ferrara, are narrated with the scruple of an urban planner, but they are *placed in a space outside time*, because the organization of objects and people takes place with his consciousness of their belonging *to a world that has ended*.)

17. Emily Dickinson and her poem "I Died for Beauty" are perfect expressions of the postmortal perspective inherent in Bassani's texts. For the persona, the doubled perspective implies an apocalyptic authority and a mournful vision of sacrificial death, whose originary referent is the Nazi death camp. It is Micòl—she who epitomizes Holocaustic victimage—who translates and effectively speaks Dickinson's poem, predicting, as it were, her own death, which intertwines with that of the poem's male speaker. Appropriated by Micòl, the poem comments on the persona's ontological status:

> I died for Beauty—but was scarce
> Adjusted in the Tomb
> When One who died for Truth, was lain
> In an adjoining Room—
>
> He questioned softly "Why I failed"?
> "For Beauty", I replied—
> "And I—for Truth—Themself are One—
> We Brethren, are," He said—
>
> And so, as Kinsmen, met a Night—
> We talked between the Rooms—
> Until the Moss had reached our lips—
> And covered up—our names—

In Micòl's translation the implicit sexual identities of the speakers are made explicit; female Beauty and male Truth are, moreover, buried in "Rooms" reminiscent of the Finzi-Continian "burial house." The speakers stay alive in death through their spoken discourse, that is, through language.

18. Geno Pampaloni's review "Io, Narciso," responding to the poems of *Segreto*, describes the author's notion of eternity as one "che non somiglia certo a quella di Dio . . . e neppure a quella della memoria: è l'eternità che la vita trova nella poesia come in una tomba, in un reliquario" (that surely doesn't resemble God's . . . or even memory: it is the eternity that life finds both in poetry and in a tomb, in a shrine), and the events of the poems "allietano un lascito sepolcrale" (gladden a sepulchral bequest). Bassani, a "Narcissus" figure, "si fa cantore postumo di se stesso e del mondo" (becomes a posthumous bard of himself and the world). Pampaloni maintains, engagingly, that in contrast with much contemporary poetry, which is self-reflexive, Bassani's is "assolutamente asser-tiva, perché si colloca naturalmente come un 'dopo' della vita" (absolutely assertive, because he naturally places himself as an "afterward" of life).

Other critics also have paid attention to Bassani's funerary vision and otherworldly stance, in response largely to the later poetry. But the posture holds even more validity — because of its greater symbolic range — for the narratives, even though their posthumous voice is less pronounced. For insights into the prose as well as the poetry, see Enzo Siciliano's reviews of *Epitaffio* and *Segreto* in "Ma la poesia non è una signorina perbene."

See also Lorenzo Mondo's "Bassani poeta."

Bàccolo, in "Città dei morti," although referring primarily to the *Romanzo*, underscores the pervasiveness of death in the total writings.

Natalia Ginzburg, reviewing *Epitaffio* in "La soddisfazione," *Corriere della Sera*, 9 June 1974, faults the poems for the very qualities essential to them. She mistranslates their poetic rhetoric into authorial (self-)"satisfaction," mistaking, for example, Bassani's ironic, distancing voice for his intent to "esiliare dalle sue terre la sua antica, seria, ebraica, tragica idea della morte" (exile from his lands his ancient, serious, Jewish, and tragic idea of death).

The most original and provocative reviews of Bassani are Pier Paolo Pasolini's. See, for instance, *Descrizioni di descrizioni* on *Dentro le mura* [*Romanzo*, I], pp. 262–66, and on *Epitaffio*, pp. 333–36; the reviews appeared originally in *Tempo*, 8 February 1974 and 21 June 1974, respectively.

19. In *Parole* Bassani takes to task the centuries-old, "idolatrous" literary fascination, especially of non-Italians, with Venice. In Montaigne he detects "il primo, in ordine di tempo, a intuire da critico il fascino, e il pericolo, dell'esotismo lagunare" (the first, in order of time, to intuit as a critic the fascination and the danger of lagoon exoticism), unlike "il giovane Shakespeare del *Merchant of Venice*, e quello un po' meno giovane dell'*Otello* (the young Shakespeare of the *Merchant of Venice*, and the not-so-young one of *Othello*), who abandons himself "senza più remora alcuna all'incanto smemorante della Sirena meridionale, sede di tutte le passioni e di tutte le voluttà" (without any further delay to the amnesic charm of the southern Siren, the center of all passion and all sensual pleasure) [p. 22; *Di là*, p. 244]. Professor Ermanno seems to represent one of the excessively sentimental "futuri pronipoti romantici e decadenti" (romantic and decadent future descendants) of Venice's "idolators" taken to task in this essay (see p. 23).

20. Sidra DeKoven Ezrahi, *By Words Alone*, pp. 68–69.

21. Bassani wrote the epitaph for his real grandfather, who is buried in the Jewish cemetery of Ferrara. Elia Corcos acts out the other's idealized life history in "Passeggiata." Here is the loving and literary real-life funeral inscription Bassani composed:

In questa tomba / Accanto a quella del figlio / È sepolto il prof. dottor / Cesare Minerbi / Per quarant'anni primario dell'Arcispedale Sant'Anna / Scienziato originale e clinico di fama / Medico curante di quattro / Generazioni di ferraresi. / Nato nel 1856 quando ancora a Ferrara / Governavano / I cardinali legati / Morì nell'autunno del 1954 / Quasi centenario / Vivendo fino all'ultimo del proprio lavoro / Passando arguto e solitario fra noi / Col sorriso del saggio e del filosofo / E lo sguardo distante di chi ha scrutato il dolore.

In this tomb / Near his son's / Is buried Dr. / Cesare Minerbi / For forty years chief of staff of the Saint Anne Hospital / Ingenious scientist and surgeon of great renown / Family doctor of four / Generations of Ferrarese. / Born in 1856 when Ferrara was still / Governed by / Cardinal legates / He died in autumn of 1954 / Almost a hundred years old / Living until the end by his own labor / Passing among us, cunning and solitary / With the smile of a sage and philosopher / And the distant gaze of one who has looked closely at grief.

Perhaps it was this epitaph that spurred the author to his epitaphic perspective in general.

22. Eugenio Donato, "Mnemonics of History," p. 2.

23. The Israeli nation has attempted to compensate for the Nazi erasure of the Holocaust victims by erecting an extensive memorial, located in a "cemeterial" space on a hilltop, significantly called Yad Vashem, the Hebrew words for "A Place and a Name."

24. Donato, "Mnemonics," pp. 7-8.

25. In Dolfi, *Sentimento*, p. 90.

26. From a line in Mallarmé's sonnet about a magnificent swan, cited on the last page of the *Giardino*.

27. The essays of *Parole*, which is divided into three parts, are emblematic of the beginning, middle, and end stages of achieved artistry. Part I, which Bassani describes as essays of a "general character" (p. 9), in fact focuses largely on cities in literature: Venice, Trieste, Milan, and a bit of Dublin. The Milanese Manzoni, to whom critics often compare Bassani and of whom Bassani is a great admirer, figures in several of the essays. The representation of cities in literature – their "concreteness" and "historicity" [p. 32] – obviously grips Bassani's imagination: without Ferrara, there would be no *Romanzo*. In these essays the reader gets a workshop view of the production of a city in words, that is, a picture of the artist setting up and studying his project.

Part II of *Parole* deals with ideologies and myths – Nazi, Fascist, bourgeois, Crepuscular – and the forms of their rhetoric: the "physiogonomy" of their *ethos* [p. 82]. In search of politico-historical veracities, these lucid essays delineate a portrait of the artist as a moralist. Part III closes in on the literary-autobiographical: the first essay memorializes Bassani's artistic "progenitor," the distinguished art critic Robert Longhi, who was his teacher and mentor at the University of Bologna; the second, in the form of a diary – lost and recovered – tells of the author's hunger, fear, and hiding in occupied Rome during the winter of 1944 (and figures his burial and resurrection). Resurrection is evidenced also in the next essay on the author's postwar work in film in the 1950s and, especially, on his firm attainment of artistic mastery: "Proprio in quegli anni, dal '49 al '57, scrissi un racconto, *La passeggiata prima di cena*, che alcuni critici continuano a considerare tra i miei migliori" [p. 237] (Precisely in those years, from 1949 to 1957, I wrote a short story, "The Walk before Supper," which some critics still consider among my best).

The two interviews that constitute part III bring the speaking "I" – the author citing himself, in a repetition of the pattern of "Laggiù" – into absolute foreground and certify his continuing presence, both in time and as poetic exemplar. Thus the writer refines the two ingredients essential to his craft – art and morality (addressed, respectively, in Parts I and II) – to reach his creative pinnacle (expressed in Part III).

Carlo Bo describes *Di là dal cuore* (the revised version of *Parole*) as an "important book." Highlighting the structural significance of Bassani's organization of his essays, Bo says: "In realtà più che di sistemazione bisognerebbe parlare di un disegno, anzi di una vocazione unitaria, anche perché sin dagli esordi lo scrittore obbediva a una volontà di costruzione, sia pure segnata principalmente dagli interessi e dalle speculazioni del narratore" (In reality one should speak not so much of arrangement as of design – indeed, of a unitary vocation – because even from the beginning of his career, the writer felt a compulsion toward construction, even if revealed primarily by his interest in and meditation on the narrator). In "Come Bassani critico continua il narratore," *Corriere della Sera* (22 May 1984), p. 3.

Bassani has pointed out in an interview that the opening and closing sections of *Di là* (which are comprised of some of his letters and a speech) deliberately focus on "existential experiences." The large but submerged existential pattern of *Parole*, described above, is thus enclosed in the revised text within an explicit existential frame. Furthermore, the choices of *Di là* emphasize the author's existential growth: the opening section is written by a youth in his twenties; the closing section, by the distinguished president of "Italia Nostra," a man in his sixties. Nico Orengo, "Le passioni dello scrittore in una raccolta di saggi," *La Stampa: Tuttolibri* (9 June 1984), p. 1.

28. In Anna Folli, *Vent'anni di cultura ferrarese*, 2, p. 347.

29. In a taped interview with me (Rome, 1978).

30. Paolo Ravenna, *Annali del Liceo-Ginnasio "Ariosto"* (Ferrara, 1974), pp. 45–47; originally part of a televised broadcast on the *Romanzo di Ferrara* (Ferrara, 14 February 1974). I am grateful to Mr. Ravenna – now a prominent lawyer and citizen of Ferrara – for a copy of his article and for spending time with me talking about Bassani and Ferrara. Carlo Rosselli, a political exile in Paris in the early years of Fascism assassinated with his brother near Paris in 1936 by Mussolini's order, is remembered as the founder of the anti-Fascist movement and newspaper *Giustizia e Libertà*, published in Paris.

31. See, for example, Siciliano, "Epitaffio," and Pampaloni, "Narciso."

32. The book received the 1982 Bagutta prize, Italy's oldest literary award, which is usually reserved for works of prose.

33. Said Renato Bertacchini, "L'importanza di *Te lucis ante*, di questa raccolta sempre meno confusa e disturbata da inframettenze ineffabili, idillico-culturali (e orientata se mai, vedremo, su temi e spunti diaristici) consiste quindi nell'assestamento della vocazione di Bassani. Nel senso che i dati biografici e le convinzioni gli si saldano infine alla necessità storica" [in *Letteratura Italiana: I Contemporanei*, III (Milan: Marzorati, 1969), pp. 800–801] (The importance of "Te lucis ante," of this collection that is less and less confused and disturbed by ineffable, idyllico-cultural intrusions [and oriented, if at all, we shall see, toward diaristic themes and origins], consists therefore of the stabilization of Bassani's vocation. In the sense that the biographical data and his convictions bind him finally to historical necessity.

See also Pasolini's keen and admiring review (1952) of "Lucis" which concludes with an observation of Bassani's shift in poetic interest "from aesthetic values to more broadly spiritual ones"; in *Passione e ideologia*, pp. 419–23.

34. The 1964 interview is reprinted in *Parole*, p. 247 and in *Di là*, p. 267. A remark about Pellico's prison diary, made by Bassani in the essay on Venice in literature – the essay that opens *Parole* and gives it its title – reflects the importance Bassani gives to "Lucis": "Ma anche le pagine veneziane delle *Mie prigioni*, forse perché ci mostrano di Venezia, quel poco che se ne può scorgere attraverso la bocca di lupo d'una prigione, *e quel poco è la vita, allora, tutta la vita* . . . anche di quelle pagine modeste ma assolute mette conto di ricordarsi" [p. 33; emphasis added; *Di là*, p. 255] (But even the pages on Venice in *My Prisons*, perhaps because they show us that little bit of Venice one can detect from the slit of a prison window, *and that little bit is life, then, all of life* . . . even those modest but perfect pages are worth remembering).

35. Pampaloni, "Narciso," finds that the inscribed addressees in the poetry of *Segreto*, that is, in poems of the seventies, are "indicati senza pudori dalla biografia, e al tempo stesso sono anonimi, confusi nella grande folla della valle di Giosafat" (pointed out shamelessly from biography, and at the same time they are anonymous, indistinct in the great crowd of the Valley of Jehoshaphat). The purgatorial and Dantesque vision roused by the critic is a social and political one, incompatible with the purgatorial modality of isolation that characterizes "Lucis." Yet the early poem, through intertextual means, also turns Bassani into a likeness of Dante.

Chapter 2. Ferrara, Real and Invented

1. Tourists in Ferrara seek out Micòl Finzi-Contini's family estate (and, with the cynical help of the locals, often "visit" it) as deferentially as they visit Ariosto's famous house. Some of the Fer-

rarese wax indignant over Bassani's "defamation" of them through characters they recognize as friends, relatives, and themselves. Specific examples were related by several of the author's old-time acquaintances during my research trip to Ferrara in the spring of 1980.

2. Attilio Milano, "Una consolazione nelle tribolazioni d'Israele," p. 251.

3. Federico Fellini, "Un'Olanda disperata," p. 195.

4. In Renzo Renzi, p. 146.

5. In ibid., p. 208.

6. Reviewing the first edition of the *Romanzo*, Luigi Bàccolo touched on this question in a lyrical style of his own, with a nod to Dantean imagery: " . . . partendo da una terra magicamente spopolata, rifare l'opera di creazione, riempire strade e case di personaggi, usurpare il compito del demiurgo che penetrato in una città deserta ne fa sorgere uomini [e donne], passioni e destini; un demiurgo che parte dalle ombre che sono le creature viventi per arrivare alle cose salde che sono le finzioni dello spazio letterario" (. . . starting with a land magically emptied, to begin the work of creation all over again, to fill the streets and houses with people, to usurp the task of the demiurge who, having penetrated a deserted city, succeeds in making men and women, passions and destinies, spring up again; a demiurge who begins with shadows that are living creatures in order to arrive at the solid things that are the fictions of literary space.) See "Bassani dentro la sua Ferrara, città dei morti," *Gazzetta del Popolo*, 21 January 1975, p. 3.

7. The archaic meaning of *barco* is an enclosed place, a park. The word *barchetto* would thus mean little park; in modern Italian it denotes a small barge. See Giacomo Devoto and Gian Carlo Oli, *Dizionario della lingua italiana* (Firenze: Le Monnier, 1971).

8. This broad and gracious street, built by Ercole and originally named Via degli Angeli, is of perfect Renaissance proportions: the height of the elegant *palazzi* on both sides of the street measures exactly its width.

9. Jacob Burckhardt, *The Civilization of the Renaissance in Italy*, pp. 66-74, passim. For the Jewish history (which Burckhardt ignores) see Milano, "Consolazione," pp. 251-53.

10. The description of Margherita is in Denis Mack Smith, *Italy: A Modern History*, p. 197. Verses from the "Canzone di Legnano" that Micòl's father, Professor Ermanno, recites in the *Giardino* are, "O bionda, o bella imperatrice, o fida" (Oh blond, oh beautiful empress, oh devoted one); "Onde venisti? Quali a noi secoli / sì mite e bella ti tramandarono" (Whence came you? Which centuries / handed you down to us, gentle and beautiful lady); and "eterno femminino regale" (regal eternal woman) (pp. 265-66).

For descriptions of Margherita di Savoia, see Federico Chabod, *L'Italia contemporanea*, pp. 72-73.

11. See the prologue of the *Giardino*.

12. Fernando Visser and Franco Zagagnoni, "Riconoscimento di un'immagine attuale della città," p. 224. It is not for mere descriptive interest, incidentally, that Bassani sends Edgardo Limentani (*Airone*) on a journey to a marshland, during which he reflects upon and radically reconstructs his life's destiny.

13. See Milano, "Consolazione," pp. 253-56.

14. See the poem "Mi avessi da bambino" in *In rima e senza*.

15. Dora Bassani, the author's mother, recounted the good fortune of having a "papà" who was one of the chief doctors of Ferrara's major hospital. The Fascists — to keep him alive for their own sakes, she told me in Ferrara, 1980 — protected and hid the "bravissimo professore" and his family after the anti-Jewish legislation.

16. In his autobiographical poem "Le leggi razziali," Bassani recalls a family tree-planting ceremony "che riuscì a metà solenne e a metà comica / tutti quanti abbastanza allegri se Dio / vuole / *in barba al noioso ebraismo* / *metastorico*" [*Epitaffio*, p. 58; emphasis added] (that succeeded half solemnly and half comically, everyone rather happy, thank God, in spite of insufferable metastorical Judaism).

17. Mack Smith, *Italy*, p. 269.

18. These were the Libyan (1911), World (1915–17), Ethiopian (1935–36), and Spanish (1936) wars.

19. " . . . [la]barba a punta nemmeno tanto ingrigita." [1974, p. 93] (his pointed beard, hardly showing signs of graying). Although the author specifies in both editions of the *Romanzo* that the only beard among the "barbe di guerra" [p. 85] (war beards) that Geo tolerates is his old Fascist uncle's (p. 81), the more precise and more cuttingly ironic phrase, cited above, is expunged from the 1974 edition.

20. See chapter 1, note 7, for observations on the subject by the historian Renzo De Felice.

21. Renzo De Felice, *Storia degli ebrei italiani sotto il fascismo*, p. 544.

22. Ibid., p. 282.

23. Ibid., pp. 541–42 and p. 559.

24. Ibid., pp. 562–66.

25. Lucy S. Dawidowicz, *A Holocaust Reader*, p. 84. For the Italian figures see De Felice, *Storia*, p. 524. Dawidowicz gives a somewhat higher Italian casuality figure of 8,000 deaths (p. 381).

26. Milano, in "Consolazione," estimates the 1938 Jewish population in the country at 65,000, which he compares with the 1911 figures of 1,300 in Ferrara and 37,000 nationwide. In 1860 as many as 2,000 Jews were citizens of Ferrara. Today many of their descendants (like Bassani) are scattered in other cities; a few are in Israel. According to Milano, those remaining in Ferrara number about 200.

See also Renato Sitti and Lucilla Previati, *Ferrara, il regime fascista*, pp. 183 and 185.

27. Giuseppe Mayda, *Ebrei sotto Salò*, pp. 184–94.

28. Giuliano Procacci, *Storia degli italiani* p. 548.

29. Mack Smith, *Italy*, p. 497.

30. Procacci's view, shared by other commentators, has De Gasperi provoking the government crisis in response to cold war pressures — primarily American — to eject the left-wingers from government; Procacci, *Storia*, p. 546.

31. Chabod, *L'Italia*, pp. 147 and 151.

32. Mack Smith, *Italy*, p. 495.

33. Of related interest is Giorgio Bàrberi Squarotti's application of a geometric metaphor to the graphic layout of the poems of *Segreto*, "che disegnano figure geometriche precise e nette, come in una matematica resa dei conti con la vita e con gli uomini" (which draw precise, sharp geometric figures, like a mathematical rendering of accounts with life and people); in his review, "La poesia di Bassani e Ceronetti," *La Stampa*, 16 June 1978, p. 12.

34. For this summary I have relied on the fine study of my colleagues Philip W. Porter and Fred E. Lukermann, "The Geography of Utopia," pp. 197–223.

35. Ibid., p. 207.

36. Mussolini, aiming to transform Italy into a totally self-sufficient nation, waged an intense campaign to have Italian industry and agriculture produce all the goods Italy required. He also spread a great deal of propaganda exhorting the "patriotic" Italian people to buy only Italian products.

37. Porter and Lukermann, "Utopia," p. 206.

38. J. M. Powell, in ibid., p. 201.

Chapter 3. Center, Periphery, Boundary, Outside

1. Giuseppe Mayda, *Ebrei sotto Salò*, pp. 115–18. This account of the slaughter of innocents also describes the weather, which Bassani modifies for the sake of symbolism, as we shall see in his setting of the scene.

2. For the first version see Pietro Secchia and Filippo Frassati, *Storia della Resistenza* 1, pp.

271-72. For the second version see Giuseppe Gelli, *Ferrara* 2, p. 180, and Eugenio Curiel, *La Nostra Lotta*, 5/6 March 1944. See also Renato Sitti and Lucilla Previati, *Ferrara: Il regime fascista*, pp. 221-22.

For a more recent account that adds some new information, see the three-part article by Bruno Traversari, *Il Resto del Carlino*, 14, 19, 28 November 1983, p. 3.

3. In Curiel, "Garibaldi in Spagna e nella resistenza bolognese," *La Lotta*, 1966, p. 13, and Ezio Antonioni, "Bologna verso la libertà," *La Lotta*, 9/10 1970, pp. 27-29. The Museo del Risorgimento e della Resistenza in Ferrara was very helpful in locating some of the sources listed in this and the preceding note.

4. The chronology is specific only in the 1974 edition; the later redaction implies an even more distant time from the massacre.

5. René Girard, *Violence and the Sacred*, pp. 101-2.

6. Marilyn Schneider, "Mythic Dimensions of Micòl Finzi-Contini," pp. 43-67.

7. Clara Falco, "I Finzi non perdonano a Bassani il 'tradimento' del personaggio di Micòl," p. 14.

When I asked Bassani about his selection of Micòl's surname, he said that he wanted a hyphenated name for its "chic" and for its "snob" value. He chose Finzi-Contini, after a family from Trieste. (Taped interview, Rome, 1978.)

8. The word "cryptohomosexual," expressly in reference to Alberto, is Bassani's. (Taped interview, Rome, 1978.)

9. The short story, "The Leather Man," gives us further insight into Geo and his odd dress. Its central character, named in the story's title, is a figure "colossally dressed, in layers of coats and shawls and pants." He is a type who "makes the world foreign. He distances it. He is estranged. Our perceptions are sharpest when we're estranged." Benjamin DeMott, "Pilgrim Among the Culturati," rev. of *Lives of the Poets: Six Stories and a Novella* (New York: Random House, 1984), by E. L. Doctorow, *The New York Times Book Review*, 11 November 1984, p. 1.

It is also worth noting that Geo's name has significance. First of all, it obviously evokes "Giorgio." The name "Girolamo" ("Muro") also appears in the *Romanzo*. In "Muro's" rewritten form as "Odore," the reconstructed "Girolamo" is "Bruno." Extratextually the author adopted the pseudonym Giacomo [Marchi] during Fascism in order to publish his *Una città di pianura*—illegally, for a Jew.

10. Yi-Fu Tuan, *Topophilia*, p. 226.

Chapter 4. Sexual Identity and Political Persecution

1. Discussing "Notte," Bassani said of Pino and his wife: "Tanto è vero che i loro rapporti . . . sono inesistenti. Stanno in camere separate, non hanno probabilmente fatto l'amore insieme" and "Tra Pino Barilari e Sciagura c'è un segreto rapporto omosessuale" [taped interview, Rome, 1978] (Their relations are obviously nonexistent. They sleep in separate rooms and have probably not made love together) (Between Pino Barilari and Sciagura there is a secret homosexual relationship).

2. Federico Chabod's "L'ascesa del fascismo," *L'Italia contemporanea*, pp. 57-66, gives a good, succinct introduction to the early years of Fascism, including some comments on conditions in Ferrara.

3. In 1925 the Fascist government passed a law prohibiting state employees from holding Masonic membership.

4. The 1974 edition diminishes the elder Barilari's pro-Fascism by noting that his support was "subito rientrata" [1974, p. 157] (immediately withdrawn). The 1980 edition, in which the character shows no hesitation of support for Fascism, adds a degree of irony to Fascism's intolerance of Masonry.

5. A review of a book on the Viennese Alma Mahler offers some observations pertinent to our

subject of day and night worlds (in which, as just shown, the erotic is central): "In German literature the terms bright (or light) and dark have designated different types of personality ever since Goethe's haunted Orestes called his friend Phylades a 'brightly colored butterfly' circling a 'dark flower' — himself. The light are better at dealing with life; the dark understand more, know more, and suffer more. The types correspond very roughly to extrovert and introvert. Thomas Mann was always juxtaposing them, most overtly in Tonio Kroger." Gabriele Annan's rev. of *Alma Mahler: Muse to Genius*, by Karen Monson, *The New York Review of Books*, 29 Sept. 1983, p. 8.

6. Philip Wheelwright, *The Burning Fountain*, p. 178.

7. The document called "Measures for the Defense of the Italian Race," written into law November 17, 1938, may be read in Renzo De Felice, *Storia degli ebrei italiani sotto il fascismo*, pp. 562–66.

8. Dominique Fernandez, "Entretien: Cassola et Bassani," pp. 22–23.

9. *Natura morta* appeared in serial form in the magazine *Paragone*. Six chapters appeared in October 1966, and six more in June 1967.

10. On a site visit to Codigoro, I discovered that the highest building in town—a modern apartment building—rose only three stories. Like the fictive one, it has arcades on the ground level. As Bassani told me in reference to another "inaccurate" textual description, "Quando [la realtà] non mi serve, la invento" (When reality is not useful to me, I invent it). [taped interview, Rome, 1978]

11. In the author's own words, "Ulderico . . . rappresenta l'uomo vitale, il contrario di Limentani" [*Epoca*, October 27, 1968, p. 12] (Ulderico represents a vital man, in opposition to Limentani).

12. The verb "sbattere" ("to bash in") replaces the still more violent "abbattere" ("to slaughter [an animal]") of the 1974 edition. Clearly belonging to the semantic field of the extermination camp that the scene evokes, the latter verb may have been rejected precisely because its meaning was so explicit.

13. "Gli appartenenti alla razza ebraica sono stranieri. Durante questa guerra appartengono a nazionalità nemica" [point seven in the Manifesto of the newborn Social Republic, approved at its founding assembly in Verona, autumn of 1943; cited in De Felice, *Storia*, p. 433] (Members of the Jewish race are foreigners. For the duration of this war they belong to a hostile nationality).

14. See note 1.

15. In the 1974 edition she also has bleached blond hair: "I suoi capelli, sempre più ossigenati, sembravano splendere nell'oscurità di luce propria" [1974, p. 184] (her hair, increasingly bleached, seemed to shine in the darkness with its own light). The entire line, enhancing Anna's charms at the same time it dissipates them, is later deleted in favor of a more objective discourse (1980, p. 160).

16. The text and translation of Dante's poem is the Charles Singleton edition of *The Divine Comedy*, 2 (Princeton: Princeton University Press, 1977; orig. 1973). Among the "speaking stones" that dazzle the pilgrim-poet on Mount Purgatory is the following scene:

> Lì precedeva al benedetto vaso,
>   trescando alzato, l'umile salmista,
>   e più e men che re era in quel caso.
> Di contra, effigïata ad una vista
>   d'un gran palazzo, Micòl ammirava
>   sì come donna dispettosa e trista. [Purg. 10: 64–69]

(There, preceding the blessed vessel, dancing girt up, was the humble Psalmist, and on that occasion he was both more and less than king. Opposite, figured at a window of a great palace, was Michal looking on, like a woman vexed and scornful.) [p. 103]

On the subject of Micòl's childlessness, see my "Mythical Dimensions of Micòl Finzi-Contini," p. 48.

17. In Petrarch's Canzone 126.

18. Joseph Cary, *Three Italian Poets: Saba, Ungaretti, Montale*. Cary gives the following account of possible meanings of the word "iride" in reference to Montale's poem of that name: " 'Iris' . . . is not only a flower . . . not only synecdoche for the eye of *coscienza* . . . not only the name of the rainbow goddess and messenger for the Olympians, but also and above all . . . the rainbow of the Promised Land, the Lord's own sign of covenant with the lost and wandering" (pp. 316-17).

19. Micòl embodies nature. The dazzling sunlight and moonlight accompanying her presence, her "majestic" lineage, the trees and plants she loves, and the earth colors and aromas associated with her—pungent garage and elevator smells, the thick elevator carpet "the color of tobacco, carrot, and oxblood" (p. 348), her leopardskin coat—all reflect her "divine" partnership with earth.

20. The verse, cited in the novel, is from Baudelaire's "Moesta et errabunda," in *Fleurs du mal*. Expressing an intense yearning for a lost "vert" ("innocent") paradise, the poem reflects a dominant motif of the *Giardino*.

21. Eugenio Montale, "Vita e morte di Micòl," p. 3, recognizes this special power of Micòl's: "Più di ogni altra persona della sua famiglia . . . solo lei è la donna che sa e che ha capito" (More than any other person in her family, she alone is the woman who knows and has understood).

22. Thomas Mann, *Death in Venice and Seven Other Stories*, trans. H. T. Lowe-Porter (New York: Vintage Books, 1963; orig. 1930), p. 134. See also note 5 in this chapter.

23. Ferdinando Camon, *La moglie del tiranno*, p. 96.

24. The medieval King Henry IV went to Canossa as a penitent; his act was immortalized in Pirandello's play named for the king.

25. Giuseppe Bardellini, "Note su Alda Costa," in "Socialismo Ferrarese" (1963). Published in Ferrara by the Museo del Risorgimento e della Resistenza.

26. According to "Anni" (p. 102), Clelia died in Codigoro during the German occupation. Also implicit in *Airone*—by mention of her death in 1944—this fact adds unspoken extensions to her victimage.

27. See "Quaderno 7: Donne ferraresi nella Resistenza" (May 1975), of which the first twenty-two pages are dedicated to Costa. Publ. in Ferrara by the Museo del Risorgimento e della Resistenza.

28. Bruno's fascination with the dreamlike young lovers is nurtured by the pervasive Fascist ideology of the time. Susan Sontag, in her essay "Fascinating Fascism," esp. pp. 92-93 and p. 102, soundly assails Leni Riefenstahl for her presumed artistic innocence of some of the features of Fascist art, such as its utopian aesthetic of physical perfection and its implied "ideal eroticism." Sontag also draws attention to the "predilections" of Fascist leaders for sexual metaphors.

Another superb essay on National Socialism, Hitler, and Mussolini was written by Bassani during the heat of war (1944); it includes some arresting comments on Hitler's sexualized rhetoric of seduction. See "La rivoluzione come gioco," *Parole*, pp. 81-91; rpt. in *Di là*, pp. 44-55.

Chapter 5. The Act of Self-Inscription

1. The first interviewer was Grazia Livi, *Epoca*, pp. 120-23; the second, Manlio Cancogni, *Fiera Letteraria*, p. 11.

2. The last line of the poem that begins "Non chiederci la parola," in Montale's first book of poems, *Ossi di seppia*; emphasis Montale's.

3. In "Storia di Dèbora," no mention is made of the Lateran Pacts. The narrative significance of the pacts grows gradually from the original simple allusion to Oreste's "respectful tone when he spoke about religious persons and matters" to increasing importance in successive writings.

For more details see Ignazio Baldelli's study of the four "Lida" texts, "La riscrittura 'totale' di un'opera," p. 180-97.

4. The epigraph is "Enfin, des années entières s'étant passées, le temps et l'absence ralentirent sa douleur et éteignirent sa passion" (Finally, after many years had passed, time and absence slowed

her pain and extinguished her passion). From *La Princesse de Cleves*; not reprinted in the 1980 edition of the *Romanzo*.

5. Bassani's fictive account blames some shady late nineteenth-century politicking for the selection of Bologna as the site of the "most important railroad center of northern Italy"; this "fatal resolution" condemns Ferrara to mediocrity and victimage forever (see pp. 54–55). The author's scenario is pure invention. Another invention—the character Gemma Brondi—is not so pure. She is modeled on Bassani's maternal grandmother, Emma Marchi, a Catholic peasant woman who spoke "almost always in dialect" (*Di là*, p. 387).

6. See his essay "Laggiù" (*Romanzo*, pp. 729–34).

7. Enzo Siciliano's "Ritorna Bruno Lattes," p. 21, is a very fine review of *Odore*. Here is its introductory judgment: "*L'odore del fieno* . . . è libro minore a confronto degli altri suoi. Ciononostante assai più rivelatore di quelli. . . . E questo accade quando, pure nel loro essere minore, questi libri mostrano una necessità, una sintesi espressiva che li libera da qualsiasi ombra di contingenza" (*L'odore del fieno* . . . is a minor book compared with his others. Nonetheless much more revealing than those are. . . . And this happens when, precisely for being minor, books such as *Odore* display a necessity, an expressive synthesis that frees them from any shadow of contingency). Siciliano felicitously describes the "musical" autobiographical sketch entitled "Ravenna"—discussed later in this chapter—as "un tutto compiuto, un improvviso schubertiano" (an achieved whole, a Schubertian impromptu).

8. After noting how the "trauma" of Jewish persecution—namely, the anti-Jewish legislation—affected Bassani, Antonio Russi rightly makes a link between Bassani's remark that he is unable to read *The Scarlet letter* "senza provare la più violenta commozione" (without experiencing an extremely intense empathy) and the "marchio imposto all'adultera" (mark forced on the adulteress). There can be no doubt that the scarlet letter "ricorda quello inflitto dagli hitleriani alle loro vittime" (recalls the indelible punctures that Hitler's henchmen inflicted on their victims). See Russi, "Sei esemplari di narrativa contemporanea," pp. 420–21.

9. Two of the others are young schoolboys, nearly strangers to Bruno and the narrator, and the third is a total stranger who is older than the narrator, not a Ferrarese, and not dressed for tennis, as are all the others.

10. The first sentence of the citation, in the 1974 edition, spells out the Fascists' "bad taste": Adriana was very indignant, "above all," because they had the "cattivo gusto di mescolare allo sport la politica" (bad taste of mixing sports and politics); a few other nearby phrases in the 1980 edition hammer in the facts of Adriana's moral vacuity and the author's contempt for her.

11. Perhaps Micòl's observation of her amorous friends inspired the film director Vittorio De Sica's erotic scene of Micòl and Giampiero Malnate making love—with the narrator as voyeur—in a cabin just like the one that sheltered Bruno and Adriana. Whatever the inspiration, it deforms the novel's delicate ambiguity. Bassani's indignant response to what he regarded as the filmscript's gross and demeaning distortions of his novel (a response that led to a lawsuit) may be read in his "Il giardino tradito" (*Di là*, pp. 311–21). The film bears the same title as the novel.

12. The relation of the Petrarchan lyric speaker and his beloved Laura is similar. See John Freccero's illuminating essay on this subject, "The Fig Tree and the Laurel: Petrarch's Poetics," pp. 34–40.

13. East is traditionally good, as opposed to West, which, like the left, is traditionally bad. One must wonder whether the actual location of the Jewish cemetery—and the nearby Catholic (communal) one—in the eastern half of Ferrara has anything to do with symbolic necessity.

14. Although the reference to these idealistic nineteenth-century figures was expunged in the later edition, their presence remains in some fictive characters, such as Salomone Corcos. See chapter 2.

15. Baldelli, "Riscrittura," pp. 180–97, is perplexed by some of the textual alterations in "Odore" as well as in "Lida," but he grasps an important literary strategy of the author: "proprio quel

'o giù di lì' ci par rilevare l'inessenzialità" (precisely that "or roughly" seems to underscore the unessentiality) of a procedure whose "risultato paradossale è spesso, nella pagina di Bassani, anzi quello di ottenere una atmosfera più mitica e misteriosa" [pp. 184-85] (paradoxical result is often, in Bassani's pages, indeed always to create a more mythic and mysterious atmosphere).

16. The transatlantic liner that passes the Rimini coast in Fellini's *Roma*, bringing the whole town out to greet it, could well have been inspired by Bassani's Adriatic tourist ship.

17. This saying supplied the title of an earlier version, written shortly after the war (1946-47). It appeared in the *Antologia del Campiello*, a volume published by the sponsors of a literary prize received by Bassani.

18. Primo Levi, *La tregua*, pp. 252-53.

19. Says Sidra DeKoven Ezrahi, *By Words Alone*, p. 74, "The *ancien régime* is delineated in the survival novels largely through physical properties, and the stripping away of the objects of a comfortable, civilized life marks the gradual denuding of the human soul of all its material and affective supports. The focus on *things* in this literature signifies a palpable foothold in a world from which the individual is about to be banished and measures the transformation of his ambience."

20. "Many writers have mourned the slaughter of Europe's Jews, but a few have transformed private mourning into the jeremiads that may endure within an ancient Hebraic tradition." Ibid., p. 96.

21. See, for example, Federico Chabod, *L'Italia contemporanea*, p. 61.

22. The image of a "used-up" or "expired" Bruno permeates the two Bruno narratives that follow "Odore": "Ragazza" and "Abbazia."

23. The title of Cesare Pavese's collection of poetry, *Lavorare Stanca* (1943), means "Work Is Tiring"; the American edition is called *Hard Labor*.

24. Elias Canetti, *Crowds and Power*, p. 227.

25. Bassani further inscribes present time into this text by replacing Corso Roma, the street name frequently mentioned in the earlier narratives, with its postwar and current name, Corso Martiri della Libertà (see p. 107). In addition, the 1974 edition begins the sentence quoted above as "*Ora* (Now) bisogna tenere presente" (emphasis added).

26. Bassani takes his title *Les neiges d'antan* from François Villon's popular fifteenth-century ballad, "Des dames du temps jadis." I am indebted to my colleague Tom Conley, whose words I cite in the text, for his allegorical reading of the poem cited above.

See also David Kuhn's allegorical study *La Poétique de Villon* (Paris: Armand Colin, 1967), which Professor Conley brought to my attention.

27. Regrettably, the American publisher of this volume, entitled *The Smell of Hay*, excluded the third apologue, "Scarpe," and "Laggiù" from it.

Bibliography

Bibliography

Works by Giorgio Bassani

Una città di pianura. Pseud. Giacomo Marchi. Milan: Arte Grafica Lucini, 1940.

Storie dei poveri amanti e altri versi (poetry). Roma: Astrolabio, 1945. Enl. ed. 1956.

Te lucis ante (poetry). Rome: Ubaldini, 1947.

Un'altra libertà (poetry). Milan: Mondadori, 1952.

La passeggiata prima di cena. Florence: Sansoni, 1953.

Gli ultimi anni di Clelia Trotti. Pisa: Nistri-Lischi, 1955.

Cinque storie ferraresi ("Lida Mantovani," "La passeggiata prima di cena," "Una lapide in via Mazzini," "Gli ultimi anni di Clelia Trotti," "Una notte del '43"). Turin: Einaudi, 1956 (Premio Strega). Oscar ed. Milan: Mondadori, 1977. Introduction by Guido Fink.

Gli occhiali d'oro. Turin: Einaudi, 1958. Rev. ed. Milan: Mondadori, 1970. Preface by Luigi Baldacci.

Le storie ferraresi ("Il murodi cinta," rev. *Cinque storie*, *Occhiali*, "In esilio"). Turin: Einaudi, 1960.

Il giardino dei Finzi-Contini. Turin: Einaudi, 1962 (Premio Viareggio). Rev. ed. Milan: Mondadori, 1974. Oscar ed. Milan: Mondadori, 1976. Introduction by Eugenio Montale. Postscript by Marilyn Schneider.

L'alba ai vetri: Poesie 1942–50 (anthology of three poetry vols.). Turin: Einaudi, 1963.

Dietro la porta. Turin: Einaudi, 1964.

Le parole preparate e altri scritti di letteratura (essays). Turin: Einaudi, 1966.

L'airone. Milan: Mondadori, 1968. Oscar ed. Milan: Mondadori, 1978. Introduction by Marilyn Schneider.

L'odore del fieno. Milan: Mondadori, 1972.

Dentro le mura (rev. *Storie*). Milan: Mondadori, 1973.

Epitaffio (poetry). Milan: Mondadori, 1974.

Il romanzo di Ferrara (collected fiction; *Storie* et seq.). Milan: Mondadori, 1974. Rev. ed. 1980.

In gran segreto (poetry). Milan: Mondadori, 1978.

In rima e senza: 1939–1981 (collected poetry). Milan: Mondadori, 1982 (Premio Bagutta). Premio
Penna d'oro (1982) bestowed by the president of Italy.
Di là dal cuore (rev. and enl. *Parole*). Milan: Mondadori, 1984.

English Translations*

By Isabel Quigly:

The Gold-Rimmed Spectacles. London: Faber and Faber, 1960.
A Prospect of Ferrara.† London: Faber and Faber, 1962.
The Garden of the Finzi-Continis. London: Faber and Faber, 1965.

By William Weaver:

The Heron. New York: Harcourt Brace Jovanovich, 1970.
Five Stories of Ferrara. New York: Harcourt Brace Jovanovich, 1971.
The Smell of Hay (with *The Gold-rimmed Eyeglasses*). New York: Harcourt Brace Jovanovich,
1975.
Behind the Door. New York: Harcourt Brace Jovanovich, 1976.
The Garden of the Finzi-Continis. New York: Harcourt Brace Jovanovich, 1977.

General Critical Works

The first seven listings below include extensive bibliographies.

Bertacchini, Renato. "Giorgio Bassani." In *Letteratura Italiana: I Contemporanei*, Vol. 3. Milan:
Marzorati, 1969, pp. 797–816.
De Stefanis, Giusi Oddo. *Bassani entro il cerchio delle sue mura*. Ravenna: Longo, 1981.
Dolfi, Anna. *Le forme del sentimento: Prosa e poesia in Giorgio Bassani*. Padua: Liviana, 1981.
(Interview, pp. 79–115).
Ferretti, Gian Carlo. *Letteratura e ideologia: Bassani Cassola Pasolini*. Rome: Editori Riuniti,
1964; 2d ed. 1974.
Grillandi, Massimo. *Invito alla lettura di Bassani*. Milan: Mursia, 1972.
Renzi, Renzo, gen. ed. *Ferrara*. Vol. 1: *Il Po, la Cattedrale, la Corte dalle origini al 1598*. Vol.
2: *La Fortezza, il Territorio, la Piazza dal 1598 ad oggi*. Bologna: Edizioni Alfa, 1969.
Varanini, Giorgio. "Bassani," in *Il Castoro* 46. 3d ed. Florence: La Nuova Italia, 1975.

The following are collections of essays on Bassani's work.

Cro, Stelio, ed. "Omaggio a Giorgio Bassani." *Canadian Journal of Italian Studies*, Fall 1977 and
Winter 1978.
Sempoux, André, ed. *Il Romanzo di Ferrara: Contributi su Giorgio Bassani*. Louvain-La-Neuve:
Presses Universitaires de Louvain, 1983.

Selected Works

The following works are either cited in the text or relevant to it. Because the number of commentaries on Bassani is extensive, works not listed here may also be of interest.

Ajello, Nello. "Arriva l'avanguardia," *Lo scrittore e il potere*. Bari: Laterza, 1974.

---

*Bassani's work has also been translated into French, Spanish, German, Dutch, Danish, Finnish,
Polish, Czech, Serbo-Croatian, and Japanese.
†Same contents as *Five Stories of Ferrara*.

Bàccolo, Luigi. "Bassani dentro la sua Ferrara, città dei morti." *Gazzetta del Popolo*, 21 January 1975, p. 3.

Baldelli, Ignazio. "La riscrittura 'totale' di un'opera: Da *Le storie ferraresi* a *Dentro le mura* di Bassani." *Lettere Italiane* 26 (1974):180–97.

——."La lingua della prosa italiana." In *Letteratura Italiana Contemporanea*, vol. 3, edited by Mariani, Gaetano and Petrucciani, Mario. Rome: Lucarini, 1982, pp. 660–62.

Bàrberi Squarotti, Giorgio. *Poesia e narrativa del Secondo Novecento*. Milan: Mursia, 1961; 2d ed., 1967, pp. 254–62.

——. "La poesia di Bassani e Ceronetti: Tragedia e apocalisse." *La Stampa*, 16 June 1978, p. 12.

Bardellini, Giuseppe. "Note su Alda Costa." In "Socialismo Ferrarese." Ferrara: Museo del Risorgimento e della Resistenza, 1963.

Bon, Adriano. *Come leggere "Il giardino dei Finzi-Contini" di Giorgio Bassani*. Milan: Mursia, 1979.

Boselli, Mario. "Ambiguità di Bassani." *Nuova Corrente* 9 (1962). n. 27, p. 11.

Burckhardt, Jacob. *The Civilization of the Renaissance in Italy*. 1929. Reprint. New York: Harper & Row, 1958.

Camon, Ferdinando. *La moglie del tiranno*. Rome: Lerici, 1969, pp. 20–24 and 85–98.

Cancogni, Manlio. Interview. *Fiera Letteraria*, 14 November 1968, p. 11.

Canetti, Elias. *Crowds and Power*. New York: Seabury Press, 1978.

Carsten, Francis Ludwig. *The Rise of Fascism*. Berkeley: University of California Press, 1967, 2d ed., 1980.

Cary, Joseph, *Three Italian Poets: Saba, Ungaretti, Montale*. New York: New York University Press, 1969.

Chabod, Federico. *L'Italia contemporanea (1918–1948)*. Turin: Einaudi, 1961.

Dawidowicz, Lucy S., ed. *A Holocaust Reader*. New York: Behrman House, 1976.

De Felice, Renzo. *Storia degli ebrei italiani sotto il fascismo*. Turin: Einaudi, 1961; 3d ed., rev. and enl. 1972.

DeKoven Ezrahi, Sidra. *By Words Alone: The Holocaust in Literature*. Chicago: University of Chicago Press, 1980.

Donato, Eugenio. "The Mnemonics of History: Notes for a Contextual Reading of Foscolo's *Dei Sepolcri*." *Yale Italian Studies* 1 (Winter 1977):1–23.

Falco, Clara. "I Finzi non perdonano a Bassani il 'tradimento' del personaggio di Micòl." *Il Tempo*, 19 May 1971, p. 14.

Fava Guzzetta, Lia. "Una scrittura al rallentatore: *L'airone*." In Sempoux, ed., *Contributi*, pp. 85–108.

Fellini, Federico. "Un'Olanda disperata." In Renzi, gen. ed., *Ferrara*. Vol. 2, p. 195.

Fernandez, Dominique. "Entretien: Cassola et Bassani." *L'Express*, 23 August 1962, pp. 22–23.

Folli, Anna. *Vent'anni di cultura ferrarese: 1925–1945*. 2 vols. Bologna: Pàtron, 1978.

Freccero, John. "Medusa: The Letter and the Spirit." *Yearbook of Italian Studies*, 1972, pp. 1–18.

——. "The Fig Tree and the Laurel: Petrarch's Poetics." *Diacritics* (Spring 1975):34–40.

Gelli, Giuseppe. "Cronache della lotta armata." In *Ferrara*, vol 2. Bologna: Edizioni Alfa, 1969, pp. 177–84.

Ginzburg, Natalia. "La Soddisfazione." *Corriere della Sera*, 9 June 1974, p. 3.

Girard, René. *Violence and the Sacred*. Translated by Patrick Gregory. Baltimore: Johns Hopkins University Press, 1977.

Hughes, H. Stuart. *Prisoners of Hope: The Silver Age of the Italian Jews, 1924–1974*. Cambridge (Mass.) and London: Harvard University Press, 1983.

Levi, Primo. *La tregua*. Turin: Einaudi, 1963.

——. *Se non ora, quando?* Turin: Einaudi, 1982.

Livi, Grazia. *Epoca*, 27 October 1968, pp. 120–23.

Mack Smith, Denis. *Italy: A Modern History.* Ann Arbor: University of Michigan Press, 1959; 2d ed., rev. and enl. 1969.

Mayda, Giuseppe. *Ebrei sotto Salò: La persecuzione antisemita 1943–1945.* Milan: Feltrinelli, 1978.

Milano, Attilio. "Una consolazione nelle tribolazioni d'Israele." In Renzi, gen. ed., *Ferrara.* Vol. 2, pp. 251–56.

Mondo, Lorenzo. "I versi di *Epitaffio*: Bassani poeta." *La Stampa*, 18 June 1974, p. 3.

Montale, Eugenio. "Vita e morte di Micòl." Introduction to *Il giardino dei Finzi-Contini.* Oscar ed. Milan: Mondadori, 1976. Reprint of *Corriere della Sera*, 28 February 1962.

———. "Non chiederci la parola." *Ossi di seppia.* 1925. Reprint. Milan: Mondadori, 1963.

Pampaloni, Geno. "Io, Narciso." *Il Giornale*, 6 August 1978.

Pasolini, Pier Paolo. *Passione e ideologia: 1948–1958.* Milan: Garzanti, 1960, pp. 325–26; 344–45, 419–23.

———. *Descrizioni di descrizioni*, ed. Graziella Chiarcossi. Turin: Einaudi, 1979, pp. 262–66, 333–36.

Porter, Phillip W. and Lukermann, Fred E. "The Geography of Utopia." In *Geographies of the Mind: Essays in Historical Geosophy in Honor of John Kirtland Wright*, edited by David Lowenthal and Martyn J. Bowden. Oxford: Oxford University Press, 1976, pp. 197–223.

Procacci, Giuliano. *Storia degli italiani*, vol 2. Bari: Laterza, 1968; 2d ed., 1983.

Russi, Antonio. "Sei esemplari di narrativa contemporanea." In *Letteratura Italiana Contemporanea*, vol. 3, edited by Mariani, Gaetano and Petrucciani, Mario. Rome: Lucarini, 1982, pp. 411–28. (Includes Bassani.)

Schneider, Marilyn. "Mythic Dimensions of Micòl Finzi-Contini." *Italica* 51 (1974):43–67.

———. "A Conversion to Death: Giorgio Bassani's *L'airone.*" *Canadian Journal of Italian Studies* 1 (Winter 1978):121–34.

Secchia, Pietro and Frassati, Filippo. *Storia della Resistenza*, vol. 1. Rome: Editori Riuniti, 1965, 2 vols.

Shapiro, Marianne. "Bassani's Ironic Mode." *Canadian Journal of Italian Studies* 1 (Winter 1978):146–52.

Siciliano, Enzo. "Ritorna Bruno Lattes." *Il Mondo*, 20 June 1972, p. 21.

———. "Epitaffio della vita." *Il Mondo*, 30 May 1974, p. 20.

———. "Ma la poesia non è una signorina perbene." *Corriere della Sera*, 21 May 1978, p. 12.

Sitti, Renato and Previati, Lucilla. *Ferrara, il regime fascista.* Milan: La Pietra, 1976.

Sontag, Susan. "Fascinating Fascism." In *Under the Sign of Saturn.* New York: Vintage Books, 1981.

Stampa, Carla. "Per scrivere ho bisogno del mare." *Epoca*, 25 April 1981, pp. 84–89. (Includes interview.)

Tornabuoni, Lietta. Interview. *La Stampa: Tuttolibri*, 17 April 1982, p. 1.

Traversari, Bruno. "La lunga notte del'43," "Un'alba di sangue," and "E fu guerra civile." Three-part article in *Il Resto del Carlino*, 14, 19, and 28 November 1983, p. 3 of each issue.

Tuan, Yi-Fu. *Topophilia: A Study of Environmental Perception, Attitudes, and Values.* Englewood Cliffs: Prentice-Hall, 1974.

Visser, Fernando and Zagagnoni, Franco. "Riconoscimento di un'immagine attuale della città." In Renzi, gen. ed., *Ferrara.* Vol. 1, pp. 222–36.

Wheelwright, Philip. *The Burning Fountain: A Study in the Language of Symbolism.* Bloomington: University of Indiana Press, 1954; rev. ed. 1968.

Index

Index

Marilyn Schneider is a professor of Italian and comparative literature at the University of Minnesota. She has served as chair of the French and Italian department and associate dean of humanities in the College of Liberal Arts at Minnesota. Her essays on modern Italian writers have appeared in *PMLA, Contemporary Literature, Yale Italian Studies,* and other journals.